Patrick A. Smythe

'The Heaviest Blow' – The Catholic Church and the East Timor Issue

LIT

Bibliographic information published by Die Deutsche Bibliothek
Die Deutsche Bibliothek lists this publication in the Deutsche
Nationalbibliografie; detailed bibliographic data are available in the
Internet at http://dnb.ddb.de.

ISBN 3-8258-7177-0

© LIT VERLAG Münster 2004
Grevener Str./Fresnostr. 2 48159 Münster
Tel. 0251-23 50 91   Fax 0251-23 19 72
e-Mail: lit@lit-verlag.de   http://www.lit-verlag.de

Distributed in North America by:

Transaction Publishers
New Brunswick (U.S.A.) and London (U.K.)

Transaction Publishers
Rutgers University
35 Berrue Circle
Piscataway, NJ 08854

Tel.: (732) 445 - 2280
Fax: (732) 445 - 3138
for orders (U. S. only):
toll free (888) 999 - 6778

Patrick A. Smythe

'The Heaviest Blow' –
The Catholic Church and the East Timor Issue

Religion und Theologie im Asien-Pazifik-Kontext

herausgegeben von

John D'Arcy May

(Irish School of Ecumenics, Dublin)

Band 4

LIT

'The Heaviest Blow'

Contents

DEDICATION

This book is dedicated to the memory of two courageous priests in East Timor who lived out
the Gospel of Jesus and the Social Doctrine of the Church by laying down their lives
in defence of the human dignity of their people:

Fr.Hilario Madeira
&
Fr.Francisco Soares

murdered by pro-integration militia as they sought to protect their parishioners
Suai, East Timor, September 1999.

Foreword

This book investigates responses within the Catholic Church to the invasion in 1975 and subsequent occupation of East Timor by the armed forces of Indonesia which interrupted the decolonisation process begun by Portugal the previous year. The East Timorese were to suffer oppression and exploitation under the Indonesian regime. Eventually a plebiscite conducted in 1999 under the auspices of the United Nations demonstrated that there was resistance to this unjust state of affairs by the great majority of the native people and the international community rallied to support the establishment of an independent and democratic nation. In the intervening years the Church in East Timor endeavoured to serve the needs of the populace and won their increasing affiliation by a courageous defence of fundamental human rights.

A number of countries were closely involved in the issue and this study explores the reaction of the local Catholic Church within the socio-political context of several of them: Indonesia, Portugal, Australia, the United States, Japan and Britain. The response of the Vatican is also observed - and the effect that this had upon the disposition of local Churches, upon the growing movement of international solidarity with the people of East Timor, and upon those national governments with an interest in the affair.

Some attention is given to the nature of the coverage provided by the mass communications media regarding the issue, and to the relations between the Church and non-governmental organisations responding to the needs of the victims of injustice. Noted also are the influence of large commercial corporations upon eventualities, and the pertinent prescriptions of International Law - but it is recognised that these several matters merit fuller exploration than is possible here.

Criteria for evaluating the response of the Church to the East Timorese plight are derived from Catholic Social Doctrine and from the personal ministry of Jesus Christ. The study discovers significant shortcomings in the Church's reaction at all levels of its operation, yet examples of an admirable faithfulness to that Doctrine, and to the role model of Jesus, within the Church in each country and in every circle of its community life are also in evidence. The question is raised as to the feasibility of applying the general principles of Catholic Social Doctrine to complex issues, and the Church is challenged to abide by its own teachings on social justice - for its own sake as well as for that of the world in which it lives.

Acknowledgements

Appreciation should first of all be conveyed to bishop David Konstant who gave his consent to this engagement of my energies and time, and authorised the measure of financial support that was forthcoming from the Diocese of Leeds to enable this study to proceed.

I would also like to acknowledge the moral support that has been afforded to me by the parishioners of St Boniface Parish, Bentham and St Mary's Parish, Rothwell to continue with this work over several years.

I am indebted to Simon Willan for technical assistance in keeping my computer functional throughout that period. Without his prompt, skilful and generous attention this work would never have been completed.

I wish to express thanks to Professor Haddon Willmer and Professor Nigel Biggar, formerly of the Department of Theology and Religious Studies at the University of Leeds, for their guidance and encouragement from the beginning to the completion of this task.

I am grateful to all those who were willing to be interviewed, especially those in East Timor and in Indonesia who did so at personal risk. I am also indebted to those who facilitated my researches both in this country and abroad, especially those who made arrangements for interviews on my behalf or who provided accommodation or access to their archives. I want to acknowledge in particular the assistance given by the following:

In East Timor: Fr. Hilario Madeira, Fr.Domingos Soares, Fr.Ricardo da Silva, the Salesian Community at Fatumaca and Fuiloro, and Sr.Gabriella at Delsos for their especial courage in co-operating with my research.
In West Timor and Oecussi: Frans Teti for great assistance with arrangements for travel and accommodation, and bishop Anton Pain Ratu for his readiness to be interviewed at length in the midst of a busy pastoral schedule.
In Indonesia: Mgr Peter Turang (now archbishop in Kupang, West Timor) and his family for their hospitality and help, and to Sr.Bernadita Guhit at the Bishops Conference National Justice and Peace Commission - and latterly at the Bishop Belo Centre for Peace and Development in Dili, East Timor - for her provision of invaluable resource material throughout the period of my investigations.

In Portugal: Padre Mauricio de Basto e Pinto and all the Community at the Salesian Mother House in Lisbon; to Christina Cruz of CDPM; and to Professor Jose Manuel Marques da Silva Pureza, and his colleagues and friends in Coimbra who provided accommodation and help in arranging local interviews.
In Australia: Juan and Maria do Ceu Federer in Darwin, bishop Hilton Deakin in Melbourne, the Servants of the Blessed Sacrament in Sydney, Fr Michael McKenna in Canberra, Rachel Harrison and Damien LeGoullon in Brisbane for their hospitality and their facilitating of interviews with key persons and access to essential resource material in each of these locations.
In Japan: Sister Monika Nakamura and her religious community for indispensable assistance with both travel arrangements and schedule of interviews, and for their inspiration and encouragement.

In the United States, for their hospitality and guidance: The Communities of Maryknoll Missionaries in Washington and New York; the pastor and parishioners of Our Lady of Fatima, Rhode Island; Fr.Justin in St. Mary's Parish, Boston; and Rev. John Chamberlain and his wife Allen at First St. John's United Methodist Church, San Francisco. I wish to acknowledge especially the considerable efforts made on my behalf by Arnold Kohen: his invaluable assistance with setting up both my research itinerary and interviews with key persons; the sharing of his rich experience of effective activism in the East Timor cause; and for the insight of a sympathetic 'outsider' into the operations of the Catholic Church in America.

In England: Estavao Cabral, Timorese in exile, and fellow expatriates, for giving me deeper understanding of the nature of the East Timorese struggle. I owe a special debt of gratitude to Catherine Scott at CIIR and Stephen Alston at CAFOD - for their continual encouragement and assistance over the whole period of my research and beyond, and for their invaluable help with accessing archives and with establishing fruitful contacts in East Timor and indeed in all the countries in which I undertook research.

Finally I wish to thank all the many people engaged in the international solidarity movement on behalf of the East Timorese who have shared their knowledge of this complex issue and passed on something of their zeal for justice. And I would like to thank my brother and my sister-in-law, and my friends in many places who have in various ways encouraged me to persist with this endeavour for the sake of the East Timorese, for the good of the Church, and for the welfare of the human family.

Glossary
Frequently used acronyms and non-English terms

ABRI	- *Anghatan Bersenjata Republik Indonesia* Armed Forces of the Indonesian Republic [from April 1999 renamed TNI, *see below*].
ACFOA	- Australian Council for Overseas Aid.
APEC	- Asia-Pacific Economic Co-operation (Summit)
APODETI	- *Associacao Popular Democratica Timor*: Timorese Popular Democratic Association.
ASEAN	- Association of South East Asian Nations.
CAFOD	- Catholic Agency for Overseas Development [England]
CCJPD	- Catholic Commission for Justice, Development and Peace [Australia]
CIIR	- Catholic Institute for International Relations [London]
CSIS	- Centre for Strategic and International Studies [Indonesia].
ETAN	- East Timor Action Network [USA]
FABC	- Federation of Asian Bishops Conferences
FALINTIL	- *Forcas Armadas de Libertacao Nacional de Timor Leste*: Armed Forces for the National Liberation of East Timor.
FRETILIN	- *Frente Revolucionara do Timor Leste Independente*: Revolutionary Front for an Independent East Timor.
Golkar	- *Golonkan Karya*: 'Functional Groups' - Indonesian political party based on social groupings: political vehicle of the *Orde Baru.*
INTERFET	- International Force for East Timor (September 1999).
KWI	- *Konperensi Waligereja Indonesia*: Indonesian Bishops Conference.
Liurai	- Traditional political and ceremonial leaders in East Timor.
MASRI	- *Majelis Serikat-serikat Religious Indonesia*: Council of the Federation of Religious in Indonesia.
MAWI	- *Majelis Agung Waligereja Indonesia*: Supreme Council of the Bishops of Indonesia [renamed *KWI* in 1987].
MFA	- *Movimento das Forcas Armadas*: Armed Forces Movement [Portugal].
Orde Baru	- New Order [Indonesian Government established by Suharto].
Pancasila	- The 'Five Principles' of the Indonesian State Constitution.
TAPOL	- *Tahanan Politik* [Political Detainee] - The Indonesia Human Rights Campaign [London]
Timor Lorosae	- Timor 'of the Rising Sun' [Indigenous *tetun* name for East Timor].
TNI	- *Tentara Nasional Indonesia*: Indonesian National Defence Forces.
UDT	- *Uniao Democratica Timorense*: Timorese Democratic Union.
UNAMET	- United Nations Assistance Mission in East Timor (1999)
UNTAET	- United Nations Transitional Administration in East Timor (1999-2002).

INTRODUCTION

The Reasons for this Book

In April 1974 the new government in Portugal initiated a process of de-colonisation in its province of East Timor. This was still to be completed when in December 1975 armed forces of the Republic of Indonesia invaded the territory with terrible brutality and began a repressive and exploitative occupation. This was to continue with varying degrees of intensity until October 1999 when the government in Jakarta finally abandoned its spurious claim to sovereignty over the half-island.

Members of religious orders working in East Timor were invited to contribute to the Council of the Federation of Religious in Indonesia (*MASRI*) in 1981. They described the painful reality of the situation they were experiencing:

> What has taken place during these five years is mostly invasion, war, looting, the destruction of the indigenous population, territorial subjection, colonial exploitation, the expulsion of the local population who are replaced by people from other islands, military occupation and attempts at mass mobilisations of people...to make war on each other...the people's way of life has been turned upside down and the basis of the community life has been destroyed...The people are experiencing oppression without end, their rights not acknowledged. They do not have a voice and live in fear...their produce is seized...even their property rights...and they get no explanation for it. But they remain in a very clear position concerning their ideals. Their faith stands firm and is strengthened...
>
> We are the religious of East Timor who together with the people were suddenly thrown into emptiness and alienation until we became the silent church of East Timor. Now we are more aware of the faith and see that this experience was very useful because our faith was deepened and more felt in life as a gift from God. This faith says that we are still one with the Universal Christian Church. It is precisely the dimensions of that universal faith which are being felt and deepened. ...
>
> We do not yet understand why the Indonesian Church and the Universal Roman Church have up till now not stated openly and officially their solidarity with the Church, people and religious of East Timor. Perhaps this has been *the heaviest blow* for us...We felt stunned by this silence which seemed to allow us to die deserted.[1]

This lament, along with subsequent appeals made from within the Catholic community of East Timor for the support of fellow believers, moved the author to investigate the nature of the response of the Catholic Church at large to the East Timorese plight.

The Encyclical Letter of Pope John Paul II *Tertio Millenio Adveniente* (1994), written to encourage spiritual preparation for the new Millennium, provided further stimulus. In this the pontiff regrets 'the lack of discernment, even acquiescence' shown by many of the faithful concerning the violation of fundamental human rights by some regimes. No doubt he had many awful situations in mind but he was certainly well aware of the sufferings of the people of East Timor. The Pope challenges the institution of the Church and every individual Christian to admit past shortcomings and amend their ways in responding to such matters:

> The Church cannot cross the threshold of the new millennium without encouraging her children to purify themselves, through repentance, of past errors and instances of infidelity, inconsistency, and slowness to act.

---

[1] *Statement of the Religious of East Timor*, (*MASRI*) 1981. Full text in: *The Church and East Timor*, 1993 Catholic Commission for Justice, Development & Peace (CCJPD) pp 13-14, Archdiocese of Melbourne. The words that evoked this book's main title are italicised.

Acknowledging the weaknesses of the past is an act of honesty and courage which helps us to strengthen our faith, which alerts us to face today's temptations and challenges and prepares us to meet them. (Paragraph 33)

Should we not also regret, among the shadows of our own day, the responsibility shared by so many Christians for grave forms of injustice and exclusion? It must be asked how many really know and put into practice the principles of the Church's Social Doctrine. (Paragraph 36)

In the Jubilee Year itself the International Theological Commission published a document entitled *Memoria e Reconciliazione: la Chiesa e le Colpe del Passato* [Memory and Reconciliation: the Church and the Faults of the Past]. This stressed the importance of discovering and facing up to the truth of the Church's involvement in historical situations of injustice and violence. Pastoral reasons put forward for such an exercise include the 'purification of memory' which is seen also to have beneficial effects upon the present because 'past sins frequently make their weight felt and remain temptations for today'. Moreover, 'fidelity to the will of God' and 'the call to bear witness to God's mercy and to his liberating and saving Truth' requires the believing community continually to appraise its own behaviour. It is hoped that such an endeavour by the Church might also evoke similar action from elsewhere in human society with positive outcome and so be 'a service to humanity'. The document then offers theological reasons for the taking of responsibility for past wrongs and shortcomings. Such action is seen as a necessary consequence of the spiritual bond which all Christians in every time and place have with each other as members of the Mystical Body of their Lord. It is also 'a kind of sharing in the mystery of Christ, crucified and risen, who took upon himself the sins of all' and it will 'produce fruits of liberation, reconciliation and joy - recognition of the truth is a source of peace'. Of course, it is equally important to acknowledge any positive efforts made by the Church in such matters. This may give encouragement to the promotion of justice and peace among the human family and also be regarded as 'a service to humanity'.

Aims of this Book

As stated already, in 1981 the religious of East Timor had lamented that solidarity on the part of the Catholic Church abroad with the suffering native people appeared to be lacking. It was evident that others within the local Church – and sympathisers elsewhere – were also of the view that the Timorese had been neglected, even betrayed, by those who shared their faith and from whom positive assistance had been expected. The author wished to defend the Church against such charges should they prove to be unfounded in reality.

When work on this project first began there were also certain practical purposes for the endeavour. These were to raise awareness of the ongoing suffering of the East Timorese and to make some contribution towards the cessation of the enduring hostility that had brought terrible anguish to so many on both sides of the conflict. The requirements of research in fact presented many such opportunities. At last a settlement has been reached, although the East Timorese have had to pay a heavy price and still face many and severe difficulties.

There is no doubt that the Church, in East Timor itself and around the world, could have a significant part to play in the long process of rebuilding a shattered society and devastated country, and in the work of reconciliation and renewal. It is hoped that the content of this book might encourage such a response. Moreover, by reflecting on the Church's response to the situation in East Timor some general directions for its present and future work throughout the world may be discovered.

Methodology

The response of the Church is recognised at various levels or circles within its hierarchical structure from the Pope and Vatican officials to the people in parishes. Particular attention is given to the disposition and influence of individual bishops, to the national and international Conferences of the hierarchy, and to the action of the agencies and organisations that bishops have established or permit to function within their dioceses. The contribution of some outstanding members of various religious congregations, of diocesan clergy, and of the laity is also noted.

The consideration of the Church's response begins with that of the Church in East Timor itself, by way of setting a standard for the subsequent evaluations. Limits of space preclude an exhaustive treatment of the response of the Church in every country with a connection to the East Timor tragedy.[2] The following are studied for the reasons given:

Indonesia, the occupying power;

Portugal, the former colonial ruler, regarded by the United Nations as having responsibility for the administration of the territory;

Australia, the nearest neighbour;

The United States of America, facilitator of the invasion and occupation through its arms supplies to Indonesia and its diplomatic influence;

Japan, largest donor of financial aid to the government in Jakarta.

Britain is considered because the extensive supply of armaments and aid by commercial enterprises and successive governments of this country provided both material and moral support for Indonesia's presence in East Timor.

The foundation of a proper pastoral and theological evaluation of the Church's response to the East Timor issue must be a thorough historical analysis - only then can it be asked whether what was or was not said and done by the Church can be understood as consistent with the Gospel. Thus in Part One a description is given of the significant features of local, regional and international politics. Other important considerations and influences are also outlined to the extent that space permits. These include reference to the relevant prescriptions of international law, and the effect upon the Church's response of the media coverage given to the issue. The operations of large commercial enterprises had their bearing upon developments and so upon the Church's effort, as did the engagement of non-governmental organisations at local, national and international level. The importance of these matters will be illustrated within the subsequent study of the Church's response in several countries of the world that is provided in Part Two. Each of these accounts is preceded by a brief presentation of the prevailing socio-political circumstances in which that Church lives. Then follows an examination of the disposition and activity of the Vatican - which also impacted upon the kind of effort made within each national Catholic Church, and beyond Church circles. An evaluation of the response of the Church is undertaken by using criteria derived from its official Social Doctrine, which is summarised in Part One while its practice in respect of the East Timor issue is observed and assessed in the chapters of Part Two.

Sources and Interpretation of Data

East Timor has been an international issue since the outset of the historical period under consideration and there is extensive archive material and literature available. But only a proportion of that was readily accessible in England during the time that could be given to research. Furthermore there was, and still is, comparatively little in print that is specifically on the subject of the Church's response to the issue, and even less in English.

---

[2] e.g. New Zealand, a near neighbour; Canada, which sold arms to Indonesia, donated aid to East Timor, and supported UN negotiations towards a settlement; ASEAN countries gave diplomatic support to Indonesia; the Lusophone nations were generally sympathetic to the East Timorese. Countries of the European Union besides the UK - Holland, Germany, and France especially - were involved for historical or commercial reasons, or through political alliance. The East Timor became truly international.

The Internet proved to be an invaluable tool of research – a number of web-sites entirely given over to the subject emerged in the 1990s, and email Conferences or 'Lists' specialising in the topic were helpful sources of information. The handling and interpretation of the sheer abundance of material on offer presented a practical difficulty. It was necessary to create a system of archiving the information so that it could be efficiently retrieved and items compared one with another, and over a period of time. The many and various contributions included statements and press releases by a range of government and military officials, analysis and commentary by scholars, reports of journalists, calls for action by campaigners, appeals and documentation by humanitarian and human rights agencies, the plans and achievements of commercial enterprises. The origin and purpose of the information affected its reliability and/or the usefulness of its content for this present work – propaganda and polemic, or the promotion of a particular or a narrow agenda, had to be recognised for what they were. Comparison revealed that some of the opinions that were expressed betokened an inadequate knowledge of the situation that actually prevailed in the half-island territory, and of the mind of the majority of the inhabitants. Notably, as with the printed material, a limited amount of attention was given in these *fora* to the Church's involvement in the issue – especially regarding that which pertained outside of East Timor.

It therefore became absolutely necessary to undertake field trips to the territory itself (1995, 1996), and subsequently to Indonesia (1996), Portugal (1997), Australia (1997, 1999), Japan (1998) and the United States (1998). These journeys provided an enhanced sense of the local socio-political scenario, and a deeper understanding of the range of demands put upon the Church both in respect of the East Timor issue and in the context of its own national, regional and global concerns. These demands can only be partially conveyed within the confines of this book. The field trips were of several weeks' duration in each instance and covered a considerable geographical spread within each country. During them it was possible to access local archives with pertinent material, and to meet with a number of government officials, academics and diplomats with a special knowledge of and engagement in the East Timor issue. Members of non-governmental organisations (NGOs) supporting the East Timorese cause, and a range of activists with different priorities and styles of operation were also interviewed. The principal interlocutors were, of course, leaders and members of the Catholic Church at various levels or circles of Church life, and some representatives of other denominations. The hospitality offered by all these persons made the research programme feasible and facilitated extended discussion and an exchange of experience.

To benefit as fully as possible from these meetings the author prepared a series of questionnaires specific to each country and to the operation of its Catholic Church. The intention was to ensure a consistency of approach and that the same areas of inquiry were covered in each instance. The questionnaires did indeed provide a helpful basis for the research and were always the initial point of reference. However, as research progressed in each country the initial questionnaire necessarily became more refined. Some areas of investigation proved to be less relevant than had been imagined, while other lines of inquiry proved to be more fruitful. In the light of information received further questions were added, while some were deleted as being of only secondary or even peripheral importance. The manner of conducting the interview also had to vary with the circumstances and the personality or role of the persons involved. Thus in East Timor, and sometimes in Indonesia, meetings had to be arranged discreetly, and the tape-recording of conversations was rarely possible because of the risks to which this would expose the interlocutors, especially the interviewee. Even the essential taking of notes in these situations had to be in brief or encrypted form and written up in full later. In locations where security issues were not such an overriding concern other inhibitions affected the expression of personal views as indicated below. In several countries there were language barriers to be overcome, although these were in all cases satisfactorily surmounted by the assistance of competent interpreters provided by Church or humanitarian agencies. The author also acquired a limited knowledge of the Portuguese and Indonesian languages which proved at least helpful in perusing archive material and in establishing positive relations with interviewees.

Of course, the material provided orally was affected by its origin and purpose as much as was that accessed via the Internet. Various pressures came to bear upon interviewees, especially - but not only - in East Timor and Indonesia. Their different responsibilities - such as the facilitation of the local Church's pastoral work, or the welfare of their families - presented them with the dilemma as to how much they could safely or properly divulge to the researcher. A perceived need for discretion and/or an unwillingness to be directly or fully quoted lest future commitment to the East Timorese cause would be restricted or jeopardised altogether could lead on occasion to an incomplete picture being presented, or to a bias in the viewpoint being expressed. It was not the author's experience in any instance that the interviewee was saying what they felt the interviewer wished to hear – all those being interviewed wanted to present their own perceptions. However, many were not so ready to listen to the contrasting views that the author increasingly became in a position to relate. The social and ecclesiastical status, professional background, and the personal history of the interviewee also affected their perception of the issue and the priorities they held as to its satisfactory resolution. Their level of education, breadth of experience, and measure of responsibility clearly affected their perceptions and judgements. Thus positions adopted varied from each other or were apparently self-contradictory either over time or even on proximate but separate occasions. For all these reasons the author considered it a necessity to conduct a wide range of interviews in order to gain a feel for the overall ethos, to avoid hasty conclusions, to complement or place in confrontation the spectrum of opinions expressed – and so work towards a balanced evaluation.

As the author's knowledge deepened through these researches an initially rather simplistic perception of the East Timor issue was steadily displaced by a growing appreciation of its complexity. For example, it was soon discovered that the East Timorese people themselves were not unanimous in their views regarding the Indonesian take-over of their country. It also became apparent to the author that his expectation of the response of the Catholic Church to the issue – within as well as outside of East Timor – had been rather idealistic. But as the momentum towards a final political resolution of the issue gathered speed the uncertainty of the eventual outcome also increased. This inculcated in the author a growing sense of the importance of solidarity on the part of the Universal Church with the Timorese cause, and with the local Church that was urging it. The research itself, and the increasing significance and pace of events, pointed to the need of a consistent attitude towards the issue within the family of the Church as a whole. It also became apparent that action by the Church would be all the more effective to the extent that it was done in co-operation with pro-Timorese sympathisers outside the Church's own community who had expertise to offer. Certainly the author was left in no doubt that the Church could (and should) make a significant contribution to any movement towards greater social justice.

PART ONE:

SETTING THE SCENE-

THE SOCIO-POLITICAL CONTEXT;
CRITERIA FOR EVALUATION

CHAPTER ONE - INDONESIA: INDEPENDENCE & REPRESSION

Indonesia is the world's most extensive archipelago with an east-west axis of about 3,500 miles and at least 17,500 islands. It is rich in natural resources, is the world's fourth most populous country, and has great significance in terms of international communication as it is located in the midst of important air and sea routes. A variety of cultural influences have been brought to bear upon its island peoples, many of whom migrated into the territory during centuries past. Hindu and Buddhist religious leaders who accompanied the early Asian traders sought and won converts to their respective faiths. These blended with traditional indigenous beliefs and continue to underlie the practice of Islam which arrived via Moslem merchants in the 13th century and to which the great majority of the people now adhere - with varying degrees of orthodoxy and orthopraxis. A number of significant kingdoms ruled by indigenous monarchs who had adopted the Hindu or Buddhist religions ran their course from ancient times until the middle of the second millennium AD. The most powerful of these was that of Majapahit in East Java (1293-1520) which traded widely across the chain of islands. Apologists of Javanese hegemony have used the historical importance of this regime to give the idea of an archipelago-wide state a respectable, non-colonial antiquity but in fact it had limited political and cultural influence beyond Java itself.[1] The Portuguese, who arrived in the 16th Century, also encouraged trade - and they won converts to Christianity (Catholicism). Gradually they lost out to the Dutch who sought to gain greater political and economic control than any previous outsiders had done and who established the Reformed Church in a number of the islands. The eastern half of Timor, however, remained under Portuguese control until 1975. There were a number of revolts against Dutch colonial rule especially in Java.

Nationalism grew ever stronger in the opening decades of the 20th century. In fact the Dutch had weak support among the inhabitants - as was revealed by the relative ease with which the Japanese were able to establish control over the country from December 1941 onwards. As the fortunes of war turned against them the Japanese sought to woo support from the people upon whose land they had encroached by promises of liberation from Western domination through the provision of military training and supplies. These efforts proved to be of no benefit to them but served to strengthen the ability of the native people to resist the return of the Dutch. Indonesian nationalists declared Independence on 17th August 1945 although the Dutch refused to recognise it and attempted to regain control by unsuccessful and costly military manoeuvres which generated international political opposition. This was especially vigorous from the United States, bent upon winding up the old European empires while increasing its own influence among developing countries in a form of neo-colonialism. Sovereignty was eventually formally transferred on 27th December 1949.[2] Ahmed Sukarno, the leading figure in the struggle for independence, was the first president of the new Republic and faced the prospect of forging a national identity and promoting the social development of his people. This proved to be a difficult task given the country's fragmented nature, lack of precedents, and the economic dislocation caused by colonialism. The national motto '*Bhinneka Tunggal Ika*'[3] was adopted calling for political unity among the diverse peoples of the archipelago.

---

[1] See: Bibliography – Ch1: Cribb, R.1992, p274-5 '*Majapahit*'. See also: Government of Indonesia Department of Foreign Affairs, Internet website: Background on Indonesia – The History of Indonesia, p.274-5: '*Majapahit*'.

[2] West New Guinea (West Papua) remained under Dutch control until 1962 when it passed to UN administration and then to that of Indonesia in 1963 until the 'Act of Free Choice' brought the territory under complete Indonesian sovereignty in 1969.

[3] Usually rendered 'Unity in Diversity'.

The period 1945-50 between the Proclamation of Independence and the actual establishment of the Republic of Indonesia was one of considerable turbulence. In his Proclamation Constitution Sukarno had envisaged a one-party model for the political process with considerable power afforded to the President. But during these years, when the armed forces, assisted by the mass of the people, resisted the attempts of the Dutch to reassert their control, he was prevailed upon by other independence leaders (such as Hatta and Sjahir) to allow a system in the style of Western democracies. This was supported by Western governments who feared that otherwise Sukarno would have too much power.[4]

The 'Liberal Democracy' which ensued (1950-59) was increasingly chaotic with numerous conflicting parties preventing the execution of coherent or consistent policies and hence national progress. Too many political groups saw it as an alien system not representing their interests. This was also a period during which the Indonesian Communist Party (PKI) increased in membership and organisational skill. Eventually Sukarno determined upon a return to the 1945 Constitution on which he based an arrangement of so-called 'Guided Democracy' within which, as leader of the national community, he could be more directive.

Unfortunately the period of Guided Democracy (1959-66) saw the mushrooming of bureaucracy, rampant corruption, and the economy slowing almost to a standstill. As a style of government it enjoyed wider support than its 'imported' forerunner but it proved unable to cope with the realities of power among the heterogeneous peoples of the archipelago and its cultural values were conservative rather than progressive. Crucially, Sukarno realised his need of help against Muslim groups favouring an Islamic or a Federal State and began openly to support the PKI which continued to grow numerically and in political ambition - much to the alarm of the Army, the Christian Churches, and the Western powers. The West was also alienated by Sukarno's leading role in the establishment of the Non Aligned Movement of nations seeking to strengthen their anti-colonialist and anti-imperialist solidarity.

In 1965 there was an attempted coup and successful counter coup which remain the subject of controversy but which are of great importance in Indonesia's post independence history.[5] It was alleged (on very dubious grounds) that the coup was planned by the PKI, and the Army promoted a wave of violence against Party leaders, members, and supposed sympathisers in which thousands of people were killed (estimates vary between 80,000 and one million) and many thousands more were imprisoned. These events had a traumatic effect upon the national psyche. Subsequently Sukarno's power waned and he was formally deposed in March 1968 by the *Orde Baru* ('New Order') government dominated by the military under the leadership of Suharto who became President.

The thirty-year presidency of Suharto was characterised by political manipulation and the de-politicisation and ideological control of the nation. Political parties were reduced in number, then reduced again; political activity was prohibited beyond the district capitals, and elections were tightly and ingeniously controlled. The ideals of Indonesian society propounded by Sukarno in the 1945 Constitution - the 'five principles' or *Pancasila* - were imposed as a practical guide for life and politics and became the ideology of a corporate state, to the exclusion or delimitation of other value systems.[6] Extensive military intervention in East

---

[4] For detail see: Bibliography – Ch1: Cribb, R. & Brown, C., 1995.

[5] For a brief account Bibliography – Ch1: Cribb, R. 1992.op.cit. p168f. *'Gerakan September Tiga Puluh – G30S, Gestapu'*. There are many studies of this contentious period. Arguments put forward suggest complicity of, variously, Sukarno *or* Suharto and defend the *PKI* against the allegations that led into its destruction.

[6] Stated in the Preamble to the Constitution as: 1) Belief in one God. 2) Just and Civilised Humanitarianism. 3) National Unity. 4). Popular Sovereignty governed by wise policies arrived at through deliberation and representation. 5) Social Justice for the entire Indonesian people. For further commentary see: Bibliography – Ch1: Cribb, R.1992, op.cit. p.340ff. *'Pancasila'*.

Timor began in 1975 and the regime formally incorporated the territory as the '27th Province of Indonesia' the following year.

Suharto's government always depended upon the support of the military who repressed dissent in the name of national unity and development while engendering deep-rooted discontent by gross abuses of human rights. A consistent feature of the political management exercised by the New Order regime was its exploitation of the 'Communist' bogey to strike down opponents or potential rivals, justify repressive measures and injustices, and cover up its own shortcomings. Economic pragmatism led swiftly to an accommodation with the capitalist powers for the advantages of investment, trade and aid - in contrast with the policy of Sukarno who had sought to cast off the reins of economic control exercised by the West. The revised relationship enabled the achievement of a notable industrial, agricultural, and social progress including an improved infrastructure, education provision, and health programme. But it also brought a renewed dependency on Western support. The military and business elite (and foreign corporations) benefited disproportionately more than the great mass of the people among whom poverty remains endemic. The population continued to increase, and national policies of birth control and of transmigration to less populated islands failed to ease demographic pressures in Java and Bali.[7] Among the sorry consequences of widespread corruption, cronyism, nepotism and mismanagement was the considerable loss of potential income from abundant natural resources, and a number of environmental catastrophes.

Despite formidable repression, dissent with Suharto's government gradually developed. The restrictive nature of the so-called 'Pancasila Democracy' was increasingly recognised, especially by the growing middle class. The demand for political liberalisation grew along with a call for diminishment of the considerable military influence that had come to pervade national politics and commerce.[8] The call for *Reformasi* grew louder, and the economic crisis that beset Indonesia in the autumn of 1997 led inexorably to President Suharto's resignation the following May.

Vice President Habibie took up the reins of office. He enjoyed the support of the commander in chief of the armed forces, an important group of Muslim intellectuals, and *Golkar* (the party given dominance by his predecessor who had made it his political vehicle)[9], but his power base was limited. Despite his links with the old regime, Habibie pursued a more open approach to government. Most significantly he proposed an option of special local autonomy to the people of East Timor which was to lead to a political crisis in that territory and ultimately to its 'uncoupling' from the Indonesian Republic. At the Presidential elections which were to follow in October 1999 Habibie was supplanted by Abdurachman Wahid, leader of the largest Muslim organisation *Nahdatul Ulama* (NU). Wahid won office by due process of election and appeared to be committed to thoroughgoing political, economic and social reform. However, he faced considerable obstruction from sections of the Armed Forces and civilian elite who had prospered under Suharto and who still retain substantial influence. Confidence in his administration steadily diminished both in Indonesia and abroad and in July 2001 the supreme legislative assembly replaced him by his vice-President Megawati Sukarnoputri, daughter of founding president Ahmed Sukarno.

This often-turbulent history has been the context in which the Catholic Church in Indonesia has had to function. It affected the policies of foreign governments and of international commerce, and so also the response of the Church to the East Timor issue especially within those countries that had vested interests in Indonesia.

---

[7] The population now numbers over 200 million.

[8] For detail see: Bibliography – Ch1: Cribb 1992 op.cit. pp133-5; Lowry, R.1996; Indonesian Armed Forces (since April 1999 *Tentara Nasional Indonesia - TNI*) Internet web-site: *'Defence & Security Policy'*.

[9] For detail see: Bibliography – Ch1: Cribb, R.1992 op.cit.; May, B. 1978, pp237f 'The *Golkar* Campaign'.

CHAPTER TWO - EAST TIMOR: OCCUPATION & RESISTANCE

Timor Island lies about 300 miles north west of Darwin, Australia. East Timor is some 14,000 square miles in area - roughly the size of Wales. A conservative estimate of the population in 1974 would number it at 650, 000. There are over thirty regional languages and dialects. A lingua franca, *Tetun*, is widely but not universally spoken. Although there are kinship links with the inhabitants of the border areas of West Timor, for much of their history the East Timorese have been a distinct community from the people living in the Western half of the island. This distinction was enhanced during the colonial period when West Timor became a Dutch possession (and in 1945 part of the Indonesian Republic) while East Timor continued under the rule of the Portuguese who had first arrived in the 16th century and laid claim to the territory in 1701.

Formerly the East Timorese belonged to various small kingdoms based on kinship, and around important cult sites with their own ceremonial leaders and political rulers known as *liurai*. The underlying social systems were resistant to Portuguese efforts at reorganisation and were a significant factor in the resilience of the East Timorese to the subsequent imposition of Indonesian rule and culture. However, divisions within East Timorese society also have a long history and were exploited by successive external rulers. This disunity has its significance for the role and response of the Church both within the territory itself and in the wider world.

Decolonisation and Political Subversion

In Portugal on April 25th 1974 the Armed Forces Movement (*MFA*) ousted the regime of Salazar's successor Caetano in the so-called Carnation Revolution and established a Government committed to capitalist modernisation and to off-loading colonial responsibilities. A de-colonisation process was soon initiated in East Timor and several political groupings emerged proposing various options to the people.

There were three parties that gained significant support. The manifesto of APODETI *(Associao Popular Democratica Timorense)* called for 'an autonomous integration into the Republic of Indonesia in accordance with International Law'. There was considerable Indonesian influence in its creation. UDT (*Uniao Democratica Timorense* -Timorese Democratic Union) was initially the most popular party standing for 'the self-determination of the Timorese people oriented towards a federation with Portugal and the rejection of the integration of East Timor into any foreign country' - a progressive autonomy under the Portuguese flag. It enjoyed the support mainly of those Timorese who had benefited from Portuguese rule: the traditional and administrative elite. ASDT *(Associacao Social Democratica Timor)*, the Timorese Social Democratic Association, was committed to 'the universal doctrines of socialism and democracy, economic reforms, and a gradually-achieved independent nationhood'. Its competent campaigning, practical programme of social reform, and identification with the common people soon won this party majority support. In September 1974 it changed its name to FRETILIN *(Frente Revolucionaia de Timor Leste Independente)* as being more expressive of the radical nature of its purposes.[1]

As already noted, the *Orde Baru* regime in Indonesia was minded to incorporate the territory into the Indonesian Republic. To this end it gave support to the pro-integration fac-

---

[1] Other parties with few adherents included: KOTA *(Klibur Oan Timur Aswain)*, 'Sons of the Warriors', which aimed to preserve the authority of village headmen and supported some form of integration with Indonesia. ADITLA *(Associacao Democratica para a Integracao de Timor Leste na Australia)* favoured some form of union with Australia but soon disbanded as it was given no encouragement by the Australian political leadership. TRABALHISTA, a 'Labour Party' comprised only the members of one extended family.

tions and contributed significantly to internal divisions amongst the East Timorese. At the international level Indonesian diplomats supported the contention that East Timor had no viability as an independent state and that its affiliation to Indonesia made geographical, economic and political sense. As these manoeuvres became more apparent a coalition was formed between the UDT and FRETILIN to prevent such a take-over. However, agents of the Indonesian Military Intelligence Co-ordinating Agency (BAKIN) operating in Timor were able to play upon uncertainties within and between the party leaders and the coalition could not be sustained. At a critical stage some members of the FRETILIN leadership, fresh from the political upheavals in Lisbon, expressed sympathies with a Marxist perspective on the social order. In East Timor it is doubtful that this ever amounted to anything more than a vigorous nationalism. FRETILIN never sought any relationship with Communist powers. But however brief or superficial this dalliance with Marxism was it had significant consequences for the people of East Timor. In the first instance the party's 'Marxist sympathies' provided Indonesia with some ground (albeit poor) on which to base the claim that FRETILIN was a Communist movement, thus stirring opposition from all those who perceived Communism as a threat to their peace and prosperity. The alleged 'Marxist character' of FRETILIN also affected the Church's response to their plight - as will be seen in all the succeeding chapters of this book.

In East Timor UDT leaders were moved into staging a coup to prevent FRETILIN from gaining political domination. A civil war resulted, lasting throughout August and September of 1975, costing several thousand lives, and intensifying the divisions of East Timorese society. The Portuguese colonial administration could not control the conflict with the limited resources available to it and withdrew to the neighbouring island of Atauro. This brief but bloody strife ended with FRETILIN in control of virtually the whole of the country, while UDT sympathisers, and many others simply taking refuge from the conflict, had fled to West Timor where they came under Indonesian influence.

Pro-integrationists fostered the belief in Indonesia and in international circles that the civil war was continuing, thereby strengthening the case for intervention in the territory. A number of tentative military incursions were made, of which the one reaching Balibo in October 1975 is noteworthy as several Western journalists were killed there. These were repulsed by FRETILIN forces but the lack of international condemnation encouraged Jakarta's intent and East Timorese anxiety. Since outright invasion seemed imminent, and in the hope that a direct appeal to the United Nations might more quickly provide defence than one routed via a pre-occupied Portuguese government, the FRETILIN administration unilaterally declared East Timor a Democratic Republic on 28th November 1975. The very next day, in Atambua (West Timor), a group of UDT-APODETI-KOTA-TRABALHISTA supporters were persuaded by Indonesian agents to sign a declaration of popular assent to East Timor's integration into Indonesia - the so-called 'Balibo Declaration'.

Thus was the stage set for an Indonesian intervention in East Timor to be presented to the world as a 'response to the request of the Timorese people', and demanded by the 'menace' of 'an unstable internal situation' and 'Communist assertion'. The details of the invasion and subsequent occupation of East Timor by Indonesian armed forces (ABRI), and the East Timorese resistance to it are amply provided elsewhere. However, its principal features should be noted and also the contrasting perspectives of Indonesian rule that were given by opposing sides during what was to prove a long-lasting conflict.

Invasion, Occupation and Resistance

FRETILIN was able to raise an army of some 20,000 men including a hard core of 2500 regular troops and a further 7000 with some military training under the Portuguese administration in East Timor or in the African colonies. These forces, called FALINTIL *(Forcas Armadas de Libertacao Nacional de Timor-Leste)*, mounted a strong resistance to the invasion and attempted occupation. At a national conference held 20 May-2 June 1976, the political and military decision was taken to fight a protracted 'people's war' against Indonesian domination. The competence of the FRETILIN/FALINTIL leadership was remarkable in outfacing an enemy marshalling an overwhelming number of troops and continually provided with arms, aircraft, and other technical support by Western powers especially the United States and Britain. Also notable was their provision for the safety and welfare of the thousands of civilians who fled into their care to escape ABRI's extreme brutality. For many of these people FRETILIN offered not only protection from ABRI but also emancipation from servitude to traditional chiefs, tribalism and superstition. But there were divisions within the leadership between the political and military wings, and additional tensions were created by some who sought a compromise with Indonesia, and by others who were in favour of a more radically Marxist purpose to the whole endeavour. Some civilians, even clergy, were dragooned into joining FRETILIN in the hills. There were a number of atrocities perpetrated by FALINTIL although these were exceptional and relatively small in scale, paling into insignificance when compared with the activities of ABRI which were near-genocidal in their effects. Nonetheless, such actions compounded the antagonism of UDT and other party supporters who had fled the Civil War. Some of these people found refuge in Portugal and Australia, and worked against support for FRETILIN in these countries and elsewhere internationally, as well as in East Timor itself. Their activities provided material for Indonesian apologists and caused confusion within Church circles deliberating an appropriate response.

By 1978 saturation bombing finally brought leader Nicolau Lobato to declare to the mass of people (about 160,000) who had sought refuge with them that FRETILIN could no longer provide protection and that they should give themselves up to the Indonesian authorities. Xanana Gusmao took command when Nicolau Lobato was killed soon afterwards and began the reorganisation of FALINTIL as a guerrilla force. Because this strategy became increasingly effective, East Timorese suspected of being supportive to FALINTIL were 'resettled' in compounds and roadside areas which could be closely supervised by the authorities but which lacked adequate food supply and were in many other ways deleterious to health. Together with the devastation caused to agriculture, killing of livestock, and disruption of social infrastructure already consequent upon the Indonesian military campaigns this counter-insurgency strategy was to create severe famine. Pictures and reports of this famine began to stir international concern, especially within the Church - but in terms of the need for humanitarian aid rather than a political settlement.[2]

Under Xanana's leadership a 'national reorganisation' began in 1981. At a National Conference held in March the *Conselho Revolucionario da Resistencia Nacional* (CRRN - National Council of Resistance) was consolidated with Xanana at the head. FALINTIL was disassociated from the FRETILIN party as such, becoming the armed wing of the overall East Timorese Resistance to Indonesian sovereignty. Although FALINTIL came to number only a few hundred soldiers these could be swiftly augmented if need be from civilian sympathisers who were ubiquitous. The Indonesian authorities were well aware of this and persistently tried (and failed) to eliminate what they described as a 'Security Disrupter Gang'[3] and to crush its extensive popular support. It was during this Conference that the Clandestine Network was set up - the *Nucleos de Resistencia Popular* ('NUREPS', Popular Resistance Centres), which became present in most inhabited areas as further elaborated below.

The revised strategy was effective and led to defensiveness on the part of ABRI and to several local treaties and finally a general cease-fire during which negotiations proceeded between Xanana and Indonesian Colonel Purwanto. Meanwhile an international appeal was made to 'all peace-loving peoples' to bring pressure to bear upon Jakarta to reach a peaceful

---

[2] See, e.g.
Bibliography – General (East Timor): Report by visiting US journalist Rod Nordland, in Retboll 1984, pp64-72; David Jenkins in Far Eastern Economic Review 29.9.78.

[3] *Gerakan Pengacau Keamanan (GPK).*

settlement and a Peace Plan was prepared notable for its generosity towards Indonesia.[4] However, Benny Murdani, a Catholic General who had been one of the inner circle of President Suharto's advisers advocating the annexation of East Timor and who had actually led the invasion force, broke the cease-fire unilaterally. Conflict between ABRI and FALINTIL was to continue thereafter with varying degrees of intensity.

Political Unity

From 1986 the East Timorese political leadership undertook a policy of 'National Unity'. This began with a *Convergencia Nacionalista* between the two major parties UDT and FRETILIN and in due course led to the birth of the *Conselho Nacional da Resistencia Maubere*[5] (CNRM), a national front embracing all East Timorese political parties and groups dedicated to securing national independence. CNRM included FRETILIN'S so-called 'External Delegation' whose members had left Dili just before the invasion to muster international support for the unilaterally declared 'Democratic Republic of East Timor' (especially from the Lusophone countries). CNRM's inclusiveness also led to increased support from the younger generation previously alienated by the old party rivalries. Another significant feature of CNRM was its purge of all left wing activists. This enabled greater support from Western and Church groups wishing to help the Resistance but previously inhibited by the 'Marxist associations' attributed to FRETILIN. However, it still had some inherent problems and although UDT co-operated at almost every level with CNRM in political campaigns it refused to be a full member of the Council.

A convention at Peniche in Portugal in April 1998, resulted in the establishment of the *Conselho Nacional da Resistencia Timorense* (CNRT - National Council of Timorese Resistance). This was the last attempt to establish an overarching political entity in which all parties, cultural groups and independent associations opposed to the Indonesian invasion and occupation could feel they were adequately represented and comfortable with the declared objectives and policy.[6]

These successive efforts reveal the difficulties experienced by the East Timorese at home and abroad in achieving the political unity necessary to resist the Indonesian project successfully. Nevertheless they were continued, thereby providing evidence of the widespread determination among East Timorese to assert their cultural and political identity.[7] This led in turn to increasing international sympathy, and encouraged the support both of secular organisations dedicated to the promotion of human rights and of Church agencies or groups committed to the furtherance of 'God's Kingdom of justice and peace' in the world.

It is important to acknowledge the sufferings endured by the women of East Timor and the crucial role played by them in the survival of their people and culture - both in the territory itself and elsewhere.[8] It is also undoubtedly the case that the work of women of other nationalities, both in East Timor and abroad, was of central importance in the overall response of all agencies committed to the East Timorese cause. This is true of those acting within or in the name of the Church and the Gospel, as will be seen.

---

[4] See Bibliography – Ch2: FRETILIN 1983, and Bibliography – General (East Timor): Retboll, T., 1984.. There were later revisions but the Peace Plan remained essentially the same in scope and tone, see: Bibliography – General (East Timor): CNRM Peace Plan 1989 - in ETAN Docs Vol 26:50f.

[5] 'Maubere' literally means 'My brother'. The word became a short-hand term for the reassertion of Timorese culture and the struggle against oppression.

[6] See Bibliography – Ch2: FRETILIN 1998.

[7] See e.g.: Agio Pereira, 'A Brief Note about CNRM' (East Timor Relief Association (ETRA) 9.2.1998); 'Timorese Political Parties Reject Indonesia's Special Status Offer', Timor Link Oct.1998, p8; and 'Statement of CNRT', ETRA Conference, 9.4.1999, Melbourne.

[8] For further details see Bibliography – Ch2: Aditjondro, G.J. 1997; Sissons, M.E. 1997; Galhos, B. 1997; Pires, M. & Scott, C. 'East Timorese Women: The Feminine Face of Resistance', in Retboll, T. 1998, pp141-152; Winters, R. (ed), 1999.

From the outset it was Indonesian policy to effect division among the East Timorese population and leadership, for example by placing some in positions of pseudo-authority, and by the recruitment of local men into the armed forces and 'civil guard' (*hansip,* or *wanra*). Some Timorese chose to collaborate with the Indonesian government, furthering its project and becoming its apologists. They included those who were disaffected with the former Portuguese administration and those who were keen to hold on to their traditional exercise of power. Some others felt particularly vulnerable to Indonesian aggression - or by what might transpire for them within an independent East Timor. There were also those who sought to advance their own interests regardless of the fate of the nation as a whole. Such persons were relatively few. A larger number of Timorese were initially persuaded (under considerable duress) of the 'good reasons' for political 'integration' with Indonesia but in due course they became disaffected. One important reason for their disaffection was the continuous brutality of the occupying forces. Another was the social marginalisation that indigenous people increasingly suffered as successive waves of migrants and transmigrants from other islands of the archipelago were encouraged by the government to settle in the territory and then came to benefit disproportionately from its resources and what opportunities there were for economic advancement.

Clandestine Resistance

By 1989 the Indonesian authorities were confident that they had achieved 'pacification'. Anxious to convince outsiders of the 'development' they had brought to the country and its people, they began to open up the territory to foreign visitors. The Clandestine Resistance seized upon the opportunity provided by the presence of such people. A series of more public activities were organised by a second generation of leaders who had grown up under the Indonesian administration but, far from accepting it, revealed themselves to be in the vanguard of dissent. The first large public demonstration was mounted during the Pastoral Visit of Pope John Paul II that took place in October that same year. It was not long before this was followed by further expressions of discontent - principally those made during the visit of US ambassador John Monro (January 17th 1990) and on the 50th anniversary of the Diocese of Dili (September 4th 1990). The underground networks also facilitated an extended interview by the Australian lawyer and journalist Robert Domm with Resistance commander Xanana Gusmao - in a FALINTIL camp in the bush (September 27th 1990). This meeting was of considerable importance in the dissemination of information to counteract Indonesian propaganda and in strengthening international sympathy for the Timorese plight.[9] Other high profile actions by Timorese student and youth groups were their entries into national embassies in Jakarta in quest of asylum, and demonstrations outside multilateral conferences hosted in Indonesia and elsewhere which drew the attention of the international media.[10]

The most renowned and tragic demonstration organised by the young leaders of the Clandestine Resistance took place during a memorial procession to Santa Cruz Cemetery on November 12th, 1991. ABRI soldiers fired indiscriminately into the unarmed crowd that included religious sisters, women and many children. Well over two hundred young people were killed and others subsequently 'disappeared', while many of the wounded were later murdered in and around the local hospital.

The reaction of the Indonesian Government to this atrocity (and of those whose interests lay in keeping its friendship) was to minimise the casualties, and dismiss the 'incident' as 'an aberration'. The Timorese, supported by their local Church leaders, claimed that, far from

---

[9] See: Bibliography - General (East Timor): Aarons, M. & Domm, R. 1992, p45f; Gunn, G. 1994, pp155-7, & 174.

[10] E.g. During the Asia Pacific Economic Co-operation meeting, Jakarta Nov.1994. Over one hundred students sought asylum in various embassies during the period 1995-6.

being exceptional, this action of the military was typical of the violent repression which had characterised the Indonesian occupation of East Timor for over twenty years.

In fact, the shocking event proved to be a watershed in the understanding of the reality of the East Timorese situation in the wider world, and indeed in Indonesia itself. This was because a number of foreign journalists and cameramen were caught up in the drama as it unfolded and were able to communicate internationally and almost immediately what they had witnessed. The Santa Cruz massacre also had a very significant effect upon the response of the Church to the Timorese plight.[11]

Contrasting Perspectives

Throughout the period under consideration the Indonesian Government and its agencies persistently declared that the entry of their forces into East Timor had been at the invitation of the 'majority' of the inhabitants whose lives had been disrupted by a civil war consequent upon the withdrawal of the Portuguese administration. Jakarta also alleged that the purpose of its actions was to protect the East Timorese, and Indonesia - and the region as a whole - from the incursion of Communism encouraged by the left wing political faction FRETILIN. Indonesian sovereignty, it was asserted, was formally 'requested' by 'representatives' of the East Timorese people on May 31st 1976 and was 'graciously agreed to' by President Suharto on behalf of the Republic on July 17th 1976. Following this 'Act of Self-Determination' the East Timorese 'confirmed their desire' to accept the status of being Indonesia's '27th Province' by participating in national and provincial elections. Thereby they came to belong to an archipelagic community with its antecedent in the pre-colonial Majapahit Kingdom.

It was claimed that the East Timor had benefited extensively from a Development budget more generous than that afforded to any other 'Province' and that dramatic improvements had been achieved there in education, health, infrastructure, and the economy as a whole. The remarkable growth in the local Catholic Church was declared to be indicative of the religious tolerance characteristic of the Indonesian State, based as it is upon the principles of *Pancasila*.

The Government regretted that 'an intransigent minority' persisted in 'separatist' rebellion, but their ultimate failure was assured because the 'population as a whole' recognised the 'advantages of Indonesian sovereignty'. The view of the regime was that those who had the 'best interests' of the East Timorese at heart should try to assist in their progressive unification within the rich diversity of the Indonesian family proclaimed by the national motto *'Bhinhekka Tunggal Ika'*.

The Armed Forces of the Republic (ABRI) were committed to securing this 'Unity in Diversity' through its dual role which included, along with intelligence and combat duties, its 'territorial' work, namely engagement in the practical tasks of national development - a socio-political function. The substantial numbers of personnel deployed in East Timor (usually noted as 'some 5,000') were justified by these allegedly benevolent 'social' purposes.

The East Timorese who continued to resist Indonesian rule (and those around the world who rallied to their cause) maintained that the military-dominated Indonesian govern-

---

[11] See:
Bibliography - General (East Timor): Krieger, H. (ed). 1997, Index – 'Santa Cruz Killings'; Dunn, J. 1996; Gunn, G.C. 1994; Carey P. & Carter Bentley, G. 1995; Kohen, A.1999;
Bibliography - Ch 2: Pinto C. & Jardine, M. 1997;
See also: 'Report of the [Indonesian]National Commission of Inquiry' 26.12.1991; 'Report on the Santa Cruz Event', UN Geneva (1995); 'Causes of the Incident at Santa Cruz', Bishop Belo of Dili, *Matra* August 1992; 'Inquiry lacks credibility', Tapol 108 (1991) pp12-13; 'The Hearing on East Timor: The Santa Cruz Massacre, 12.12.1991', Parliamentary Human Rights Group, London; for Photos by Steve Cox see Bibliography – Ch2: Cox, S. & Carey, P. 1995; Video footage by Max Stahl, 'In Cold Blood', First Tuesday, Granada TV, UK.

ment was set upon the incorporation of the territory purely out of self-interest. Jakarta wished to gain access to the substantial oil and natural gas deposits in the southern sea, to the aromatic sandalwood, and to the renowned '*arabica*' coffee grown in extensive plantations established by the Portuguese. In their understanding of the situation it was Indonesian military agents who had provoked the civil war between the rival political factions which had emerged when Portugal initiated the de-colonisation process. This war had been concluded and the victorious and popular socialist-inspired FRETILIN party was effecting beneficial government in the absence of the Portuguese administration - which it acknowledged, and which it had requested to return and complete the de-colonisation. There had been no links with international Communism at any time.

This account asserted that Indonesia had endeavoured to impose its control: through force of arms; by disruption of the existing social order; through a deliberate strategy of terror; and by a variety of repressive measures. These actions had resulted in the deaths of a third of the population (at least 200,000 people, the great majority civilians) either in direct conflict or as a result of malnutrition, disease, or from trauma related to the upheaval and devastation. The Indonesian military presence in the territory was calculated by the Resistance to be at least 20,000 strong, even as late as 1998 - long after 'pacification' had supposedly been achieved (numbers that were to increase the following year). The military presence was described as intimidating, responsible for continual and gross violations of human rights, and presenting a major obstacle to any satisfactory resolution of the conflict. It was judged to be in the territory to effect Indonesian rule against the wishes of the great majority of the population who continued to oppose the occupation in every possible way. The so-called 'territorials' were engaged in information gathering and could be called upon for combat duties as required.

In this perspective there had been no 'Act of Self Determination' acceptable by United Nations criteria. Local people had been coerced into participation in the national and provincial 'electoral process' in order that Indonesia might win international acceptance for the 'legitimacy' of its rule. The alleged 'developments' in the territory had not been to the general advantage of the original inhabitants. Rather they had benefited 'outsiders', including the many who had come to live there as economic migrants or on the Indonesian Government's 'Transmigration' programme and who in due course comprised nearly a quarter of the overall population of 750,000. The significant growth in membership of the local Catholic Church (from 30% – 90% between 1975 and 1998) was credited to its faithful service of the people during the many years of oppression, including the courageous defence of their human rights as individuals and as a nation. [12]

But the response of the universal Church to the plight of the East Timorese people must be considered not only in the context of such conflicting perceptions and accounts. Attention must also be given to the international context that has prevailed during the quarter of a century that has elapsed since the catalyst of the Portuguese revolution in 1974.

---

[12] For the Indonesian Government perspective, see Bibliography – Ch2: Department of Information: 1979, 1987, 1991; Department of Foreign Affairs: 1977, 1981, 1983, 1985, 1997.
See also Statement by Foreign Minister Ali Alatas to the National Press Club (Washington DC) March 1992 (cited by, *inter alia,* Simpson, G. 'Judging the East Timor Dispute' in Hastings International and Comparative Law Review, Winter 1994); Statements of RI Embassy Officials: UN (Agus Tarmidzi) Geneva, March 1997; USA (Arifin Siregar) 10.12.96 and 24.1.97; Canada (Benjamin Parwoto, with F.Lopez da Cruz), April 1997 and (Moses Tandung) to Editor of 'The Press' 9.1.97.
For the contrasting perspective, see Bibliography – General (East Timor): Barbedo de Magalhaes, A. 1990, and 1992; Horta, J.R.1987, especially Ch19; Bibliography – Ch2: Aditjondro, G.J., 1994, (1); Mubyarto, Sutrisno, *et al.,*1991; de Sousa Saldhana, J.M.,1994; Turner, M. 1992; Bibliography – Ch8: CISET 1994.

CHAPTER THREE - INTERNATIONAL RELATIONS[1]

Action and Inaction

The United Nations General Assembly condemned the Indonesian invasion of East Timor immediately, adopting Resolution 3458 (12.12.1975) which recognised the right of the East Timorese to 'self-determination, freedom and independence', and calling on the Republic of Indonesia to 'withdraw its forces without delay'. Responding to the recommendation that it take 'urgent action' the Security Council unanimously repeated this condemnation and called upon 'all States to respect the territorial integrity of East Timor', a position that had a firm basis in International Law already established at that time. However, these Resolutions were ignored by Indonesia, and there was no commitment by member States to carry them into effect, while there was considerable diplomatic lobbying favourable to the position of Indonesia. The GA Resolution was repeated annually until 1982 when it was shelved because of diminishing international support. Instead the Secretary General was charged to 'explore avenues for achieving a comprehensive settlement' which led in due course to 'Tri-partite Talks' with Indonesia and Portugal. Years of fruitless negotiations were to follow until a determined input from Secretary General Kofi Annan and the proposals of Indonesian president B.J.Habibie stimulated developments, as will be seen. It is necessary to give further attention to this apparently unsympathetic response from the international community for two reasons: it casts further light upon the predicament of the East Timorese people (and their local Church); it is in such a context that the Church elsewhere has had to operate.

In the first place East Timor is somewhat remote from the centres of political power, and culturally isolated. Apart from that of Portugal, and to a much lesser extent Australia - and the relatively short, if bloody, occupation by Japan in World War II - there had been a lack of international involvement historically in the territory, and there was a general lack of interest in its future. There had not been any active indigenous political elite or independence movement before 1974, and in so far as the attention of the world was directed towards the disintegration of the Portuguese maritime empire it focussed on African states such as Mozambique and Angola. The FRETILIN radio cries for help at the time of the invasion were paid no heed, and subsequently their reception in Darwin was prevented by the Australian government's confiscation of the necessary equipment.

More fundamentally, Indonesia is of strategic importance both commercially and militarily, and has therefore benefited from the sycophancy and anxieties of its neighbours and the self-interest of the Western capitalist powers. The Suharto regime found favour with the 'business community' because of its openness to foreign investment and trade, and because its suppression of internal dissent created a stable economic environment. With over 200 million inhabitants the Indonesian archipelago presents a huge market for western goods, immense natural resources, investment opportunities and cheap labour. Moreover, Indonesia has considerable influence in the maintenance of Western access to the consumers of the whole SE Asian region. Especially during the Cold War period Indonesia's location - spanning important air and sea routes - and its political affiliation was of great military significance. As already noted, the Western powers viewed Sukarno's association with Communist forces with alarm, and backed the displacement of his government by Suharto's *Orde Baru* regime. The weaponry and military training that was part of this support was to be deployed against the unprovided East Timorese both in the invasion of their homeland and in several subsequent campaigns attempting to achieve their subjugation. Also of considerable impor-

---

[1] For detail see: Bibliography - General (East Timor): Carey, P. 1996; Dunn, J., 'The Timor Affair in International Perspective', in Carey, P. & Carter-Bentley, G. 1995, pp59-72; Chomsky, N., 1996, Ch.7 & Ch.8; Horta, J.R.1987, Ch.14 & Ch.15; Krieger, H.1997, Introduction xxiv-xxv, Ch5 & 6, and Index - Arms, International Court of Justice; Tanter, R. (ed), 2001, Part III (pp 127-188).

tance militarily was access to the deep water passage afforded by the Ombai-Wetar Strait to the north of Timor which reduced the journey time for submarines from the Pacific to the Indian Ocean by several days. Furthermore, Australian military intelligence on the situation in East Timor was shared with Britain and the United States, addressing Western/Indonesian rather than Timorese concerns. The ideological opposition to Communism on the part of the Church also had a bearing upon the outcome, as will be seen.

For these reasons Indonesia was to receive considerable diplomatic support in international forums where Indonesian envoys and delegations pushed the view that the annexation of East Timor had been requested by its people and was to their benefit and also to that of the region as a whole. As the largest Muslim nation in the world Indonesia received the support of other Islamic countries. As a founder member, Indonesia found favour within the Non-Aligned Movement, even winning the backing of India - which might otherwise have been critical of such blatant neo-colonialism. Indonesia could count also on the good will of the other countries within the Association of South East Asian Nations (ASEAN).[2]

The Mass Media

It is important to give consideration to the role of the communications media in the level of international understanding of the East Timor issue, although it can only be summarised here. In Indonesia the Suharto regime exercised tight control over the mass media and dissent from the government's account and justification of East Timor's integration was exceptional until the authoritarian president was ousted in 1998.[3] But journalists in Western democracies also demonstrated a considerable degree of compliance with the priorities of their government and social elite -themselves dominated by corporate and/or military interests. They were constrained by what were considered to be the parameters of acceptable discourse – an 'institutional pressure'.[4] At the practical level coverage was dependent upon the amount and quality of information to which journalists had access. Good relations with government sources had to be both cultivated and maintained, and any assessment of the situation within East Timor itself was very difficult during the fourteen-year period when the territory remained closed to outsiders. Coverage was also affected by the degree of popular interest in the issue. The most able of professionals who were committed to the East Timorese cause found it difficult to discover fresh 'angles' on the story that would evoke the attention of the readership. Outside of Portugal and Australia it was also hard to sustain interest over a prolonged period of time in a complex and distant issue that competed for public attention with other significant international affairs of more evident pertinence to the reader.[5] The paucity of visual material was a significant factor in the lack of coverage especially on television – but even when this was provided (as in the case of the Santa Cruz massacre) its deployment had a limited duration. In short, the full truth of the situation in East Timor was an early casualty, and for years the reality was either concealed, or misrepresented, or lacked balanced or ade-

---

[2] The categories of international recognition of Indonesia's sovereignty in East Timor are detailed in Krieger, H. 1997 op.cit. The positions held by the countries studied in this book were: *de iure* (Australia); *de facto* (USA, Japan); non-recognition (Portugal, United Kingdom) – further detail in Part 2. NAM condemned the invasion at Colombo in 1976 but thereafter its position varied, see: Horta, J.R.1987, op.cit. Ch15. For detail of ASEAN response see: Bibliography – Ch3: Inbaraj, S. 1995.

[3] See, e.g.: 'The Press Under Siege: Censorship in Indonesia', 10.11.1994, Article 19, London; 'The Indonesian Propaganda War Against East Timor', Cabral, E. 1996, Paper to Conference '*Formacao para a democracia em Timor*', hosted by University of Oporto.

[4] Noam Chomsky to the author, MIT Boston, Sept 1998. For detail see: Bibliography – Ch3: Herman, E.S. & Chomsky N. 1994; Parenti, M. 1993; Pilger, J. 1998, Part VIII 'The Media Age'.

[5] Arnold Kohen; John Sharkey (Assistant Foreign Editor, Washington Post 1969-94), Don Southerland, (Washington Post 1976-84), Alan Berger (Editorials, Boston Globe) to the author, Washington and Boston, Sept. 1998.

quate coverage in many leading outlets of information.[6] It must also be admitted that although the Church has always acknowledged the importance of the mass media and drawn attention to its moral dimension[7], the statements of Catholic officials on the East Timor issue were rather sparse and apparently inconsistent. They provided little material for sympathetic journalists to use as a peg for articles on the subject. Overall the Church gave limited coverage to the subject of East Timor in its own broadcasting or printed publications, thereby falling short in its proclaimed responsibility 'to furnish the missing information to those deprived of it and to give a voice to the voiceless'.[8] Some attention was given to the humanitarian dimension of the East Timorese suffering, but little to the political causes and remedies until late in the day. Indeed, there were some Catholic writers who argued in support of the Indonesian annexation. Although the Church as an international community with religious personnel actually present in the territory had special insight into the nature of the situation that prevailed there, Catholic journalism more often echoed rather than led the secular media in its treatment of the issue. But, as in secular circles, there were notable exceptions to this general pattern whose contribution was of critical importance in the eventual outcome.

Developing Circumstances

Finally, it is important to recognise that the international scene and international perception of the East Timor situation changed considerably over the years since 1975.

The growing appreciation of the reality of Indonesian rule in the territory was in part due to the persistent resistance of the great majority of the indigenous inhabitants, and to the testimony given by Timorese refugees in the various countries of their dispersion. Of great importance was the witness, testimony and growth of the local Church, as will be seen in Part 2. The 'opening' of the territory to foreign visitors in 1989 which at last allowed some direct communication with the inhabitants, albeit under the scrutiny of Indonesian intelligence agents, also helped in the dissemination of fuller information. The same year Pope John Paul II made a pastoral visit to the Church in East Timor – which drew international attention to the situation there. Another significant development that impacted upon the issue began with the entry of Portugal into the EEC (now EU) on 1 January 1986. This led in due course to a heightened awareness and positive action on behalf of East Timor in the European Union and other related forums.[9] The emergence of an international organisation of Parliamentarians for East Timor (founded June 1988) began to have influence in the corridors of diplomacy. Most significantly, in 1989 the Cold War ended affecting the nature and priorities of numerous international alliances. The subsequent liberation of the Baltic States focused attention on the continuing captivity of East Timor.

International Law

A number of universally obligatory standards known as *ius cogens* or 'peremptory norms' had long been acknowledged by the legal community, for example in respect of the aggressive use of armed force, violations of human rights, and denial of the right to political

---

[6] See: Bibliography – General (East Timor): Chomsky, N. 1978; O'Shaughnessy, H. 'Reporting East Timor, etc' in Hainsworth, P. & McClosky, S. 2000, Ch3; Bibliography – Ch3: Ball, D .& McDonald, H. 2000; Burke, A. 1990; Tiffen, R. 2001. See also: Woods, T. 1992, 'Propaganda: Press, Policy and East Timor', BA (Hons) Thesis (unpublished), University of Canberra.

[7] See Bibliography Ch4: Papal Encyclical Pius XII, *Miranda Prorsus* (1957); II Vatican Council, *Inter Mirifica* (1963); Pastoral Instructions (Pontifical Council for the Instruments of Social Communication) *Communion et Progressio* (1971), *Aetatis Novae* (1992).

[8] *Aetatis Novae* (1992), op.cit. paragraph 4. Text in Briefing (CBCEW) 1992, Vol 22, No9, pp4-11.

[9] e.g. European Parliament, Joint Assembly ACP/European Union, APEC, ASEM. Countries of the Lusophone community (e.g. Brazil) raised the issue at fora in which they were participants, e.g. Ibero-Latin America Summit, etc. Indonesian officials acknowledged the impact of this upon international attitudes – see: Director General for Political Affairs Nugroho Wisnumurti, EU Ambassador Atmono Suryo, *Realitas*, Jakarta, Feb.1999.

self-determination. Experts contended that the manner of the Indonesian invasion and annexation of East Timor offended against both customary and humanitarian international law - but the International Community did not bring these principles to bear effectively. This was partly because its members had to contend with skilful Indonesian diplomacy in defence of the 'integration' of the half-island territory but also (and principally) because the vested interests of the most powerful nations meant that the political will to enforce the law was lacking. There were also weaknesses within the legal system itself which inhibited a satisfactory resolution of the East Timor issue. These included its decentralised nature and the lack of clarity and precision in many of its norms – particularly in respect of the right to self-determination. But the clarification of the legal norms and of their application had been on-going and the invasion of Kuwait by Iraq in 1990 highlighted their violation by Indonesia in regard to East Timor and re-invigorated efforts to challenge the status quo.[10] However, bearing in mind the regular exhortations it makes for these crafted prescriptions to be honoured by the community of nations, the institutional Church's own application of them and appeal to them in the case of East Timor was less than satisfactory, as will be seen.

Solidarity Groups

Certainly the massacre in the Santa Cruz cemetery (November 1991) had international impact - and a stimulating effect upon NGO and Church activists on behalf of the Timorese cause. A valuable partnership steadily developed between 'faith-based' and secular groups in their advocacy of 'justice and peace for East Timor'. While these had distinctive approaches to the issue their objectives were broadly shared and a productive fusion of effort and inter-mingling of membership came about even in those countries where there had been a historical divide between such organisations. However, on occasion, tensions arose because of the belligerent public style of some single-issue groups who also seemed insensitive to other pressing concerns which Church people were obliged to address and generally to the Church's burden of wide-ranging institutional responsibilities. There were also grounds for anxiety on the part of Church groups that their personal dedication and 'moral capital' was being used to serve the sometimes narrow agenda of secular organisations. At the same time it has to be acknowledged that the direction given by the Church leadership was far from clear. Tardy, often hesitant and ambiguous, it diminished the confidence of committed activists, Gospel-motivated and secular alike. But there is no doubt that the work of such solidarity groups internationally was a primary factor in achieving the liberation of the people of East Timor from oppressive Indonesian rule.[11]

Corporate Responsibility

Another pertinent event was the conduct of the case in the International Court of Justice in 1995 in which Portugal contended the legality of the treaty (1989) between Australia and Indonesia in respect of the exploitation of the oil and gas reserves in the Timor Sea.[12] These substantial deposits had undoubtedly been a major factor in evoking the East Timor project in the minds of the *Orde Baru* regime, and in the complicity of the Western powers with the Indonesian take-over of the territory.[13] The Church has made frequent pronouncements (in general terms) on the just distribution of natural wealth with an especial regard to the prior needs of the poor, and on the responsibilities of both governments and the business

---

[10] See: Bibliography – Ch3: CIIR/IPJET, 1995; Leite, P.P. (ed) 1998. Key texts are in Kreiger, H. 1997.op.cit. The Timorese perspective is expressed by (e.g.) Horta, J.R. 1987, op.cit. especially Chapters 13,17 & 18.

[11] See Bibliography - Ch3: Baranyi, S., Kibble, S., Kohen, A., O'Neill, K. 1997.

[12] For documents see Bibliography – General (East Timor): Krieger, H.1997.op.cit. Ch7; for technical legal discussion of issues see Bibliography - Ch3: CIIR/IPJET 1995, Section V.

[13] See Bibliography - Ch3: Aditjondro, G.J.1999.

community for the promotion of general human welfare.[14] But this author discovered few overt challenges by the Church hierarchy to the planned exploitation of these Timorese resources. This was also true in respect of the export of coffee beans, sandalwood, marble and other local assets that enriched the Indonesian military and their civilian associates in the *Orde Baru*. It was the case even in those nations whose economies would directly and substantially benefit from such stolen goods – Indonesia, Australia – or which were the home of the large industrial companies which would likely (and profitably) undertake the extraction of the mineral and gas deposits (such as the United States). The other principal Western commercial connection with the East Timor issue was the extensive supply of arms and equipment to the Indonesian Military (especially by the United States & Britain). Again the Church had shortcomings in the application of Social Doctrine to this practice, as will be seen.[15]

The award in 1996 of the Nobel Peace Prize to two East Timorese leaders was of considerable importance as it stirred international media and public interest in the issue. One of the laureates was Jose Ramos Horta, the foreign minister of the short-lived Democratic Republic of East Timor, who had toiled in exile to raise awareness of the injustices suffered by his people. His co-laureate was East Timorese diocesan bishop Carlos Belo and consequently the award had important repercussions at all levels within the Church.

Meanwhile in Indonesia itself a pro-democracy movement gradually grew in strength, receiving much inspiration from young East Timorese students attending institutions in the Republic. The collapse of the economy in the autumn of 1997 not only led to the resignation of Suharto the following May, but was to have significant implications for the future of East Timor. An immediate consequence was the wish of international business interests to see the matter settled so that the desirable stable environment for investment, productivity, marketing and profit would be achieved.

The Year of Crisis

By the end of 1998 political pressures within and upon Indonesia were favouring the 'uncoupling' of East Timor and, on January 27th 1999, president Habibie surprised everyone by repeating his earlier offer of 'wide-ranging autonomy' but adding that, should this be rejected, Indonesia should 'let East Timor go'. Within the long-established and hitherto largely fruitless tri-partite dialogue under the auspices of the UN Secretary General, Portugal seized upon this opportunity with the full support of the Timorese pro-independence umbrella organisation CNRT. An Agreement was reached in New York on May 5th between all parties principal, that is: Indonesia, Portugal and the United Nations.[16] According to this Agreement, the details of an autonomy proposal acceptable to both Indonesia and Portugal would be put to the East Timorese and a 'popular consultation' of the native people's wishes would be conducted under the supervision of a special United Nations mission, UNAMET. Security for the whole process was to be entrusted to the Indonesian armed forces.

The dramatic and violent events that took place during this 'year of crisis' are elaborated elsewhere (see below, Note 17). Significant elements of the Indonesian Military - in an attempt to safeguard their vested interests in the territory - tried to intimidate the population into voting for a continuation of the status quo. At the same time some pro-Jakarta East Timorese politicians established several 'pro-integration' groupings in a bid to hold on to their power and status. Nonetheless, 98.5% of the people registered to vote and on August

---

[14] From Leo XIII's encyclical *Rerum Novarum* onwards, especially in the Papal Encyclicals *Mater et Magistra, Pacem in Terris* (John XXIII), *Populorum Progressio* (Paul VI), *Solicitudo Rei Socialis, Centesimus Annus* (John Paul II), in the II Vatican Council Decree *Gaudium et Spes*, and in the Statement of the Synod of Bishops (1971) 'Justice in the World'.

[15] For the Doctrine see, e.g.: 'The International Arms Trade: an ethical reflection', 1994, Pontifical Council for Justice & Peace; Catechism of the Catholic Church, 1995, para. 2316.

[16] 'Agreement Between the Republic of Indonesia and the Portuguese Republic on the Question of East Timor, etc', UN New York, 5th May 1999.

30th rejected the autonomy proposal by a majority of 78.5% in the UN supervised ballot. This courageous action vindicated the long-upheld claim of the pro-independence East Timorese leadership and their international supporters that in anything approaching a free vote the people would show their disaffection with Indonesian rule.

Despite this truly democratic outcome, the intransigent and powerful elements of the Indonesian armed forces that opposed East Timorese independence engaged their militia proxies in a campaign of 'political cleansing'. In a highly organised operation over 250,000 people were deported within a matter of *days* into neighbouring West Timor or to other Indonesian islands. Many thousands more fled unprovided into the mountainous interior. Pro-independence sympathisers were sought out and murdered, including a number of diocesan clergy and men and women belonging to different religious orders working in the territory. The great majority of UNAMET personnel were intimidated into emergency evacuation - in breach of the UN commitment to 'remain after the ballot'.

However, the UN 'consultation' process had given access to the territory of many foreign journalists and the international personnel of the UN itself and of numerous NGOs. All of them witnessed the severe intimidation before the ballot and a few bravely remained *in situ* to report on the dreadful aftermath. Unprecedented extensive coverage was given in the international media to the crisis and public demand for action intensified around the world. Military and economic sanctions were at last brought to bear by the international community. These included the suspension of military training and the supply of weaponry and equipment for the Indonesian Armed Forces, the implicit threat of a halt to governmental aid, and the immediate suspension of loans by the principal international financial institutions. Such measures persuaded president Habibie and his Cabinet, and even the Military, to allow an international force - approved by the UN Security Council (Resolution 1264) and led by Australia - into the territory to establish order. By September 27th the Indonesian Army and most of its militia proxies had left the territory, although they undertook a 'scorched earth' policy as they did so, wrecking the social, administrative and communications infrastructure. Meanwhile the departure of Indonesian migrants who had held most executive positions had left the country largely devoid of a managerial class. On October 20th the upper house of the Indonesian parliament (MPR) accepted the outcome of the August ballot and formally revoked its 1976 Decree of Integration by which East Timor had been incorporated into the Republic. In a subsequent letter to the UN Secretary General president Wahid relinquished all Indonesian claims to the territory. The administration of East Timor was then entrusted by the United Nations Security Council (Resolution 1272) to a temporary executive authority – UNTAET. This administration was tasked with arranging a democratic process for the people to elect their own national government and to develop the economic and social viability necessary for political independence. [17]

Thus ended the twenty-five years of Indonesia's illegal, exploitative and frequently brutal intervention in East Timor. During that period a third of the native population had lost their lives as a direct or indirect consequence of the conflict, and as many as twenty thousand Indonesian military servicemen had been killed, to say nothing of the virtual destruction of a unique and remarkable indigenous culture. The international community played a key role in the whole course of events. The Church too has its measure of responsibility for what took place.

---

[17] See: Bibliography - General (East Timor): Cristalis, I. 2002; Kohen, A. 2000 (Revised edition of 1999 publication) – Epilogue, p277f; Taudevin, L.1999; Bibliography - Ch2: Kingsbury, D. (ed) 2000; Taylor, J. 1999, pp.xi-xxxvii; Bibliography - Ch3: CIIR 1999; Dunn, J. 2001; Martin, I. 2001.

See also: Amnesty International Reports: ASA 21/26/99, 21/49/99, 21/186/99, 21/191/99, 57/001/2001; Government of Indonesia, Office of Attorney General: '[Secret] Report of the Special Commission on Militia Violence in East Timor in 1999'; *Tapol* Bulletin 1998, Nos.149/150, 1999, 151-155; 1999, Nos. 151-155.

CHAPTER FOUR - CRITERIA FOR EVALUATING THE CHURCH'S RESPONSE

The Church in Modern Times

In modern times the Catholic Church has been in the process of redefining its relationship with the world in general and with the secular powers in particular. Before Vatican II, the Church tended to identify itself with the ruling authority, even when these were not explicitly Catholic. It sought to enter into formal arrangements or "concordats" with secular regimes, in order to preserve its freedom of operation. Concern for its religious liberty and for that stability in society which is conducive to its pastoral work prompted many Church leaders to associate in some measure with right wing regimes which seemed to promise such an environment but were to prove oppressive in nature. The Church perceived the spread of Communism as the greatest threat to its mission and message and this led some to demonise Marxist ideology and its political expressions and indeed to regard all left-wing movements and sympathisers with suspicion and disfavour. There has been an ongoing debate within the Church at all levels in respect of priorities for action in carrying out the Gospel mandate. Some have emphasised the religious nature of the Church's work while others have stressed the moral obligation to become engaged in matters of social justice. This controversy has hinged upon the question as to whether action for justice is 'constitutive' or 'integral' to the mission of the Church i.e. absolutely essential to the life of the Church, or pertaining only to its fullness. There has been a common endeavour to avoid the mistake of idealising particular historical movements which aspired towards an improved social order – and some instances when there has been an over-identification of such movements with the establishment of God's kingdom on earth.

The Emergence of Catholic Social Doctrine

The challenges that the teaching and actions of Jesus presented to the religious and the secular authorities of his day are apparent in the Gospels. The Acts of the Apostles and the Letters of Saints Peter, Paul and James indicate how the young Church began at the outset what was to be a gradual, continuing and demanding process of discovering its identity and role within human society. The Church's engagement in socio-political affairs still remains an issue within the believing community as well as within society at large.

Down the years various efforts have been made within the Catholic Church as a whole to respond to a wide range of social and political issues and these constitute the evolution of its **social thought**. Historically the Church has always had some form of actual **social teaching** - considered evaluations that have been made in respect of the morality of particular social, economic or political practices in the light of the sources of faith, *viz.* Scripture and Tradition. However, the idea of a *corpus* of social teaching that could be described and promoted as a distinctively Catholic **Social Doctrine** did not emerge until more recent times. In the 20th Century Catholic leaders, theologians and social activists often used the phrase "Social Doctrine" to signify that the Church had a comprehensive series of teachings, promulgated by the *Magisterium,* by which Catholics could understand their social and political responsibilities and guide their actions within an increasingly secular society.

The systematic formulation of this Doctrine is first evidenced in the seminal encyclical of Pope Leo XIII, *Rerum Novarum* (1891). It has been elaborated ever since – most prominently (but not exclusively) in the teachings of successive pontiffs, in certain decrees of the Second Vatican Council (1962-65), and by the Synod of Bishops meeting in Rome. Various authors have provided commentaries upon the Doctrine and its most significant elements are expressed in the Catechism of the Catholic Church (1995).[1] A summary of its main principles

---

[1] See Bibliography Ch4 for key texts and selected commentaries.

is given at the end of this chapter. The Teaching Authority of the Church – i.e. the *Magisterium* – regards this Social Doctrine as having an inner coherence and to be of universal application because its principles are intrinsically related and because they derive fundamentally from recognition of the innate dignity and social nature of the human person. Catholic theologians do not regard these principles and the general directives that flow therefrom as having the status of 'infallible' teaching. However they do generally hold the view that the Doctrine is to be accepted and obeyed by the faithful because it is part of the 'ordinary' teaching of the *Magisterium* on moral issues and therefore has considerable authority.

Since Vatican II certain regional Bishops Conferences – as in Latin America and Asia - have made significant reflections upon the social issues immediately confronting them and have also commented upon the pertinence of the Doctrine as it stands to their social situation. To some extent their perceptions have been integrated by the *Magisterium* into the *corpus* of Social Doctrine but, as this study will indicate, further accommodation of such insights and experience deserves consideration because of the benefits that may accrue.

There is no doubt also that the development of the Catholic Church's Social Doctrine has been stimulated from the outset by the organised efforts of its laity to deal with various problems within human society – and that its formulation has in its turn encouraged the endeavours of such 'social movements'.[2] It is important to note that these movements do not themselves exhaust the contribution made by Catholics to social action, reform and reconstruction. This study will provide evidence that greater attention on the part of officialdom to the activity and the reflections of committed ordinary members of the believing community towards the achievement of greater social justice would assist in the development of a sound and efficacious social ethic within the Church.

The Importance of the Second Vatican Council [3]

The decrees of this twenty-first Ecumenical Council, which met in Rome from 1962-65 reveal that a significant change in the Church's perception of its relationship to the world had occurred. For the first time major documents of such a Council dealt in depth with social issues. They are characterised by an attitude of openness to and respect for wider human society and declare a readiness for 'dialogue' with the world outside the Church.[4] This posture encouraged a somewhat more positive appraisal of the Church's role and competence to offer comment upon social affairs from those who were not of the Catholic community.

The social encyclicals of Pope John XXIII *Mater et Magistra* (1961) and *Pacem in Terris* (1963) were an important factor in bringing about this disposition for dialogue. In contrast to the general form of previous Papal expositions on social matters these appeared as *appeals* from *within society* to 'all men of good will'.[5] Attempts to establish more constructive relations with the temporal powers can be traced back to Leo XIII, but it is John XXIII who can be said to have re-opened the door to participation in liberal and pluralistic societies that had been practically closed since the anti-modernist stance of Pius IX.[6] A development in ec-

---

[2] For a brief presentation of the influence of such movements in the 19th & 20th C see:
Bibliography - Ch4: Zahn, G.C., 'Social Movements in Catholic Thought', in Coleman J.A. (ed) 1991.
See also: McGraw-Hill (eds), 1961, *New Catholic Encyclopaedia*, Catholic University of America, Washington DC - Social Movements; Jocists; etc; Newman, J. 1962, *The Christian in Society*, Baltimore; O'Connor, D.A., 1956, *Catholic Social Doctrine*, Westminster, MD; Somerville, H. 1933, *Studies in the Catholic Social Movement*, London.
[3] See: Bibliography – Ch4: Charles, R. *SJ*, & Maclaren, D. *OP*, 1982; Charles, R. *SJ*, 1998, Ch22; O'Brien, D.J. 'A Century of Catholic Social Teaching', in Coleman, J.A. (ed) 1991 op.cit
[4] *Gaudium et Spes*, paras 91-93.
[5] *Mater et Magistra*, para 221; *Pacem in Terris*, Address.
[6] Expressed, e.g., in his *Syllabus of Errors* (1864).

clesiology had encouraged the notion of the Church as the 'sacrament of human unity' – a perception expressed in Vatican II's foundational decree *Lumen Gentium*. This indicated a sense of *solidarity* with the world to be further elaborated in the pastoral decree on the Church in the Modern World, *Gaudium et Spes* – a document that would serve to invigorate social engagement by the Church as a whole. Since this Council the Church as an institution has defended its perceived right to speak and act in the social arena mainly by exercising it broadly and vigorously. But the social engagement of the Church as a *community* can be further developed, as this study will reveal.

While the Council was still engaged in its deliberations Paul VI became Pope and he too appealed in his encyclical *Ecclesiam Suam* (1964) for the Church's relations with the world to be characterised by a spirit of confident but respectful 'dialogue'. He was convinced that the Church had much to offer the human family but urged that its approach must be made in humility and love. He contended that while the Church must carefully avoid 'relativism, syncretism and irenism' it would be better able to communicate its message fruitfully to the world in which it lived by listening attentively to voices from beyond its own community.

At the Council there was also a methodological development. The revival of Thomism in the late 19th Century had given rise to a deductive approach in discerning the principles of Social Doctrine. As these were understood to be discoverable at least to some extent simply from a study of the essential constitution of human nature – that is, to express a 'Natural Law' – there was considerable confidence within the *Magisterium* as to the universality of their application. Vatican II, however, favoured a more experiential process of 'reading the signs of the times' – that is, discerning significant social phenomena - along with action for greater social justice. The inductive approach to a social ethic that this expressed and encouraged was more attractive to many people - within the Catholic Church as well as those outside of it - who had not been comfortable with the former method, although that too has a practical value as will be seen.

As noted already, the Catholic Church had also been steadily disentangling itself from old political alliances and this enabled the Council to clarify its position vis-à-vis current political situations. Thus the Council describes the Church's mission as transcending the affairs of this passing world but properly including the promotion of human welfare in history. The Church is exhorted to avoid political partisanship but may properly be supportive of any government seeking to serve the general welfare. Church and State are regarded as collaborators in upholding the essential dignity of the human person. At the same time the Church is perceived to have a moral obligation to draw to the attention of the secular authorities any shortcomings it might discern in their provision for the people in their charge.[7]

Moreover, it was at the Second Vatican Council that the *global nature* of the Catholic Church was more fully appreciated - as remarked by Karl Rahner in his essay 'Toward a Fundamental Theological Interpretation of Vatican II' (1979). The recognition that the Church was not European in essence, and that a European notion of how to be Church should not - indeed, could not - be imposed elsewhere in the world, was of significant importance. After the Council earnest efforts were made to express the Church's presence and activity in the cultural forms appropriate to the people living where it was located and the importance of such 'inculturation' was increasingly accepted by the ecclesial community as a whole. Encouraged by theologians of the stature of Yves Congar the Catholic Church actually present in these other cultures came to see that it had both the right and the duty to address directly the social issues with which it was confronted. This gave rise to a further development of Catholic social thought and so to further expressions of Catholic social teaching. In turn this has raised the issue as to how the Church's Social Doctrine (as a systematic formulation) should properly be reached and effectively lived out, as this study may serve to illuminate.

---

[7] *Gaudium et Spes*, para 76.

To mark the eightieth anniversary of *Rerum Novarum* in 1971 Pope Paul VI wrote the apostolic letter *Octogesima Adveniens* in which he readily acknowledged the diversity of situations in which the Church lived. While expressing confidence that the Church had something valuable to say on social matters the Pope admitted the difficulty of 'offering solutions that had universal value'. He invited each local Church to 'scrutinise the true situation in their own region' and to discuss the options and commitments that were called for – no one, he opined, could do this on their behalf. Nonetheless, in his view, 'principles of reflection, norms of judgement and guidelines for action could be derived from the Social Doctrine of the Church' (*OA*, paragraph 4). That same year the Synod of Bishops meeting in Rome stated that 'work for justice was a constitutive dimension of the preaching of the Gospel'.[8] These declarations have been of considerable significance for the development of the Church's social engagement around the world. Their implications for the formulation, expression, and effecting of Catholic Social Doctrine are also of importance, as the following two regional experiences bear out.

The Church in Latin America

The Bishops Conference of Latin America declared their response to the social injustices manifest in that region in their statements at Medellin (1968) and Puebla (1979). The concern of the hierarchy over the suffering of the poor majority in society and of their 'irruption' into the sphere of politics is manifest in these documents. The influence of the emergent 'Liberation Theology' was evident in the bishops' reference to 'structural sin' and in the 'preferential option for the poor' that they urged – and which subsequently found greater expression than previously in the Social Doctrine emanating from the *Magisterium*. The hierarchy in Latin America did not echo the views of some of the 'liberationists' in their region who were inclined to see the poor as the principal shapers of secular (and ecclesial) history.[9] But they did call for a practical solidarity with the poor and for full attention to be given to the special insight of the poor into the challenges that the Gospel presented to society as a whole and to the Church itself. The bishops were convinced that the Church should participate in an ongoing cyclical process of practical action to achieve greater social justice and in reflection upon that 'praxis' as necessary preparation for further activity. They were certain that only in this way would the Church appropriately and effectively help the poor to become agents of their own integral development as human beings. They were equally sure that this was also the best way for the Church to increase its own awareness of important social values and be in a position to promote them.[10] It is noteworthy that this positive appreciation of the role of the poor featured to some extent in the Instruction of the Congregation for the Doctrine of the Faith 'On Certain Aspects of Liberation Theology'. Negative criticism of a perceived Marxist influence upon some of the liberationists was uppermost in this document which nonetheless acknowledged that 'in the praxis of working for the advancement of the poor one becomes more aware of certain aspects of the Truth'.[11]

The Church in Asia

In Asia too, the Church faced particular and serious challenges. In November 1970 the bishops of Asia met together for the first time to encourage mutual support in facing up to a demanding reality. They observed that the region was home to two billion people (two thirds

---

[8] Statement *Justice in the World*, 1971.
[9] e.g. Boff, L. 1985. *Church, Charism and Power*. SCM: London, pp8-11.
[10] See CELAM: Medellin, 9, 14; Puebla 1134, 1142, 1147
[11] See CDF, 1984, *Libertatis Nuntius*, XI, 9, 13. Cf. CDF, 1986, *Libertatis Conscientia*, paragraphs 21 & 22. For more detail see: Smythe, P. 1994, 'Certain Aspects?' and 1995, 'Some Echoes of Liberation Theology in the Catechism of the Catholic Church'. Unpublished *MSS*, University of Leeds.

of humanity) of whom sixty per cent were under 25 years of age. In particular, only 3% of this huge population was Catholic and 50% of those Catholics lived in the Philippines. The bishops then declared their hopes for the Church they represented. It was to be 'more truly the Church of the poor...to speak out for the rights of the disadvantaged and powerless against all forms of injustice...to uphold and promote the realisation of human rights and defend them whenever, wherever, and by whomsoever they are violated'. They pledged 'not to tie our hands by compromising entanglements with the rich and powerful in our respective countries' and committed themselves 'to the total development of our peoples.' They also acknowledged that 'it remains for us to muster the effective will to eradicate entrenched injustice and replace oppressive structures'.[12] At the institutional level the regional hierarchy established the Federation of Asian Bishops Conferences (FABC) and in due course various subordinate organisations including the Bishops Institute for Social Action (BISA), for the Missionary Apostolate (BIMA), for Inter-religious Affairs (BIRA), and the International Congress on Mission. FABC also created the Office of Human Development as its social action arm.

At the time of writing FABC has met in plenary session seven times and its Statements have continued to express the highest ideals in respect of social justice and the Church's commitment to solidarity with the poor and oppressed.[13] Certain central themes and thrusts have been recurrent. The overarching concern has been to develop the local Church – that is, 'to embody and activate the presence of Jesus and his Gospel in the Asian region'. An immediate consequence of this has been the sustained effort towards indigenisation and inculturation of the Church. This 'in-rooting' has called in the first instance for a genuine dialogue with the great religions of the region and with the rich and ancient cultural expressions shaped by them – 'and especially with the poor who constitute so massive a part of our peoples'. The bishops have urged that this concern for the poor be nourished by a life of prayer and, at the practical level, that it engage the Church in efforts towards their integral development as persons. Such an effort, they have declared, must include action on behalf of greater justice and encourage greater participation by the poor in socio-political affairs - so that they can become 'authentic subjects of their own future and history'. The principal instrument adopted for these related endeavours has been the so-called 'Dialogue of Life' in which Catholics are to come alongside the poor of all faiths in humility and trust and be engaged in a process of 'conscientisation'. This involves shared action/reflection in which all concerned are facilitated to discover and address the structural causes of poverty and injustice, and be directly involved in effecting positive change.[14] With increasing determination the effort has been made to express the Church's life as a 'communion of communities of authentic participation and co-responsibility'. In practice that means to respect and engage the contribution that each and every member can make to the Church's mission - which must include the embodiment of the Asian vision and values of life.[15]

The inspiration of Vatican II is clearly evident in these purposes (and often cited in the Final Statements of FABC Plenary Assemblies). The concurrent response to the needs and giftedness of the poor by the Church in Latin America is likewise clearly influential. The developing 'Feminist' theologies certainly helped the Asian Church to appreciate more fully the manifold injustices experienced by women whose distressful situation – and giftedness – have

---

[12] See: Bibliography – Ch4: 'Meeting of the Bishops of Asia', in FABC 1984; Eilers, F.J. (ed) 1997.
[13] For Statements of Sessions I-III see: FABC 1984 op.cit. For subsequent sessions see UCANews internet website. Especially pertinent are: FABC I Taipei, April 1974, Resolution 5; FABC II Calcutta, Nov.1978 – Briefer Statement paras 16-18; FABC III Bangkok, Oct.1982, Syllabus of Concerns III; FABC IV Tokyo, Sept.1986, para 3.1.7; FABC V Bandung, July 1990, para 1.7; FABC VI Manila, Jan 1995, para4; FABC VII Bangkok, Jan 2000, Part III, Introduction.
[14] For an elaboration see: Bibliography – Ch4: Chia, E. (ed) 2001.
[15] See: FABC VII, Samphran, Thailand, January 3-12, 2000, Part 1, A. 'A Vision of Renewal'; Part 3, 'The Challenge of Discerning the Asian Way'. Ucanews Online – FABC, Index.

been acknowledged. The emergent 'Third World' theology encouraged an awakening sensibility to the moral riches to be found among its diverse peoples. Within the Asian region itself responses of committed Christians to the needs of outcastes and of the marginalised and dispossessed were to find expression in the so-called *Dalit* and *Minjung* theologies of India and Korea respectively – and these too were an influence upon the regional Church's social thought and teaching.[16] The experience of the Basic Ecclesial and Basic Human Communities in which local groups have sought to respond to pressing social needs through an ongoing process of action/reflection have also been a significant element in this development. Indeed, they have become regarded as foundational to the 'new way of being Church in Asia', as is a 'holistic' vision of life and a sense of the immanence of the Divine 'even in mundane affairs' - which are characteristic of the indigenous religious heritage. Increasing trust has also been placed in the ability of the Youth, the majority age group, to be effective agents of the Gospel of Jesus and in the building up of his Kingdom in history. The engagement of the Church with - and within - the mass media of communication has been urged as an essential means of bringing Gospel values to bear in Asian society.[17]

The Pertinence of the Church's Social Doctrine

As a consequence of such developments - and as part of them - there has been criticism in the Asian Church of Catholic Social Doctrine. Its formulation appears to many to be a prisoner of the European cultural context in which it arose. With its concepts couched in Western European intellectual and theological categories alien to the Asian mind it is seen as failing to enter into potentially creative and mutually enriching dialogue with the social wisdom of Asian culture. The question has been put as to whether its principles and directives should be taken as 'universal norms' or simply as 'magisterial indications' to be interpreted and adapted according to different contexts.[18] Asian critics of the Doctrine have recognised the difficulty the *Magisterium* has in formulating its teaching to cover all eventualities: it must remain truly 'Catholic', be somehow relevant to all contexts, yet at the same time it should touch concrete situations. Western theologians have also articulated this dilemma:

> Catholic Social Doctrine can fly so high in the stratosphere of principles that, from above, the whole landscape was flattened out and no details could be perceived; or – more rarely – it could fly so close to the ground that its particular statement was too localised to be applicable elsewhere.
> The problem…[is] how to relate Christian faith to ongoing history.[19]

However, the fact that Catholic Social Doctrine hitherto has for the most part not sprung from the situation of non-European peoples, or directly addressed them, does not mean that it is irrelevant to their experience. It has been acknowledged by the Church in Asia that the Catholic Church is precisely that (i.e. universal) and there is an expectation that the Teaching Authority of such a Church will make pronouncements that can be applied in a general way to all situations. Indeed, the prophetic nature of these declarations - that is, the chal-

---

[16] On *Minjung* ['little people'] theology see: *Minjung Theology – People as Subjects of History*, CCA Commission on Theological Concern (ed) 1983, Zed Books, London.
[17] See: Bibliography – Ch4: FABC 1984, op.cit.; Eilers, F.J. (ed) 1997, op.cit.
See UCA News online, Hong Kong for FABC Plenary Assembly III-VII Statements and also 'Communion and Solidarity: A New Way of Being Church in Asia', FABC Colloquium on the Church in Asia in the 21st Century, Pattaya, Thailand, August 1998. See also: 'Synod of Bishops Special Assembly for Asia: *Instrumentum Laboris*, in East Asian Pastoral Review, Vol 35, No.1 (1998), p4ff.
[18] See: Tirimanna, V. *CSSR*, 'The Relevance of Catholic Social Doctrine in a non-European World', in Vidyajyoti Journal of Theological Reflection, Vol LVI, No 10, October 1992, pp 534 – 542.
[19] Peter Hebblethwaite *SJ*, 'The Popes and Politics: Shifting Patterns in Catholic Social Doctrine', in Readings in Moral Theology No5, p272.

lenges they put to human society and to its various forms of ordering - is recognised and considered to be of value. What is being called for is a formulation of the Doctrine that would demonstrate sensitivity to diverse socio-economic, political and cultural situations - and to the Church's own enhanced self-awareness as a global entity with local expressions.[20] While in some measure the Doctrine can and should be 'universal' in its derivation and application its pertinence also depends upon an emergence from and an immediate relevance to local context. Inevitably this must involve fresh consideration as to the method by which Social Doctrine is reached, the manner of its proclamation, and the means by which it can best be put into effect.

The evidence gathered in this study on the Church's response to the particular plight of the people of East Timor supports the contention that these are issues needing to be addressed. Its narrative reveals the truth of a *dictum* of Thomas Aquinas regarding the interpretation of general norms:

> In the case of the practical reason which is concerned with contingent matters such as human actions, even though there be some necessary truth in the common principles, yet the more we descend to what is proper and peculiar the more deviations we find.[21]

But it also underlines the importance of having a Social Doctrine with clear general principles, and norms that are derived therefrom, for the effective defence of human rights and the promotion of social justice. Such principles and rules help to justify - both within and beyond the Church - certain courses of action, and they also assist in the communication of moral wisdom from one situation to another. The evidence provided in this book certainly does not lead to the conclusion that all norms of Social Doctrine should be drawn from the context. But it does urge that the relationship of moral reason to particular historical situations is a dynamic affair in which a certain negotiation or dialectic between general norms and contextual circumstances should be encouraged.[22] Primarily this book is a study of the degree of consistency that pertained between the theory and practice of the Church's Social Doctrine in respect of the issue of East Timor. In doing so it draws attention to the importance of there being a continuous dialogue on issues of social justice both within the community of the Church itself and between the Church and agencies outside of it that are involved in those same matters. Before beginning this exploration a summary account should be given of the norms of Catholic Social Doctrine as they have been expressed by the *Magisterium* since the time of Pope Leo XIII. From them Criteria can be derived for evaluating the Church's response to the issue of East Timor.

The Ultimate Measure: the Person and Role of Jesus

At the heart of Catholic Social Doctrine is the person of Jesus who is regarded as the exemplar of how the Church should act because it receives its mandate from him and it is his redemptive work which the Church is called upon to continue in and for the world. The ministry of Jesus is perceived to have various dimensions – he acts as Pastor, Prophet, Disciple, Evangelist, and Intercessor. These roles, which are inter-related and overlapping, are to be taken up by the Church at all its levels of operation: they are the forms that the mission of the Church can take in different circumstances.

---

[20] See: Bibliography – Ch4: Asian Theologians and Catholic Thinkers, 1993; Lobo, G.*SJ*, 1992; 'The Relevance of Catholic Social Teaching in a Non-European World', Tirimanna, V.*CSSR*, in Fernando, T, & O'Sullivan H. *MM* (eds) 1993, pp27-33; FABC Statement of the Colloquium on Social Doctrine of the Church in the Context of Asia (Jan 20-24 1992).
See also: 'The Changing Anthropological Basis of Catholic Social Ethics', Curren, C.E. in Readings in Moral Theology, Paulist Press, New York, No5, p188.
[21] Summa Theologica I-IIae, Q.94, art 4.
[22] On the importance of the practice of such casuistry see: Bibliography – Ch4: Biggar, N.1989.

The **pastoral** ministry of Christ that the Church continues is to lead humanity from a situation of sin to one of grace; to effect an increasing orientation towards and participation in the life and love of God. In its exercise the Church is to be concerned with integral human development which includes a religious dimension and looks beyond present experience to a future which is expected to transcend it. In fulfilling its pastoral ministry the Church can properly be a partner in nation-building if this leads to an improvement in the welfare of all but it should avoid becoming involved in the pursuit of partisan ambitions which disadvantage or imperil other groups and communities. Its pastoral engagement can provide the Church with a special insight into the effects of government and other institutional policies and it has a corresponding obligation to use this knowledge in the achievement of greater justice and in the defence of human rights. The Church must be concerned for its institutional survival so that its mission might continue for the benefit of all, but it should also be ready to put its corporate life on the line for humanity's sake, in imitation of its Lord.[23]

For the Church to be truly **prophetical** it must be inspired by the Divine Spirit and apply the Gospel in judgement upon its own life and on that of contemporary society, gauging to what extent they align with God's will and purpose for humanity. The Church is thus called to judicious criticism of the secular authorities – a practice that will certainly reveal its strength or vulnerability in the prevailing social order. Again the ultimate test of the Church's prophetical character is its readiness to 'lay down its life' for the sake of the Kingdom of God.[24]

In imitation of Jesus, the faithful Servant who 'listens like a disciple' (Isaiah 50:4-7; cf.Matt 3:17; Lk 4:17-21), the Church is called to discover over and again the mind of God in a given historical situation.[25] For the Church to contribute effectively to the building up of justice and peace it must therefore undertake a dialogue with the secular world. In this it should be willing both to learn from social analyses that are offered by experts in the field and to query the appropriateness of social policies that are being pursued by the authorities. Crucially the mark of true **discipleship** is that humility and courage which is prepared to learn and obey God's will via the costly path of suffering, ready to risk all – even death itself – in the trusting faith that in God all will be secure.[26]

Evangelisation constitutes 'the essential mission of the Church'.[27] It comprises the mediation of God's grace to achieve personal renewal of life, a proclamation of the life hereafter and of humanity's salvation in Christ. It includes the concern to liberate human beings from *all manner of oppression* and it requires of both evangelist and recipient a radical change of heart and wholehearted responsiveness to God's directives in a spirit of trust and self-sacrifice.

Intercessory prayer is central to the work of the Church in the world. In general, prayer is the means by which the will of God, and the strength to abide by it, are sought in particular historical situations. To pray is to participate in the filial response of Jesus to the Father's loving plan for humanity; to avail of the power of the divine Spirit to bring the Kingdom of God into the world; and to orient the world more into the life and love of God. It is of prime importance in the remedying of the world's disorders. Intercessory prayer specifically ex-

---

[23] See: Vatican Council II, *Gaudium et Spes*, Preamble, & Part I, Ch4; Pope John Paul II's Encyclicals *Redemptor Hominis* (1979) Part II Sections 10 &11, *Christifideles Laici* (1989) Ch1&3, *Redemptoris Missio* (1990) Ch1, 2,&5; VII Synod of Bishops (1987) Part I Section 1 and Part II Section 1&2; *Catechism of Catholic Church* (CCC) 1995, paras 871-5, 897-913.

[24] See: Vatican II *Gaudium et Spes* Part I, Ch2; John Paul II *Redemptor Hominis* Ch4, para 19, *Christifideles Laici* Ch1, para 14; Synod of Bishops 1987 *Instrumentum Laboris* Part II, Section II, para 52. See also: Bibliography – General (Theology): Clements, K. 1997, Ch4.

[25] See: Pope Paul VI Encyclical *Evangelii Nuntiandi* (1975), para 15,29,63,75.

[26] Hebrews 2:17; Cf. Clements, K. 1997, op.cit. Ch5.

[27] See: Paul VI *Evangelii Nuntiandi*, op.cit., Ch3.

presses and furthers the spiritual bonding of Christ's disciples with their Lord and with each other that they have as members of his 'Mystical Body', and is mutually supportive. The activity of prayerful **intercession** is one that is not undertaken by secular agencies engaged in issues of justice and peace, but it belongs at the heart of all efforts made by the Church for those in need. And just as the intercession of Christ was most perfectly expressed upon the Cross 'where prayer and the gift of self are one', so the intercession of the Church is at its most authentic when it is wholly inclusive - and when its own survival is thereby put at risk.[28]

Principles of Catholic Social Doctrine

Within this doctrinal tradition of the Church's continuation of the Mission and Ministry of Jesus, which is inspired by his own teaching and example, several particular ethical principles have emerged as reference points for the Church in dealing with the socio-political issues that confront it. All these principles are rooted in a fundamental respect for the human person and are seen as expressing the mind and heart of Christ and as the means of building up his Kingdom on the earth. They may be briefly delineated as follows. The '**Common Good**' is always to be sought – meaning that the general welfare must be given full consideration even when the immediate purpose of an enterprise is to meet the needs of the social majority or of any minority group in society. The principle of '**Subsidiarity**' requires that no function should be taken over by a higher authority that can be efficiently performed by lower groupings. There is a fundamental '**Solidarity**' between all members of the human family based upon their shared human nature and common identity as children of God created in the Divine image. Because human life has an essentially social dimension sin is not only manifest in the lives of individuals but also in the structures of society. Such '**Structural Sin**' - that is, institutional injustices that prevent people from realising their full potential - must be confronted and overcome. All persons have fundamental political and socio-economic '**Rights**'. These include the right of a people to political self-determination, to resist oppression, and to participation in decision-making processes affecting their daily lives. Human '**Development**' is to be promoted and must be 'integral' or holistic - that is, it must meet the needs of body, mind and spirit and serve social as well as individual needs. In all matters a '**Preferential Option**' is to be exercised in respect of the poor, namely the impoverished, the dispossessed and the marginalised. They are to be given priority. This is not only because of their especial need but also because they have special gifts to offer in the building up of a truly just society - one that is in accordance with the mind of God. In its official Doctrine the Church has also been critical of the exploitative nature of **Colonialism** and **Neo-colonialism** and has considered both **Socialism** and **Capitalism** to have internal shortcomings which are ultimately detrimental to the welfare of society as a whole but especially to the poor. Integrity requires the Church to apply these standards to its own internal life and, while seeking to preserve its identity and independence, to be ready both to dialogue with other ideologies and systems of belief and to be critical of their socio-political expression.

As others have remarked, various kinds of response to issues of social justice are possible and proper for the Church in different circumstances. There is a time and place for formal declarations from the highest Church authorities. Such observations can take a variety of forms including pastoral documents, statements of Church leaders, resolutions by assemblies and councils and Church organisations, press releases, etc. Their effectiveness may depend upon the breadth of their base of support within the Church community as a whole, and upon appropriate follow-up - and consistency in internal Church practice. There are other acts of the Church community which can impact upon the resolution of a social issue and include such seemingly 'spiritual' activities as prayer services, public acts of repentance or reconciliation, devotional processions, funerals, etc. All of these bear witness to the possibility of an alternative history more in accordance with the mind and heart of God. Furthermore, participation by

---

[28] See: CCC 1995, op.cit. paragraphs 2570-84, 2599-2606, 2634-36, 2820-1. Cited is paragraph 2605.

Church people in the efforts of non-Church groups engaged in the same cause can serve it well and be mutually beneficial. But it is important that the Church contribution somehow retains a distinctive character and that opportunity is thereby given for relationship with Jesus to be sustained and so for the realm of God to impinge in order that mere activism is avoided. Silence - or delayed comment - on the part of the Church can be a positive as well as a negative response to a particular socio-political issue for in the matter of 'speaking out' there can be a moment of optimum advantage. But there is also the risk that such restraint will amount to - or be interpreted as - complicity in the *status quo* to the detriment of the cause of justice.[29]

Some Questions to Ask

This *précis* of Catholic Social Doctrine expressed as fundamental principles and in terms of the Church's continuation of the ministry of Christ in the world suggests a number of questions by which the response of the Church to the East Timor issue can be evaluated.

In general terms it should be asked:

In what circles of the Church's operation has there been a response, and can it be said to have been supportive to the East Timorese cause in any sense? Has the response been from the leadership, or the membership, or both, and what has been its nature and effect (so far as this can be assessed)?
Have internal differences over priorities for action, and the Church's concern for its own security and the furtherance of its mission in the world affected its response at any of the levels of its operation?
How has the response of the Church to the East Timor issue been affected by the socio-political context and competing ideologies in which it functions?
What ambiguities have there been in the Church's faithfulness to its own standards?
What status has been afforded to this particular effort for justice and peace within the overall *corpus* of the Church's concerns?

With regard to the fundamental principles of its Social Doctrine as summarised above it should be asked:

Has the Church actually stood by these principles in respect of the East Timorese? Has it expressed *solidarity* with them and given *due preference* to their needs as an oppressed, marginalised, impoverished people?
Has it urged for the East Timorese the *rights* it proclaims belong to all people to political participation, self-determination, and integral development, and to resist an unjust and exploitative government?
Has the Church in its dealings with and on behalf of this abused people perceived and challenged *structural injustices* impacting upon their welfare?
Has the Church given due respect to their insights and capacities and operated according to its own principle of *subsidiarity*?

In terms of its task of continuing the redeeming work of Jesus Christ in the world it should be asked if the Church served the people of East Timor in any way as a *Pastor, Prophet, Disciple, Evangelist*, and *Intercessor*:

Is there evidence within the Church of efforts to improve their present circumstances while seeking to enhance their participation in the life and love of God?

---

[29] See: Bibliography – General (Theology): Clements, K., 1997. op.cit.

Has the Church called the people to greater faithfulness towards God while also striving for a re-ordering of their situation of injustice, defending their dignity and promoting their human development in every respect?

Has the Church listened to the people of East Timor, sought a thorough social analysis of their predicament, questioned the secular authorities regarding the manner of their rule, and looked for fresh solutions in the light of God's grace and truth?

Has the Church urged the liberation of the people of East Timor from *everything* oppressing them, and called for the recognition that such renewal requires a radical conversion of heart?

Has the Church offered intercessory prayer on behalf of the Timorese, for all who are engaged in their cause - and for their 'enemies'? Has a sense of spiritual communion as members of Christ's Mystical Body been in any way in evidence?

Crucially, in applying the message it is called by its Lord to proclaim, has the Church any-where appeared willing to *lay down its own life* for the sake of the suffering people of East Timor?

PART TWO:

RESPONSES OF THE CHURCH

CHAPTER FIVE - THE CHURCH IN EAST TIMOR:
A 'PEOPLE'S CHURCH'

The Church in the Colonial Era[1]

Catholic missionaries first arrived on the island of Timor in 1515 along with Portuguese merchants. The mission became more consolidated after the foundation of the Diocese of Malacca in 1558. At first the missionaries were received warily by the native tribes who were uncertain of their motives, but during the period of colonial rule they came to hold a special place in the hearts and lives of the inhabitants, as in due course did the indigenous clergy and religious. They were esteemed as God's representatives and for their long-term commitment to the welfare of the people. They were also appreciated for their defence of the islanders against the severe treatment meted out by some of the Portuguese traders and government administrators, and for their critique of unjust colonial policies. This activity sometimes extended even to siding with them in their political rebellions. The Church offered some limited medical care, and, through the establishment of schools, exercised an influence beyond its network of mission stations. Around these small Christian communities developed, remaining faithful in their commitment as best they could even when the Portuguese and other foreign clergy withdrew during World War II.

But as an institution the Church was heavily involved in the power structures and struggles of the colonial regime. Although its relations with the state were often testy and sometimes broke down altogether, the Church was party to the implementation of government policies. It played a central role in bringing Lusophone culture to bear among the East Timorese, but conversions were mainly among the elite and even then tended to be syncretic in character. Some missionaries limited their ministry to the townships and rarely ventured into the interior. In 1940 the Concordat between the Vatican and Lisbon entrusted the Church with the prime responsibility for education in the colonies and it became the principal agent of Portugal's 'civilising mission'. It enjoyed certain privileges: an annual grant, tax exemptions, provision of extensive tracts of land for building and plantation, and assistance with clergy travel expenses. By the Papal Bull *Solemnibus Conventionibus* the Diocese of Dili was established as a suffragan of the Diocese of Goa, becoming part of an ecclesiastical province and remaining to some extent dependent on its (Portuguese) metropolitan See. Dom Jaime Goulart was given oversight. Throughout the colonial period the Church was obliged to accommodate itself to many traditional practices and, despite occasional surges of pastoral growth, its adherents never numbered much in excess of 30% of the total population even by as late as 1975.

Nonetheless, the Church's activity was the most significant factor in social development during the Portuguese era. Furthermore, a number of missionaries were critical of the Church's own ambiguous role in East Timor, observing that it seemed to concentrate more on helping its flock come to terms with their plight than on pressing for positive reforms. The Jesuit community, in particular, raised awareness of nationalist movements occurring elsewhere in Asia and the Portuguese colonies. They stimulated thinking about issues of social justice, and introduced ideas concerning adult education that had proved effective in the literacy programmes of Paulo Freire in Brazil. They took over the seminary of Our Lady of Fatima at Dare in 1958 and it became the *alma mater* of all the future nationalist leaders. It also sup-

[1] For detail see: Bibliography – General (East Timor): Dunn, J. 1996, pp7, 13-15, 43-47; Kohen, A. 1999, pp32-47; Bibliography Ch2: Jolliffe, J. 1978; Bibliography – Ch3: Carey, P. 'The Catholic Church, Religious Conflict & the Nationalist Movement in East Timor', in Leite, P. (ed), 1998, pp265-284; Bibliography – Ch5: Boxer, C.R. 1968, and 1990; Carey, P. 1997; Crowe, L. 1996; Gunn, G.C. 1999.

plied writers for the Catholic 'Seara' newspaper that flourished in the 1960s and early 1970s, providing a focus for political dissent until it was closed by PIDE[2] in 1973. However, some of the staff at Dare were included among those who were to see in FRETILIN the seeds of a Communist movement.

The Decolonisation Period

In theory the Church adopted a neutral stance in respect of the political parties author-ised by the new government in Lisbon after the 'Carnation Revolution' of April 1974. In practice bishop Jose Joaquim Ribeiro, who succeeded Jaime Goulart in 1966, and many clergy and religious inclined towards the UDT with its declared aim of retaining close ties with Por-tugal.[3] A few East Timorese priests who had links with the neighbouring Catholic communi-ties in Indonesia were present at the inaugural meeting of APODETI, and some of those from India also supported this party, influenced perhaps by the earlier Indian incorporation of the Portuguese colony of Goa. It has been asserted that within the hierarchy some favoured a po-litical merger with Indonesia in preference to government by FRETILIN.[4] However, the ef-fective work of FRETILIN among the common people impressed others, especially some of the native clergy. Generally speaking, the indigenous clergy and religious tended to align pri-vately with the preferences of their own families. A conscious effort was made to 'keep de-bates within the ranks of the clergy and publicly demonstrate unity and loyalty to the bishop...to be above the personal clashes of viewpoint that were inevitable. We saw our mis-sion as being to serve the people - which included trying to bring them together.'[5]

Undoubtedly there were considerable misgivings within the Church leadership in re-spect of FRETILIN's intentions, especially when the party became influenced by the return of students from Lisbon. These young scholars had come under the spell of Maoists in the *Movimento Revolucionaro Proletario Portuguese* and had been impressed by the revolution-ary nationalism of Amilcar Cabral in Guinea Bissau and the advance of the independence movements in Angola and Mozambique. The FRETILIN programme was radical enough al-ready - without the acquisition of a 'Communist' label - including as it did a critique of the Church's involvement in colonialism and of its large land holdings, and the proposal of social reforms that seemed to pose a threat to certain ecclesiastical interests. Bishop Ribeiro regarded FRETILIN as 'communistic' and promulgated a Pastoral Letter that referred to Pope Pius XI's Encyclical on 'Atheistic Communism', *Divini Redemptoris* (19.3.1937). He declared that the Church forbade Catholics to vote for Communists or Socialists, defended the right to private property, and warned against 'the materialism and atheism of Marxism which is seeking to extinguish the positive values of the Timorese people'.[6] Ribeiro also alluded in his sermons to the existence of 'certain people' who wanted to 'discredit the work of Catholic priests'.[7] He believed the Indonesian propaganda that FRETILIN was receiving help from Communist China and Vietnam and he put his faith in the seemingly benign purposes of ABRI. He was also affected by a small group of Portuguese officers who supported UDT. His views influ-enced Vatican officials and were carried beyond Timor, notably to Portugal and to Australia

---

[2] *Policia Internacional e de Defesa do Estado* - an agency of repression during Salazar's rule.

[3] Non-indigenous clergy in Timor came mainly from Portugal, Spain, Italy, and Macau.
The Canossian Sisters engaged their pupils in sewing UDT flags for the political rallies of the time, although the order withdrew its personnel during the Civil War in August-September 1975 (as it had during World War II) on the grounds of political neutrality - Maria do Ceu Federerer (then a Timorese exile) to the author, Darwin, Sept. 1997.

[4] Aditjondro, G.J., 1994, 'East Timor: an Indonesian Intellectual Speaks Out', Development Dossier 33, ACFOA, Canberra, pp55-56 who cites *Tempo* 6.10.1975, pp 9 and 12.

[5] Frs. Reinaldo Cardoso (Portuguese missionary in East Timor) and Domingos da Cunha (a native East Timorese) to the author, Rhode Island USA, Sept.1998.

[6] *Uma Nova Situacao*, Diocesan Offices: Dili, East Timor, 25.1.1975.

[7] See: Bibliography – Ch5: Boavida, J.F. 1993.

where they certainly impacted upon the reaction of the local Church in these countries, as will be seen.

The violence of the Civil War had negative consequences for the image of FRETILIN within Church circles, even though the party cannot be held solely responsible for its outbreak or for the atrocities perpetrated within it. Bishop Ribeiro stayed aloof from the political fray, which perhaps was regrettable as he was held in high regard and his intervention might have effected reconciliation between the contending factions. The flood of refugees to West Timor seeking to escape the strife came under the influence of the Catholic leadership there - which was already susceptible to the manipulation of the Suharto government elite. They also entered into a situation where it was prudent to assert opposition to FRETILIN and its policies, whether or not such sentiments were genuine.

Invasion and Aftermath

With the arrival in the territory of Indonesian forces and civil administration the Church sought to maintain a neutral position in respect of the political situation. This was acknowledged by the new regime and the authorities afforded a degree of trust to the Church and allowed it to continue its pastoral work. Clergy who had indicated their support for 'integration' were given certain responsibilities within the new social order and all were expected to help the mass of the people to accommodate themselves to it.[8] However, the barbarous excesses of the invasion forces caused bishop Ribeiro to express criticism but his complaints and interventions on behalf of the people, forthright but generally discreet, were ignored or dismissed. Overwhelmed by the slaughter and destruction he successfully asked the Vatican for permission to resign and he retired in 1977.[9] As the devastating military campaigns continued into the interior, the letter of a priest was smuggled out which vividly describes the reality of the suffering:

> The war is entering its third year...the barbarities, cruelties, theft...are now part of everyday life...insecurity is total... the sabotage and the lies are spread out...oppression is a reality... Against the force there is no resistance...Freedom is a word without meaning...the liberation they announced means slavery...Commerce is just exploitation....
> Timor was not integrated, it was annexed...it was not liberated from 'communism' but given to the Indonesians...
> Do something positive for the liberation of the Timor people. The world ignores us and it is a shame. We are on the way to a genocide...the war is to exterminate...Ask the justice-loving people to save Timor, and to pray to God to forgive the sins of the people of Timor.[10]

The information and appeal in this letter, although disseminated within Church-related support groups, generated limited response within the institutional Church outside East Timor.

Bishop Ribeiro's retirement provided the Vatican with the opportunity to change the status of the Diocese of Dili. It was brought under the direct administration of the Holy See and placed in the local charge of an 'Apostolic Administrator', Mgr. Martinho da Costa Lopes, formerly assistant to the Bishop and a native East Timorese.[11] For a while Dom Martinho attempted to protect the people from maltreatment by quiet diplomacy with ABRI but as

---

[8] E.g. Fr.Jose Antonio da Costa became head of the Department of Education and Culture, and Fr.Apollinario head of the Department of Spiritual Matters.
[9] For further detail on Ribeiro see Bibliography – General (East Timor): Dunn, J. 1996, op.cit.pp80, 143, 146-7, 240 & 304; Retboll, T. 1980, p42; Kohen, A.1999, op.cit. pp61-2, 84-85, 90.
[10] Published in Nation Review January 1978, and Timor Information Service No 23, February 1978, filed with ACFOA, Fitzroy, Melbourne. For detail of these military operations see: Bibliography – General (East Timor): Dunn, J. 1996, op.cit. Ch10; Taylor, J. 1994, Ch5-10; Bibliography – Ch2: Budiardjo, C., & Liem, S.L. 1984, Ch 3-7.
[11] For the life and ministry of Dom Martinho see: Bibliography – Ch5: Lennox, R. 1999.

this proved to be of little avail he decided to speak openly and also to pass on information about the atrocities being perpetrated to the wider world. He chose the Feast of Our Lady of Fatima, May 13th 1981, for his first public denunciation when he addressed a rally attended by some 12,000 Timorese people. Carefully avoiding partisanship he condemned the abuses perpetrated by the occupation forces without naming Indonesia.[12] It was about the same time that he charged the Military with genocide in a letter to friends in Australia. This letter, which made specific reference to a recent massacre at Lacluta, was publicised. Dom Martinho also wrote a letter to Australian Catholic Relief in which he described the impending famine that was the direct result of the Indonesian military strategies of widespread aerial bombardment and population 'resettlement'. Later that year he wrote a personal request to Pope John Paul II for a private meeting but received a reply from a Vatican official that such an audience was 'neither timely nor necessary'. This perhaps was 'the heaviest blow' for Costa Lopes whose critique had led to his interrogation by military Intelligence and to assassination attempts.[13] However, he maintained his humble faith in the institution of the Church, still refused to support 'integration', and continued publicly to denounce ABRI brutality while trying to keep a place in his heart for the oppressor.[14] In March 1983 General Benny Murdani, a Catholic, became ABRI Commander in Chief and brought pressure to bear upon the Papal envoy to Jakarta, Pablo Puente, to effect Lopes' resignation - which was indeed tendered only a few weeks later. The removal of Mgr Costa Lopes from East Timor was distressing to the clergy and people there, who were especially devastated by the role of fellow Catholics in the intrigue.[15] But the exile himself saw his removal as an opportunity to present his information first hand to an international audience: 'It is God's design so I can speak for my people to the rest of the world'.[16] He visited all the major cities in Australia, then went on to five Pacific countries, the United States, and Great Britain.

In 1984 Dom Martinho sent a message to the US Bishops Committee for Social Development and World Peace, clarifying the stance of the Church in East Timor, describing how (and why) the local people and the Church were becoming mutually identified, and appealing for support from the countries of the West:

> In the face of the cultural and psychological genocide that the Indonesian army has imposed on us, the large scale deaths, whether directly from the war or indirectly from starvation and disease, the Catholic Church has emerged as the only one organisation that the East Timorese people trust. There is a special and profound respect for the Church. Everything the people know they tell to the priests. The East Timor Church has listened intently for nearly nine years since the Indonesian invasion. With the highest authority the East Timorese Church can say that it knows the plight as well as the deepest aspirations of the people.

[12] Pat Walsh, 1983, East Timor Report, Melbourne; see also Bibliography – General (East Timor): Retboll, T. 1984, pp180-1.

[13] Lopes was subsequently given a Papal audience (after leaving Timor) about which he remarked that 'the Pope is well aware of East Timor' - Interview for *Diario de Noticias* and *Libertas Oporto*, Lisbon, July 1983.

[14] He told the local Military commander of his 'irrepressible need to tell the whole world about the genocide being practiced in Timor'– but he tended wounded and dying ABRI soldiers in hospitals in Dili and Jakarta, and visited their wives. A delegation from the WCC visited Timor in 1982 and reported: 'The leader of the Catholic Church in Dili did not hesitate to speak out in the presence of the security officials and dared to criticise the negative aspects of Indonesian Government policy, concluding that the problem of East Timor is not a military problem but a political and humanitarian one and, consequently, cannot be resolved by the use of guns.' (Citations in Catry, J-P.,1994, 'The Church in East Timor - Voice of a Silenced People', 6th Christian Consultation on East Timor, Strasbourg, June 17-19).

[15] 'Statement of Solidarity ', 13.5.1983. See Bibliography - Ch2: Budiardjo & Liem 1984, op.cit. p121.

[16] See Bibliography – General (East Timor): Citation in - Horta, J.R. 1987, p203.

The Church in East Timor would have no objection if the people, free of all pressure...freely chose to be part of the Republic of Indonesia...but more than 90% if not 99% would be against it.... Only through dialogue, not military means, can there be a just and lasting solution... Western nations that proclaim the principles of justice, liberty and self-determination cannot fail to support such a process...

Humanitarian aid and material things will not by themselves solve the question of East Timor...No material goods can compensate for the denial of self-determination and independence, and for the unending bloodshed and violence...

The Church is persecuted in East Timor because of its moral authority and institutional strength...and because it refuses to call on *Falintil* to lay down its arms...
We in the Church in East Timor live with the consequences of this war every day...we know what we see... We know that the resistance of the East Timorese continues at all levels - in their hearts and souls, and in their prayers to God.'[17]

To the United Nations Human Rights Commission in Geneva he asserted: 'This war will go on and on for as long as natural justice and freedom are denied to the East Timorese people.'[18] In Australia he remarked upon the keen sense of isolation from the Universal Church he and his fellow East Timorese had experienced:

During eight years I only received one letter of support [from a Justice and Peace Commission in a French parish]. One letter only during eight years! But it was good for us, because this letter gave us comfort in our suffering, [that others] understand and are in solidarity with our suffering...so the priests were very, very happy about it.[19]

The welcome he was given by the Church in Portugal on his return to that country (where he died in 1991) also left much to be desired, as will be seen.
There were other factors besides the Church's effort to respond to the manifold needs of a severely oppressed population that led to an unprecedented identification of the local Church with the native people. These included the 'Timorisation' of its clergy that resulted from the withdrawal of many Portuguese and other missionaries. Significantly, the young generation of indigenous clergy were contemporaries and former fellow students of the Timorese political leadership, notably that of FRETILIN. Also pertinent was the isolation imposed on East Timor by the Indonesian regime. The whole process gathered pace during the ministry of Dom Martinho da Costa Lopes and was to be further consolidated under his successor Mgr Carlos Felipe Ximenes Belo.
Before giving attention to the response of the Church in East Timor as a whole it will be helpful to proceed directly to a summary of the ministry of Mgr Belo, the second Apostolic Administrator of the diocese of Dili and the third bishop to have charge of this Catholic community during the period of Indonesian occupation.[20]

---

[17] IDOC Internazionale, 1987, International Documentation Centre (IDOC), Rome, Introduction: p1-2; Pro Mundi Vita Dossier 'East Timor' 1984, Brussels, pp36-7.
[18] UNHCR 21st February, 1984.
[19] East Timor Report Nov 1983, ACFOA, Melbourne; See also: Bibliography – General (East Timor): Retboll, T. 1984, op.cit.p180.
[20] For more information see: Bibliography – Ch5: Belo, C.F.X. 1987, 1993, 2001; Tuekan P. & de Sousa D. (eds.) 1997; Smythe, P. 1998, pp163-169 and 1999, pp99-120; Bibliography – General (East Timor): Kohen, A. 1999, op.cit *passim*.   See also: Belo's 'Message' to UNHRC, February 1997.
For journalists' interviews with Belo see especially: *Kompas* March, 1990; *Matra* August 1992 (ETAN docs Vol 16:7-13); UCANews Sept 1993 (ETAN docs Vol 24:25); Asia Focus April 1994; *Tempo* Sept 1994; *Publico* May 1995; *Gatra* Sept 1995; 'Bishop with charisma to unite squabbling E.Timorese factions', by J.Jolliffe, Irish Times 5.6.1995; *Jawapos* Dec 1996.

Carlos Belo, a native of East Timor, had been out of the country during the period of invasion and the early years of occupation.[21] No doubt the authorities in Jakarta (and perhaps in Rome) hoped that Mgr Belo, who was obliged to take Indonesian citizenship in order to return to East Timor, would prove more 'understanding' of the changed situation. His appointment was made without the proper consultation of the local clergy by the Vatican's envoy to Jakarta, Pablo Puente, and initially Belo's reception by them was not positive. He strenuously sought to avoid any political partisanship such as had been perceived in the attitude of his two immediate predecessors. But it was not long before his comprehension of the prevailing situation led him into challenging the manner and legitimacy of the Indonesian rule in East Timor. At first these criticisms were expressed in private and by continual approaches to the military and civilian authorities on behalf of suffering or vulnerable individuals and groups of Timorese, or they were couched within the carefully worded Diocesan statements to which reference will be made shortly. In due course, as his people continued to suffer abuse and exploitation of all kinds, he was compelled to become more outspoken and unequivocal. He sought to highlight the fundamental causes of tension between East Timorese themselves and with the Indonesian administration and immigrant population. He often pointed to the need for an authentic plebiscite in respect of East Timor's political status and for the completion of a proper process of self-determination in accordance with International Law and the Charter of the United Nations.[22] He appealed for an open and honest dialogue between all parties concerned. He called for a development process that was truly participatory, for the preservation of Timorese cultural and social identity, and for a reduction in or even complete withdrawal of the Indonesian military presence.[23] He proposed a number of bridge-building options over the years including giving East Timor special status or autonomy within the Indonesian republic. But Belo always stressed the necessity of fairly consulting the people over such matters as independence or autonomy, and the importance of giving adequate time to any transition so that local resources, both material and human, could be provided to meet the demands of any new social order.[24]

Bishop Belo had continual recourse to Catholic Social Doctrine. His adherence to it was exemplified in his Pastoral Letter prior to the planned visit to East Timor by the Portuguese Parliamentary delegation in late 1991. In this document he quoted extensively from the Second Vatican Council's Decrees *Gaudium et Spes* and *Apostolicam Actuositatem*, from the Encyclicals of Popes John XXIII (*Pacem in Terris*) and Paul VI (*Populorum Progressio*), from Pope John Paul II's Apostolic Exhortation *Christi Fideles Laici*, and from the Code of Canon Law. Belo addressed in turn the political leaders of Indonesia, Portugal, East Timor, the Timorese Resistance, and the Timorese people as a whole. His overriding emphasis was that the Church is politically non-partisan but is concerned with 'the Common Good' - that is, with furthering social justice and peace and the integral development and freedom of every human person - which must involve respect for human rights including proper political participation and expression. Pointing to Jesus as the model to be emulated he called for mutual respect, for dialogue, and for reconciliation.[25]

---

[21] Born 3.2.1948 Belo was ordained a priest in Lisbon in 1980. From 1975 - 1981 he received his education and formation as a priest and as a member of the Salesian religious congregation in Macau, Lisbon and Rome. Appointed as Apostolic Administrator of Dili Diocese May 1983 he was consecrated titular bishop of Lorium in 1988.

[22] See esp. 'Letter to UN SG Peres de Cuellar', Feb.1989 - cited ubiquitously, and ' Letter to a European Church Organisation' 1984, in 'East Timor: an international responsibility', CIIR 1992, p.28.

[23] See: 'A Time for Justice', Millennium Lecture (7.6.1997) CAFOD, London; Letter of bishops Belo and Nascimento to President Habibie 23.6.1998, Timor Link Aug.1998, p8.

[24] Examples in the 'Year of Crisis' 1999 include: Homily, Dili Cathedral (16.5) Globe & Mail (19.1); LUSA (29.1); 'Belo warns against rushing independence', Wendy Pugh, Reuters 16.2.1999; 'Time to prepare is necessary', Andrew Nette, IOPS, Melbourne 22.2.1999; Antara 2.5.1999; etc.

[25] See, e.g. Bibliography - Ch5: Belo, 1991 (1).

It is important to highlight bishop Belo's recognition of the divisions which existed between Timorese themselves and his continual appeal to them to overcome their differences in the name of God, as well as to keep their hearts open to the possibility and importance of reconciliation with Indonesia. Two homilies given in Dili Cathedral during Lent 1984 and at Christmas 1994, quoted below, and echoed at Christmas 1998, are indicative of his concern for the unity of his people:

> Blinded by the idea of liberty, ambition and power, we lost the sense of brotherly love and human solidarity. We ranged ourselves into parties, confronted other Timorese as adversaries…We have contributed to the continuation of hatreds, revenge, accusations, murders, exile, torture…and to the climate of insecurity in which freedom is lacking…

> We must start a journey of repentance and collective conversion… We must ask for forgiveness and forgive offences… The Church and Christians must be agents of peace, creating a climate of reconciliation, of encounter, of fraternity, of welcome…cultivating virtues of justice, equity, charity, prudence…
> (Dili, 11.3.1984)

> Peace is a gift of God… We are divided, but unity must reign. Divisions are a negative reality, a wound, a sin. The Timorese have never been united… There were fights between kingdoms and tribes…divisions which were increased by economic, religious and political interests…external forces…factions and antagonistic groups… Our leaders do not understand each other… There is no-one who seems able to unite the Timorese…
> In the midst of this vacuum Jesus Christ and his Church try to present the moral and spiritual values of peace, reconciliation, justice and love. The Church proclaims [that] it is necessary to create a mentality of union and unity - Division is a sin! Union and communion are gifts of God.
> Live in unity, build peace…work for the Common Good!   (Dili, 12.12.1994)

Belo's conciliatory disposition towards Indonesia is well illustrated in his speech on the occasion of his receiving the Nobel Peace Prize in Oslo, on December 10th 1996:

> To make peace a reality we must be flexible as well as wise. We must truly recognise our own faults and move to change ourselves in the interests of making peace…let us banish anger and hostility, vengeance and other dark emotions, and transform ourselves into humble instruments of peace…
> The people in East Timor are not uncompromising. They are not unwilling to forgive and overcome their bitterness. On the contrary they yearn for peace -within their community, and within the region. They wish to build bridges with their Indonesian brothers and sisters. They wish to find ways of creating harmony and tolerance.
> Stop the bloodshed, I say. Stop oppression. Stop violence. Stop conflict. Let us sit down around a table and understand each other.[26]

Such sentiments were also those Basileo do Nascimento, consecrated bishop by the Pope in January 1996 and appointed in March to the newly created East Timor diocese of Baucau.[27] Together with Belo, bishop Nascimento repeatedly called for a ceasefire.[28] The two leaders submitted a letter to Indonesian President Habibie on June 23rd 1998. This carefully avoided proposing 'concrete solutions' but urged an end to the so-called 'security approach' adopted by the Indonesian armed forces and for 'a mechanism to collect the aspirations of the entire

---

[26] Full text see: Bibliography – General (East Timor): Retboll, T. 1998, op.cit. pp72-83.

[27] See e.g. 'Dialogue the best way forward' Interview by Manuela Paixo, *Diario de Noticias*, Lisbon 6.1.97; 'Inaugural Address', *Kompas* 20.3.97.

[28] E.g. At the Third UN All Inclusive Intra-Timorese Dialogue (AIETD) Meeting, Krumbach, Austria, October 1997. See: Timor Link Feb 1998, p5.

society of East Timor'. The bishops called for freedom of expression and movement; for genuine dialogue, respect for local culture, release of political prisoners, and access to the territory for international human rights organisations. The letter also appealed for a just settlement 'acceptable to the international community' to be arranged through the United Nations Organisation.[29] The bishops presided jointly over two gatherings of a 'Reconciliation Dialogue' held in the seminary at Dare outside Dili. 'Dare I' (September 10-11th, 1998) adopted an eleven point statement acknowledging the right to differences of opinion and the need for further efforts 'to realise a common platform to unite the people of East Timor and lead to the establishment of a representative forum.' 'Dare II' (June 28-30th 1999) sought to build bridges with the Indonesian regime, bring an end to decades of conflict, and achieve harmonious relations in advance of the UN plebiscite. The two bishops were also invited to be 'observers' in the 'East Timor Consultative Commission' set up by the Indonesian authorities to bring all parties into joint deliberation after the UN ballot of August 30th. All these efforts were entirely frustrated by the disruptive and murderous activities of the pro-Jakarta militias created and supported by the Indonesian National Defence Forces (*TNI*) as described already.

In the dreadful mayhem that ensued after the ballot Belo had to flee the country for the sake of his people, describing the 'cyclone of violence' which threatened to destroy them utterly in words immediately published (16th September) in *The Washington Post*. In this impassioned plea Belo drew the attention of the free world to the 'wholesale slaughter' faced by his people, 'a monstrous effort to annul the people's choice', and the 'systematic persecution of the Catholic Church' which had sought to protect them. 'What is the world waiting for?' he cried, 'An international peacekeeping force is urgently needed if an even more cataclysmic situation is to be avoided that would be a permanent stain on the world's conscience'. Perhaps 'the heaviest blow' for Bishop Belo was the devastation and vengeful murders perpetrated by the 'pro-integration' militias backed by the Indonesian Military - even within the sanctuary of his own home where many defenceless people had fled and a number were brutally killed. But over the years his anguish had been deepened by the apparent lack of solidarity from within the Vatican itself.

During a visit to Australia in 1993 Belo elaborated on the role of the Church in East Timor. It was, he said, 'to be with the people...to speak out about human rights...to put it into the hearts of the young that we must live in hope to become a new society...to help in justice, peace and reconciliation, to be the '*voice of the voiceless.*'[30] The clergy in East Timor undertook this task during Belo's administration as they had during that of his predecessor Costa Lopes. A little over one year into his ministry, on January 1st 1985, the Dili Diocesan Council of Priests published a significant Statement drawing the attention of the Indonesian authorities to the current sorry situation in the country and asserting the Church's right and duty to do so. Reference is made to the doctrinal principles which underpin the Statement and which relate to 'the sovereignty of the people over their own destiny' and to the respect owed to their human rights as individuals and as a nation 'which alone endows legitimacy to any regime'.[31] The document acknowledges aspects of development achieved by Indonesia 'in several sectors of social life in East Timor' (schools, agriculture, media, transport, health) but then attends to 'the roots of all the ills' which continue to beset the populace. These are described as 'the violation of fundamental human rights of the people' including that of 'choosing and directing their own future' and preserving their 'social and cultural identity'. The Statement lays emphasis on the 'sacred duty' incumbent upon the Church to highlight these issues 'in faithfulness to its Divine mission' and 'in fidelity to the people to whom it preaches the gospel

[29] Full text in Timor Link, August 1998, p8.
[30] 'Homily', St. Patrick's Cathedral, Melbourne, 12.11.93. In Timor Link 28 Jan 1994, p.7.
[31] Quotations in the documents referred to here are from the Vatican II decree *Gaudium et Spes*, and from the Papal encyclicals *Populorum Progressio* (Paul VI) and *Redemptor Hominis* and *Christi Fideles Laici* (John Paul II).

message of Truth, Justice, Love, and Human Dignity.' It concludes with an appeal to the Indonesian authorities for total respect for these 'fundamental human rights' and for 'the conditions for an open, frank and fruitful dialogue between the different parties involved, inside the country or abroad, free from any form of coercion'.

Nearly a decade later another document clearly indicative of the local Church's stance was the 'Statement on the East Timor Catholic Church Nowadays' published in Dili on 7th August 1994. This began with the declaration that the Church is 'not a political institution', is 'not tied to any particular political system', and will accept the situation 'chosen by the people of East Timor'. Again the Statement quoted the teaching of the Universal Church in support of its contention that there is a duty on the part of the local Church to 'promote the progress of the people in justice, peace, love and freedom' and to 'submit political structures' to 'a moral assessment.' This document went on to level criticism at 'the imposition of institutional force', 'excessive control', human rights violations, 'extra-judicial institutions and actions', and the 'worsening cultural conditions'. Again, the Church indicated its readiness to abide by the choice of the people by suggesting 'the holding of a Referendum as the most democratic option', or - to avoid possible bloodshed - the offering by Indonesia to East Timor of a 'greater autonomy' or the status of 'a special territory'. And again the Church urged 'dialogue with all political groups' - which it 'calls to reconciliate [sic]'- and offered its own services 'if asked', to be 'with open hands' the 'mediator for such talks'. The Church appealed for 'the reduction of Indonesian armed forces and extra-judicial authority' in the territory and emphasised the importance of 'a conducive atmosphere' for 'freedom of expression', and 'true information on current events without hiding the facts dishonestly'. The Statement concluded by urging:

> Co-operation by the government of Indonesia with the UN Secretary General, the government of Portugal, and resistance groups, so as to allow effective progress towards a settlement...by a series of dialogues in order to achieve peace, justice and an internationally acceptable solution.

In the same year attention was given to a specific issue, that of Development - *Pembangunan* – which was regarded as the prime objective of the New Order government under President Suharto who himself delighted in being known as 'Father of Development'. In 'The Outlook of the Catholic Church on Development: Development that has Value and the Morality of Its Implementation' the local Church was so courageous as to call into question the supposed benefits of this policy in respect of East Timor. As the title suggests, this document was rooted in Catholic Social Doctrine - especially the Encyclical of Pope John Paul II, *Solicitudo Rei Socialis* (1987). It acknowledged the need for local development but required that this be carried out in a proper manner, namely one that 'avoids social alienation, forced (quasi) stability, and fear'. Development must be seen 'as a process of freeing human beings from poverty and injustice'.[32]

This theme was further elaborated in a statement 'East Timor in the Catholic Church's Perspective' presented on the Church's behalf by Bishop Belo at the first meeting of the UN All-Inclusive Intra-Timorese Dialogue (AIETD)[33] that took place at Schlaining in Austria

---

[32] Dili Diocese 9.8.1994.

Cf. Essays on ET Development in: *The East Timor Project, Vol 1.*, 1995, Monograph Series 3/95, Centre for SE Asian Studies, NT University, Darwin. A Timorese critique in: Gomes, R.A., 1997, 'East Timor "Development" or Colonialism?' in *VII Journadas* 17-30 July, University Oporto. At the time of writing the RI govt provided an account of *Pembangunan* policy on its internet website.

[33] Set up by the UN Secretary General to make progress under the mandate given him (1982) by the UNGA to encourage dialogue between the Portuguese and Indonesian governments.

during June 1995. This text also summarised the overall concern of the Church for effecting those changes in the situation that alone could bring about a just settlement:

> As long as the Timorese are treated as a defeated people and are turned into hostages in their own land, this will constitute a very significant obstacle in the way of their real, just and un-impaired development as human beings, as members of a family, and as Timorese...
> Material development cannot be considered development at all if it does not go hand in hand with respect for basic rights which enable people to express their own feelings and give vent to their creativity...When authority is based exclusively on threats, fear, intimidation and cor-ruption, the Common Good suffers...
>
> The Timorese feel that they are annexed (conquered) and not integrated with a civilisation which is respectful of and in harmony with International Law...They strive towards being masters in their own homes and in their own land...
> The Church appeals to Timorese politicians and leaders to learn from the lessons of the past...harmonise their own ideologies and interests with the basic and civil rights of the peo-ple as a whole...
>
> The Church, to which most Timorese belong, seeks no privileges for itself except the freedom to serve the faithful and promote the moral virtues of justice, peace and reconciliation...
> The Church is willing to co-operate with all individuals of good will, as well as with the pub-lic [Indonesian] authorities, on the basis of moral order, for the sake of the dignity of the East Timorese, and in the interests of comprehensive development, harmony, peace and justice.

It is important to note that the clergy who composed these published statements did not enjoy complete unanimity in their opinions as to how best to respond to the situation of oppression in which they and those to whom they ministered had to live. As the populace continued to suffer, and in their various needs to have recourse to the Church, priests and religious became increasingly identified with the people to whose anguished tales they listened. Inevitably they became embroiled in the tensions and divisions prevalent within their society. Within the ranks of Church personnel a variety of attitudes were to be found arising out of their various backgrounds over and above such as might normally result from theological preferences or age differential. These dispositions can be summarised as follows.

There were divergent opinions as to the primary role of the Church. Some perceived this as to further the work of salvation and principally a spiritual enterprise. Others were con-cerned to improve the conditions of the people by seeking to redress their impoverishment and marginalisation and political frustration and regarded such action as the 'preferential option' expected of the Church's ministry according to Catholic Social Doctrine. Continual effort was made to achieve a better balance between the Church's proper religious focus upon sacred rit-ual and its urgent practical concerns about serving the people's needs and advocating their le-gitimate social and political aspirations. But tensions persisted within the community of faith in respect of the image and practice of the Church.[34]

Native pastors belonged to families who had identified with the views of the parties which came into existence in 1974-5 and whose ideology remained influential. For all East Timorese, clergy and laity alike, the issues revolved around the fundamental question: is po-litical self-determination feasible, or is it unrealistic? Those who aspired to its achievement proposed a variety of paths that focused on the choice between autonomy within Indonesia or outright independence. It was expected that the great majority of the people would favour the latter option if a truly free ballot could be arranged.

---

[34] Such divergences were observed by Indonesian scholars in 1980, and in 1989-90: see Bibliography – Ch2: Mubyarto, Sutrisno *et al.* 1991. From this author's discussions with priests and religious in East Timor in 1995 and 1996 it was clear that these issues had still to be satisfactorily resolved.

As membership of the Church grew, and government restrictions on foreign missionaries were tightened, the numbers of native clergy and religious were deemed insufficient to meet pastoral needs. Bishop Belo was minded to invite more Indonesian priests and religious to assist in ministering to the people. This policy decision was later considered by many East Timorese and those in solidarity with them to have been a strategic mistake. The Indonesian pastors were a homogeneous group and, together with their lay catechists, they generally accepted the Indonesian government's official position that East Timor had expressed its desire for 'integration' with the Republic by an 'act of self-determination' in July 1976. Thus they regarded any moves towards a further referendum as illegitimate. Many of the Indonesian clergy and religious engaged earnestly in valuable pastoral activity but there is little doubt that the regime sought to use their ministry as an instrument of its policy. While the East Timorese respected them for the sacred functions they performed, they had little confidence in their political impartiality and a disinclination to place trust in them in matters of any sensitivity.[35]

A third group was composed of the foreign missionaries who included Italians, Spaniards, Indians, Portuguese, Filipinos, Czechs, Slovaks, Mexicans, Americans and others. Because of continuing uncertainties in respect of the renewal of their visas these men and women had to exercise great care in expressing or even intimating their political views. Of course these were mixed but in general it could be said that they occupied the middle ground between those of the Indonesian and the Timorese clergy.

Clearly, attitudes towards the fundamental issue of self-determination determined the way that other questions were dealt with and had an influence on the way the priests and religious worked and to whom they felt accountable. Thus there were different views on the nature of the relationship between Church and State. Such practical subjects as development and health care - and even purely pastoral matters - were approached in radically different ways according to whether the problems faced by the Timorese were regarded as due to a fundamental deprivation of liberty, or to a backwardness and difficulty of adaptation. Foreign priests too, for all that they might sympathise with the Timorese, would carry out their work quite differently if their private view was that Timorese aspirations were unrealistic. Thus different sections of the Church leadership, approaching their work from different perspectives, inevitably tended to pull in different directions. Such tensions were clearly in evidence within the ranks of the Diocesan clergy and within particular religious communities.

The fact of such divisions within the ranks of Church officials - entirely understandable in a situation of extreme social disorder - should not be allowed to obscure the remarkable courage these leaders demonstrated. This was shown in their sustained efforts to defend the people from harm and to put legitimate claims to the international community in furtherance of what they saw as 'the Common Good'. Nor should it diminish the consistency, clarity and urgency of their appeal for support from the world-wide family of faith.[36]

This call was made initially from within the territory by letters and messages passed out with the help of fellow clergy and religious. In later years, following the 'Opening up' of the territory in 1989, it was effected via contributions to the reports prepared by individual or teams of investigative journalists, or by development and humanitarian agencies. In each and every instance such communication was fraught with risk for all concerned, as the author's own experience confirmed in many ways.

---

[35] For further detail see below, Ch.6.

[36] This author received generous and courageous hospitality from all these categories of clergy and religious. Within the Diocesan fraternity of priests as well as in that of Religious houses (especially if they included Indonesian personnel) a variety of views were expressed. With one notable exception - to whom reference will be made in Ch.6 - their political views were subordinated to their religious commitment of dedicated service to all.
See also: Bibliography Ch2: Sword, K. & and Walsh, P. 1991; Bibliography – Ch5: Archer, R.1991, and 1995; Crowe, L. 1996, op.cit. pp121-2.

In time it became possible for detailed first hand information to be presented to state officials, media outlets and to the general public in a number of countries having a direct connection with the East Timor issue.[37] These were important opportunities for the Church in these localities, and universally, to become better appraised of the situation and to respond more vigorously to the plight of the Timorese people. This study aims to make some assessment as to whether such opportunities were indeed seized and exploited to the extent that they deserved - from the viewpoint of those living in the territory itself it certainly appeared that they were not:

> What grieved us was the silence of the world and of the church. We suffered and died, and nothing was said...From the spiritual point of view but for my faith in Christ I could not have stood it...I would either have taken to arms or left the country.[38]

The Indonesian government expected the Church to be subservient to its project, or at least to limit its activity to the purely religious sphere. For this reason it gave visible support to the Church by funding certain high profile projects such as the building of a new cathedral, the raising of a statue of Christ in Fatukama Bay, and a number of grants towards church premises. But the repressive policies of the Military pushed the people towards the Church and laid upon it the moral obligation to serve their needs, act in their defence and advocate their cause. Church leaders were at pains to avoid political partisanship. Nonetheless they became the 'voice of the people', acting as trusted mediators and repeatedly calling on the Indonesian government to respect the dignity of the indigenes by affording them the opportunity of an authentic plebiscite, and a genuine participation in the political processes affecting their daily lives. As a result the Church itself was to suffer from the repression experienced by the community as a whole and the bonds between them strengthened all the more.[39]

As an institution the Church in East Timor had limited means at its disposal but it endeavoured to provide food and clothing for impoverished families, support for widows and victims of physical and sexual abuse, care of orphans, and basic medical attention through a network of 'polyclinics' based on parishes. It defended the right of parents to determine the

---

[37] e.g. The visits made by Mgr Costa Lopes to Australia, the Pacific, the United States, the United Kingdom and to Portugal after his resignation in 1983; the several visits of Mgr Carlos Belo to Portugal, Australia, the USA and to other Western nations after he was awarded the Nobel Peace Prize in 1996; the testimony given by Fr.Francisco Fernandes and Fr.Leonetto do Rego in the late 1970s and during the 1980s in various countries including the United States. Information about the continuing human rights violations in the territory came via various internal channels of the institutional Church. Such evidence is of historical and political significance and represents an important dimension of the international Church's response to the East Timorese plight.

[38] Fr. Martins SJ. Interview with CAFOD/CIIR 1994 - copy on file with the author.

[39] A summary follows - for further detail see:
Bibliography – General (East Timor): Smythe, P. 'The Catholic Church in East Timor', in Retboll, T. 1998 (cited here); Bibliography – Ch2: Budiardjo & Liem 1984, op.cit., pp119-124;
Bibliography - Ch5: Archer, R. 1991 and 1995; Boavida, J.F. 1992 op.cit.; Crowe, L. 1996, op.cit.; Federer, J. 1994; Smythe, P. 1995, 1998 and 1999; Bibliography – Ch8: Hull, G. 1992.
See also Smythe, P. 'The Braving of the Church', in Timor Link No34 Nov.1995, pp1-2, 7-8, and 'Bishop Belo: the essentials for peace' in Timor Link No 38 Jan.1997, p6.
For an appraisal by Indonesian scholars see: Bibliography – Ch2: Mubyarto, Soetrisno, et al.1990 op.cit.; Bibliography – Ch4: Aditjondro 1994 (1), Ch6.
For an assessment by an East Timorese scholar see: Bibliography –Ch2: Saldanha, de Sousa J.M. 1994.
For a description by a Catholic Church scholar in neighbouring West Timor see: Bibliography – Ch5: Neonbasu, G.SVD 1992, and 1998.

number of their children and also the manner of their 'family planning'.[40] The Church continued - even expanded - its educational provision maintaining a relatively high standard despite the difficulties of resourcing such an establishment. Thus the 'Externato San Jose' in Dili played an important role in preserving the Portuguese cultural heritage with its respect for freedom of thought.[41] The development by the Salesians of specialist training facilities such as Fatumaca Technical College, Fuiloro Agricultural College, Venilale Professional & Vocational College and the Comoro Technical Institute were remarkable achievements. Religious congregations of women such as the Canossians established Boarding Schools for girls in an attempt to offer them some protection against the rape that was perpetrated continuously by Indonesian armed forces. Church orphanages cared for large numbers of children.[42] The author visited several such institutions in 1995. Church premises also provided sanctuary to those in danger, and within them could be found mutual encouragement and the discreet counsel of the clergy.[43]

Pastors and religious offered to the Timorese people whatever consolation and fellowship they could in their times of grief, and a spiritual context for their experience of suffering.[44] They comforted the bereaved, encouraged the fearful, and gave fresh hope to those in despair. They eased the consciences of those disturbed by thoughts of hatred and revenge, or troubled by their coerced participation in betrayals, torture, and executions. The congregations of religious sisters especially strove to restore a sense of dignity and integrity to those women who had experienced sexual abuse at the hands of Indonesian military personnel.[45] In general, such pastoral ministry was able in no small measure to discover, articulate, and soothe the people's pain. Furthermore, the Church's corporate preaching of the Gospel generated a 'spirituality of resistance', namely a deep-seated determination to achieve justice and freedom together with the conviction that such an effort was according to the mind and heart of God. Gatherings for prayer, liturgical ceremonies, funerals and anniversaries of death, and religious celebrations generally, were times not only of consolation but also of consolidation for the community. At the sametime, the teaching and communal practices of the Church, which engaged traditional customs and ceremony when appropriate, contributed significantly to a remarkable spirit of reconciliation and to the enduring efforts to bring about a peaceful and honest settlement of the conflict.[46]

As the only public entity surviving from former times the Church provided a degree of continuity, a link with the past. It became the keeper and guardian of the traditional values of the people, defending the nation against its being assimilated or overwhelmed by a foreign

---

[40] See: Bibliography – Ch5: Belo, C.F.X. 1985, and 1993 (2). Both these Pastoral Letters were responses to the social policy of birth prevention being imposed upon Timorese girls and married couples by the Indonesian authorities.

[41] These were important factors in sustaining a resistance to the dominance of Indonesia - and the reason for the enforced closure of the Externato by the Military after the Santa Cruz demonstration in November 1991.

[42] *Viz* The bereaved, and those whose parents simply could not provide for them, or whose fathers were in the armed resistance, or for youngsters who had been 'fathered' by Indonesian soldiers during their tour of duty in East Timor.

[43] In a number of the church premises where the author was accommodated shelter was being provided to persons at risk of maltreatment by the Military.

[44] See e.g. Bibliography – Ch8: CISET, 1994; Visitors Report in Timor Link, No.27 (Oct.1993) p4; Bibliography – General (East Timor): Barbedo de Magalhaes, A. 1990, p112-113 (observation by US Episcopal Bishop Paul Moore).

[45] e.g. *inter alia* Canossians, Carmelites, Sisters of St. Paul of Chartres, Sisters of the Holy Spirit, Maryknollers.

[46] For elaboration see Bibliography – Ch5: Smythe, P. 1999, op.cit. pp99-120.

culture.[47] As the sole institution to function independently of the Indonesian State it enjoyed the special confidence and loyalty of the native people. Church membership became a symbol of Timorese identity to such an extent that there was a fusion of the religious and the secular, a merging of Catholicism and nationalism. As an organisation with international bonds the Church sought to maintain contact with a universal family of faith, and belief in the reality of that spiritual fellowship deepened despite the many disappointments which this study examines.[48] The institutional Church's corporate link with the Universal Church also afforded it significant (but not complete) protection against the malevolence of the occupying forces and helped it to be the sole 'moral force' capable of critical comment on the Indonesian administration.

Beyond the workings of Divine grace, it is for these reasons that applicants to the ordained ministry and to religious congregations became ever more numerous in East Timor. As a group of seminarians in their final years of training expressed it in written responses to questions put by the author (East Timor September 1995):

> The most important work of the Church in East Timor is to protect the Timorese from the oppressors, and to defend their human rights, and to struggle for justice and truth according to the Gospel...
> In the Gospel it is said that all of man in the eyes of God is the same, but in East Timor it is contrary, so we must struggle for the dignity of the people...
> The most pressing work of the Church in East Timor today is the education of the youth, the refuging of the poor, the defending of the truth, and the justice to the small people [sic].

Despite the claims that were made by the Indonesian authorities, it was for these same reasons that the Catholic Church in East Timor as a whole grew apace during the period of Indonesian occupation until it truly represented - because it included - the great majority of the people (over 90%).[49] The Church's numerical, organisational, and especially its moral strength gave it considerable socio-political significance. It had become a 'People's Church' and its membership served - and suffered - accordingly.[50] The laity became actively involved in social welfare and in catechesis through 'lay apostolate' movements fostered by the religious congregations and at the Diocesan Pastoral Centre at Becora. Also, through their partici-

---

[47] An important aspect of cultural preservation was the introduction (in Mgr Costa Lopes' ministry) of a catechism in *Tetun*, and (during bishop Belo's administration) the adoption of this *lingua franca* for the Church's Liturgy. The Church also sought 'inculturation' by the incorporation of elements of traditional Timorese family and social life in its ceremonial.

[48] Indicated, e.g., by the sentiments expressed by the Religious of East Timor (with which this study began): 'Our faith says that we are still one with the Universal Christian Church. It is precisely the dimensions of that universal faith which are being felt and deepened.' Bibliography – Ch5: MASRI 1981.

[49] Indonesia attributed the Church's numerical growth to:
Increased funding afforded under the government's Development Programme or by Indonesian commercial agencies and private individuals;
The principles of *Pancasila* which awarded 'freedom' to the Church to undertake its pastoral work and 'encouraged' conversions by the people from their former animist beliefs.
See Bibliography – Ch2: RI Department of Information - 1984 pp146-7, Department of Foreign Affairs - 1986 p10 and 1992 p19-20. See also: *Statement of the Permanent Mission of the Republic of Indonesia to the UN on Religious Life in East Timor*, 5.4.1985; *Facts on East Timor*, Embassy of Indonesia, Washington DC; etc.

[50] See Bibliography – General Works (East Timor): Pro Mundi Vita 1984, p25; Bibliography – Ch5: Walsh, P. 1982, p.11.

pation in the diocesan Justice and Peace Commission, some were able to become involved in the work of systematic investigation and reporting on human rights violations and in promoting conflict resolution through dialogue.[51]

Of course, many people remained illiterate or at best semi-literate and could bring only limited skills and perceptions to bear upon problems and needs, and there were also limits as to what could be achieved in a situation of considerable political and social repression. There was a continuing need to develop a sense of self-sufficiency, and the understanding many people had of their Catholic faith was far from developed and not free of superstition. But their pastors, though concerned to remedy such defects, by no means deemed such faith superficial.[52] On the contrary, they respected the depth of its sentiment which, through the practice of various populist devotions (especially those honouring the Blessed Virgin Mary), evidently sustained the people during their long anguish and achieved a spiritual unity between them. So the Church leadership encouraged the organisation of religious gatherings in houses, processions and festivals, the erection of Stations of the Cross, and the placing of statues of Christ the King, the Virgin Mary, and patron saints in various prominent locations. This author witnessed the spiritual sustenance all these gave to participants.[53]

The identification of Church and people in East Timor during the period of Indonesian occupation is attested by outstanding representatives of two generations of the Resistance. Xanana Gusmao opined in the early days of the occupation that 'the prophetic mission of the Church requires that it be engaged in the people's struggle for liberation' and that its support had been 'given and guaranteed' and had in fact been 'indispensable'.[54] On a later occasion he was to declare:

> [The Church] is very important to the resistance fight, even though from the outside it might be difficult to fully appreciate it. The Catholic Church in East Timor has played an essentially moral role in regard to the popular resistance. This almost unseen action is felt deeply by our people…strengthening patriotic consciousness…and increasingly the people have enormous trust in the Church… They feel that it isn't isolated from their suffering but in solidarity with us.[55]

Constancio Pinto, who grew up under Indonesian rule and became a significant leader in the Clandestine Resistance, asserted:

> The Church is helpful because the Church is the people… When the people suffer the Church also suffers…The Church is the only East Timorese institution that is outspoken about the atrocities committed by the Indonesian army in East Timor…
> The East Timorese put their hope and trust in the Church. It's the only institution we can complain to about our suffering. The Church has made the resistance even stronger. It gives inspiration to the East Timorese to continue to resist and to fight.[56]

---

[51] Tense circumstances delayed the institution of the Commission until 1995. See its Report (11.12.1998) on human rights violations, land and labour issues, enforced removals, etc.

[52] e.g. In 1981 the religious of East Timor testified: 'The people are experiencing oppression without end, their rights are not acknowledged. They do not have a voice, and live in fear…but their faith stands firm and is strengthened, although it is not always able to be expressed in words.' In 1989 Bishop Belo told the Pope: 'Our people have a simple faith, but are very, very profound in this faith. It is not intellectual, not theoretical, but a kind of emotional faith, a living faith'. See Bibliography – General (East Timor): Kohen, A. 1999, op.cit., pp144, 257.

[53] See also: CIIR interview with Belo, Timor Link Sept.1993; Kohen, A. 1999, op.cit., pp257-276.

[54] See: Letter from 'a priest of East Timor' 17.6.86, on file with CDPM, Lisbon.

[55] Gusmao in interview with Australian lawyer Robert Domm - 'Background Briefing', Radio National Broadcast, ABC, Australia, October 1990.

[56] Bibliography –Ch2: Pinto, C. & Jardine, M. 1997, p238; and expressed personally by Pinto to this author, New York, Sept.1998.

At this point it is important to note that although the Church in East Timor never actually condemned the armed wing of the Resistance, FALINTIL, as the Indonesian authorities would have wished, neither did it provide the guerrillas with much beyond humanitarian support[57], and 'moral support' *in the terms already outlined*. Thus there was no public defence of FALINTIL's activities by the Church leadership in East Timor on theological grounds, although a cogent argument could have been raised to that effect with a basis in International Law and in consistency with traditional Catholic Social Doctrine on what constitutes a 'just war'.[58] There were times when the Indonesian authorities urged Bishop Belo and other clergy to undertake 'negotiations' with FALINTIL to effect their surrender and to facilitate their rehabilitation should they respond to offers of 'amnesty'.[59] However, the Indonesian Military failed to keep the pledges they had made and so the Church's co-operation became limited to a repetition of calls for a non-violent solution to the conflict and for general disarmament.[60] This stance adopted by the Church in East Timor received strong support from many within the international movement.[61] Certainly the Church had a restraining influence upon the youth and had much to do with the Resistance never adopting terrorist practices.[62] In later years the Church refused permission for its premises to be used for any demonstrations and religious events would be cancelled if such plans were suspected.[63]

But the greatest testimony to the significance of the Church in meeting the needs and furthering the legitimate aspirations of the East Timorese were the various efforts made by the civilian and military agencies of the Indonesian government to diminish its influence. Attempts were made to discredit Church leadership in East Timor and abroad; there were restrictions on, or prohibitions of, its meetings and assemblies, and surveillance and intimidation of worshippers. Lay church workers were harassed, sometimes suffering arbitrary arrest, detention and torture. The movement of pastors was inhibited and the provision of foreign missionaries obstructed. There was the prevention of any real social dimension to Church life. On occasion there was physical abuse of priests, and threats of imprisonment or expulsion

---

[57] That is: food, clothes and medicine, and the care of their bereft or bereaved families.

[58] The legality of Falintil's armed struggle can be argued on the basis of UN GA Resolutions 3070 (xxviii) and 3324 (cited by J.Ramos Horta as 'endorsing the use of violence as a legitimate form of struggle for Independence' – See Bibliography: General (East Timor): Horta, J.R.1987, p182. See also Papers by Professors Andre de Hoogh and Alberto Azaredo Lopez, Symposium *VII Journadas*, University of Oporto, Portugal 17-20 July 1997. Taken overall the official teaching authority of the Church latterly has weighed against the 'violent option' in responding to aggression, see:
Pope Paul VI: Encyclical Letters *Populorum Progressio*, 1967,para 30-31, and *Evangelii Nuntiandi*, 1975, para 37; *Address to Campesinos* in Columbia, AAS, 1968 (60) p.263. Bishop Belo and other Church leaders in East Timor consistently adopted this stance during the many years of Indonesian occupation.

[59] e.g. General Abdul Rifai (Regional Commander): 'Belo has the power to end the conflict - he can call for the guerrillas to come down…they are Catholics too'. Straits Times 26.11.96; cf. Timor Link 15/16:6 Jan-Feb 1989; 18/19:7 Oct 1989; UCA Dispatch 679/B. 14-15.1.1993.
[60] 'Our trust was betrayed and *Falintil* soldiers suffered the consequences. We will not repeat the same mistake. If we are asked to 'mediate' we say 'this is not our function'. There has been no 'mediating' since 1993' – East Timorese clergy to the author, Suai, East Timor Sept 1996. 'For me it is better to fight with diplomacy, with intelligence, with discussion, rather than with guns and bullets'. Bishop Belo to Jonathen Head, BBC World Service 15.2.99.
[61] Cf. Vlazna, V. 1997. 'The Value of Non-Violence in East Timor Activism', Paper to *VII Journadas* International Conference on East Timor, Oporto, 17-20 July 1997.
[62] East Timorese clergy to the author, East Timor 1995. See also: Bibliography – General (East Timor): Kohen, A. 1999, op.cit. pp150-1, 156, 159, 197, 213-4, etc: Bibliography – Ch5: Gunn, G.C. 1999, op.cit.p297.
[63] See Bibliography – Ch5: Belo, C.F.X. 1991 (2). Also: Kohen, A. 1999, op.cit. pp182, 191.

from the country, or to bodily integrity or life. Tensions and suspicions between local church personnel, or between Catholics and other faith communities in the country were fostered or provoked. Indonesian diplomats in Jakarta and in Rome also made efforts to bring about the subdivision of the Diocese of Dili or to have it incorporated within the Indonesian Bishops Conference, and to have outspoken Timorese Church leaders subdued or replaced. But all of this only stiffened the resolve of the Church in East Timor and united it still more intimately with the people among whom it lived and worked.

A Blighted Hope

Whatever this study reveals about the response of the Church in the wider world to the plight of the Timorese people, there can be little doubt that the high expectations which the leaders of the Church in Timor had of the universal family of the Christian faith were sorely disappointed:

> As we were approaching 1975 we felt that there was on the part of the churches a rather con-descending attitude which favoured the direct intervention of the neighbouring power... This attitude ... was not dissipated in 1974-5, and continued to express itself...almost up to recent years....

> The preoccupation of the Church in those days was international Communism which exerted extreme pressure on the minds of the Church hierarchy, who considered an intervention, even an armed one, preferable... They even made Christians believe that 'integration', sacrificing the right of self-determination and independence, would be better than Communism....

> What happened from 1975 to 1995 has finally become known by the entire world... The real-ity is that silence transformed itself into an attitude of connivance [with] an armed interven-tion... which has cost the innocent people of East Timor the genocide of thousands of victims ... a number which keeps on growing; the destruction of human and cultural and Christian values...of Timorese identity ...

> [These are] facts which authenticate the phrase of Mgr. Belo to the United Nations: 'We are dying as a people and as a nation.'[64] This cry, let out by the Bishop, has been said and re-peated down the years... in the appeals by the diocesan Priests Council and by religious communities... This cry has been lost in the desert of silence of the majority of the churches... An appeal to truth and justice which continues without sufficient echo from the Church and churches, which gives us the impression that they are inconvenienced by the fact that the Timorese people have continued to stand up and resist...

> But we think that there is still time - as not all the Timorese are dead yet - that the Church, in the knowledge of what it has done, and what it has not done, since the beginning of this trag-edy, demonstrates now, more strongly than at the beginning, a clear position in denouncing the crime, and in influencing the international community and governments ... It will be the only way for the Church to record itself in history, and to human consciousness, with clean hands.'[65]

The Church in East Timor: an Evaluation

Referring to the criteria previously delineated it can be argued that the Church in East Timor, during the period of Indonesian occupation, fulfilled to an impressive degree the prin-ciples of Catholic Social Doctrine. Church leaders were always ready to dialogue with the secular authorities with open mind and heart. At the same time they were courageous enough

---

[64] Citation from Belo's Letter to the UNSG (Peres de Cuellar), February 6th 1989.
[65] Excerpts from 'Reflection on East Timor, from East Timorese Clergy for the 7th Christian Consul-tation on East Timor, (Brussels) 26-28 January 1996.

to pass critical comment upon the management of socio-political affairs, inviting the government to search for better ways of fulfilling its perceived responsibilities while properly urging the Church's own distinctive religious nature and programme. As an institution the Church sought to preserve its own identity and independence, not for its own sake but for the sake of those whom it was called to serve.[66] Its principled actions were rooted in a fundamental respect for the human person, expressing the mind and heart of Christ, and as an effort to build up his Kingdom on earth. The religious purposes of the Church were never forgotten, and given priority by some, but the overall thrust was surely to give 'preference to the poor' who were the abused and marginalised majority of the indigenous people. The Church in its teaching and practice highlighted the rights of the people - to political self-determination, to resist oppression, to participation in the decision-making processes affecting their daily lives, and to 'integral development'. It was 'the Common Good' that the Church sought - i.e. not just the welfare of the native people but that of all who came to live in East Timor during those years. The growing numbers of East Timorese who became Catholics (with a profound if 'unlettered' faith) indicated the Church's solidarity with the people. This was also affirmed by the Resistance leaders, and recognised by the Indonesian authorities - who consequently sought to diminish the respect in which the Church was held and the influence it had with the people. Included in the Church's critique of the Indonesian regime was its account of the injustices inherent in the very structures of social order which were imposed upon the people and which denied them opportunity for economic advancement or even to provide adequately for their ordinary needs. In its efforts to meet those needs the Church endeavoured to devolve responsibility. Although such 'subsidiarity' was not fully achieved the reasons for this lay substantially in the colonial heritage and in the present oppression which prevented so many from acquiring the necessary skills to take proper charge of their own affairs.

Measuring the Church in East Timor against the highest ideal of all - that of the ministry of Jesus himself - it can be fairly judged to have emulated the character of that commitment to a high degree.

The Church was a true *Pastor*, leading the people to a greater participation in the life of grace while attending to their human needs in every possible way. The Church sought to avoid an identification of the Kingdom with any specific political order and hence lent its support to the Resistance only in a clearly circumscribed way. At the same time the Church determinedly refused to become an agency for the Indonesian authorities, despite the negative consequences this had for its personnel and upon its institutional operation.

The Church fulfilled its calling as *Prophet* by subjecting to criticism not only the Indonesian rule but also the efforts of the Resistance when these contravened the Gospel imperative, compromised the independence and message of the Church, or failed to effect the non-violent principles of Catholic Social Doctrine. More fundamentally, the Church's call was to a trust in and obedience to God's will. This was not to the passive acceptance of a new social order but to justice and holiness, virtues requiring a spirit and practical expression of mutual respect and support, to resistance against evil, and to reconciliation of those in opposition.

The Church surely 'listened like a *Disciple*' - to the cries of the poor, to the proposals of politicians, to the representatives of humanitarian and development agencies, and to the authorities of the Church Universal - who were sometimes quicker to propound their expectations than to offer practical support. The Church in East Timor had to learn anew what its response should be, and was ready to express this humble disposition by offering to search

---

[66] cf. Bibliography – Ch8: Walsh, P. 1980 (1), p10. Walsh opines that an important motivation for the ET Church's great [educational] efforts was its own survival.

alongside the Indonesian authorities for an improved social order - inviting shared reflection on how things could be better for all.

Carrying out Christ's mission as *Evangeliser* the Church was concerned to liberate the people from 'all manner of oppression' - failing hope, the burden of guilt, the heart hardened against the perpetrators of great cruelty, social and economic disadvantage, cultural imperialism, political oppression.

As *Intercessor* the Church was continually gathered in prayer, for her members in need - and for their oppressors. This prayer was not only offered in the formal Liturgies presided over by the ordained clergy or consecrated religious. It was also raised in the humble homes of the faithful where the rosary was recited and the statues of the Virgin and other patron saints became a focus of devotion and renewal of faith, hope and love. Through the celebration of the Sacrament of Reconciliation, frequently participated in by many, a spirit of forgiveness was engendered. In the daily celebrations of the Eucharist, attended by great numbers, the Church's intercession was effectively united with that of Jesus to his heavenly Father, helping the people to discern what God was asking of them and to obey God's will.

Most important of all was the readiness of the Church to *lay down its life* for the sake of the suffering people of East Timor. This was demonstrated not only in the manifest courage of the leaders but also in the commitment of so many of the laity who, by their very association with the Church, became identified as '*GPK*' (rebels) - in the minds of the Indonesian authorities, especially the Military. The readiness of Church personnel to suffer death for the sake of the people was clearly in evidence during 1999, the year of *kairos* for East Timor.[67] In those fearful months a number of the diocesan clergy, religious personnel, young seminarians, and Catholic laity were done to death by the marauding militia groups as they tried to protect their defenceless people from harm or to serve their needs. There can be no doubt that the religious faith of the East Timorese both evoked and supported the courageous vote when 78.5% rejected Indonesian rule. Those who died can surely be regarded as martyrs, not only for *Timor Loro Sae* but also for the Gospel and the Kingdom of Christ.

---

[67] See Bibliography – General (East Timor): Taylor, J. 1999, (revised and updated edition of 1991 publication) pp xi-xxxvii; Kohen, A. 2000 (revised and updated edition of 1999 publication), p293-295.

CHAPTER SIX - THE CHURCH IN INDONESIA:
'PARTNER IN NATION-BUILDING'

A Lament and Allegation

In 1983 a group of priests of the Diocese of Dili made an appeal on behalf of the East Timorese people to Episcopal Conferences world-wide. The text expressed their distress concerning the neighbouring Church in Indonesia:

> We feel disappointed and profoundly hurt, knowing that members of the Indonesian Catholic Church have joined in the *chorus of campaigns* carried on inside and outside Indonesia and in the defamation of its Prelate [Costa Lopes], accusing him presumptively of falsehood, exaggeration and irresponsibility ... when his is the only voice raised in defence of the people ...
> This group affirms its solidarity with the martyred people of East Timor and with the clear position assumed by its Prelate in defence of those denied their fundamental human rights.[1]

To discover whether this critique was justified at the time of its composition, and thereafter during the ensuing seventeen years of Indonesian occupation, it is necessary first to describe the situation of the Church in Indonesia in modern times.

An Historical Overview[2]

A Catholic community established itself on the island of Sumatra as early as the 7th century. In the 14thC Franciscan missionaries started working in Java and Borneo as well. Portuguese and Spanish colonial expansion led to the eventual extension of missionary activities to other of the more populous islands of the archipelago. The missionaries were expelled from those territories that subsequently came under the rule of the Dutch but this policy was changed early in the 19th century. By 1842 all the Catholics in the territory came within one Apostolic Vicariate. An outstanding missionary at the turn of the century was Fr.van Lith S.J. who wholly identified with the indigenous people and culture and whose principles were to have a significant impact upon the subsequent development of the Catholic Church in Indonesia.[3] By 1900 there were 50,294 Catholics in Indonesia and during the 20th century this number continued to grow until by its end the total had reached over three million in an overall population of 200 million. The Indonesian Catholic hierarchy was installed by Pope John XXIII in 1961.

Situated in a pluralist but predominantly Muslim society the Church in Indonesia has always felt insecure. Not long after the first significant nationalist movement *Budi Utomo*, 'Noble Endeavour', was inaugurated in 1908 Catholic political organisations began to be formed to protect the Church and its work and to ensure that Catholics were party to national developments. One of the earliest was the Catholic Political Association of Java with an outstanding leader in the person of I.J.Kasimo, a former pupil of van Lith. The promotion of Indonesian rights and interests by van Lith and Kasimo gained the attention of nationalist leaders, notably Sukarno, who experienced the dedicated care of Catholic missionaries at first hand. The extensive social work organised by the church - especially its educational provision, health care, and assistance to the poor also impressed the nationalists.

---

[1] 'Statement by a Group of Priests of Dili Diocese' 13.5.1983. Author's italics; copy on file.

[2] For detail see: Bibliography – Ch6: Muskens, M.P.M. 1973, and 1979; Coomans, M. 1988 'The Catholic Church in Indonesia', East Asian Pastoral Review, Vol 25, pp379-390.

[3] See: Van Lith, Pamphlet 1922. Archive, Bishops Conference of Indonesia (*KWI*).

During the turbulent period in which Independence was finally gained (1945-50) the Catholic Church played a significant role in the task of building up the nation both politically and socially. The Manifesto of the newly formed *Partai Katolik Republik Indonesia* declared 'a will to defend the Republic and strengthen its condition...to preserve the unity of the people as necessary for progress and self-sufficiency'. The Apostolic Vicar, bishop Sugyapranata, a native of Java, was anxious that the loyalty of Catholics should be in no doubt and he called on the faithful to give the young Republic their support and co-operation urging them to 'fight *pro ecclesia et patria*'. Many Catholic students volunteered to take up arms in the struggle against Dutch colonial rule - and many of them were to lose their lives in doing so. This spirit of self-sacrifice for the sake of the nation further enhanced the Church's standing in the eyes of the political leadership.

After Independence was achieved all the existing Catholic parties which had come into existence across the archipelago were merged into one *Partai Katolik* (*PK*). The statutes of the Catholic Party declared that its objective was 'to work for the progress of the Republic of Indonesia and the welfare of its people' and its operations were to be based on 'belief in God, Catholic Social Doctrine, and *Pancasila*'. The State ideology was accepted as at least consistent with the Christian gospel and its principles were considered to be a safeguard for the continuation of the Church's presence and ministry. Such identification with the aspirations of the young nation state brought favourable regard on the part of the secular authorities.

During the period of so-called 'Liberal Democracy' the influence of the Church was great considering its relatively small size. Through its educational provision the Church had ensured that Catholics were numerous among the administrative class who were prominent partners with the government in the practicalities of 'nation-building'. The bishops encouraged the fullest participation of all Catholics in political and social life. They were especially concerned about the growing influence of Communism perceiving it as a form of 'neo-colonialism' and a destructive force, not only in Indonesia but in other Asian nations. They doubted Sukarno's ability to contain the growing Indonesian Communist Party (*Partai Komunis Indonesia, PKI*) within the co-operative relationship he envisaged.[4]

The system of 'Guided Democracy' that Sukarno subsequently introduced was supported by the Catholic Party with a view to preserving the *Pancasila* and so protect the Church's presence and operation. The Bishops Conference declared:

> The Church can co-operate with any form of government as long as the fundamental rights of belief in God and humanity are respected and as long as people are not pressured into a society of materialism or atheism'.[5]

During this period the *Partai Komunis Indonesia* was openly supported by Sukarno - who needed its help against Muslim groups favouring an Islamic or a Federal State - and it grew dramatically in numbers and in political ambition. The bishops and the leaders of the Catholic Party were alarmed by its growing assertiveness and influence. Hitherto they had aligned with the secular nationalists to safeguard the Church against a politically dominant Islam but now, as a polarisation of ideology developed between 'communist people' and 'religious people', they sought the cultivation of relationships with the Army in defence against revolutionary Marxism - receiving a positive response. They also encouraged a militant Catholic political activism: archbishop Djajasepoetra exhorted the Catholic community to 'unite, protect *Pancasila*, and defend the life of the Church'. The *Partai Katolik* sought to counteract the Communist Party's vigorous and effective information barrage

---

[4] Viz. *NASAKOM*, i.e. *Nationalisme, Agama* [religion], *Komunisme*.
[5] See: Bibliography – Ch6: Muskens, M.P.M. 1979 op.cit. p267.

and were instrumental in the establishment in 1965 of *Kompas* - destined to become the leading national newspaper with a significant number of Catholic journalists. At the same time Fr.J.Beek *SJ* established an influential training programme for Catholic youth to prepare them for political leadership. This had a strongly anti-Communist tone.[6]

The bishops were attending the Second Vatican Council at the time of the alleged 'Communist coup' in the autumn of 1965 but they addressed a letter 'To our Fellow Countrymen' some eight months later. In this they expressed sentiments of distress at the 'many victims' of the purge of '*PKI* activists' and asked pardon for 'any negligence or irresponsibility of theirs' which might have contributed to the disaster. They called for the principles of *Pancasila* to be honoured as offering a good basis for a tolerant and inclusive society.[7] If the hierarchy had misgivings about the manner in which the *Orde Baru* was established and was operating they appear to have been relieved by its opposition to Communism and its control of Islamist assertion. It is also evident that they wholeheartedly supported the new regime's proposed development programme that seemed to propose practical remedies for the nation's economic and social ills.[8] Meanwhile the Catholic Party made no bones about its participation in the destruction of the *PKI* and about its backing for Suharto. It celebrated what it called 'a return to the Rule of Law and a clear and consistent adherence to the *Pancasila* and the 1945 Constitution'.[9] The General Secretary of the *Partai Katolik*, Harry Tjan Silahi, became General Secretary of the *Front Pancasila*. Young Catholic activists such as Liem Bian Kie (Jusuf Wanandi), Liem Bian Kun (Sofyan Wanandi) and Cosmas Batubara (Chairman of the *PK* youth wing) joined the United Action Front of University Students (*KAMI*) where they were very influential. They used other opportunities besides to help build close relationships with Army personnel, later opting - along with many others - to leave the *Partai Katolik* in favour of *Golkar*. Clearly, both the bishops and the Catholic politicians considered that the developments which had taken place, and their political alignment with the Military, would be to the advantage of the Church and safeguard its place in and mission to Indonesian society.

At first the co-operation of the Catholic community with the Military - which certainly assisted the *Orde Baru* to become established - seemed to be to the reciprocal advantage of the Church whose political leaders were afforded influential positions in Suharto's government.[10] Opportunism supplanted defensiveness as the motivation for the continuation of Catholic involvement in political training and activism: Catholics intended to secure a niche for themselves at the centre of the new emerging power structure and they were generally supportive of government policies domestically and abroad. Thus Frans Seda - who as a student had fought in the war of Independence against the Dutch and had been Chairman of the *PK* since 1960 - became Finance Minister in Suharto's first Cabinet, and Jusuf Wanandi was appointed assistant to Ali Murpoto, Suharto's right hand man. Wanandi thereby became closely associated with the special operations unit *Operasi*

---

[6] See: Bibliography - Ch6: Hadi, A.I. 1990; Stuart, C. 1991. Hadi and Stuart discern direct connections (e.g. financial) between Fr.Beek's enterprise and Bob Santamaria's NCC organisation in Australia, see Ch 8.

[7] Muskens, op.cit. pp279-80. This was the only major statement of the hierarchy on the issue.

[8] e.g. 1) Pastoral Letter 'A Joint Declaration on Socio-Economic Development', October 1966; 2) Address of Cardinal Justinus Darmojuwono 'To all the people of Indonesia', 1.4.1969. Cited in Muskens, op.cit. p299.

[9] For details see: Muskens, op.cit. p281, and cf. Muskens, op.cit. p316; Stuart, C. 1991, op.cit.; Hadi, A.I. 1990, observes that many lay Catholics 'forgot the principles of Social Doctrine and went on an anti-Communist rampage' (op.cit. p74).

[10] Stuart, C. 1991, op.cit. pp45, 47.

Khusus (*OPSUS*) which had masterminded the overthrow of Sukarno and which was to engage in the manipulation of the political parties in and the 'integration' of East Timor as Indonesia's '27th Province'.[11] There is also no doubt about the significant influence of Harry Tjan Silali in persuading Suharto to intervene in East Timor.[12]

In 1973 the *Orde Baru* required the amalgamation of the existing political parties, a policy supported by some leading Catholic politicians on the grounds that it would overcome developing factionalism. The bishops had already indicated in their 'Action Guidelines for Catholic Indonesians' (1970) that they considered it expedient for Catholics to join other parties, especially *Golkar*. But the negative effect this merger had upon Catholic influence in national affairs, and the regime's manipulative use of *Golkar*, subsequently cast doubt upon the wisdom of such judgements. The Suharto administration attempted to impose *Pancasila* as the sole ideology of all political parties and social organisations (including religious ones) which caused Church authorities considerable concern. The strong Catholic opposition to Communism was a critical factor in the achievement of a mutually satisfactory outcome to this problematic issue.[13] Likewise, the laws introduced in 1978, 1984 and 1988 prohibiting proselytism and limiting both foreign funding for Church activities and the activities of foreign missionaries heightened the hierarchy's sense of the continuing vulnerability of the Church. The growing influence of the Muslim majority upon national politics and in social relations made many in the Catholic community feel increasingly insecure.

However, the hierarchy and lay leaders - including the Catholic media and the Catholic journalists of the leading national newspaper *Kompas* - did not vigorously challenge these developments. They were convinced that for the welfare of the Church it was necessary to adopt a co-operative rather than a confrontational relationship with the Government. The bishops therefore took pains to emphasise publicly the spiritual purposes of the Church, its desire for social tolerance and harmony, its promotion of humanitarian values, its recognition of the principles of *Pancasila*, and its desire to continue to contribute to the up-building of the nation. They tended to avoid explicit political directives, eschewed political partisanship, and warned against the politicisation of religion.[14] These sentiments were reiterated in the Catholic Press.

There were times when the Bishops Conference appealed for integrity and openness in public affairs and invited Catholics, Indonesian citizens in general, and the Government in particular, to consider the wisdom and humanity of some of the regime's policies and to reflect on the state of the nation.[15] And there were dissenting voices within the Church community who expressed their dissatisfaction with the conciliatory posture adopted by the hierarchy towards the Suharto regime. As a number of clergy, religious and laity across the archipelago remarked to the author in 1996: 'it adds up to the defence of the

---

[11] See: Bibliography – General (East Timor): Taylor, J. 1991, pp23, 30 n44, 200.

[12] Revealed in Australian government documents declassified in December 2000. See: 'Gough got gamble wrong', Paul Monk, Canberra Times 18.12.2000. Tjan Silali later regretted the 'meaningless violence' which had ensued: 'Can history pass a fair East Timor ruling', H.Tjan Silali, Editorial & Opinion, Jakarta Post 2.10.2000.

[13] Decree of Consultative Assembly March 1983. Cf. Bishops Conference: Pastoral Letter, May 1984; Guidebook 1985 'Indonesian Catholics in the *Pancasila* Society'.

[14] e.g. Pre-General Election Pastoral Letter, 1976 (cited in Muskens, op.cit. pp300-301); Lenten Pastoral, 1997.

[15] e.g. 1) Pre-General Election Statement (June 1971); 2) 'Observations on Developments in the Nation and in Society' (Nov.1977). 'An Open Letter' by Cardinal Darmaatmadja (Aug. 1996) on recent riots in Jakarta, appealed for a 'spirit of humanitarianism and solidarity', criticised 'lack of accurate information' and referred obliquely to 'vested interests'. The government's response was to call on all religious leaders to 'support national unity' and caution them against being seduced by the 'siren calls of democracy.' Cf. 4) Lenten Pastoral Letter, 1997, cited later in this text.

institution and the neglect of justice'. But a need for foreign missionaries remains and the general situation of the Church can still hardly be described as 'secure'. From 1998 onwards, serious conflicts arose between Christians and Muslims in the Moluccas especially, but also elsewhere in the Republic, with many hundreds killed and Church property destroyed or damaged, even in Jakarta itself. Many political analysts were of the view that the Military were responsible for provoking such confrontations in order to justify their continuing social control and to maintain their political influence. A fair appraisal of the response of the Church in Indonesia to the issue of East Timor must be made in this context.

The Relationship of the Church in Indonesia with East Timor

The Bishops Conference
There was certainly a symbiotic relationship between the *Orde Baru* and the Catholic Church leadership at the time of the invasion of East Timor. But the Church had little actual control over government plans and the manner of their execution. Indeed, it is clear that it was the regime's intention to use the Church as an agency in its policy of *Integrasi* (integration) from the start. An armed forces chaplain described in 1977 how Catholics had been preferred for military and civil service positions in East Timor. He also said that the army had put helicopters at the disposal of the (local) priests to help them visit outlying areas 'to spread the good word about Indonesia and development, and to coax FRETILIN to give up the struggle'.[16] The government also exercised control over the relief programme organised by the Indonesian Church - 'for reasons of security and to educate the public'. This exercise in propaganda actually had negative consequences upon the programme's effectiveness.[17] Furthermore, the information about the situation in East Timor was conveyed to Indonesian citizens by a mass media that was closely supervised by government agencies. Such coverage was both limited in its extent and entirely positive in its account of the 'accelerating development' integration was supposedly bringing to the local people. It referred to the lack of popular support for the 'dwindling band' of FRETILIN 'separatists'.[18] Such sentiments were echoed in the Catholic media outlets. Yet the Church, through its own internal communications, was better appraised of the situation than the Indonesian populace at large. In September 1976 a delegation of Indonesian priests had visited East Timor and reported on how the great majority of East Timor's people had demonstrated their feelings about the arrival of the Indonesians - they had fled into the mountains. The visiting priests also gave a clear description of the genocide that was taking place:

> The number of people in the towns and villages occupied by Indonesian troops is about 150,000, out of a total population of 650,000. They told us that so far about 60,000 Timorese had been killed. We had thought this was a very high figure as it meant that 10% of the population had been killed. However, when we spoke of these numbers to two priests in Dili, they told us that, according to their calculations the number of dead was nearer 100,000.[19]

---

[16] 'Report 1', Timor Information Service Nos 18/19 April 1977, Darwin.

[17] 'East Timor: Some Experiences and Thoughts', Alex Dirja *SJ,* Inter-Nos, Journal of the Society of Jesus, Indonesia, Year xxiii/1979, No.2 Issue (April May June).

[18] 'Report 1', Timor Information Service April 1977, op.cit. See also: Bibliography – Ch2: Budiardjo & Liem. 1984, p49.

[19] Report of the Parliamentary Library/Legislative Research Service, Australia. 22 Nov.1976; See also Bibliography – General (East Timor): Chomsky, N.1978 'Statement delivered to the Fourth Committee of UNGA (cited in Retboll, T. (ed) 1984, p12).

Dom Martinho da Costa Lopes had written to the bishop of Jakarta[20] detailing the killings and had attended gatherings of the Bishops Conference where he provided a first hand account of the human rights violations being perpetrated in East Timor. These unequivocal reports embarrassed the bishops at their meetings, especially when Suharto was present, and they remained silent on the issue in public.[21] At the same time they were persuaded by government officials to support the attempts being made to consolidate the integration of East Timor by making a discreet appeal to the Vatican for the Diocese of Dili to be incorporated into the Indonesian Church:

> Since 1976 the government and the people of Indonesia officially recognise East Timor as constituting an integral part of the Indonesian nation. Although the Catholic Church in East Timor is not yet part of the Indonesian Hierarchy, co-operation between the Catholic faithful in the two places is an accomplished fact. Since 1977 the Bishops Conference has invited the Apostolic Administrator of Dili to take part in all sessions of the annual meeting of the Bishops Conference as an observer. The Conference serves as a contact and distributor of aid to East Timor from outside the country. There is now a priest from Atambua and two sisters from Java who are helping the Church in East Timor...
> We ask that the Holy See weigh and consider the status of the Catholic Church in East Timor so that it might enter fully into the Indonesian Bishops Conference....
> With such a change in status we could expect that the co-operation which has already begun would be intensified, and relations between the Conference and the Government of Indonesia would likewise be enhanced.[22]

In May 1983, in their appeal at the time of Mgr Costa Lopes forced resignation, the priests of Dili diocese described the violations of human rights then widespread:

> Moral and physical violence; arbitrary imprisonment; the resettlement of families and whole villages; the execution of those who surrender; execution without trial or after summary judgement; disappearances and the destruction of families; the execution of whole groups of those captured; hunger and disease throughout all of East Timor.

In November of the same year bishop Belo attended the Bishops Conference annual assembly and presented his own first hand report. The Conference was moved to make a compassionate written response, but carefully avoided any wording that might be perceived by the regime as confrontational:

> We do not want our solidarity with and our concern for the Church and the people of East Timor to be interpreted as any movement inspired by worldly considerations: our attitudes and actions are based on 'the collegial nature and meaning of the episcopal order...by which bishops are linked...by the bonds of unity, charity and peace (*Lumen Gentium* 22)...
> There is a relationship among the Faithful from all places and it is because of this that we cannot refuse to face up to the events that are happening among the people...

---

[20] Letter, July 12th 1980. For citation see also Bibliography - General (East Timor): Taylor, J. 1990, p189; Bibliography - Ch2: Budiardjo & Liem, op.cit. p137.

[21] See Bibliography – Ch5: Lennox, R. 2000, p178-8; Bibliography – General (East Timor) Chomsky, N.1978, op.cit. p12.

[22] *Ad limina* Report of the Bishops Conference of Indonesia to the Holy See, May 1980. The bishops were continually under pressure from high-ranking government officials - even from President Suharto himself - to persist with this proposal. See e.g.: UCA News Dispatch 107, 16.9.1981; Walsh, P., 1982, 'Church may hold key to Timor's future' in Outlook Vol.4 No.1 Jan 1982. Fr.Kartasiswaya, Bishops Conference pro-secretary remarked on the occasion of Mgr Belo's episcopal ordination in 1988 that such an incorporation was 'only a matter of time.' For citation see: Bibliography – Ch8: CCJPD. 1993, p8.

We reaffirm that 'the role and competence of the Church being what it is, she must in no way be confused with the political community nor bound to any political system' (*Gaudium et Spes* 76)...

The Catholic Church of Indonesia, ...in spite of all restrictions, has made every possible effort to express its solidarity and friendship with the Faithful and people of East Timor who are being deluged by most bitter trials both physically and spiritually...

We present [them] with the most precious gift that we can give: 'our efforts towards the application of justice and charity within and between nations' (*Gaudium et Spes* 76)...

We struggle so that with respect for all persons we may attain first and foremost a return to peace for all...and through various ways to enforce acknowledgement and respect for those things which are considered most sacred by the people of East Timor: their religion, their family, and their land...

The sympathy and solidarity of the Church in Indonesia...is expressed not only in our prayers, but also in the form of material assistance...

Moreover we request understanding from all who control the decision-making that any changes which will lead to a better situation can only be successful if they are carried out with a spirit of honesty...

We are conscious that the road to justice and peace demands an extraordinary sacrifice of feelings....and we believe that for some time the root of the problem is the level of ability to understand the world of reason and feelings of the other party...

We pray and hope for a lasting peace and a return to true harmony...[which is] 'an enterprise of justice' (*Gaudium et Spes* 78, 32, 7).[23]

The Bishops were evidently at pains to base their statement safely and securely upon the Social Doctrine of the Universal Church. At the same time they appealed to the principles of *Pancasila* and evoked the most fundamental of Javanese cultural values, 'harmony'. They intimated that all parties would find it beneficial to give further consideration to the issues that divided them - but what this statement lacks is a forthright challenge of a grave and persisting injustice. First hand accounts of continuing oppression continued to be presented directly to representatives of the hierarchy[24] but this restrained letter remained the strongest expression of dissent with government policy in East Timor for years to come.

Thus in 1984 bishop Hadisumarto (Conference Chairman) declared only that 'the Church hopes the heritage of value systems, culture, and uniqueness of tribes in East Timor will be preserved and developed for the benefit of the whole Indonesian nation'. The same year archbishop Soeketo (Conference Secretary) expressed the view that the Church was concerned to provide humanitarian assistance but not with the political question of East Timor's status. Foreign reports on the situation in East Timor, he opined, were 'deliberately exaggerated'.[25] When bishop Belo's letter to the UN Secretary General (1989) became public knowledge, archbishop Darmaatmadja *SJ* (Conference Chairman) was quick to remark that 'it must be interpreted as a personal letter and not on behalf of the Church or in the name of Catholics'.[26] Notably, the Indonesian Catholic Weekly *Hidup* commented: 'The political and legal integration of East Timor is not reversible and disputable any more. But the full realisation of the integration likely takes time [sic]'. In May that year Darmaatmadja was to observe that the way the Catholic Church in

---

[23] 'To the Apostolic Administrator & the Priests, Brothers and Sisters of the diocese of Dili'. Jakarta (17.11.1983). Notably, this letter was never disseminated in Indonesia itself.

[24] e.g. 'Statement made by Seminary Students on the Occasion of the Visit of the Indonesian Episcopal Conference President to the Territory of East Timor' (Jan.1984) made reference to forced recruitment for counter insurgency operations, massacres of children, and the aggressive treatment of priests by the Military. See Bibliography – Ch8: CCJPD. 1993, op.cit. p15-16.

[25] UCA News Dispatch 262, 12.9.84, p3-5.

[26] *LPPS Forum* July 1989, No.8, p.14.

Indonesia got things done was 'by the wisdom of silence'. He asked the Vatican not to give too much attention to 'one-sided campaigns by a certain party'.[27] When the Pope made his pastoral visit to East Timor in October, after his journeys in Indonesia, the hierarchy urged that he kiss the ground only once, in Jakarta and not in Dili. They had received warnings that 'if things go badly Catholic schools and hospitals in Indonesia will suffer'.[28] The hierarchy's *ad limina* report to the Holy See that year referred to various 'burning problems' but East Timor was not included among them.[29] Of course, the Vatican did not require the Indonesian Bishops to report on East Timor since it undertook 'direct' administration of the territory. But at least an oblique reference to the situation was warranted since the Indonesian Church had been extensively engaged in humanitarian and religious assistance in the territory. However the Bishops did raise their concerns privately with the Pope.[30]

Even after the Santa Cruz Massacre in November 1991 the reaction of the Bishops Conference was notably weak - their Statement used the government term 'incident' to refer to the atrocity. They questioned the veracity of received reports and expressed confidence that the shootings were not a policy of the government, or of *ABRI* as an institution. Their view was that 'some members of the armed forces had regrettably put at risk the moral integrity, dignity and credibility of the nation in the eyes of the world and of the people of East Timor'. 'It is most pressing' they declared, 'that the people's feelings of security, and trust in the Government be restored'. The massacre did not have much impact either upon the conservative and powerful sections of the Catholic laity in Indonesia who remained pre-occupied by the need to preserve the long-term interests of the Church. But the bishops did list some questions that the Government should pursue indicating that they felt further inquiry into what actually happened would be generally helpful. They also sent their own fact-finding team which discovered numbers of deaths which the Military had blatantly denied.[31]

From then on a change of tone in the hierarchy's pronouncements became discernible. Early in 1995 President Suharto appealed to the Conference of Bishops to help in solving the problem of East Timor because 'the continuation of the issue would harm everyone - including the Catholic Church'. The bishops assured the president that they were already giving assistance 'not in political but in humanitarian and religious affairs', but afterwards they publicly attributed the discontent of the East Timorese to 'a deeper feeling of frustration, disappointment and hopelessness. Many feel as if they are being marginalised in their own home.' However, they did not challenge Indonesian sovereignty in East Timor, continuing to affirm it - at least by default.[32]

In 1997 the bishops' Lenten Pastoral included a significant paragraph inviting 'all parties concerned to make a profound introspection and ask why, after twenty years of integration, some East Timorese have yet to live it'. The letter continued:

> The key to the settlement of the problem is a transition from the 'security approach' to the creation of a social milieu in which the people of East Timor feel that their cultural, religious and historical identity is recognised and safeguarded. It is of the utmost importance to heed the real aspirations of the East Timorese.

No longer was there the outright acceptance of the Government claims that the Timorese political wishes had been satisfactorily fulfilled, nor was there a complete compliance

---

[27] UCA News Dispatch 508. May 31, 1989 p24-5.
[28] Walsh, P. Memo-12.9.89, ACFOA; Bibliography – General (E.Timor): Kohen, A.1999, p143.
[29] See also *ad limina* Report 1996.
[30] UCA News Dispatch 506, May 17 1989, p26.
[31] Full text in CCJPD, op.cit. p52-3. Report in Timor Link CIIR London No22, Feb 1992. p7.
[32] Internews 1995, Vol 2. No.3 p5, Jakarta; Timor Link, CIIR London. Nov.1995, p2.

with the Military's repressive policy of social control in the territory. Cardinal Daarmatmadja elaborated further in a contemporaneous interview:

> It is clear that many [Timorese] still do not want to join Indonesia. They have been handled with the 'security approach' with all its consequences. If this does not change I am afraid that the younger generation will not respect and join Indonesia. They will inherit only hate.... An open dialogue is essential.[33]

These words indicate some measure of change in the position adopted by the bishops but there is little sign of penitence for the erstwhile complicity of the Indonesian Church in the government project.

The bishops' Easter Pastoral of 1999 was an impassioned appeal to the faithful then preparing for a General Election to face up to a national 'moral decline' and 'break the shackles of the power of evil.' The Pastoral called for 'solidarity, especially with the poor', for honesty in public affairs, truth in the media, and for trust in the power of God. A section of the letter attended to 'special regions' (surely including, *though not naming*, East Timor) and called for peaceful attitudes, dialogue, the involvement of the people, and the eschewing of 'manipulative practices'.[34] The Conference was represented at the Dare II Dialogue in East Timor by its president bishop J.Suwatan who declared its support of the efforts of East Timor's bishops Belo and Nascimento who had sponsored these efforts at reconciliation between pro-Integration and pro-Independence East Timorese. On the occasion of the 54th Anniversary of Indonesian Independence' (17 August 1999) the Conference publicly criticised the country's political elite accusing them of failing to take care of the people's interests and future. This Statement made specific reference to East Timor:

> We very much hope that what has been agreed upon will be respected and realised whatever risk it entails to provide the Timorese [with] a just opportunity to be self-determined in the spirit of freedom and peace.[35]

When the post-ballot violence was let loose in East Timor the Indonesian bishops invited all Catholics in their nation to express solidarity with, and intercession for, the suffering victims by participating in a Requiem Mass on Sunday 12th September.[36] In a Pastoral Letter emanating from their annual meeting in November the Bishops indicated the reasons for their more forthright critique and exhortation:

> We feel the need to interpret the new situation that demands from us a new attitude and a new movement...The crisis that has impinged on all aspects of our life...cannot be separated from the legacy of the *Orde Baru* (the Suharto regime)....
> Money has played a significant role...for money's sake the rich natural resources of our land are being destroyed through unchecked exploitation...violence has become the norm in a militaristic system...the mass media which should reveal the truth have become silenced....democratic life has been stultified....
> Signs of hope must be generated by the [new] government showing its willingness to leave old ways of thinking behind which gave priority to group interests over the Common Good...We invite the whole people of God to place their hope in their faith in God...
> We maintain a critical and pro-active attitude in struggling towards the Indonesian dream of the people, in particular the little people...

---

[33] AFP 1.2.1997.

[34] Pastoral Letter, 'Arise and be Unwavering in Hope', *KWI*, Jakarta, Easter 1999.

[35] Jakarta Post 17.8.1999.

[36] 'Urgent Appeal'. email disseminated internationally by Mgr.J.Suwatan *MSC* (Chairman), and Mgr. J.Jadiwikarta, (Secretary General) Bishops Conference, 10.9.1999.

Let us work together to create a democratic Indonesia where the participation of each group and everybody is valued…

Let us also remember that the changes we hope for in the country and the nation should also happen first in the Church, in its openness and in the role of the laity.[37]

During the *Orde Baru* regime the Catholic leadership had never taken the lead and rarely been forthright in challenging the priorities and operations of the government, despite the increasing restrictions upon the operation of the Church. Such dissent had for the most part been expressed from outside the Church. Now that the regime was discredited and ousted from office the hierarchy identified itself with the seemingly inexorable movement for socio-political *Reformasi*. Only then did they acknowledge the human rights of the people of East Timor, so long denied by the government with which they and the lay Catholic leadership had aligned in their concern to defend the interests of the Church.

Beyond the Bishops

Other leading clergy also favoured *integrasi* and were of the view that the Timorese could only benefit from the Indonesian presence. Thus Fr.Kartasiswaya, administrative secretary for the Bishops Conference opined in 1987: 'the recognition of integration is the best solution and will facilitate assistance by the Conference to the Dili Diocese in pastoral, educational, socio-economic and health projects'. Fr.Hardaputranta, Director of the Bishops Conference Institute of Social Research and Development, praised the 'progress' that had been achieved in East Timor since its 'incorporation'. He declared that the Timorese were 'becoming realistic' about their situation; that FRETILIN had 'made many mistakes which had hurt people'; and that the Bishops Conference, while 'not interfering in political matters', were able to help communicate 'the correct information' about East Timor to 'people outside'.[38] East Timorese clergy and foreign missionaries working in the territory often observed that the mind set of Indonesian pastors and religious was that the annexation was good for East Timor.[39] Indeed, bishop Belo had to appeal to the Religious Superiors in Indonesia to ensure that their personnel came to assist in East Timor 'with a true spirit of inculturation, to see with the eyes of the people'.[40]

Other groups and individuals within the Catholic community were also engaged in the outcome, for good or ill. Foremost chronologically, and in terms of their influence upon the issue, must be the Catholic members of the Jakarta-based Centre for Strategic and International Studies (CSIS). This was the 'think tank' associated with General Ali Murtopo (1924-84) and affiliated to *OPSUS* which played a major role in developing the

---

[37] 'Let us Change', Bishops Conference, Jakarta, Nov.1999. cf.
1) Conference meeting with interim President B.J.Habibie on June 1st 1999 at which they pleaded for 'a thorough and total reform of the county'. The Tablet UK, 143.6.99, p789.
2) Conference Statement 14.11.98 expressed concern over rising violence in an attempt by the establishment to prevent political reform; and Statement 18.11.98 'Bishops Call for and End to Island [Moluccas] Killings' - The Universe 18.11.98.
3) 'Resume of the Third National Conference Secretariat for Justice and Peace' (Feb 11-19th 2000) – cited later in this text.
4) Jose Ramon Perez Araguena, 1997, 'Flourishing in an Intemperate Climate' in *Palabra*, Feb 1997, Madrid (also in The Catholic World Report, April 1997 p32-39).
[38] UCA News Dispatch 421, 30 September 1987.
[39] Remarks by members of various religious congregations to the author, e.g. Claretians, East Timor 1995; (Timorese) Maryknollers , New York, September 1997.
[40] Request to Indonesian Major Religious Superiors (*MASRI*) Meeting Aug.1986 *A Paz e Possivel* Lisbon, Dec.1987; summary in Timor Link CIIR London, No12/13, April 1988, p7.

political format for 'New Order' Indonesia, especially its various tools for political control and in advising the Military strategists.[41] Established by conservative Chinese Indonesian Catholics in the mid 1960's this group had included Fr.Beek, Harry Tjan Silali, and Jusuf Wanandi and was instrumental in the propaganda war and diplomatic campaign designed to prepare world opinion for the invasion of East Timor in 1975. On various occasions the CSIS paid for the UDT leadership to travel to Jakarta to undermine their coalition with FRETILIN.[42] Tjan Silali and Wanandi discreetly visited Western Europe and North America and maintained close links with Bob Santamaria's right wing National Civic Council organisation based in Melbourne, Australia. In April 1975 Jose Ramos Horta was delegated by the FRETILIN administration to convince the CSIS to pursue a 'hearts and minds strategy in respect of the incorporation of East Timor and cease their hostile clandestine operations'. He had to relate that 'all our assurances of friendship and co-operation fell on deaf ears'.[43] Wanandi was the Director of CSIS at that time and was party to an orchestrated campaign 'to destabilise East Timor, undermine the process of decolonisation and weaken the Portuguese presence.'[44] CSIS organised short and carefully stage-managed visits to East Timor of Australian Prime Minister Gough Whitlam in 1982 and of journalist John Hamilton in 1983. These evoked from Whitlam a dismissal of Mgr Costa Lopes' graphic accounts of East Timorese suffering and from Hamilton a glowing description of Indonesian 'development' in the 'province'.[45] In 1989 Jusuf Wanandi was to remark in respect of the East Timorese: 'forget this generation, they will never love us'.[46] Another member of the Wanandi family, Marcus, a Jesuit priest, appeared in East Timor after bishop Belo's appointment as Apostolic Administrator. He worked earnestly to encourage acceptance of *integrasi* among the clergy and people who, with good reason, suspected him of being a spy for the Military.[47]

Within the Indonesian Armed Forces the Catholic General Leonardo Benyamin Murdani played a central role in the incorporation of East Timor into the Republic.[48] As assistant head of the Military Intelligence Operation *INTEL* he was involved in *Operasi Komodo*, Ali Murtopo's campaign of political subversion in East Timor during 1974. In 1975 Murdani was to head up the planning and execution of *Operasi Seroja* (the invasion force) and the three subsequent major offensives. In 1983 he became *ABRI* chief, the second most powerful man in the country, and brought an end to the cease-fire then operative with FRETILIN. On that occasion he rallied his troops with the words: 'this time no fooling around, we'll hit them without mercy', while in a message to Xanana Gusmao (July 26th) he admonished the Timorese Resistance:

---

[41] See Bibliography – Ch1: Cribb, R. 1992, pp75-6.

[42] See Bibliography – Ch2: Cox, S. & Carey, P.1995, pp17-18.

[43] See Bibliography- General (East Timor): Horta, J.R. 1987, p66. Horta also indicates that Jusuf Wanandi had met with Australian Foreign Minister Andrew Peacock in September 1974 to ensure that Australia would not protest Indonesian intervention in East Timor. (p.79). cf. Gunn, G. 1994, p122.

[44] See Bibliography-General (East Timor): Jose Ramos Horta, in Carey, P. & Carter Bentley, G. 1995, p163.

[45] See Bibliography-General (East Timor): Dunn, J.1996, pp294-5.

[46] For citation see Bibliography-General (East Timor): Kohen, A. 1999, p.136.

[47] In 1995 this author witnessed at first hand Fr.Wanandi's pro-Indonesian bias. To him is attributed the drafting of bishop Belo's aberrant Pastoral Letter for Christmas 1990 which calls on the faithful to 'put aside all unrealistic desires...and cease all activities and initiatives which could cause disturbance'. See also: 'Indonesian Jesuit Speaks to Journalists' Catherine Napier, BBC Dateline, Dili Feb.16th 1994, in ETAN Docs Vol 27, 1994, p.7; East Timor News (*CDPM*) Lisbon, 10.6.1990; 'East Timor people need example', *Kompas* 25.3.1990.

[48] For a contrasting account of Murdani's career see Bibliography - Ch6: Pour, J. 1993.

Don't think you can disentangle yourselves...or receive assistance from other countries...no-one is going to help you...We are prepared to destroy you if you are not willing to co-operate with our Republic.

Directly responsible for the deaths of thousands, Murdani preached to his men at Christmas 1985: 'Christ's doctrine is to love peace and not destroy lives'. To all outward appearances he devoutly received Holy Communion from Pope John Paul II during the Papal Mass at Tacitolu, the notorious killing fields outside Dili in October 1989 – an action that startled the Timorese present but about which they were not inclined to be judgmental.[49] However, following the small and peaceful demonstration that was mounted during the visit to East Timor of US Ambassador John Monjo in January 1990, Murdani had no qualms about berating assembled Timorese civilian administrators and religious leaders and warning them to give up all notions of future independence:

> Don't dream about having a state of Timtim [*Timor Timur* - East Timor]...there is no such thing! Timtim is part of Indonesia...
> In the past there were some small states that wanted to stand on their own...without hesitation the Indonesian Government took steps to stop that...This also applies to Timtim...
> If there is a movement to create your own nation it will be crushed by the Armed Forces. Any such movement will be destroyed. We will crush them! I repeat, we will crush them all![50]

Murdani had control over the family reunion programme and was to be a principal agent and major beneficiary of the commercial monopolies established by the Indonesian military in East Timor.[51] This Catholic General played a significant part in persuading the Indonesian Bishops to urge the Vatican to include Dili diocese within their Conference and also in effecting the resignation of Dom Martinho Costa Lopes through his close relationship with Apostolic Nuncio Pablo Puente.[52] He attempted (but failed) to control the East Timorese students at Indonesian Universities by requiring them to join a single organisation (*IMPETTU*) which was closely watched by Army Intelligence. Besides his efforts to mobilise a Catholic network against bishop Belo at the Vatican, Murdani also had influence upon the policy of the Government and Catholic Church in Australia through his meetings with successive Foreign Affairs Ministers, and by contact with Bob Santamaria's National Civic Council.[53] During the political manipulation attempted by *TNI* in East Timor in 1999 Murdani was alleged to have defied President Habibie (and the UN New York Agreement) by contributing large amounts of money to fund the militia terror campaign.[54] He was also reported to have declared that 'in four to five months the Armed Forces will be ready to crack heads once and for all in East Timor'.[55]

Leading Catholic politician Frans Seda held the unique distinction of being an adviser for Presidents Sukarno, Suharto, Habibie and is still influential in Indonesian politics. He was a consistent supporter of *integrasi* for East Timor. Together with former *PK* chairman Ben Mang Reng Say (then Indonesian Ambassador to Lisbon), Frans Seda

---

[49] Source: Maria do Ceu Federer to the author, Darwin, August 1997.

[50] Text of speech in: Inside Indonesia June 23, 1990.

[51] See Bibliography-General (East Timor):Taylor, J. 1991, op.cit. pp125-7

[52] See, e.g. Bibliography-General (East Timor): Dunn, J. 1996, op.cit.Index; Bibliography - Ch2: Budiardjo & Liem 1984, Index.

[53] Bishop John Gerry to the author, Brisbane 1997; see also Bibliography - General (East Timor) Kohen A. 1999, op.cit. p153.

[54] See: 'TNI's dirty war in East Timor', Tapol, London, June 1999.

[55] 'Habibie's Fatal Flaw: failing to end military privilege', G.Van Klinken, The Age, Melbourne, 15.4.99.

(then Indonesian Ambassador to the EU) lobbied the transition government in Lisbon to let East Timor fall into the hands of the Indonesian Government, introducing them to Ali Murtopo.[56] In 1985 he brought his influence to bear at the General Assembly of the Pontifical Commission *Justitia et Pax* and the information he provided, favouring the Indonesian annexation, subsequently circulated among the Justice and Peace commissions of several countries which had a significant interest in the issue. In his address to the Assembly he claimed integration was the will of 'the majority' in East Timor and alleged that 'Communist-inspired' FRETILIN was 'responsible for the war, had little popular support, but was receiving arms from Marxist sympathisers in Portugal and Australia'. He described foreign media coverage and recent reports by Amnesty International as 'excessive, improper, negative, lacking objectivity and failing to recognise the significant development that had taken place under Indonesian administration' which he contrasted with the 'primitive state' of the people under Portuguese colonial rule. He criticised the 1983 Bishops Conference Letter of Solidarity to bishop Belo as 'a big one-time mistake' and open to the misinterpretation that the Conference had accepted 'the genocide claims'. In Seda's view the inclusion of the diocese of Dili into the Indonesian Bishop's conference would be 'good for East Timor' - because it would enable the Indonesian Church to speak and act on its behalf with the Vatican, and 'good for Indonesia' - because it would add a substantial number of Catholics to the national population.[57] In 1988 he was to defend the Indonesian regime against the allegation of the US Catholic Conference of Bishops that religious freedom was not fully respected in East Timor.[58] In 1989 his personal, diplomatic and business links with Australian politicians secured him a place aboard the RAAF Boeing 707 with those who were celebrating the signing of the Timor Gap Treaty which divided the natural gas and oil resources of the Timor Sea between Indonesia and Australia. When an anthology of bishop Belo's sermons and speeches was prepared for publication in 1997 the editors invited Seda to write an introduction. He asserted:

> The problem in East Timor is not integration, which is widely accepted, but how to manage the integration... Complaints against the handling of the integration process have been taken as anti-integration sentiments.[59]

At the outset of East Timor's 'Year of Crisis' Seda was finance adviser to President Habibie. He argued against the idea of the country being awarded an autonomy as a prelude to independence (the path urged by both Church and Resistance leaders in East Timor as the best way of precluding political strife) because the Indonesian State system 'did not allow for a 'Province' to dissolve'.[60]

Catholic students had been prominent in the *KAMI* organisation that helped to topple Sukarno and bring Suharto to power in 1966 - and in due course their national organisation (*PMKRI*) lobbied in support of East Timor's incorporation into Indonesia – for example at the international assembly of Catholic Students in Belgium (1986). In that same year the students passed a letter to Pope John Paul II via the Papal Nuncio to Jakarta (Canalini) alleging that the Resistance under FRETILIN was 'a tool of Portuguese colonialism' which was 'terrorising' the 'majority of the population who favoured integration'. They called for the immediate 'unification of the Catholic Church in East

---

[56] Aditjondro, G.J., 1995, 12 November. Article: 'It is not a matter of military or civilian, but a choice between fascists or democrats'. ETAN Documents Vol 41-2, p 177.

[57] Address to General Assembly, Pontifical Commission Justitia et Pax, 7-12th Nov.1985.

[58] *LPPS Forum*, No. 6 Dec. 1988. Jakarta.

[59] Bibliography – Ch5: Tukan, P & de Sousa, D. (eds) 1997, Introduction.

[60] *Antara* 29.1.1999. Jakarta.

Timor with the Indonesian Bishops Conference'. These ideas and activities were publicised through the Indonesian Catholic journal *Hidup.*[61] But the students were shocked by the massacre of the young people at Santa Cruz in 1991 and criticised the army for 'the shooting of innocents'.[62]

Dissenting Voices

In the midst of this *'chorus of campaigns'* there were also those who had the independence of mind and heart together with the moral and physical courage to challenge the Government account and the Church's compliance with its policies. They sought a solution to the East Timor issue that fully respected truth and justice. To express dissent in such repressive circumstances as those created by the *Orde Baru* was indeed perilous. It was these (few) Catholics who were in touch with the courageous activists of the non-governmental organisations in Indonesia which had suffered under or were evoked by the repression effected by the *Orde Baru.* They were in the forefront of the movement towards *Reformasi* in Indonesia - indeed there was a developing co-operation between the advocates of these related causes.

An outstanding example of the Indonesian priests and religious committed to these associated ends was Fr.Yohannes Baptista Mangunwijaya who 'worked for a genuine democracy literally to the last breath of his life'.[63] 'Romo Mangun' dedicated his life to the cause of the *wong cilik,* the 'little people'. His political ethics and activity were rooted in Catholic Social Doctrine. Manguwijaya's involvement with the East Timorese cause began in a veiled way through his novel *Ikan-ikan Hiu, Ido, Hoa* (1983). In this he drew parallels between the bloody massacres of the inhabitants of Banda Island by the Dutch VOC in the 17th century and the Indonesian occupation of East Timor from 1975. He pointed to the ideals of the founders of the Republic. His passion for justice and his revulsion against any kind of human rights abuse moved Mangunwijaya to become one of the first to speak publicly in favour of a just solution to the bloody strife in East Timor. Along with Abdurrachman Wahid, then chairman of the large Muslim organisation Nahdahtul Ulama and subsequently (November 1999 – July 2001) President of the Republic, he was the only other Indonesian to be invited by bishop Belo to attend the Nobel Peace Prize ceremony in December 1996.[64] In an article explaining Belo's stance to a largely Muslim readership Mangunwijaya argued that politics should be regarded as 'the forging of all human endeavour for the sake of the Common Good'. He asserted that the principles of *Pancasila* 'put upon bishops and all spiritual leaders the duty to speak out and act on behalf of duty and morality' and he compared Belo's defence of Timorese well-being with the advocacy of Pastor Martin Niemoller against Nazi oppression.[65] In an article withheld from publication by nervous editors he asserted that:

> The political domain is part of normal human activity and the struggle of the Kingdom of God against the Kingdom of Darkness is also fought in the political sphere...
> Bishop Belo is therefore not only allowed but obliged to be active - as had been bishop Sugyapranata in the Indonesian national struggle - for the public interest and well-being... for the weak, the poor and downcast who are the majority in East Timor...

---

[61] *Tapol* No 81. June 1987. P6-7.

[62] Eglises d'Asie, No122, 1.12.91.

[63] 'Romo Mangun, activist', obituary by Nico Schulte Nordhold, 1999, Inside Indonesia, July-September, 1999, p13. For articles by 'Romo Mangun' see: Mangunwijaya, Y.B. 1998, *Menuju Indonesia Serba Baru* [Towards a Completely New Indonesia], Gramedia. Jakarta.

[64] Some points drawn from the obituary written by Schulte Nordhold, 1999, op.cit.

[65] Jakarta Post 22.11.96.

defending human rights, justice, humanity…including those related to the behaviour of Indonesian Armed Forces towards those living in East Timor.[66]

In August 1998 Romo Mangun wrote an open letter to his long-time friend, B.J.Habibie (then President). In this message he appealed for the authorities to 'act with nobility and take the path of atonement, reconciliation and rehabilitation of the peaceful people of East Timor…and in all sincerity return to the East Timorese the freedom they had attained for themselves before Indonesian troops attacked them.'[67] As the fraught progress towards the 1999 East Timorese plebiscite began Mangunwijaya wrote in the national newspaper *Kompas* that 'East Timor was a moral, political, economic and military disaster for Jakarta.' He highlighted the fact that the Indonesian government's argument that it should retain control of the territory where it had expended so much in 'development' was based on the 'superior belief that the people of East Timor were too poor, culturally backward, and too divided to rule themselves'. This, he pointed out, was 'exactly the kind of argument the Dutch had used to justify continuation of their rule over Indonesia'.[68] When he died two weeks later he was mourned by Timorese and Indonesians alike.

Fr.Ignatius Sandyawan Sumardi *SJ* of the Jakarta Social Institute was another consistent and persuasive advocate for the Indonesian poor and for the marginalised people of East Timor. He was arrested in 1996 for giving shelter to pro-democracy activists. His *Tim Relawan Untuk Kemanusiaan (TRK)*, Voluntary Team for Humanity, responded to the needs of Chinese Indonesians attacked in the Jakarta pogroms of May 1998. These atrocities he compared to the heinous crimes carried out in East Timor and as likewise having their roots in the elitist, militarist politics of the *Orde Baru*.[69] His critique of *Pembangunan* (development) in Indonesia, equally applicable to the situation in East Timor, echoed the principles of Catholic Social Doctrine:

> For thirty years the *Orde Baru* regime has carried out its Development project…and we have to see that the crisis of the country is a product of this government's policies…
> The government does not respect the 'message of the people's suffering' ['*Ampera*' - the title of Suharto's first cabinet]. It has marginalised many people and rendered them inhuman… The maintenance of society's structure which ignores the existence of the poor and is prioritised more than the consideration of the participation of the poor themselves…
> For the future of this country and this nation there is no other choice but returning the people's rights, especially to those who have been marginalised, and listening to the voice of the victims, not to the voices of those in power.[70]

In July 1999 Sandyawan's was among the signatures of various Catholic organisations and individuals which were appended to a public Petition organised by the Indonesian Solidarity Forum for the People of East Timor (*FORTILOS*).[71] This pleaded for the Indonesian Military 'to disarm the pro-autonomy militias and end its campaign of

---

[66] Subsequently disseminated on email conference > indonesia-l@igc.apc.org, 5.12.1996. For an appreciation of Mangunwijawa: 'Romo Mangun', C.Mills, Inside Indonesia Oct-Dec 2001, p10f.

[67] *Kompas* 11.8.1998

[68] *Kompas* 28.1.1999.

[69] *Tapol* Bulletin No 147, July 1998, and No 149/150, Dec.1998; email conference > indonesia-act@igc.apc.prg < 16.6.98, 6.7.98; Sandyawan Sumardi, 'Rape is Rape' Inside Indonesia Oct-Dec 1998, p19-21

[70] 'The Duty of the State: Immediately return the rights of the poor'. Address by I.Sandyawan Sumardi *SJ* on the occasion of a Meeting and Prayer of Concern for the Urban Poor, Bantar Gen-bang, Bekasi, West Java, 22.3.1998.

[71] 'Petition of the Indonesian People Regarding the Resolution of the East Timor Problem', *FORTILOS*, Jakarta July 5th, 1999.

violence and intimidation against the East Timorese people'. *Tim Relawan* was involved in taking care of the East Timorese refugees who fled the violence in their homeland and its repercussions in Jakarta and assisted with their repatriation while pointing up the shortcomings of the UNHCR provision.[72]

Non-episcopal representatives of the Indonesian Bishops Conference Secretariat for Justice and Peace also signed this Petition. Some of these persons had been discreetly and courageously involved over many years in providing protection and succour to East Timorese students (and others at risk of maltreatment by the Military). They had participated in national and regional advocacy of the East Timorese cause and provided support for various humanitarian projects in East Timor itself - including care of the families of those who had been imprisoned or who were 'in the mountains'. At its Third National Conference this Secretariat drew attention to several matters of key importance. These included the 'unjust social structures' which evoked violence in regions such as East Timor and West Papua; the stifling of democracy by the repressive government which created human rights violations and criminal acts; the forced evacuations from East Timor after the UN supervised referendum; and the general moral degradation which had come about during the *Orde Baru* regime. The Conference stated:

> The Church encounters these challenges with hope, and wants to renew her commitment in the light of God's Word and Catholic Social Teaching, which are the sound bases upon which the struggle for justice and peace can get its spirit.[73]

An Indonesian Catholic layman outstanding for his critique of the *Orde Baru* in general and its East Timor project in particular, and forced into political exile as a consequence, is academic George Aditjondro some of whose many writings are cited throughout this text.[74] Another is Dr.Arief Budiman. But however admirable such a commitment has been on the part of a few, the fact is that there remained many lay Catholics in Indonesia who, along with their clergy, were not engaged in issues of justice and peace at all. They were 'concentrating on the institution, the sacramental church, choirs, liturgy, *et cetera*, while the prophetic function of the Church [was] being lost.'[75] In 1984 an Indonesian Jesuit priest had made this observation and realistic comment:

> The decision we make on East Timor - to speak out or not to speak - will determine in large measure what we will be as a Church. Are we another bloc in society seeking prosperity and influence, or are we a religious community led by the Gospel? Right now it seems we've got them mixed up. ...
>
> [But] we're not a heroic community. We're a cross section of society, weak and fearful like most people.[76]

By 1996 only six out of thirty-four dioceses had a Justice and Peace Commission and the criticisms made at the level of the national Commission concerning the Church's public posture were 'not received with enthusiasm by the hierarchy':

---

[72] Letter from *TRK* to Representatives of the High Commissioner for Refugees, UN Office, Jakarta.10.11.1999. email conference > east-timor@igc.apc.org < 20.11.99.

[73] Resume of the Third National Conference Secretariat for Justice and Peace, Prigen - Malang Diocese, 19.2.2000.

[74] Dr.Aditjondro examines especially the commercial ramifications of the Suharto regime and the East Timor issue. For his critique of the response of the Indonesian Catholic Church see: Bibliography – Ch6: Aditjondro, G.1995 (reprinted in ETAN Docs. Vol 39, 1995, p.15-18), and 1996.

[75] Fr.John Prior *SVD*, to the author, Jayapura, West Papua, Sept.1996.

[76] In IDOC International Bulletin, No3.1984, pp16-17.

While the Church has its prophets it is not sufficiently assertive and it is also a self-serving institution. Those in power in the Church are mostly concerned with the institution.[77]

But a Statement made in the autumn of 1998 by members of a Pastoral Consultation of Church leaders assembled at St.Paul's Seminary in Flores should be noted. This gathering included thirty-two priests, vicars general, directors of pastoral centres and diocesan secretaries, both clergy and laity. A frank and public admission of Catholic compromise with the discredited Suharto regime was made, and the group called for a formal act of repentance and for the formation of a Truth and Reconciliation Commission to investigate abuses since 1966.[78] An English missionary and academic with many years' experience in Indonesia had claimed earlier in the same year:

> If for the hierarchy nothing much has changed, for Catholic intellectuals and members of religious orders, everything has. The sinful collusion of Church and State for the last thirty-two years is being redeemed by the biblically inspired social activism of the laity and religious today.[79]

The more recent disposition of some among the Church leadership suggests that such a redemption might be taking place – but only time will tell. It is significant that in 2001 long-serving Catholic member of the CSIS Jusuf Wanandi was minded to blame 'the loss of East Timor' only on the 'weakness of the Habibie presidency' and the long-term abuses perpetrated by the Indonesian Military in the territory. He gave no indication whatever of repentance for the key role that had been played by leading Catholic politicians including himself in the whole tragic tale.[80]

The Church in West Timor

It is important to note the response to the East Timor issue of the Catholic community in the other half of the island. The Church in West Timor presents on a smaller scale the reaction of the Indonesian Church as a whole, and it influenced the reaction of the Catholic Church in other countries, especially Australia and Portugal. There are a number of factors in the political and ecclesiastical history of West Timor which are pertinent.

Matters of political significance include the following. There have been long-standing ethnic and family links between East and West Timorese, especially in the border region where there is widespread sharing of a common language, *Tetun*. The artificial divisions of the colonial era which ignored these ties were sustained and deepened when West Timor became part of Indonesia in 1950 while East Timor remained under Portuguese administration. In common with the inhabitants of other 'outer' islands in the *Nusa Tenggara Timor* (*NTT*) region the majority of West Timorese are impoverished farmers. They resent the Javanese dominance that developed after Independence and especially under the Military-led *Orde Baru*, in the face of which the farmers found themselves largely powerless. Some traditional leaders in the areas on both sides of the

---

[77] Sr.B.Guhit *SPC*, Secretary *KWI* J & P Commission, to the author, Jakarta, Sept.1996.

[78] 'Catholics confess collaboration in Suharto regime', The Tablet 31.10.1998, p 1446-7.

[79] Fr.John Prior *SVD*, 1998 'Redeeming the Time', in The Tablet 6.6.1998, p729.

[80] 'Indonesia must face facts on East Timor saga', Jusuf Wanandi, Jakarta Post, 15.6.01.

border saw in the prospect of *Integrasi* a means of holding on to, even consolidating, their power as already noted.[81] Subjected to the extensive propaganda purveyed by the *Orde Baru* regime, especially during *Operasi Komodo*, the West Timorese understanding of developments in East Timor was at best confused and at worst completely in line with the Military-dominated government's own self-serving account. The influx of substantial numbers of refugees from East Timor during the brief civil war (August-September 1975), and during the countdown to and execution of the brutal invasion in December 1975, served to compound such misunderstandings. This was because the refugees, who came under close military supervision in the camps which were established, were in grave fear for their safety and were (understandably) inclined to declare anti-Communist, anti-FRETILIN, pro-*integrasi* sentiments. These declarations certainly influenced the attitude and actions of the leadership and faithful of the local Churches, amongst others, who also passed on their interpretation of the situation further afield in Indonesia and (importantly) to other countries concerned over events. The arrival in due course of Muslim immigrants from the over-populated 'inner' islands (Java, Bali) and from Sulawesi increased their sense of political and economic vulnerability and their inclination to avoid challenging government policy in matters not immediately related to their own concerns.

In the early history of Catholicism in the Indonesian archipelago there was contact between the communities of believers across Timor and on other nearby islands. After Timor was divided between the Portuguese and the Dutch such contact drastically diminished and in due course different styles of ecclesiastical management were to develop. In 1961 the Diocese of Atambua was formed to serve the pastoral needs of the 90% Catholic population of the eastern region (about 380,000 people).[82] Largely as the long-term consequence of the former Dutch government's 'Peace and Order' policy which restricted proselytism, the western half of West Timor remains about 80% Protestant (110,000 Catholics).[83] Some *NTT* Catholic politicians -such as regional Governor Dr.(later General) Aloysius Mboi and his successor Dr.Fernandes - were inclined to see only advantages in East Timor's integration, for its native people and for the strengthening of the Catholic Church in the region and in the Republic as a whole.[84] In 1989 the Catholic Diocese based on the capital city of Kupang, together with the bishoprics of Weetabula and of Atambua became an Archdiocese and an Eccesiastical Province which, together with the Province of Ende (Flores), make up the ecclesiastical administration within the Indonesian Province of *NTT*. The Church in the eastern Diocese of Atambua continues to have some influence upon the local Government because of the numbers of civil servants and Military personnel who are still Catholics. But this is not the case in the western half of the territory and the Church has everywhere been affected by the influx of Muslim immigrants, especially among the leadership in the administrative (civilian and military) and commercial circles of society.

For these reasons the Church in West Timor was anxious about its own survival and primarily concerned to serve the religious and social needs of its own people. Inevitably these considerations weighed heavily upon those in positions of responsibility when they were faced also with the manifest distress of the East Timorese. In their

---

[81] In West Timor an example would be Catholic *liurai* Louis Taolin who was recruited by *BAKIN* and worked in collaboration with Jose Martins of *KOTA* and *liurai* Guilherme Goncalves of *APODETI* (see above Part One Ch 2) to further *Operasi Komodo*. He gathered information in East Timor for Military Intelligence, promoting the Petition to President Suharto for Integration (May 31st 1976), and secretly visited Portugal in 1980 to build up political support for the annexation. For further details see Bibliography – General (East Timor): Dunn, J.1996, op.cit. pp 65-6, 81, 100, 102-3, 160, 336; Bibliography – Ch2: Aditjondro, G. 1995, p90 (Notes 47-8).

[82] 386,353 in 1995. *Septennial Report to the Holy See*, 1989-1995, Diocese of Atambua.

[83] 106,179 in 1995. *Ad Limina Report to the Holy See*, 1995 Archdiocese of Kupang.

[84] See Bibliography – Ch5: Federer, J. 1994, p20-21.

conscientious efforts to give due attention to these suffering people the Church leaders in West Timor became more or less unwitting agents of Indonesian government policy and propaganda.

Thus from 1974 the bishop of Atambua Theodore van den Tillart *SVD*[85] (adopted Indonesian name Theodore Sulama) prepared a report on possible collaboration between his diocese and that of Dili in the event of Portuguese withdrawal. The *SVD* Provincial was already prepared in November 1975 to send more than a hundred Catholic teachers from West Timor to East Timor in the event of 'integration'.[86] In December 1975 bishop Tillart wrote earnestly to Cardinal John Knox in Melbourne presenting an account of FRETILIN'S 'Marxist character'. He drew attention to the support that he had been told it was receiving from international Communism and he elaborated on its extensive human rights abuses among the East Timorese and its 'border violations'. Tillart also remarked upon the 'irresponsibility of Portugal in abandoning its government in the territory'; the request of 'the majority' of East Timor's people for Indonesian intervention; and the benevolent intention of the Indonesian government to 'restore order and then leave it to the people to decide their future'. This account clearly echoes the principal features of Indonesian propaganda.[87] In June 1976, in a letter to the Australian St.Vincent de Paul Society (SVP) appealing for humanitarian aid for East Timorese refugees in Atambua, bishop Tillart again attributed destruction of Catholic Church property in the border area to 'FRETILIN elements'. He asserted that the Indonesian Government was 'doing its utmost to help the refugees' and he described the extensive support being provided by the Diocese of Atambua for the people from East and West Timor displaced by the ongoing conflict. An appeal for assistance had already been made in the first week of October 1975 to the Australian SVP by the local Conference in Kupang. The chaplain stated that '36,509 refugees had run to Indonesian Timor' and were in a 'very distressing condition' while 'in Portuguese Timor the Catholic Church was experiencing damages, cruelty and violation with the action of the FRETILIN Communist party which in rude manner has done shameful actions'.[88] Further correspondence from bishop Tillart in June 1977 again attributed the large number of refugees to their desire to 'seek security from the bands of FRETILIN people'. It is noteworthy that in this letter the bishop revealed that the actual distribution of emergency aid to the refugees was prohibited to Church personnel and was being handled by the Indonesian Red Cross 'as government policy'. Yet at the same time a deported French photo-journalist, Denis Reichle, reported that, while the refugees were suffering from military oppression in the camps, the invasion forces were 'systematically wiping out the populations of villages known or suspected to be FRETILIN supporters':

> Catholic missionaries, led by the bishop of Atambua, were the only voices in Timor trying to stop the systematic killing-off of East Timorese... The bishop had been trying to get an interview with President Suharto for two and half months but his requests had been ignored. A German priest had been driven insane by the constant killings in his area.[89]

---

[85] *SVD* is the (Latin) acronym for the Divine Word Missionaries who predominate in the Diocese of Atambua.

[86] 'Notes on East Timor following incorporation and implications for Australian Churches', Dunn, J. 1976. Prepared (Nov.) for the national committee of Australian Catholic Relief (ACR).

[87] This perspective, immediately published in the Indonesian Observer 19.12.1975, was comprehensively challenged by Wm.C.Byrne, national executive director of ACR, but his critique was dismissed by the Archbishop of Canberra, Thomas Cahill. More detail in Ch8.

[88] The author of the letter, Fr.Daniel Siga *SVD*, admitted his information came from the Indonesian Red Cross, and the Government of *NTT*, as well as 'from our own investigations'.

[89] See Bibliography – General (East Timor): Chomsky, N. 1978. See also Bibliography – Ch7: Dunn, J. 1977. The situation of the refugees in Atambua was so described to this author by Fr.Apollinario Guterres (who had been among their number), Lisbon, June 1997.

After the formal declaration of annexation on 17th July 1976 many Church personnel from the Atambua district were to serve educational and health needs in East Timor, thereby contributing to the government's 'pacification' intent. Among them was Fr.Anton Pain Ratu, who was to succeed bishop Tillart as diocesan Ordinary in Atambua. It was hoped by his superiors that he would be able to 'bridge the gap' between the Military and the Church in East Timor and so reduce the suffering of the people but he could not succeed in this because of the human rights violations in which the Military persisted. Bishop Pain Ratu's efforts were evaluated negatively in East Timor - in particular by the indigenous clergy who regarded him as just another agent of Indonesian government policy.[90]

The bishop's own view of the effort made by the Church in West Timor was that its humanitarian aid and pastoral support had been both necessary and generous in the years (1976-83) before outside help was given easier access - bearing in mind the limited resources it had to offer from its own impoverished community. He was convinced that those favouring *integrasi* were in the great majority among the refugees who had fled to West Timor and that FRETILIN had only minority support among the people - mainly that of the students who had returned from a left-wing political scene in Portugal. Pain Ratu opined that it was difficult for the Church in the western half of the island to show solidarity with that in East Timor. This was because the clergy there had a different sense of their standing *vis-a-vis* the people (i.e. they were 'aloof and authoritarian') and because their relationship with the Military was necessarily different as they were in a territory under 'special security arrangements' - and most of the commanders were Protestant (in the early years) or Muslim (latterly). Besides the difficulties these factors presented there was also division among Catholics in Indonesia as a whole (and so in West Timor) as to the best course of action in respect of Government policies generally. There was dispute over the merits or otherwise of *Pancasila* as a safeguard for the Church's work and over the propriety of engagement by the Church in 'political issues' as opposed to 'purely religious' concerns. There was also the question of identifying a political partner should such an alliance be considered proper. Even the manner of any dissent that might be made was a matter of unresolved dispute within the Bishops Conference itself: should it be in the Javanese way of 'implied criticism' or in the more confrontational style accepted by people of the eastern islands? The Church in West Timor, as elsewhere in Indonesia, was increasingly conscious of the decline in its influence within the Government compared with that which it had enjoyed (and earned) formerly. It was also aware of the growing resentment among the populous Muslim constituency at the disproportionate degree of power that the Catholic Church had hitherto enjoyed in the affairs of the nation relative to its small size numerically. Meanwhile, in contrast to that of the Church, the power of the Military had steadily grown under the *Orde Baru*. This regime was quick to depict as 'Communists' those who voiced any criticism of their actions, thereby deliberately evoking the blood bath of 1965 that continued to haunt the national psyche and dissuading most people from further dissent. Other Catholic Church leaders in West Timor mostly shared these sentiments.

In the Diocese of Kupang response to the plight of the East Timorese tended to be left to the neighbouring Diocese of Atambua where there was a predominantly Catholic population. Students for the priesthood from East Timor received training at the seminary in Kupang but the government 'filtered information' and prohibited demonstrations on any educational campus. Political meetings of any kind invited Military investigation, and sermons had to be judiciously worded for the same reason: to be 'outspoken' would be 'to

---

[90] Source: Indigenous priests (Frs. Hilario Madeira, Domingos Soares, Antono Goncalvez, interviewed in Dili, Sept.1996) who also contradicted most of Bishop Pain Ratu's views as expressed to the author in Besikama, West Timor, Sept.1996 and recounted here.

invite difficulties'. The Church in this region was very vulnerable and mistrust between Catholics and the more numerous Protestants and Muslims 'would only have been encouraged by relating stories of rebellion against the government in East Timor'. In any case, the Church in West Timor was fully engaged in the struggle to provide for the various needs of its own impoverished people and relations with the Church in East Timor remained undeveloped.[91] Mgr Peter Turang, national director of the Pontifical Mission Aid Societies expressed to the author (Jakarta 1996) his conviction that 'only humanitarian help could be given to the Church in East Timor while the diocese of Dili remained outside the Indonesian Bishops Conference'. Mgr Turang was to become Archbishop of Kupang in 1998. Likewise, a leading West Timor Church academic, Fr.Gregor Neonbasu *SVD*, maintained a sympathetic view of the integration policy while being critical of human rights abuses by the Military and their practice of laying all blame for social unrest in the 'Province' upon the long-suffering East Timorese.[92]

In Atambua other leading clergy stressed the decreasing influence of the Church in local and national government affairs; growing friction with Muslim incomers; and their fear of a deliberate policy of 'Islamicisation' on the part of the regime. Although there had been an all-out effort in the early years of 'integration' (1976-83) to provide humanitarian aid and deploy the West Timor Church's human resources to assist the people of East Timor this had 'ceased long ago'. Even members of the same religious congregations that had communities on both sides of the border 'had little to do with each other'.[93] Fr.Benyamin Y.Bria, then Vicar General and Chairman of the diocesan Justice and Peace Commission (and in due course bishop of Bali), acknowledged that some of the teachers and catechists who went from Atambua to assist in East Timor subsequently became *pegawai negeri* (government workers). However, he claimed that the Church in West Timor (and in Indonesia at large) did its best to assist the Church in East Timor despite the difficulties. 'Fraternal support' was given by 'affording bishop Belo opportunity to speak about the situation in East Timor at the Bishops Conference annual assembly'; by 'asking the Government for further information' about 'incidents' that occurred in East Timor; and through 'co-operation between the Justice and Peace Commissions in Dili and Atambua'. He highlighted the problems involved:

> It is difficult to know how best to respond...the Church must be prudent...it is vulnerable... Catholics are a minority in an overwhelmingly Muslim state.[94]

The Provincial of the SVD religious congregation, Fr.Joseph Sievers, criticised the 'refusal' of the Diocese of Dili to become part of the Indonesian Bishops Conference: 'They prefer to maintain their independence'. 'Young Timorese', he opined, 'are fanatical. They will not accept annexation to Indonesia. They have not known the war, and yet they oppose the government'.[95] Perhaps the most enlightening comments were those made to

---

[91] Mgr.Gregious Manteiro Archbp of Kupang (d.1998), Dr.A.Kerans (Rector St.Michael's Major Seminary, Kupang), Fr.Gregor Neonbatu *SVD* (Academic, Diocese of Kupang), Fr.Julius Bere *SVD*, (Pastor, Kupang-Soe); Fr.Marianus Kobatoyo *SVD*, lay catechist Melchior Timu, and Sr.Damiani *CIJ* (Parish of Kapan) - to the author, W.Timor 1996.

[92] Neonbasu, G. *SVD* 1995. 'Indonesian Priest Raises Questions' in Jakarta Post 24.2.1995 (in ETAN Docs Vol 35, Jan 17-March 12, 1995, pp59-60. See also Bibliography – Ch5: Neonbasu, G. 1992.

[93] Various interlocutors in Kefamenanu, Besikama, Atambua, including Fr. Jacobus Kusi, and Fr. Gerry Lanigan *SVD*, Fr.Wolfgang Jeroa *SVD*, Fr. Benyamin Seran, to the author, West Timor, Sept.1996.

[94] Fr.Bria to the author, Atambua, Sept.1996.

[95] To the author, *SVD* Provincial House, Atambua, Sept.1996.

the author by a group of women religious who had been engaged in work in East Timor in the late 1970s. One of them was present in the Santa Cruz Cemetery during the massacre in November 1991, and others had recently been deployed again in the territory:

> Relation between the Churches in West and East Timor? There is no relationship to speak of - it is a lack...
> Our Sisters were engaged in the humanitarian work in East Timor in the late 1970s. Our priority then was to respond to the immediate human need, not to inquire into politics.
> In any case most of the people themselves were unclear about what was happening - they were simply fleeing the war. Our Sisters gained little understanding of the East Timorese political parties - time would have been necessary for such an appreciation, and time they did not have for such things...
> A few years ago some of our Sisters again assisted in East Timor. They were followed everywhere by the Military...and realised the extent to which the people were under control. We were not fully aware of the situation until recently when a visit by some of our Sisters to Europe gave them the opportunity to watch a video about East Timor.[96] It is a matter of 'those who are closest knowing the least'...
> Why has there not been stronger support for bishop Belo - and for 'dissent' in Indonesia by the Catholic Church? Because people are afraid for themselves. Also there is the fear that the necessary work of the Church will be obstructed or prevented. Confrontation with the government in a Muslim majority state would most likely lead to further limitation upon the Church's work...
> Besides, it is certainly questionable as to whether such confrontation would achieve anything.[97]

The mass of the people in West Timor, poor farmers for the most part, knew little about the disastrous events at the other side of the island, except when they were directly affected by the influx of refugees. Nonetheless, in the Year of Crisis for East Timor the Catholics of West Timor generously responded to the needs of the latest wave of displaced people to arrive in their midst. Bishops Anton Pain Ratu and Peter Turang opened the doors of Church property and offered sanctuary to the East Timorese refugees.[98] The bishop of Atambua threw caution to the winds in a world-wide appeal for humanitarian help and openly advocated the East Timorese cause, charging the Military 'elite' force *Kopassus* with responsibility for the creation and deployment of the pro-integration militias. He declared in conclusion:

> It is necessary to stress that the crimes against humanity in East Timor for more than twenty-four years are the total responsibility of the Military and individuals within the Indonesian government, not the Indonesian people...
> The paradox of twenty-four years of Indonesian inhuman involvement in East Timor is that the Military has not forced integration on the East Timorese people...but it has left them no alternative other than to choose independence, when a peaceful humane integration with their neighbours and kin would have been the ideal solution.[99]

---

[96] *viz*: 'Death of a Nation: The Timor Conspiracy'. John Pilger 1994, Central TV, England.

[97] Sisters of the Holy Spirit (*SSPS*) to the author at the Mother House, Atambua, Sept.1996.

[98] 'Catholic Church in W Timor says refugees facing militia harassment', AFP Jakarta, 12.9.1999; 'Fears Refugees will be used as bargaining chips', Craig Skehan (Kupang) and Greg Roberts (Brisbane), The Age, Melbourne, 11.9.1999; & other international coverage.

[99] 'To whom it may concern: the Refugee Situation in East Timor', bishop Anton Pain Ratu, Atambua, Sept.15th 1999. Disseminated via email Conference >reg.easttimor@igc.apc.org< and subsequently via UCA News, Thailand, and international media.

Even so, the response from the hierarchy in the neighbouring ecclesiastical Province was hardly forthright in support. Three bishops of Flores decided not to make any public statement. 'Things will work out without our intervention' explained one, and another requested the religious in his diocese not to work with the deportees brought by *TNI* to Flores 'because it is too risky'.[100] In contrast a non-governmental organisation - formed in Flores in February 1999 to carry out advocacy for human rights on the island and including priests, nuns, students, medics, nurses and others - did respond to the needs of East Timorese displaced in East Timor during July that year, and of those forcibly deported to Kupang and Flores itself after the plebiscite on August 30th.[101] In October John Prior *SVD*, a forthright missionary and academic observed in *The Tablet:*

> Many nuns and male religious are doing remarkably brave work, some with encouragement from their superiors. Looking at the indifference of the many and the quiet courage of the few, one might ask what has happened to Gospel idealism. The verse buzzing through my head is: 'Those who try to save their lives will lose them' [Matthew 10:39] (op.cit.)

The Church in Indonesia: an Evaluation

Apologists for the position of the Catholic Church in Indonesia towards the East Timor issue have argued that the Church was not sufficiently appraised of the facts about human rights violations in the territory. This was due to government propaganda and control of the media, and because of the isolation of the region during the period of invasion and in the first years of occupation. The result was that there were various misconceptions of which the principal one was that the efforts towards political independence on the part of the Timorese were those of a 'Communist-inspired separatist minority' who were responsible for many human rights abuses and engaged in terrorist activity. It is difficult to accept such an argument when the Church authorities, through their own structure of communications and actual visits to the East Timor - during some of the worst periods of killings and oppression by the Military - were directly appraised of the actual political and socio-economic situation by leaders of the East Timorese Church and other experts.[102] Moreover they could have discovered more details by way of the personnel they deployed in the territory as pastoral assistants after annexation was formalised in 1976. It was also declared that for the Church in Indonesia to become more involved than it already was in the affairs of East Timor would have been improper as the Vatican would have regarded this as interference in the concerns of a Church that did not belong the Bishops Conference. As both the Indonesian hierarchy and leading Catholic laity, both military and civilian, sought to bring their influence to bear upon the Vatican in respect of the status of the Church in East Timor this argument is particularly weak.

In justifying the position adopted by the Indonesian Church it has been argued that its leaders and the faithful at large were as concerned as every other Indonesian was with the importance of sustaining the fragile 'unity of the nation'. Catholics were especially committed (and expected to contribute) to this effort since they had played a significant part in the achievement of Independence. Moreover they continued to have an important role in the social and economic development of the Republic, particularly through the Church's educational and health provisions and other pastoral institutions, and through its media outlets. The incorporation of East Timor was regarded as being supportive of that

---

[100] 'Oil is Thicker than Blood', John Prior *SVD*, The Tablet, 2.10.1999.
[101] *Viz: Tim Relawan Untuk Kemanusiaan-Flores (TRUK-F)*. See: 'West Timor Reflections', Charmain Mohammed, 12.4.2000 via email conference >reg.easttimor@igc.apc.org.
[102] See Bibliography – Ch8: Walsh, P.1980 (1), p17-18. Walsh cites a paper delivered that year to Indonesian Church leaders on the economy in East Timor indicating the monopolistic exploitation already in operation under Military auspices.

'national cohesion' and of benefit to the people of the poor and undeveloped territory. This position ignores the distinct history of East Timor and the fact that no authentic plebiscite of the people's own wishes was ever arranged (until 1999 - when the UN referendum indicated by a huge majority that the annexation was most definitely *not* so desired). It also pays no regard to the social and economic marginalisation of the Timorese in their own country which was the actual outcome of *integrasi*.

There were those who urged that the Church should be more confrontational and challenge the *Orde Baru* regime over the injustices it was perpetrating in East Timor (and within Indonesia itself). Such critics were to be found within the Church itself, as well as outside of it in Indonesia, and abroad. But they were constantly reminded by the Catholic leadership, and by their peers, of the vulnerability of the Church in its predominantly Muslim context and of its powerlessness in the face of Military socio-political domination. There is substantial truth in this perception of the Church's circumstances - but the hierarchy and lay elite had deliberately cultivated positive relations with the Military to protect the Church's missionary enterprise and to safeguard its position in Indonesian society. Besides, Catholic politicians had benefited personally (and extensively) from such co-operation, and the Church's complicity had allowed - even facilitated - the regime's political manipulation and social control. Although numerically small the Church remained a respected institution in Indonesian society, and by the government, with some influence to bring to bear if it had chosen to do so. However, the Catholic Church in Indonesia certainly never restricted its activity to the 'purely religious' (as some other Christian denominations tended to do) and was always engaged in matters of social welfare across the archipelago.

It was also argued defensively that the confrontational approach was not appropriate in Javanese culture where criticism of the authorities was not to be aired publicly and forthrightly but should be presented discreetly and 'by implication'. But the Javanese ethos is not the only cultural expression in Indonesia and indeed was not so dominant in the 'outer islands' where Catholics were present in some strength. Another cultural justification for avoiding direct challenge of government policy was offered in respect of the 'ministry of prophecy'. This, it was urged, should be exercised in the Indonesian context not by outspoken individuals, even bishops, but in a manner comparable to the *musyawara-mufakat* process of dialogue leading to consensus by which decisions were traditionally reached within village communities.[103] But evidence of such attempts on the part of Church members with the *Orde Baru* regime is sparse.

Another defensive suggestion was that the government published very little in respect of its intentions to which Catholic critics could appeal for theoretical support. But the principles of *Pancasila* and the traditional ideals of *Gotong Royong* (mutual help) which were exploited by the regime also opened the way for the Church to introduce pertinent elements of Catholic Social Doctrine (which indeed was done in respect of issues other than that of East Timor).

A more pragmatic reason for the bishops not to criticise the Government too openly or persistently was that they would not have received wholehearted support from the Catholic laity who were desirous of securing their place in society, and because a positive outcome was far from sure. In fact negative repercussions were always a distinct possibility and had been on occasion either intimated in Javanese style, overtly threatened, or actually brought about by the imposition of certain restrictions on the Church's pastoral mission and institutions. Thus Archbishop of Jakarta Leo Soekote *SJ* remarked on one occasion:

---

[103] See Bibliography – Ch6: Muskens, M.P.M. 1979. op.cit. pp316-7.

We have no wish to cry 'Victory' for two or three days and then have everything return to normal. Nothing would happen. We have to work with this government since, more and more, all power is in its hands. [104]

Therefore there is truth in the observation that the Church in Indonesia, for these various internal and external reasons, and also on account of its uneven demographical spread, 'lacked the capacity to protest in a manifest way injustices in Indonesia'. Thus 'it was correspondingly unable to reject, correct or change the Government's policy on East Timor'.[105] But it must be emphasised that some influential Church leaders had accepted and even urged the incorporation of both West Papua and then East Timor. This was in striking contrast to the posture the Catholic community as a whole had adopted in the efforts towards the creation and consolidation of the Indonesian Republic. Moreover, the general silence of most of the other leaders in respect of the policies of the *Orde Baru* - a silence which prevailed within the Catholic community as a whole including its media institutions - surely made the Church complicit in the government repression and in the regime's exploitative and abusive oppression of East Timor. Only when the popular movement for *Reformasi* gathered sufficient momentum to oust the *Orde Baru* did the Church become more assertive, and even then it did not speak with one voice. The fundamental reason for this lay in the Church's desire for its own institutional survival especially when confronted, as it was, with the perceived threat of the assertion of Islam on the one hand and that of Communism on the other. All these considerations have to be borne in mind in applying the criteria for evaluation of the Church in Indonesia's response to the East Timor issue which have been derived from Catholic Social Doctrine.

In the light of all that has been recounted it is evident that this response had variations within the overall Catholic community with noteworthy dissenting elements present in certain circles of Church life. However, the most significant proportion of the lay leadership, both civilian and military, went along with - and even promoted - the *Orde Baru's* East Timor project and the hierarchy accommodated it until political developments in Indonesia itself altered the context in which the Church was operating. Thus it should be admitted that the Church in Indonesia failed to give due preference to the most marginalised, oppressed and impoverished people in the orbit of its concern, namely the East Timorese (and West Papuans). It did indeed seek to relieve their suffering and to provide for their spiritual needs with word and sacrament, and for their material and social requirements with humanitarian aid and educational and health facilities. But far from urging their right to full political participation, integral development and self-determination, and to resist an unjust and exploitative rule, for the most part Catholic Church authorities and personnel acted in effect as agents of their government's policy (albeit generally with good will and intentions). In West Papua the Church had the difficulty of being faithful to her own Social Doctrine while operating within a set of circumstances which, though unjust, had nonetheless been accepted as legitimate by the international community. But in respect of East Timor there was no such excuse for the question of that country's political status remained unresolved until the outcome of the United Nations 'popular consultation' was finally accepted by all parties in the autumn of 1999. The Church in Indonesia did not forthrightly challenge the structural injustices that impacted upon the East Timorese welfare, marginalising and impoverishing them in their own country. On occasion it did invite the government to question the appropriateness of its policies and investigate more closely the reality of the East Timorese experience.

---

[104] Cited with other of the above arguments in 'The Church in Indonesia: to speak or not to speak?', Information on Human Development, Feb 1984. FABC: Manila.
[105] Bibliography – Ch8: Walsh, P. 1980 (1), op.cit. The Church's demography is elaborated in *Pro Mundi Vita* Bulletin 'The Catholic Church in Indonesia' Jan-Feb 1977.

Although information was received from representatives of the Church in East Timor, and from Indonesian and other pastors working in the territory, the leaders of the institutional Church, clergy and lay alike - with notable exceptions - failed either to attend or to respond to its content. Only those who were most fully engaged already with issues of social justice in Indonesia itself concerned themselves with the disorder pertaining in East Timor. The silence of the majority was explained by reference to the constraints under which the Church had to function, and justified by appeals to 'prudence', but it made the Church complicit in a dreadful injustice for which it inclined to hold the Military solely to blame.

The ambiguities of the Church's experience have been recounted. In accordance with the example of Jesus, effort was made to improve the circumstances of the East Timorese and to help them grow in the life and love of God through a conscientious *pastoral* care. But the Church largely failed in its *prophetic* task of exposing the fundamental crisis in East Timor society which was the disorder of an imposed, repressive, exploitative and alien rule, a polity in which the people's participation was only pretended. The Church was in receipt of thorough social analyses and its leaders listened to - but mostly did not hear - the East Timorese voices of dismay. Although the hierarchy sometimes adopted an interrogative demeanour towards the policies of the secular authorities this was spasmodic and was weakened by their general attitude of accommodation to the government's will. Dissenting voices were the minority in the circles of those who claimed Christian *discipleship*. No doubt the Church at every level was concerned for the liberation of the people of East Timor - but more from what were perceived as the limitations of their cultural and colonial inheritance, and from the bonds of personal sin, than from the persisting structural injustices and social disorder. These remained unrecognised, or regarded as the consequences of colonial rule, or as self-inflicted, inescapable, or not subject matters to be addressed by *evangelists*. The Church in Indonesia surely interceded with God for the people of East Timor, and thereby entered into a spiritual solidarity with them, but that *intercession* was not matched with practical advocacy of their cause with human authorities, in Indonesia or elsewhere. With notable exceptions, such as have been named above, this task was left to people outside the Church and outside the country.

In the mayhem that ensued in East Timor after the results of the UN ballot were publicised, a young Indonesian priest, Fr.Tarcisius Dewanto was among the many who were slain in and around the Church premises at Suai, a small town on the south coast.[106] With the East Timorese parish priest Fr.Hilario Madeira and his co-pastor Fr.Francisco Soares, Fr.Tarcisius was trying to protect the people who had sought sanctuary there from the murderous attacks of the marauding militias created and directed by Indonesian *Kopassus* and Army Intelligence personnel. The Church in Indonesia until then had lacked a martyr. Perhaps this young pastor's willingness to *lay down his own life* for the sake of the suffering people of East Timor may serve powerfully in their ultimate deliverance from all evil. Maybe it will also contribute towards the complete redemption of the Church which had sent him to their aid and which, for a while, seemed to put its own survival before its Gospel mission.

---

[106] Louise Williams, Sydney Morning Herald, 10.9.99, and widely in the international press.

CHAPTER SEVEN - THE CHURCH IN PORTUGAL:
A CHURCH PRE-OCCUPIED?

Expectations Unfulfilled

Not long after his public denunciation of the human rights violations being committed in East Timor Mgr Costa Lopes was invited by the Vatican authorities to tender his resignation as Apostolic Administrator. He left East Timor for Portugal, no doubt in expectation of a sympathetic hearing and positive response from the local Catholic Church that had first brought the Gospel and the ecclesiastical institution to his native land. However, within a few years he was to die in Lisbon, drained of energy and with any such hopes disappointed.[1] To appraise the response of the Church in Portugal to the Timorese plight it is necessary to give some initial consideration to the changing socio-political situation in which it had to operate and to the nature of the relationship between Portugal and East Timor.

The Church in 20th Century Portugal

The Catholic faith was endemic to the Portuguese character but the institutional Church had become identified with the privileged classes during and after the Age of Reason and its general condition during the 19th century was far from healthy. When the Republic was established in 1910 the Church suffered severe deprivations as the secular authorities sought to curtail ecclesiastical power. But this policy actually stimulated a purification of the Church and, together with the political turmoil that was to last for the next two decades, and the lasting impact of the extraordinary events at Fatima in 1917, stimulated a new national assertion of the primacy of the spirit. When Antonio de Oliviera Salazar became Prime Minister in 1932 there was a general consent to the authoritarian character of the *Estado Nuovo* he sought to establish which purposed national stability and socio-economic development. Salazar's vision of a corporative State had found much of its inspiration in Catholic Social Doctrine and he further won the confidence of the hierarchy by protecting the interests of the Church and restoring its influence. However, the repressive and interventionist nature of his enduring regime eventually evoked dissent, with some bishops and clergy adding their voices to the mounting criticism from the 1950s on and especially after the Second Vatican Council.

During the 1960s the nationalist movements in the Portuguese African colonies grew apace. The government in Lisbon failed to subdue such sentiments or to deflect international criticism of its continuing rule by designating these territories as 'Overseas Provinces'. Military efforts to crush the armed liberation forces became increasingly costly in Portuguese lives and to the national economy. In a best-selling book, *Portugal e o Futuro*, General Spinola challenged the belief in Portugal's divinely-mandated 'civilising mission' and called for a realism that would recognise the African people's right to political self-determination. Meanwhile the *Movimento das Forcas Armadas* (*MFA*) had emerged within the lower levels of the officer corps to become a vanguard of protest. It was the *MFA* that brought an end to the *Estado Nuovo* in a bloodless coup – the 'Carnation Revolution' - on April 25th 1974 and immediately inaugurated the process of decolonisation in East Timor as elsewhere.

After so many years of political repression in Portugal there was a flurry of activity and, although the principal political organisations were the new young parties of the centre

---

[1] See Bibliography – Ch5: Lennox, R. 2000, pp227-235.

and right, left wing elements were very visible and voluble.[2] Among them was the Portuguese Communist Party with which the *MFA* soon began to collaborate in various policies of attempted social control and land appropriation. These caused widespread alarm and provoked a political crisis during the winter of 1974-5. Meanwhile the liberation struggles in Africa became more bloody and internationalised in the ideological contention of the Cold War and hundreds of destitute refugees arrived in Lisbon. Church and civil leaders in the centre and north of the country joined in an anti-Communist alliance with Socialists and military moderates to break the power of the far Left but there was political instability for several more years thereafter. During this period the shape of events in Portugal became of major concern to the Western Alliance including Australia. NATO was anxious to retain access to the strategic islands of the Azores and the ports of Portuguese African 'Provinces'. From the USA Henry Kissinger despatched a new Embassy team to Lisbon, fearful of a 'domino effect' in the Iberian Peninsula and the Mediterranean. These fears were fostered within the Western Press.

In order to secure economic reform and development the politicians turned increasingly to the external stimulus of the European Community and an historic shift in foreign policy took place: the five hundred year Oceanic and Atlantic-facing international posture gave way to one which looked towards continental Europe. In 1986 Portugal was integrated into the EC and in 1988 into the Western European Union. Marxist-Leninist elements were removed from the Constitution and during the concluding decade and a half of the 20th Century Portugal's economy strengthened, social stability was sustained and a sound democracy achieved by a remarkable triumph of political moderation. But the Church, which had been re-invigorated by its opposition to Communist assertion in the mid-1970s, steadily lost social and political prestige. Attendance at religious services and other events diminished in direct correlation to the increase among the people of the materialist values, secularism, relativism and individualism pervading Portugal as in Western Europe generally.

Thus, during the years of East Timor's invasion and occupation, the Church in Portugal anxiously faced an uncertain future. An era of forty years during which its social importance had been restored and its institutional security had been assured by the *Estado Nuovo* came to an end. This was followed by an alarming period of general political instability reminiscent of the early years of the Republic, and the menace of Communist assertion. Then, as the country became politically more settled and economically stronger the Church found itself within an increasingly affluent, confident and irreligious society and saw its influence upon the outcome of important issues significantly diminished.

Portuguese relations with the people of East Timor

Detailed accounts of the colonial period are provided elsewhere and are not necessary here.[3] Fuller information about the relationship between Portugal and East Timor from the time of the Carnation Revolution in 1974 is provided in various sources.[4] However, it should be noted that there were two facets to the Portuguese disposition - that of the government, and that of the people at large – and two situations in which the East

---

[2] Many students (including East Timorese) became attached to Marxist-Leninist and Maoist groupings such as the *Movimento Revolucionario Proletario Portuguese*.

[3] Bibliography – General (East Timor); Bibliography - Ch5: Gunn, G.C. 1999; Bibliography – Ch7: Texeira, M. 1961; Biblioteca Central, *A Historia de Timor etc*; Pelissier, R. 1996.

[4] Bibliography – General (East Timor): e.g. Taylor, J.G. 1990; Kohen, A. 1999, *passim*; Krieger, H. 1997, Index: Portugal; Barbedo de Magalhaes, A. 1998, 'Portugal and East Timor', in Retboll, T. (ed) 1998, Ch16.

Timorese looked for Portuguese assistance – in Timor itself, and in Portugal, where many came seeking refuge.

Although Colonel Lemos Pires, representing the *MFA* administration in East Timor, strove to advance the process of decolonisation in a non-partisan way, the government in Lisbon was preoccupied with pressing affairs in Portugal itself and with developments in the African provinces. The UN continued to regard Portugal as the Administering Power in East Timor, and the national Constitution as revised in 1974 and 1976 included an unequivocal obligation to respect the right of the former colony to political self-determination and independence.[5] Nonetheless, the government had to some extent been complicit in the Indonesian take-over and between December 1975 and September 1980 Lisbon did very little on behalf of the Timorese either in Timor or at the United Nations.[6] Many Portuguese people had considerable sympathy for the East Timorese plight and felt sorrow and guilt that little seemed to have been done to prevent atrocities in the former colony. But there were sharp ideological differences between the Timorese refugee communities in Portugal - and between their support groups - that evoked some confusion and disaffection among the general populace.

In time, FRETILIN's continuing resistance and persistent reports of the harshness of the Indonesian rule in East Timor prodded the consciences of politicians. From 1980 government efforts began for the achievement of a diplomatic solution. These were to include talks with Indonesia and successive attempts to internationalise the issue. The government was critical of pro-Indonesian partiality on the part of Western powers and Lusophone countries in various UN forums mounted opposition to the Indonesian occupation of the territory.[7] When Portugal became a member of the European Community in 1986 the government found new opportunities besides that of the UN to press home its campaign.[8] A particularly significant action was taken in 1991 when Portugal filed a case against Australia at the International Court of Justice claiming that Canberra's negotiations with Indonesia over maritime resources - which had concluded in the Timor Gap Treaty (1989) - had breached its authority as Administering Power.[9] That same year the Pope made a pastoral visit to the Catholics of Portugal during which a poll organised by the national Press indicated that 68% of the population hoped that he would publicly denounce the situation in East Timor.[10] Popular concern – and pressure on the government - was soon roused to new heights by the massacre in the Santa Cruz cemetery in Dili that followed upon Jakarta's denial of access to a Portuguese parliamentary delegation scheduled to visit the territory.[11] The award of the Nobel Peace Prize to Jose Ramos Horta and bishop Belo in 1996 had the greatest impact – outside of East Timor itself – in Portugal,

---

[5] See: UNGA Resolution 1542 (XV); related Resolutions 647 (VII) 648 (VII) 742 (VII); UN Charter Chapter XI 'Regarding non-Self-Governing Territories'. For further details see Bibliography – Ch3: CIIR/IPJET. 1995, Ch 2, 4, 11, 15, & 16; Bibliography – Ch7: Assembleia da Republica, 1992; Gouveia, J.B. 1993.

[6] For a critique of the government see Bibliography – Ch7: Costa Alves, M. 1998. For the difficulties experienced by the governor see his own account: Pires, L. 1991. Portugal's ambassador at the UN was instructed (Oct 23rd 1979) not to actively solicit support at the UN for the East Timor issue which might have obstructed the achievement of diplomatic objectives given higher priority such as Portugal's acceptance into the EEC.

[7] e.g. At the annual (July/August) hearings of the UN Decolonisation Committee.

[8] For a collection of material related to Portuguese efforts on behalf of E Timor from 1988-91 see Bibliography – Ch7: Assembleia da Republica 1991, *Factos e Documentos*.

[9] For legal analysis see Bibliography – Ch3: CIIR/IPJET 1995, Ch12 - 14, and 15 (pp286-9).

[10] *Publico, Diario de Noticias, etc.*,10.5.1991.

[11] Bibliography – General (East Timor): Krieger, H. 1995 op.cit.pp285-289; Kohen, A. 1999, op.cit. pp174, 247.

among politicians and the people at large.[12] The efforts of several non-governmental organisations and of academics within a number of prestigious universities gave focus and direction to the national sympathy.[13] Expatriate Portuguese in the USA and elsewhere also came to act in solidarity with the East Timorese people, and the emergence of a 'Lusitanian Commonwealth' gave further strength to Portugal's advocacy of East Timorese rights under International Law.[14]

Successive waves of East Timorese refugees presented the government and people of Portugal with another problematic situation that called for their response. The first two thousand arrived in 1975 in flight from the civil war and then from the impending and actual Indonesian invasion at a time when the authorities already faced the challenge of half a million homeless and a similar number of unemployed among the Portuguese themselves. 800,000 more people were returning from the African colonies. Provisions made for the Timorese by the government were far from adequate, although the internal divisions among the refugees themselves hardly helped in evoking a better response.[15] In subsequent years a further four thousand Timorese refugees were able to reach Lisbon, bringing with them their traumatic experiences under Indonesian rule and an image of Portugal that bore little relation to its present historical reality. They were dispersed beyond Lisbon to various localities in the region. In 1995 proposals for very necessary improvements to the welcome and settling of Timorese refugees in Portugal were put to the government by a number of Portuguese NGOs concerned about their plight.[16] These recommendations evoked some important positive measures in response.[17] But the East Timorese recipients, sympathetic NGOs, and government workers involved in effecting these prescriptions, all observed serious limitations in the official arrangements and the severe hardships which refugees continued to suffer.[18] A subsequent report commissioned by the government highlighted such shortcomings.[19] From 1996 especially, East Timorese students at Indonesian institutions who opposed the oppressive rule in their homeland sought asylum in foreign embassies in Jakarta and were directed on to Lisbon. Their priority was the ousting of Indonesia from East Timor and their presence in Portugal com-

---

[12] See: 'Reactions in Portugal to Peace Prize Award', *Diario de Noticias*, 12.10.1996; and 'Communique of the Portuguese Ministry of Foreign Affairs on the NP Prize awarded to Mgr Belo and Mr. J.R.Horta'. Assembleia da Republica, 11.10.1996, Lisbon.

[13] e.g. NGOs *A Paz e Possivel em Timor-Leste*, and *Comissao Para os Direitos do Povo Maubere (CDPM)*; the Universities of Oporto and Coimbra were especially active.

[14] The Community of Portuguese Speaking Countries (*CPLP*) [former colonies] was established in Lisbon in July 1996. East Timor was formally included in the *CPLP* after Indonesia abandoned its claim to sovereignty over the territory in November 1999 but East Timorese welfare had been a principal item on the *CPLP* agenda from its inception.

[15] See Bibliography – Ch7:Dunn, J. 1977. cf. Bibliography – Ch8: Walsh, P. 1980 (1), p 26f.

[16] '*A Comunidade Timorense em Portugal Proposta Para um Plano de Acolhimento e Insercao*'. Advanced in Lisbon 12.11.1995 by: *A Paz e Possivel em Timor-Leste; Associacao Academica de Coimbra; Associacao Academica de Lisboa; Associacao 12 de Novembro; Centro de Informacao e Documentacao Amilcar Cabral (CIDAC); Civitas; Comissao Para os Direitos do Povo Maubere (CDPM); Conselho Nacional de Juventude (CNJ); Grupo Universitario de Apoio a Insersao dos Timorenses; Movimento Cristao para a Paz (MCP)*

[17] e.g. The establishment of an agency to attend to the matter (*Comissao Permanente Para O Acolhimento e Insercao Social da Comunidade Timorense - CPAISCT*), and improved Social Security provisions for East Timorese along with other refugees of Portuguese nationality (*Ministerio da Solidariedade e Seguranca Sosial, Decreto-Lei 133/97, 9.5.1997*).

[18] Observations made to the author by Maria Theresa Abrantes and Pasquale Barreto (*CPAISCT*), and Christina Cruz (*CDPM*), Lisbon, June 1997. cf. 'The Timorese Community in Portugal: Socio-economic Characterisation and the Integration Process'. Paper by Zito Soares (Timorese refugee) to *CDPM* Workshop, Lisbon, Dec.9th 1997.

[19] 'Study of the Socio-economic situation of the Timorese living in Portugal', 1996.

pounded the rather contentious ideological mix already manifest among their compatriots and increased the burden upon the government. Political militancy among such younger immigrants also tended to distance them from Portuguese society at large in which they perceived a limited understanding of Timorese (and indeed, Asian) culture and experience.[20]

During East Timor's 'Year of Crisis' Lisbon's determination to exploit the 'window of opportunity' opened up by President Habibie's offer of 'autonomy within or de-coupling from Indonesia' was manifest in the tri-partite negotiations conducted with Indonesia under the auspices of the United Nations. Following the formal termination of Indonesian sovereignty in November 1999 the Portuguese government and people was especially generous in its financial and other support to the fledgling nation of Timor Loro Sae. But the situation of the many Timorese refugees in Portugal remained difficult, as did that of their compatriots in the homeland.

The Portuguese Church and the East Timorese people

The critical events in East Timor took place during a period of acute anxiety in the Portuguese Church and this mood affected its response to the crisis - and upon the interpretation of events that it conveyed to the Church elsewhere. But even though such fears subsided when the government in Portugal moved to the political centre and a stable democracy was gradually established, the Church's concern for the East Timorese proved to be limited in its extent. An important external reason for this, as already noted, was that the ethos of secularism, individualism and relativism pervading Western Europe weakened corporate action by the Church. But there were internal factors also and these give grounds for criticism. Yet there were also within the Catholic community overall some admirable examples of effective action characterised by prudence, generosity and courage. In attending to this variety of reactions within the Portuguese Church to the East Timorese plight it is important to distinguish between the efforts made to resolve the political issue, and those which were a response to the humanitarian needs of the Timorese. Before appraising the response of the Church in Portugal itself, it is apposite to remark briefly upon the actions of the few Portuguese missionaries who continued to serve in East Timor throughout the period of Indonesian occupation and the effort made by the Church in the wider Lusophone Community. The practical concern of expatriate Portuguese Catholics residing elsewhere in the world - particularly in the United States and in Australia – should also be noted.

Portuguese Missionaries in East Timor

Missionaries accompanied the traders who were the first Portuguese to arrive in East Timor and during the succeeding centuries these evangelists enjoyed generally good relations with the native people. Although some Church leaders were rather patronising, others had high regard for local traditions.[21] When Salazar gave the Church prime responsibility for education in the *ultramar* it came to play a central role in Portugal's 'civilising mission'. Positive aspects of the Church's educational provision were that it was enriched by the broad heritage of European culture, developed students' faculty for

---

[20] e.g. Levi Corte-Real Bucar, interviewed by Jill Jolliffe, 'Back from the Dead', Sydney Morning Herald 19.6.1999; 'Exiled East Timorese youths long to go home', Linawati Sidarto, Jakarta Post 25.6.2000.

[21] One Portuguese bishop had remarked 'the Timorese need only to read and write, then we should give them a hoe and an axe' (Bibliography – General (East Timor): Horta, J.R. 1987, p13) but bishop Jaime Gulart loved the people and respected their customs (Kohen, A.1999. op.cit.pp45-6).

intellectual analysis and evaluation, and imparted a moral awareness and sense of justice.[22] Local appreciation of the Church's gift to the Timorese was revealed by the successful efforts of the indigenous laity to sustain the Catholic faith and maintain ecclesiastical property during the years of Japanese occupation when the Portuguese clergy were withdrawn.

The political upheaval in Portugal after the Carnation Revolution in 1974 and the subsequent efforts in East Timor to effect a proper decolonisation process gave rise to a certain ambiguity in the leadership given by the clergy. Bishop Riberio was not in favour of the Revolution in Portugal and he was of the view that the Timorese were 'not sophisticated enough' to be engaged in the complexities of the political process of decolonisation. His partiality for UDT has already been remarked upon, and his opposition to FRETILIN derived in large measure from his concern that under their administration the Church would lose its position and influence in local society. Yet Ribeiro did appeal to UDT to bring an end to the killings in the civil war and eventually gave recognition to the positive qualities of FRETILIN's perceptions and policies.[23] The clergy were also concerned about the influence of the political left but among them were those who were well-informed about the positive dimensions of the popular 'conscientisation' already taking place in Latin America. Some of them were acquainted with the emerging Liberation Theology and its emphasis on the 'preferential option for the poor', a notion to be taken up in due course (if less radically) by the Universal Church. Among the Portuguese missionaries there was also an understandable desire for the preservation of their national cultural heritage in East Timor, aspects of which already featured within local language and traditions. But in general the clergy endeavoured to adopt a non-interventionist posture in local politics. During the civil war in the summer of 1975 almost 90% of the missionary priests and religious brothers and sisters returned to Portugal, provoking FRETILIN leader Xavier do Amaral to comment regretfully upon this second 'flight of the shepherds'.[24]

After the onslaught of the invasion those few Portuguese priests who remained in the territory were to become, along with a number of indigenous pastors, outstanding examples of the local Church's courageous defence of the native people's human rights. In the early years of the occupation they were under close surveillance by the military and their movement was very restricted. They were in constant danger of arrest, or at least of severe delimitation to their pastoral ministry, if their activity aroused the slightest suspicion that they were providing any support for the Timorese Resistance. One of the discreet ways in which they acted on behalf of the welfare of the people was in supplying information, through ecclesiastical channels of communication, about the atrocities committed by the Indonesian military. In the later years of the occupation when this became (relatively) easier, detailed daily records of human rights violations - and of the effects of the inundation of East Timor by Indonesian migrants - were conveyed to the outside world by every means available on a regular, even weekly, basis.[25] The sympathy of the Portuguese missionaries with the spirit of resistance to Indonesian rule was suspected by the Military who intimidated them in various ways. Their attendance was

---

[22] The lack of these qualities in the Indonesian education provision after 1976 was often remarked upon to this author by Timorese students and tutors able to make comparisons.

[23] Source: E Timorese exile Roberto Seixas to author, Lisbon July 1997.

[24] Bibliography – Ch2: Budiardjo and Liem 1984, p117.

[25] e.g. By the Jesuits Fr.Joao Felgueiras & Fr.Jose Martins from a religious community which included Indonesian *confreres* sympathetic to the Suharto regime's E Timor policy. They were threatened with expulsion from E Timor in 1987, *Tapol Bulletin* No 81, June 1987. Fr.Martins was described to the author by a Timorese student in Lisbon (1997) as 'the Apostle of Liberation'. Not even all the indigenous Timorese priests undertook such perilous action.

required at the barracks where they were abused, sometimes physically, and they were unjustly accused of 'illegal activities' in order to provide the government authorities with an excuse for retaining or not renewing their visas.[26] The missionaries' criticism of the Indonesian occupying forces was sometimes more overt - Fr.Carlos da Rocha Perieira, an elderly secular priest (born 1910) publicly denounced the military and the regime they represented in his sermons during Mass. 'Jakarta is Hell', he declared loudly, and (pointing to the soldiers positioned around the church) 'There are the thieves and the devils... Suharto is the chief devil'. The rank and file troops were afraid of Fr.Carlos who had a reputation among the Timorese for sanctity and thereby possessing supernatural powers.[27] The personal experiences of Fr.Leoneto Vieira de Rego who spent three years (1976-79) ministering to the people who fled with the FRETILIN forces into the mountains of East Timor - which he later recounted in Lisbon, New York and Washington - provided testimony of significant importance in raising international awareness of the Timorese plight.[28]

The Portuguese Church outside Portugal

The Portuguese Church's presence in Macau was of significant importance for East Timorese welfare. In earlier times the Church in East Timor had been administered from this location and during the years of Indonesian occupation this last colonial outpost of Portugal was to offer a regional safe haven for Timorese in flight from the oppression. Its Catholic ecclesial presence also offered a channel for two-way communication between the Church in East Timor and the Church in the wider world. Fr.Francisco Fernandes, a Timorese priest who cared for the refugees in Atambua (West Timor) and then in Lisbon, was able to avail of Church resources in Macau while testifying in East Asia to ongoing events in East Timor. He was to settle in Australia for several years where he attended to the East Timorese refugees there while ministering to the supportive expatriate Portuguese community in Perth, eventually taking up permanent residency in Macau.[29]

The United States was another location where Portuguese Catholics had a significant presence and were able to become engaged in discreet and overt advocacy of the East Timorese cause. There were expatriate communities in Rhode Island, Massachusetts, and elsewhere. In Rhode Island, former Portuguese missionary to East Timor Fr.Reinaldo Cardoso played a key role.[30]

---

[26] e.g. Fr.Joao de Deus Pires *SDB* suffered all these experiences. See: Gema Warta, Radio Report, Radio Nederland 15 May 1981 – copy on file; 'News from East Timor' Information Section Canvisti, Jakarta, 27 October 1992 – copy on file; Timor Link Jan 1994, p8; 'I was forced to spy on the Church', Carlos da Conceicao 28.5.1996 for *CNRM* - copy on file.

[27] Related to the author by Maria do Ceu Federer, Timorese exile in Darwin, September 1997. See also Bibliography – Ch2: 'Lourenco' in Turner, M. 1992, p112.

[28] See: 'A Portuguese Priest's Sad Tale about the Situation in East Timor' Strechts Nieuwsblad, 20.8.79 – copy on file; 'Interview with Fr.L.V.de Rego', by Jill Jolliffe, Canberra Times, 22.8.79; Bibliography – General (East Timor): Chomsky, N. 1979, 'Statement delivered to the UNGA 4th Committee, October 1979' (in Retboll, T.(ed) 1980, p109f); Dunn, J.1996, op.cit. pp 269, 278, 280; Kohen, A. 1999, op.cit. pp93-4, 96; Northern Territory News, Australia, 26 Sept.1979; etc.

[29] Fr.Fernandes testified to the UN 4th Committee on Decolonisation in 1979 and to the Congressional Hearing on E Timor in Washington in 1980. CIIR arranged for him to visit Britain July 12-17th 1980 when he met Archbishop Runcie among other dignitaries. He was based at Macau when he addressed the CCA of the World Council of Churches in 1985. James Dunn notes his indebtedness to 'Chico' Fernandes - Dunn, J.1996, op.cit. p.xv.

[30] Kohen, A.1999, op.cit.pxiii; Fr.Cardoso to the author, Rhode Island USA, Sept. 1998 (detailed below, Ch9).

The Church in the Lusophone Community also expressed some limited concern for the East Timorese plight, but of course it faced severe and more immediate socio-political problems in all its locations – especially in Angola, Mozambique, and Brazil.[31]

The Church in Portugal – Links with East Timor

Former missionaries in East Timor provided key points for reception of information from the territory channelled via church contacts or, as communications technology developed, directly via the internet. One such discreet role was exercised by Fr. Joao Canico, a Jesuit who had taught in the seminary at Dare between 1966-69 and whose pupils had included Carlos Belo and Basileo do Nascimento, subsequently bishops of the East Timor Dioceses of Dili and Baucau. Fr.Canico spent thirteen years in the Caritas Press Office in Lisbon and provided the influential Portuguese NGO *Paz e Possivel em Timor Leste* with a substantial proportion of the information it was able to deploy in its advocacy and humanitarian campaigns. He sent weekly faxes to Belo on the socio-political situation in Portugal especially regarding any responses to the Timorese plight, and regularly exchanged material with the Portuguese Jesuits in Dili, Fr.Felgueiras and Fr.Martins. As mail from Portugal was thrown into the sea by government operatives in East Timor and across Indonesia, such links were of great practical and psychological importance to the Church and people there.[32] Fr.Canico was able to travel to East Timor in person on one occasion in later years, a visit that provided him with further insights into the real situation there.[33]

Another resource for East Timorese welfare was provided by the Salesian Provincial House in Lisbon where bishop Belo was accommodated during the occasional visits to Europe permitted him by the Indonesian Government.[34] The religious community here was wary of political involvement - and especially of political partisanship (with regard to Portugal as much as in respect of East Timor). Following the award of the Nobel Peace Prize to bishop Belo and Jose Ramos Horta in 1996, the political Left had become more assertive in Portugal and wished to be associated with the Laureates. Moreover there were a large number of Indonesian spies in Lisbon and Abilio Araujo, a former FRETILIN leader who had sided with Indonesia, resided in the city and was also considered to

---

[31] e.g.
In July 1982 the bishop of Nampula (Mozambique) disseminated a Note denouncing the oppression experienced by the 'Maubere people' ('*Carissimos Amigos*' 9.7.82) – copy on file. In May 1996 delegates from the Portuguese-speaking countries met in Lisbon to formalise the establishment of a Lusophone Catholic Community. This meeting invited a Church representative from E Timor and expressed the 'solidarity of our bishops with the diocese of Dili' and 'the wish of all to see the problem of E Timor resolved...with regard to the rightful autonomy of the E Timorese based on respect for human rights.'('Solidarity with Timor, etc', *Publico*, Lisbon 10/13.5.1996).
In July 1997 a delegation from the Church in Brazil participated in the *VII Journadas* in Oporto, one of whom - Frei Joa Xerri OP - had recently intervened on behalf of the E Timorese with the Brazilian Minister of Foreign Affairs, L.F.Palmeira Lampreia. (See 'Conversa com o Ministro das Relacoes Exteriores', Brasilia 11.6.97 - copy on file). In 2000 the Brazilian bishops promised an aid mission to E Timor (BBC - Summary of World Broadcasts, 5.4.2000).
[32] Fr.Canico did not have an official appointment to this work from his Order and had to undertake it in his spare time from several other pressing responsibilities.
[33] See: 'The daily martyrdom of the Church in East Timor', Fr.J.Canico, in *Voz Portugalense*, Diocese of Oporto, 4.1.1996. Translated by Jose Barros Basto in ETAN Docs Vol 43, p94.
[34] East Timor was formerly included within the Salesian Portuguese Province, and 1976-83 contact was maintained through the diplomatic mail of the Portuguese Papal Nuncio. But in 1983 the Salesian General in Rome moved E Timor into the Philippine Province because dialogue, correspondence, etc., was proving very difficult to maintain. The Holy See had also prevailed upon the Portuguese Nuncio to stop acting as a postman 'as it was causing difficulties for the Nuncio in Jakarta' (Source: Salesian Superior to the author, Lisbon 1997).

present a security risk. If the significant Salesian-organised contribution was not to be jeopardised, the utmost discretion was necessary and overt political discussion and advocacy of the East Timorese cause was therefore avoided. However, this necessarily prudent disposition did not prevent the discreet exchange of important social and political information and the supply of very substantial financial and material support for the Church's pastoral and humanitarian work in East Timor through various ecclesiastical channels.[35] Such provision undoubtedly contributed positively to the Timorese spirit of resistance against the oppression being effected there by the Indonesian military.

A very detailed account of the East Timorese plight was provided by Dom Martinho da Costa Lopes when came to live in Lisbon in 1983, exiled from his homeland but continuing to receive crucial information from the territory. His commitment to the Church was unquestionable and his former role as East Timor's representative in the National Assembly had given every evidence of his Portuguese patriotism,[36] but his appeals in Portugal were to receive comparatively little attention from officialdom in either Church or State. Besides giving in person his own urgent and detailed testimony Dom Martinho publicised other communications he received about the prevailing situation in East Timor including those from such eminent sources as his successor Carlos Belo and Resistance leader Xanana Gusmao.[37] His efforts received some attention in the Portuguese media[38], notably when he uncharacteristically expressed criticism of Pope John Paul II's apparent 'compliance' with Indonesia's East Timor policy.[39] But the forlorn circumstances of his death in 1990, and the criticism by pro-Timorese NGOs of the seeming disinterest of the Portuguese hierarchy in his welfare which this event prompted, evoked at least as much coverage as anything he had done since his arrival in the country seven years earlier.[40] It would seem that Dom Martinho's earlier patriotic fervour for Portugal caused some alienation from FRETILIN supporters in Lisbon, from whom he chose to distance himself on the grounds of impartiality. Yet he was still regarded as a worthy representative by FRETILIN in East Timor - a credibility which, perversely, caused him to be in disfavour with the UDT faction in Portugal. Many in the Portuguese hierarchy declined to acknowledge him as their equal since, though formerly Apostolic Administrator in the Diocese of Dili, he was never ordained a bishop.[41] Dom Martinho's understandable desire to minister to the Timorese exiles in preference to a

---

[35] Salesian Superior Padre Mauricio de Bastos e Pinho to the author, Lisbon 1997.
Appeals for and evaluations of the Salesian pastoral/humanitarian provision to East Timor featured in the congregation's publications *Boletim Salesiano* (Lisbon) and *Novos Horizontes* (Evora).

[36] For citations from his patriotic speeches at Sao Bento in 1957, 1958, 1960 see Bibliography – Ch5: Lennox, R. 2000, op.cit. pp58-67.
[37] For communications received by Dom Martinho in 1986, 1986, 1988 see Bibliography – General (East Timor): Taylor, J.1990, op.cit. nos 366, 444, 666. For Mgr Belo's Letter to Costa Lopes see Bibliography Ch8: CCJPD, p16.

[38] e.g. In a debate on 'E Timor: Autonomy or Integration' organised by *Associacao para o Desenvolvimento Economico e Social (SEDES)*, in *O Seculo*, and *Diario de Noticias*, Lisbon 25.2.1888. See also Bibliography – Ch7: Assembleia de Republica 1991, *Factos e Documentos*, op.cit.p15.
[39] See: *O Jornal*, and *O Diario*, Lisbon 11.7.1989
[40] See: *Diario de Noticias* Lisbon, 3.3.1990; *Publico* Lisbon 15.3.1990 - recounting the critique of Jean Pierre Catry on behalf of NGO A Paz e Possivel; *Diario de Noticias*, Lisbon 27.3.1990. (See also *Factos e Documentos*, op.cit. pp 406, 409, 415).
[41] Bibliography – Ch5: Lennox.R. 1999. op.cit. p202. Cardinal Ribeiro insisted Costa Lopes be addressed only as 'Father'.

broader pastoral appointment was not encouraged: he was deployed in general parish work. Nor was he participant in the hierarchy's general activity, some of whom considered him to be tainted by Communism.[42] Costa Lopes was alert to the danger that Portuguese as well as Timorese political opportunists were seeking to use him for their own ends. However, the unsettled political climate in Portugal and the divisions within the expatriate community of Timorese in Lisbon frustrated his earnest attempts to urge his people's rights to self-determination and independence.[43] His appeals in the other countries to which he travelled in 1983 and 1984 and at the United Nations Human Rights Commission in Geneva (1984) were arguably more fruitful in the long term.

The Bishops Conference

The bishops of Portugal received a statement written in defence of Mgr Costa Lopes by the priests of the diocese of Dili. This reached them at the time when the Vatican envoy and Church officials in Indonesia were accepting the defamatory accounts of his activity in East Timor which were being promoted by the Military leaders (in reaction to his public denunciation of the human rights violations they were committing). In this appeal, disseminated to Catholic Bishops Conferences throughout the world, the clergy listed the injustices being suffered by their people:

> Moral and physical violence; arbitrary imprisonment; resettlement of whole villages; extra-judicial executions; disappearance of whole families; hunger and disease throughout the territory.[44]

It has to be admitted that the corporate response of the Portuguese hierarchy to this letter, and to the subsequent and persistent appeals made in their own country by Dom Martinho in person was minimal. A year later in March 1984 the Bishops Conference released a Statement declaring 'its living and deep solidarity with the people of this martyred country' and affirming that 'the pain of the Timorese is also the pain of the Church'. In this document the bishops recognised the Timorese 'consciousness of a strongly felt national identity' and went on to declare that:

> To hinder this individuality...signifies not only a physical genocide but also a cultural genocide - this last being more grave because it affects as much the people who survive as those who are dying, and not only the present generations but also those of the future.
> In the Timor drama the Portuguese Church feels involved because of the historic responsibility which, although indirect, the Church had during the appearance of Timor's national consciousness....

> Convinced simultaneously of its divine authority which comes from its specific mission, and of its human authority, which comes from its historic activity, the Church can and should make its voice heard so that the injustices suffered by the Timorese people will cease, and that the Timorese people can, by themselves, in peace and in liberty, determine their own future...

> This is why, while on the one hand we denounce the hateful exploitation which some try to make of the suffering of the Timorese people for the purpose of ideological propaganda, we on the other hand welcome all sincere efforts already undertaken to find a just solution to the problem....

---

[42] Other influential clerics were of this persuasion, e.g. Fr.Jorge Duarte, a former representative for East Timor on the National Assembly. See: Lennox, op.cit. p217.

[43] The self-serving tactics of Abilio Araujo contributed to Dom Martinho's isolation – Bibliography – Ch5: Lennox, 2000, op.cit. p220.

[44] Statement by a Group of Priests in Dili, 13th May 1983. A longer citation is in Ch6.

In particular we embrace the efforts of the Holy See in the actions it has carried out for the relief of the Timorese population and in defence of their human and religious rights...

We appeal to the Portuguese Government...to the Indonesian Government...to international organisations...to the political leaders of Timor in their homeland or in exile...to dedicate their forces to obtaining rapidly and efficiently the end of this painful situation which seems to be lasting forever...

Safeguarding the legitimate interests of each of the parties involved, it should be guaranteed to the Timorese people that they will have continuity as a historic entity, with both self respect and the respect of neighbouring peoples...

Finally we exhort the faithful to pray for the comfort and mercy of God for those in Timor who in one way or another continue to suffer.[45]

This statement clearly acknowledges the special duty of the Church in Portugal to do all it can to bring the injustices being endured by the Timorese to an end with all urgency, and calls for their right to political self-determination and their unique historical identity to be to be respected. But the appeal it makes to governments, international organisations, and Timorese political leaders was unprecedented and was not pursued with any noticeable vigour thereafter. Nor was the Bishops Conference exhortation to faithful Portuguese Catholics given expression in any subsequent national campaigns for action on the Timorese behalf until East Timor's 'Year of Crisis' (1999), although greater interest was shown in individual dioceses after the Santa Cruz Massacre. A further 'Pastoral Note' on the situation in East Timor was published at Fatima on 9th June 1989 occasioned by the pending visit of Pope John Paul II to the territory. This Note did little more than recall the previous Statement to mind and express the hope that the Papal visit would 'contribute to the establishment of justice', and was the least that could have been expected in the circumstances.[46] In 1990 the Bishops Conference rose up to defend itself against the criticisms made in the press that Dom Martinho had died of hunger and neglect.[47] They declared that this allegation was 'injurious' since the former Apostolic Administrator was 'provided with a pension by the Vatican, and was in receipt of other economic supports'. In 1991, after the Santa Cruz Massacre, the bishops added a brief paragraph to the final *communiqué* of their annual Conference (underway at the time) which simply recalled the appeal of their two previous statements for the Timorese right to autonomy and national identity to be protected. Their 'expression of affectionate and fraternal solidarity' was renewed and the hope was again expressed 'for a just solution to the problem which had persisted so sadly over all these years'.[48] One gesture of such 'solidarity' was the arrangements made by the Bishops Conference for East Timorese seminarians to receive free accommodation and tuition - always supposing that the Indonesian government gave the students permission to come to Portugal, which could hardly be presumed. In the Spring of 1996 the chairman for the Conference, Joao Alves, publicised the intention of the bishops to again 'call for the urgent resolution of the [Timor] problem, without forgetting the recognition of the Timorese people's inalienable right to self-determination'.[49] Later that year, Mgr Alves expressed the view of the Conference that the award of the Nobel Peace Prize to bishop Belo and J.Ramos Horta was 'the public and unequivocal acknowledgement of the legitimacy of the East Timor cause'.[50]

---

[45] '*Nota do Conselho Permanente do Episcopado sobre a situacao de Timor Oriental*', Lisbon 28.3.1984. English translation: CCJPD 1993, op.cit. p20-21.

[46] '*Nota Pastoral Sobre Timor Leste*', Fatima 9.6.89. See also: *Journal de Noticias*, Lisbon 15.6.1989; *O Seculo*, Lisbon 20.6.89; *Factos e Documentos*, op.cit.p178

[47] *Publico*, Lisbon 15.3.1990; *Factos e Documentos*, op.cit. p409.

[48] *Conferencia Episcopal Portuguesa - Comunicado Final*, Fatima, 14.11.1991.

[49] *Publico*, Lisbon 15.4.1995; also cited in ETAN Docs, Vol.43, p174.

[50] *Diario de Noticias*, Lisbon 12.10.1996.

The evident paucity of the corporate response of the Bishops Conference met with severe criticism from others within the Church in Portugal and elsewhere,[51] and it was not fully representative of the response of the Portuguese Catholic community - or even of the Bishops - as will be seen. Several reasons can be offered in explanation of the very limited action taken by the hierarchy collectively, but they offer only a partial excuse.

The most pertinent factor was the social and political turmoil in Portugal prevalent at the time of East Timor's aborted decolonisation, the Indonesian invasion and the early years of occupation. The inundation of the metropole by *retournados* from the other 'overseas territories'; the general anxiety over the leftward swing in the transitional government; and the Marxist dimension to the struggles in Mozambique and Angola - all contributed to an ethos of confusion and alarm within the local Church. The poor who needed the attention and assistance of the Church were already numerous in Portugal, and their number increased in this time of economic weakness and political instability. The Timorese issue, with its left wing connotations (FRETILIN was easily, if mistakenly, associated in many minds with FRELIMO in Mozambique and MPLA in Angola) and the internal divisions among the Timorese refugees in Lisbon did not encourage a confident response even among sympathetic Catholics. Besides, the population generally had been discouraged from engaging in political deliberations for a generation.

But in due course Portugal achieved political stability and a stronger economy and the exploitative oppression being suffered by the Timorese in their homeland became manifest - and the very limited attention given to the East Timor issue by the hierarchy is less justifiable. It seems that the Cardinal Patriarch of Lisbon, Antonio Ribeiro, had a significant personal influence upon the restrained nature of the bishops' response. He discouraged any 'speaking out' on this 'political' issue and apparently regarded the situation in East Timor as 'irreversible'.[52] It is of interest to note that the former FRETILIN leader Abilio Araujo met with Cardinal Ribeiro to discuss the East Timor issue. This was at the very time Araujo, whose business interests were benefiting from his pro-integration posture, was urging the Church to support the Jakarta-backed 'Reconciliation Meeting' that he was facilitating in London between East Timorese factions and the Indonesian regime (December 1993).[53] The Cardinal was also under considerable pressure from the Papal Nuncio to Portugal. The Nuncio often intimated that the Holy See was not in favour of the question being raised publicly and placed obstacles in the way of whatever pro-Timorese initiatives were attempted by individual bishops (such as Dom Martins of Setubal) and others.[54] He barred all reference to East Timor in the Portuguese hierarchy's *Ad Limina* reports to the Holy See. In these some allusion could have been made to the situation prevailing in the occupied territory even though the diocese of Dili (since 1976 under the direct administration of the Vatican) was no longer the pastoral responsibility of the Portu-

---

[51] Source: The author's interviews with individual Portuguese bishops and priests engaged in providing for East Timorese welfare or in advocacy of their political rights, and Catholic academics and leaders of pro-Timorese NGOs in Portugal and in other countries.

[52] Fr.Joao Canico *SJ*, P.Maurico de Bastos e Pinho *SDB*, Christiana Cruz (*CDPM*) and Jean-Pierre Catry (*A Paz e Possivel*) - to the author, Lisbon July 1997. Cardinal Ribeiro had also indicated that in his opinion 'the occasion was not propitious to speak on the subject' at the time of the Papal Visit to Portugal (May 1991) - *Publico*, Lisbon 30.3.1991.

[53] *Publico*, Lisbon May 1993 (also cited in ETAN Docs, Vol 22, p82).

[54] On March 13th 1990 the NGO Peace and Justice for East Timor delivered 1025 letters of solidarity to the Church in East Timor to the Nuncio, Mgr Luciano Angeloni, for him to forward by diplomatic channels to the Apostolic Administrator in Dili. The Nuncio accepted only one letter on the grounds that to take all the correspondence 'could be interpreted as a political attitude'. See Bibliography – General (East Timor): Barbedo da Magalhaes, A. 1990, pp155-6 - Fr.Jose Luis Baptista.

guese bishops.[55] Other members of the hierarchy also came under the Nuncio's influence. For example, in 1991 the assistant bishop of Lisbon, Albino Cleto, aligned himself with the Nunciature which had declined (for reasons of 'delicacy') to pass on to the Pope a letter signed by prominent Catholic figures in Portugal calling on him to make a pronouncement in favour of Timorese rights.[56]

Individual Bishops

A few bishops however, and some clergy, manifested their concern for the East Timorese plight in various ways, especially as the situation in Portugal itself stabilised and international concern for a peaceful and lasting resolution of the issue developed. The archbishop of Braga provided seminary education for Timorese students after 1976 (initially the tutelage was led by the former bishop of Dili Jose Ribeiro who resided in Braga after his return to Portugal), and undertook some advocacy of the East Timorese cause.[57] The bishop of Coimbra appealed for a just settlement of the issue during the pilgrimage devotions at Fatima on October 13th 1989 – this was during the Papal visit to Indonesia and East Timor. His words were striking: 'The situation of the Maubere people, despised, humiliated and oppressed, is one of the great crimes of our era'.[58] Jaime Goulart - the former and first bishop of Dili - urged the continuing responsibility of Portugal for the situation in East Timor and compared its invasion by Indonesia with that of Kuwait by Iraq - a position supported by International Law.[59] In a few dioceses a Lenten collection was taken on behalf of East Timorese needs - a humanitarian effort which became promoted by most bishops after the Santa Cruz Massacre (1991) in response to the manifest concern of the lay faithful. In 1997 archbishop Maurilio Gouveia of Evora, where Basileio do Nascimento had studied philosophy and theology and after ordination had administered the pre-seminary, presided over the installation of his former student as the first (titular) bishop in the newly established East Timorese diocese of Baucau, east of Dili.

In later years bishop Januario Torgal Ferreira, together with his co-auxiliary in Lisbon (soon to become Cardinal Patriarch) Jose Policarpo, associated themselves with a request made by the Principals of Oporto and Coimbra Universities and Professor Barbedo de Magalhaes (instigator of the annual symposia *Jornadas de Timor Leste*). This was made to President of the Republic Mario Soares for 'a significant amount of money to be allocated for actions to promote and secure the self-determination of East Timor'.[60] He also endeavoured to win the support of the delegates to the European Bishops Conference (COMECE) at which he represented the Portuguese hierarchy, with only limited success.[61]

---

[55] Januario dos Reis Torgal Ferreira, auxiliary bishop of Lisbon to the author, Lisbon July 1997.
[56] East Timor News, Lisbon 27.5.1991.The Nuncio opined that such a means of communicating with the Pope was indiscreet and inappropriate.
[57] See: *O Comercio do Porto*, 13.9.88, and the author's interview with *UDT* Vice President Melina Pires and Alfredo Silva, Lisbon 1997. Two Timorese priests exercised their ministry in the Archdiocese of Braga.
[58] *O Dia, Diario de Noticias, Jornal de Noticias*, Lisbon, *O Comercio do Porto*, Oporto, 14.10.1989; cited by Fr.B.Q.Alves in Barbedo da Magalhaes, A. 1990, op.cit.p156. However, 'this was Mgr Alves one and only statement [on East Timor]' (Jean Pierre Catry of A Paz e Possivel, to the author Lisbon 1997).
[59] *Diario de Noticias*, Lisbon 16.10.1990 and 17.10.1990; *Factos e Documentos* p353-4.
[60] *Publico*, Lisbon 22.2.1994. Actions included support for Timorese prisoners, the clandestine resistance, refugees, political lobbying, promotion of the Luso-Maubere culture, & dialogue between E Timor, Portugal and Indonesia. (Full text ETAN Docs, Vol.27, p97.)
[61] 'There is no comparison between the response of the European Bishops and that of the American Bishops Conference, although all expressed interest. Many do not know where East Timor is' - Dom Januario, to the author, Lisbon July 1997.

In December 1996 Dom Januario co-signed, along with seventy two other leading public figures in various sectors of Portuguese political and social circles, an Open Letter to the heads of state and government assembled at the OSCE Summit Meeting in Lisbon. This letter called for 'a redoubling of efforts to find a solution to the [Timor] conflict' and urged pressure to effect 'the release of all Timorese political prisoners, an end to arms sales to Indonesia, and the establishment of a permanent UN presence in the territory of East Timor'.[62] Earlier that year, at the time of the opening of the new seminary in Dili, Dom Januario had personally visited East Timor (the first Portuguese bishop to do so in twenty years of Indonesian occupation). He described the situation he encountered as a 'living Hell' and appealed in his homily for the 'establishment of democracy such as was now enjoyed in Portugal'.[63] In 1999, as secretary of the Bishops Conference, Torgal Ferreira denounced 'the abominable massacre' in Liquica and expressed the 'solidarity of the hierarchy with the martyred people of East Timor'.[64] Dom Jose Policarpo, by then Patriarch and head of the Conference, promised mobilisation in favour of the Timorese cause:

> The Portuguese Church is committed to helping the people of Timor. The Episcopal Conference will ask international organisations, the UN in particular, to pressure Indonesia to maintain public order and create the conditions for a free and peaceful consultation process.
> Lisbon's branch of Caritas has already sent five million *escudos* to its Dili counterpart, an example which Dom Jose Policarpo hopes to promote in other dioceses...
> In his message to Dom Ximenes Belo in Dili, Dom Jose expressed spiritual support for all Timorese...several prayer meetings involving youths, university students and parish communities are being organised to pray for peace in East Timor...A special bank account has been set up for public donations. ...Dom Ximenes Belo said he was moved by the speed at which his appeal for help was answered.[65]

In Timor's Year of Crisis the Portuguese hierarchy thus reacted corporately and comprehensively and with commendable (if untypical) zeal and alacrity.

However, the bishop of Setubal, Dom Manuel da Silva Martins, had consistently undertaken a forthright advocacy of the East Timorese cause even though it had been with minimal (if any) support from his peers and was in the face of positive opposition from the Papal Nuncio. Setubal was (and still is) a region with severe social problems. Inspired by Dom Antonio Ferreria Gomes, a former Bishop of Oporto and an 'apostle of the poor'[66], Dom Manuel had been attentive to the needs of his own impoverished people, acquiring the nickname 'the red bishop' for his pains. His efforts compensated in some measure for the alienation from the Church of the local people when the Church had seemed to forget them during its years of alliance with the Salazar regime.

Dom Manuel's principal actions towards a just resolution of the Timor issue were fourfold. He organised a collection of pro-Timorese signatures in the streets of Setubal for presentation at the United States Embassy in Lisbon. He made a presentation on behalf of Pax Christi Portugal at the United Nations Decolonisation Commission in 1987.[67] He disseminated a request for signatures to a letter to UN Secretary General Peres de Cuellar

---

[62] Open Letter to the OSCE Summit, 2 December 1996.

[63] *Publico*, Lisbon 5.2.1996; *Diario de Noticias*, Lisbon 1.2.1996 and 9.2.1996 (See also ETAN Docs Vol 43, p95-98). Details of this visit were provided by Jose Lius Ramos Pinheiro, Information Director of the Catholic radio station *Renascenca* who had accompanied Bishop Torgal Ferreira on the journey - *Diario de Noticias*, 17.2.96

[64] *LUSA*, Macao 7.4.1999.

[65] Reporter, *Radio Renascenca*, Lisbon 29.4.1999.

[66] Bibliography – Ch7: da Silva Martins, M. 1995.

[67] Text (in French) in *Em Timor-Leste a Paz e Possivel*, Lisbon, No 22, October 1987, pp7-8.

to three hundred fellow bishops all over the world.[68] And he made countless statements in the mass media - including, latterly, Radio Vatican itself (when the Holy See's strictures on such comment relaxed somewhat).

Dom Manuel's attempt to collect signatures for the letter to Peres de Cuellar was inspired by bishop Belo's own letter to the Secretary General (which Belo asked him to forward and follow up)[69] and by a collection of 118 episcopal signatures acquired by bishop Soma of Japan. Although he managed to obtain 160 signatures overall only about 6 were provided by the 30-plus Portuguese bishops, and the Vatican Secretary of State Cardinal Casaroli forbade him from sending the letter to the UN Secretary General.[70] Cardinal Casaroli also prohibited him from speaking publicly about the East Timor issue - although this did not deter the indefatigable Dom Manuel da Silva Martins, any more than the pleading of his brother bishops 'not to take initiatives in opposition to Vatican policy'. In addition to giving talks in schools and other institutions, and writing articles for the Press,[71] Dom Manuel contributed to the Fourth Christian Consultation on East Timor held in Portugal in January 1988 at which he forthrightly declared:

> We did not come here for a friend's get-together but came with two deeply human and very noble objectives...
> On the one hand we want to share in the suffering of a people gagged body and soul but which the iniquitous force of cruelty has not managed to kill...
> On the other hand we want to shout out good and loud - because the noise of economic and political interests is loud itself - and say to the civilised world that this cannot go on. This inhuman and shameful situation has lasted long enough...
> The true civilisation is that in which man is the centre and criterion of its concerns... A society, people, country languishes, loses its reasons to really live when it becomes insensitive in the face of violation of these values...
> Peace is not built by force...peace is not the same as a *fait accompli* situation [East Timor claimed as its 27th Province by Indonesia] ...justice is not built by injustice...
> It is necessary to shout together louder: today more than ever before. It is our shouting which makes the powerful tremble most. If we keep quiet Timor will eventually die, but the sin will remain with us.[72]

After the Santa Cruz Massacre the Vatican position modified and the Bishop of Setubal was no longer forbidden to speak out on the Timor issue. But it was clear that the Vatican preferred it when he was silent and the Secretary of State continued to inquire into the contents of his public addresses.[73]

---

[68] Copy on file.

[69] Texts of letter from bishop Belo to Dom Martins 27.6.89, and of Dom Martins to UN Secretary General 6.2.1990 on file with the author.

For Portuguese press comments upon Dom Martin's mediation see: (e.g.) *Diario de* Noticias, Lisbon 13.5. and 17.5.1989; *O Jornal*, Lisbon 2.6.89. Further details in *Factos e Documentos*, op.cit.pp 166, 167, 174.

Belo turned to Dom Martins again for help during the campaign of terror conducted by the Indonesian military in East Timor preceding the planned Portuguese delegation to the territory in 1991 (Kohen, A. 1999, op.cit.p156).

[70] Noted in *Expresso*, Lisbon 7.5.1991.

[71] e.g. *Seara, O Dia* 8.12.1989; *Diario de Noticias*, Lisbon 1.1993 (ETAN Docs Vol 20, p66) cf. also *Factos e Documentos* p166 (14.5.89), p250 (8.12.89) etc.

[72] Address at Fourth Christian Consultation on East Timor, Lisbon 22-24 January, 1988. For full text see Bibliography – Ch8: CCJPD 1993, pp34-5.

[73] Dom Manuel to the author, Setubal July 1997.

Responses of the Laity

Advocacy of East Timorese self-determination and independence within the Church but outside the ranks of the hierarchy was principally undertaken by Catholic members of staff or supporters of determined non-governmental organisations such as *Commissio Para os Direitos do Povo Maubere (CDPM)* and *A Paz e Possivel*.[74] These received the assistance of internal Church networks of communication in acquiring accurate, detailed and current information on the prevailing situation in East Timor. They also experienced most acutely the disappointment and frustration of all those in sympathy with the Timorese cause at the lack of public support forthcoming from the Portuguese bishops both corporately and individually. Catholic members of faculties at the Universities of Coimbra and Oporto, which advocated the human rights of the Timorese as individuals and as a people through the Internet and regular symposia (such as the *Jornadas*) played a most significant role in the gathering of international as well as Portuguese support.[75] Statements of concern were published by the Setubal Diocesan Justice and Peace Commission and the National Commission – whose President also raised the matter with the Pontifical Commission in Rome.[76] Lay Christian organisations such as *O Centro de Reflexio Crista* and *Movimento Cristao Para a Paz* also promoted solidarity with East Timor.[77] Portuguese Christians who had lived in East Timor (the majority being former missionaries) were active in urging justice for the Timorese from the earliest years of the Indonesian occupation.[78] Later, young Timorese exiles won the support of a number of their Portuguese peers who demonstrated with them during the Papal Visit in 1991.[79] Portuguese Catholic students regularly urged action at their annual Congress on the Timorese behalf. For example, in 1989 they appealed for the civil and religious authorities to have greater concern for the question of East Timor. Again, in 1990, they supported the planned Portuguese delegation to the territory, condemned human rights violations perpetrated there by the Indonesian military, and were critical of Portuguese diplomacy on the issue.[80] A year later the Santa Cruz Massacre stirred the Catholic faithful to even greater ardour, hearing as they did the sound of the Timorese

---

[74] The illustrated publications of *A Paz e Possivel* facilitated public understanding of the East Timor issue, e.g. *East Timor: 20 Years of Occupation, 20 Years of Resistance*; *East Timor: Santa Cruz*; *East Timor After Santa Cruz*, Lisbon, Portugal.
The socio-political analyses provided by *CDPM*s 'East Timor Observatory' and posted on their Internet web site supported the work of academics, activists, and journalists.

[75] Bibliography – Ch7: Barbedo de Magalhaes, A. 1995, and 1996.

[76] See: Timor Link, No.1 January 1985, p7; *Comunicado da Comissao Nacional Justica e Paz Acerca de Timor Leste*, Lisbon 21.3.1984; *Factos e Documentos*, op.cit p52 (23.6.1988).

[77] *O Centro de Reflexio Crista* organised a colloquy on 'The Rights of the Timorese in the International Context' in Lisbon 18 November 1988 (*Diario de Lisboa*, 16.11.1988; *Factos e Documentos*, p52) and a 'Campaign of Solidarity with Bishop Belo' in October 1989 (*O Seculo*, Lisbon 25.10.1989).
Movimento O Cristao Para a Paz launched 'A Week of Solidarity with E Timor' in May 1989 (*Diario de Noticias*, 25.5.1989), various initiatives marking 14 years of Indonesian occupation in E Timor in collaboration with the *Associcao Academica de Coimbra* in 1989 (*Jornal de Noticias*, 1.12.1989); and mounted a photographic exhibition at the *Camara Municipal de Coimbra* in 1990 (*Jornal de Noticias*, 11.7.1990).

[78] e.g. In a letter to Pope John Paul II on the eve of his visit to Portugal 12-15 May 1982, cited in *Pro Mundi Vita* 1984, p30. During the papal visit over 1 million pilgrims prayed at Fatima for East Timor. In 1989 a deputation made an approach to Pope John Paul II via the Papal Nuncio, Mgr.Salvatore Asta, expressing their concern over the situation in East Timor (*Factos e Documentos*, p155; *O Independente*, 7.4.1989).

[79] Reuters Lisbon, 10.5.1991; *Diario de Noticias*, 11.5.1991.

[80] *O Comercio do Porto*, 20.9.1989; *Diario de Noticias* 10.9.1990; *Factos e Documentos*, p212, 522.

young people praying in Portuguese as they were murdered by the Indonesian military in full view of the camera. From that time on mounting popular pressure for advocacy of the Timorese cause brought a noticeably more positive response from the Portuguese hierarchy as indeed it did from the politicians.

The efforts of the Catholic laity to provide humanitarian support for the people in East Timor succeeded in reaching the needy largely through the discreet operation of religious orders working in the territory. Foremost among them were the Salesians, to which congregation bishop Belo belonged, and which benefited greatly by the increased profile (and security) given to its work in East Timor by the award of the Nobel Peace Prize to its now internationally famous member. Even aid from the Portuguese government (including pensions to former civil servants) reached the territory by such routes.[81] As noted already, spasmodic and local collections taken in some churches during the earlier years developed into more a regular and national effort after Santa Cruz. Public prayer also gathered momentum, reaching peaks during the Papal visits to Portugal and East Timor, and in later years on significant anniversaries such as November 12th (Santa Cruz), and December 7th (Indonesian invasion).

East Timorese Refugees

The attention given by the Church to the needs of Timorese refugees in Portugal was varied. At first the influx of so many people from the *ultramar* prevented any special attention being given to those from East Timor. In due course what limited efforts were made tended to be by the parish communities in which the exiles came to reside, or which had Timorese pastors. Although several Timorese priests were to take up appointments in Portuguese dioceses only one, Fr.Apollinario Guterres, was given special responsibility for his compatriots.[82] Lay Catholics in non-governmental organisations such as *CDPM* (and indeed some within the government agencies themselves) had a significant role in focusing attention on the shortcomings of government provision for the refugees already described. Regrettably they also had to point out that the Church itself had no agreed policy of welcome or strategy of provision for the Timorese who arrived in Portugal. It was apparent to them that the Timorese experienced perhaps their greatest disillusionment regarding the Metropole in the sad realisation that the Church there lacked the vigour, popular participation and immediate relevance of the one they had known in East Timor. This was especially true for the young Timorese, most of whom soon became alienated.[83] Nonetheless, the help that Catholic parishes did give towards the reception and assimilation of the refugees was appreciated by government social workers as by the Timorese themselves, and it remained important that the Church did not take on a responsibility which belonged in the first instance to the government itself.[84] Amongst educated Catholics, some of those who were not involved in the issue gave as their reason that it was now first and foremost an international matter which was not best served by the

---

[81] Salesian Superior P.Mauricio de Basto e Pinho, to the author, Lisbon July 1997.

[82] At the time of the author's visit (1997) Timorese clergy were appointed as parish priests in the archdiocese of Lisbon (1), archdiocese of Braga (3), diocese of Viama do Castelo (1).

[83] One student lamented: 'neither the State nor the Church in Portugal has any power over what happens in East Timor' - to the author, Coimbra University, July 1997.

[84] Source: Author's interviews with: Christina Cruz & other staff of *CDPM*; Maria Theresa Abrantes & Pasquale Barreto of government agency *CPAISCT*; P.Apollinario Guterres, Timorese chaplain to Timorese community, Lisbon July 1997.
Church institutions that helped with the needs of Timorese refugees included: the parishes of Alfragide and of Camp Grande (Lisbon), Cascais (Carcavelos), and the Gulbenkian Foundation at Fatima which provided support for Timorese national identity and cultural heritage.

Portuguese assuming the greatest responsibility in its settlement. Those who were active in advocacy or in the humanitarian efforts for the Timorese opined to the author that the response of the Church in Portugal was still affected detrimentally by the ethos of apathy or timidity which had developed during the Salazar regime. They also remarked that the institutional Church was generally conservative and not much engaged in social issues even in Portugal itself. Most Portuguese, it was felt, were sympathetic to the plight of the Timorese - but not to the extent of more generous provision being made for the refugees in Portugal itself at the cost of social services to the community as a whole.

The Church in Portugal - an Evaluation

In the estimation of committed members at all its levels of operation the response of the Church in Portugal to the plight of the Timorese people left much to be desired. Strong criticism was forthcoming from bishops such as Dom Manuel of Setubal and Dom Januario of Lisbon and from Portuguese priests struggling under oppression in East Timor or undertaking pastoral ministry in Portugal or elsewhere in the Lusophone Community. It came from members of religious orders charged with - or undertaking of their own volition - action in respect of humanitarian provision for the Timorese and advocacy of their cause. It came from Catholic laity in academic situations, or engaged in the ongoing and determined campaigns of non-governmental organisations, or personally contributing towards the improvement of conditions experienced by Timorese refugees in Portugal. They all pointed to the shortcomings of the Portuguese government's efforts in respect of Timorese welfare, but they also listed the many failures of the Church itself to live up to its own ideals in their regard. 'The Church leadership in Portugal', they said, 'was conservative and timid' in its disposition and 'not committed to serving the needs of the poor - even in its own country, still less elsewhere'. 'The majority of the bishops had shown little interest in the East Timor cause, especially in the political issue but even in matters of humanitarian provision'. Their 'restraint' was in part consequent upon their 'fear of a Communist reassertion in Portugal', but it also amounted to a 'timid subservience to the expectations of the Vatican' in so far as these were urged by the Papal Nuncio to Lisbon.

It was evident that those Church leaders who had been forthright in their concern for the Timorese were the exceptional few who were already involved in matters of social justice on the home front. The clergy who were engaged in the Timorese issue were those who had direct connections with the native people either through the pastoral work of religious orders to which they belonged or because Timorese refugees resided in their localities whose needs were manifest. There were outstanding leaders among the Catholic laity within the institutions of the Church itself (such as its Justice and Peace Commissions) or active in academic circles, student organisations, or within governmental agencies and non-governmental organisations - but the engagement of these relatively few people revealed the disinterest of the many more who were not so committed.

Over the two decades plus of Indonesian rule in East Timor the sympathy for the Timorese plight - always present to some degree among the Catholic faithful - grew, as it did in the Portuguese population at large. This sentiment expressed itself with some national vigour in prayer and action at the times of special events (such as the Papal visits to the country, or the Santa Cruz massacre, or the Nobel Prize awards). But most of the time it was evident only among the people of particular parishes in particular dioceses or on the part of exceptional individuals and families. Concern for the needs of Timorese resident in the country as unprovided political exiles and refugees extended to actual personal sacrifice only by small proportion of Portuguese Catholics. Nonetheless, it can be argued that the increased engagement in the East Timor issue of the institutional Church in Portugal towards the end of the Indonesian occupation was motivated by the growing and active concern of the ordinary faithful. This paralleled the popular pressure in society at large that brought about a more determined effort on the East Timorese behalf by Portuguese politicians.

Applying the criteria derived from the Church's own Social Doctrine the following observations can be made. The Bishops Conference drew attention to the significant contribution the Church had made historically to the Timorese cultural identity but this institution was not engaged in the defence of that identity through a concerted effort of either discreet or public advocacy, or in the collectively organised provision of humanitarian aid. Such enterprises were the initiative of particular religious orders or of individuals, clerical and lay. The social marginalisation and impoverishment of the Timorese in their own land, and indeed in Portugal itself, were not included on the agenda of the Church's national policy. Concern over the Timorese experience of oppression and the denial of their fundamental human rights was not manifest among the Portuguese Church leadership and faithful in a truly corporate way for most of the period that it was suffered. While there were certainly some Church persons who were wholeheartedly engaged in such matters the Church in Portugal as an institution and as a community seemed preoccupied with pressing concerns in its own locality. These included political upheaval, economic difficulties, social instability, the perceived threat of Communism, and - latterly - a crisis of identity consequent upon declining numbers in attendance and a diminishing influence within the national life.

If the Church in Portugal were to be judged in terms of its imitation of the various aspects of Christ's own public ministry a similar conclusion could be drawn. The Church was a 'good *pastor*' in the person of those missionaries who bravely cared for their oppressed people in occupied East Timor *at the risk of life itself*, or who sought to give spiritual and material support to the refugee communities in Portugal. In those bishops, priests, religious and laity who publicly urged the rights of the Timorese to political participation and self-determination and denounced the unjust structures established by the Indonesian regime in East Timor, or the personal abuses carried out by its agents, the Church was both *prophet* and *evangelist*. There were those who ventured into the territory to investigate the reality of the Timorese predicament, or who maintained in Portugal (and elsewhere in Lusophone communities) archives of information received from those who ministered in East Timor. They worked their knowledge into an orderly analysis of the prevailing situation and called for appropriate action in response. In them the Church exercised its ministry of *disciple*: listening carefully, and acting in the light of what was learned. All who engaged in prayer for the Timorese - at Fatima, in the company of the Pope, or in their local parishes and schools, on anniversaries of special significance to the Timorese or as a regular practice, and especially in the Eucharistic celebration - were one with Christ the *intercessor*. But the response of the Church was ambiguous in so far as the exercise of such ministries was not a corporate endeavour shared by all but the work of only some individuals and groups.

In 1980 a Portuguese missionary in East Timor had grieved at 'the silence of the world and of the Church': 'We suffered and died, and nothing was said'. By 1994 he was to assert: 'That has now changed'.[85] Nonetheless, as late as 1992 - that is after the Papal visits to East Timor and (twice) to Portugal, and after the Santa Cruz massacre - Xanana Gusmao was still moved to criticise the Portuguese Church for 'this silence, this indifference, this policy of complicity which is no longer justifiable'. From the mountains of Timor he asked: 'Does the Church in Portugal no longer know how to sing *Herois do Mar*?'[86]

---

[85] Fr.Jose Alves Martins *SJ* to UK bishop Victor Guazzelli in 1994 – author's file.

[86] Portuguese national anthem. Gusmao interviewed by Oscar Mascarenhas in East Timor interior, *Diario de Noticias* 27.9.92.

CHAPTER EIGHT - THE CHURCH IN AUSTRALIA:
DEMANDS AND DIVISIONS

Australia's Relations with Indonesia and East Timor

A very great deal has been written about the role played by successive Australian governments in the story of East Timor's invasion and occupation by Indonesia, and its eventual liberation by the Australian-led military coalition INTERFET. Irrespective of their viewpoint authors commonly draw attention to the supremacy of pragmatism over principle that characterised this role in the years 1974-99. A summary of the most significant elements follows in order to provide a context for the response of the Australian Catholic Church to the East Timorese plight. This includes the reaction to government policy within the Australian media, by non-governmental organisations, commercial enterprises, and by the populace at large.[1]

Security Concerns

National security had been a significant motivation for the federation of Australian colonies into the States of the Commonwealth in 1901. During the Second World War the government feared that the Japanese might use the territory of East Timor as a base for operations against Australia and sent a contingent of some four hundred commandos to disrupt any such development. In February 1942 the Japanese moved to occupy the country with 20,000 troops. The assistance given to the commandos by many East Timorese enabled nearly all of these troops to survive but after their withdrawal in 1943 the Japanese exacted a terrible revenge upon the native inhabitants of whom 60,000 were to perish. Some Timorese retained an almost mystical belief that one day the Australian soldiers, who had promised to return in gratitude, would indeed come again and save them from an even worse oppression.[2]

After the War security was the principal reason for the new immigration policy that encouraged many thousands from mainland Europe to Australia in order to increase the population and so to develop (and defend) the country. The apparent post-war success of Communism in Eastern Europe and in China aroused fresh concerns. With the demise of Britain as the dominant imperial power Australia looked for support to the United States and in no small measure became subject to American foreign policy priorities, at times engaging in their execution. Thus Australia was a military partner of the United States in the Vietnam War and tacitly approved the covert CIA operation against the Indonesian President Sukarno. Canberra also supported the consortium of Western 'development aid' to Suharto's authoritarian and anti- Communist 'New Order' regime.

'Batik Diplomacy'

After twenty years in opposition the Labor Party was returned to power in 1972 under PM Gough Whitlam. His administration averted to the fundamental political importance of Australia's geographical location and was concerned with fostering socio-economic relationships with countries of the region. Significant immigration from Asian countries was to follow. In particular a positive liaison with Indonesia was encouraged in a policy of so-called 'Batik diplomacy'. Besides recognising the importance of Indonesia's role in preventing the spread of Communism in the region, Australia also acknowledged - along with other Western countries - the capacity of the *Orde Baru* to impose a political stability upon the widespread archipelago that was conducive to profitable investment and trade. The regime in

---

[1] See Bibliography – General (East Timor): Krieger, H.1995 – Index, & Ch 6, 7, 8; ETAN Documents, *passim*; etc.; and Bibliography – Ch8.
[2] See Bibliography – Ch5: Gunn, G. 1998, pp223-239; Bibliography – General (East Timor): Dunn, J. 1996, pp19-21; Bibliography – Ch8: Callinan, B. 1953 & 1985.

Jakarta was also perceived as a welcome ally in developing fruitful relations with all the countries of ASEAN.

Strategic Option

In August 1975, while the civil war provoked by the Indonesian *Operasi Komodo* was raging in East Timor, Australia's ambassador to Jakarta, Richard Woolcott, cabled his advice to Canberra. He noted the 'interest' of the Defence department in the developing situation – and drew attention to that of the Department of Minerals and Energy. Substantial mineral resources lay within an area beneath the Timor Sea for which borders had yet to be defined – the 'Timor Gap'. Woolcott suggested that negotiations delineating the borders could be undertaken more easily with Indonesia than with Portugal or an independent East Timor and recommended the government 'leave events to take their course'. He continued:

> If and when Indonesia does intervene we should act in a way designed to minimise the public impact in Australia and show privately understanding to Indonesia of their problems. I know I am recommending a pragmatic rather than a principled stand but that is what national interest and foreign policy is all about.[3]

This advice, which Woolcott was to repeat and persistently defend, evidently held sway.[4] Canberra's lack of reaction to the murder at Balibo in East Timor in October 1975 of several Australian journalists who were attempting to report on the developing conflict already indicated which direction the government would take.[5] The complicity of Whitlam's Labor administration with the Indonesian project was even more evident on the part of the Liberal-Country coalition after they took office with Malcolm Fraser as PM at the end of 1975 - despite their unease over the bloody way in which Indonesia was set on taking control in East Timor. It was Fraser's government that was the first to give *de facto* recognition (12th January 1978) to Indonesian rule in the territory they had occupied. While in opposition the Labor Party challenged this position but after Labor were returned to power in 1983 with Bob Hawke as PM Canberra awarded Indonesia's annexation of East Timor *de iure* status (18th August 1985). Such recognition was unique among nations of the Western alliance, inconsistent with Australian policy in respect of other comparable situations, and in contravention of the International Law that Australia had itself been instrumental in establishing.[6] In 1989 Labor foreign minister Gareth Evans was to conclude the Timor Gap Treaty which shared the maritime mineral resources of the occupied country between Indonesia and Australia. Hawke's Labor successor PM Paul Keating pursued with even greater zeal the perceived benefits of the Canberra-Jakarta liaison through new commitments in economic and security co-operation. When the Liberal-Country coalition was returned to power in 1996 under the leadership of John Howard - a former senior member of the Fraser government - the acceptance of East Timor's 'integration' into Indonesia was again pronounced 'irreversible'. It was determined that concerns about the situation in the half-island territory should not to be allowed to 'undermine the broader relationship'.[7] Politicians

---

[3] Bibliography – Ch8: Munster, G & Walsh, R. 1980, p197f.

[4] In January 1976, see Munster and Walsh, 1980, op.cit. Thereafter see (e.g.) 'Myths and realities in our approach to Indonesia', R.Woolcott, address to The Sydney Institute, 26.5.1992; and 'Jakarta must deal with own issues', by Michael Day, The Western Australian, 5.3.1997; 'East Timor policy was right for the time', R.Woolcott, The Age, 25.9.2000.

[5] See Bibliography – General (East Timor): Dunn, J. 1996, op.cit.pp206-222; 'The Balibo Murders: Balibo and beyond: an international cover-up', by Hugh Dowson in Retboll, T.1998 pp44-55; Horta, J.R. 1987, p72-4; ETAN Docs Vol. 40pp6-14.

[6] See Bibliography – Ch3: CIIR/IPJET 1995, Ch5, and 13 - 15.

[7] See (eg): 'Australia's PM defends attitude to Indonesia', ABC International News, Sydney, 13.6.97; 'Downer tells Horta Australia will not review its policy on E Timor', Antara (Jakarta) 17.2.1997.

raised objections in respect of the pro-Indonesia policy when they were in opposition[8] but successive governments - dissenting voices notwithstanding[9] – persisted in the same strategy. In order to sustain good relations with Indonesia evidence of the severe oppression of the East Timorese people was persistently contradicted, belittled or rejected altogether.[10] Ministers dwelt on what they considered to be the 'positive outcomes' of East Timor's 'integration'.

The government option in favour of the perceived 'national interest' had drastic consequences for the people of East Timor. It created serious difficulties for the Resistance.[11] Moreover, its backing of Indonesia's policies in the territory presented a considerable obstacle to the organisation of international support on the East Timorese behalf. Thus Australia obstructed a mission of inquiry by a UN envoy in 1976 and provided substantial development aid to Indonesia along with arms supplies and military training for *ABRI*. Government delegates offered diplomatic support for Jakarta's policy in various domestic and international forums. At the United Nations Australia's diplomats steadily withdrew their support for the resolutions pertaining to Indonesia's withdrawal from the country it had illegally occupied and annexed and instead became apologists for the 'fact' of Indonesian rule over the territory.[12] The countries of the Western alliance looked to Canberra for some guidance as to the stance they should adopt and were urged to follow its lead and exercise restraint in any criticism of Jakarta's rule in East Timor. ASEAN countries already undertook a certain loyalty to each other and this was given a boost in respect of Indonesia's East Timor project by Australia's sympathetic attitude towards Jakarta's 'integration' of the territory.

Canberra's intransigent attitude also inhibited the growth of support for the East Timorese cause among ordinary Australians, most of whom were at first in ignorance of and/or uninterested in the issue (one geographically remote except for people living in the Northern Territory). At the critical period of November-December 1975 Australians were preoccupied with a domestic political/constitutional crisis as the Senate withheld supply from Whitlam's Labor government and a dissolution of both houses was ordered by the Governor General. There were relatively few people who were well informed and active in their efforts to defend the East Timorese from the pending invasion of their homeland and then from the oppressive occupation of it.[13] They had to contend with a campaign of erroneous comment and misinformation provided not only by Indonesian diplomats and government agencies but also by articulate and influential fellow citizens who supported Canberra's policy for ideological reasons, from military concerns, or out of commercial interest. Mass media accounts of the situation in East Timor were much influenced by the so-called 'Jakarta-Lobby'

---

[8] The Labor caucus urged E Timorese independence and a due process of self-determination in March 1975, and the Party agreed a strongly pro-Timorese manifesto in 1982.

[9] Some joined the international lobbying group Parliamentarians for East Timor (PET).

[10] For examples see Bibliography – General (East Timor): Dunn, J.1996, op.cit., Ch 7 (pp117-145) and Ch 12; Gunn, G.C.1994, Ch 4, 5 & 7. The defence of the Canberra-Jakarta relationship persisted even during the 1999 post ballot mayhem perpetrated by TNI and its proxy militias - 'See no Evil', Kerry Brewster for SBS 'Dateline', 16.5.2001.

[11] e.g. The Fraser government obstructed medical provisions to E.Timor and confiscated the Fretilin radio equipment in Darwin which was conveying a non-Indonesian account of the military confrontation and the conditions being endured by the people. Falintil suffered from Canberra's pressure upon Radio Australia to reduce its coverage of Timor. (See Bibliography – General (East Timor): Paulino Gama, 'The War in the Hills, 1975-85: a Fretilin commander remembers', in Carey, P. & Carter Bentley, G., 1995, p102).

[12] See Bibliography – General (East Timor): Krieger, H. 1995, op.cit., pp xxv-xxvi, 77-8, 104-5, 134-5, 152, 163, 337-340; Horta, J.R., 1987, op.cit. pp43-4, 75-83, 110, 115, 129-132.

[13] Informed people included members of the Campaign for an Independent East Timor (CIET) and of the Australia East Timor Association (AETA). The Australian Congress of Trade Unions urged the East Timorese right to self-determination after its Executive Decision 19.2.1976.

which was active in the Indonesia-Australia Institute and academic circles.[14] The Australia-Indonesia Business Co-operation Committee (AIBCC), founded in 1971 to promote trade and investment with Indonesia, continually urged support for Jakarta's East Timor policy during the key period 1975-76.[15] Indeed, there were many business links between the two countries.[16] As respected analysts have remarked, what really concerned many of the Australian elite 'was not reality but realty'[17]; in Australian foreign policy on this issue 'law, principle - even mere fact - was irrelevant.'[18]

However, as authenticated reports of East Timorese sufferings began to accumulate, and especially after the Santa Cruz massacre in 1991, a popular movement for bringing an end to the violations of East Timorese human rights gathered momentum.[19] Existing non-governmental organisations promoted the cause and new groups emerged which gave high profile to the fundamental deprivation of the Timorese right to political self-determination.[20] Among the most forthright critics were a few former members of 'Sparrow Force', the contingent of commandos whose survival in East Timor during World War II had depended upon the support of Timorese villagers and who were ashamed at Australia's betrayal of former 'mates'. Foremost among them was Paddy Kenneally, still campaigning as an octogenarian.[21]

Some within the media community had been disturbed by the murder of fellow journalists at Balibo in October 1975, and were stirred by reports of the distressful situation in East Timor emanating via Church sources, to attempt further investigation. The uncovering of the oppression in East Timor - and of the corruption of the Suharto regime - by reporters such as Jill Jolliffe, Rod Norland, David Jenkins and Lindsay Murdoch, had some significant effect upon international opinion.[22] Robert Domm's interview with Xanana Gusmao in 1990, broadcast by radio from the Resistance leader's mountain hide-away was especially important in this respect.[23] But all too often, even after the Santa Cruz Massacre, the Australian media

---

[14] e.g.. The Lobby established by the government 1989 included journalists such as Milton Osborne, Patrick Walters, Greg Sheridan and ANU economics professor H.W.Arndt. See Bibliography – General (East Timor): Gunn 1994, op.cit.pp135-40; Bibliography – Ch8: Walsh, P. 1981.

[15] See: Walsh, P. 1981, op.cit. p17.
[16] See: 'Australian Business Links with Indonesia', Newcastle Trades Hall Research Group for AETA (Queensland) - June 1977.
[17] Bibliography – General (East Timor): Dunn, J. 1996, p346.
[18] Bibliography – General (East Timor): Chomsky, N. 1996, Ch.8, p212.
[19] See (e.g.) Bibliography – Ch2: Aditjondro, G. 1994, p17.

[20] e.g.: Australians for a Free East Timor; Action in Solidarity with East Timor and Indonesia; East Timor Action Coalition; East Timor Human Rights Centre; East Timor Foundation; East Timor International Support Centre; East Timor Justice Lobby; East Timor Relief Association; Friends of East Timor; Hobart East Timor Committee; Timor Aid for Children; University Students for East Timor. NGOs with more general purposes also took up the Timorese cause or brought to it a renewed vigour, e.g. Australian Council for Overseas Aid; Australian Forum of Human Rights Organisations; Community Aid Abroad; Australian Campaign Against the Arms Trade; Campaign Against Militarism; Australian Anarchists; Australian People for Health, Education and Development Abroad.

[21] See Bibliography – Ch2: Turner, M.1992, pp13f, 60f, 198f. cf. Bibliography – General (East Timor): Dunn, J. 1996, op.cit. pp141-2, 232. Meanwhile RSL member B.J.Callinan had urged E Timor's 'integration', see Bibliography – Ch8: Walsh, P. 1981, op.cit. p19.
[22] See Bibliography – General (East Timor): Gunn, G.C.1994, op.cit. Ch 6 & 7; Retboll, T.(ed) 1980, and 1984.
[23] Full text in: 'East Timor: Keeping the Flame of Freedom Alive', ACFOA Development Dossier No29, Feb.1991 pp17-29; for Domm's own account see Bibliography – General (East Timor): Aarons, M. & Domm, R. 1992, pp55-59.

capitulated to the government pressure that set the parameters of acceptable debate. The plight of the East Timorese was considered to be of less importance than sustaining good relations with Jakarta.[24] In due course the government's response to the circumstances of the several thousand Timorese refugees in Australia - who had fled the civil war and the Indonesian invasion and occupation - came under increasing public scrutiny and criticism.[25] When the Immigration Authority argued (after 1995) that the responsibility for looking after the most recent wave of escapees lay upon Portugal a determination grew among members of the general public to act in civil disobedience and offer 'sanctuary' to these exiles in their own homes and premises.

However, circumstances were to change. The Australian public was outraged at the malevolent response by the Indonesian military and their proxy militias to the outcome of the 'popular consultation' organised under UN auspices in 1999. Severe pressure was then put upon John Howard's government - which had already supported interim Indonesian President Habibie's proposal for a referendum on 'autonomy or independence' and had formally recognised its result. At last Canberra gave the fullest practical support to East Timorese independence by authorising Australian leadership of INTERFET and by subsequent military, civilian and financial assistance to the United Nations Transitional Authority for East Timor.[26] This *volte face*, which had a negative effect upon Canberra-Jakarta relations, had been encouraged by Washington which saw the resolution of the issue as of key importance for Indonesian and therefore regional stability, and thus in the military and commercial interests of the United States.

The pragmatic disposition of the government towards the Indonesian take-over in East Timor, the interests of big business in sustaining harmonious relations between Australia and Indonesia, and the support of the 'integration' by many in the mass media had all impacted upon the response of the Australian Catholic Church. Besides these factors the Church was already beset by other pressing demands and was in a state of considerable internal division.[27]

The Response of the Australian Catholic Church to the East Timorese plight

Demands upon the Church

After World War II belief in God had declined and consequently so had trust in the authority of religious teachings and in Church leaders who urged their prescriptions. Many Australians - whose forebears had been inspired by liberal dreams as much as by a Christian vision - adopted a moral relativism. Growing affluence had encouraged the emergence in Australian society of consumerist and hedonistic attitudes. But not all citizens had benefited from the prosperity and there was considerable inequality of income and of service. In the 1980s two million out of a population of sixteen million were to fall below the poverty line, and in the 1990s homelessness and unemployment became widespread. The break-up of family life, an increase of drug abuse especially among the young, and a growing national dependency upon income from gambling evidenced serious social sickness.[28] The Church endeavoured to respond in practical ways to the various social problems while at the same time engaging in the vigorous defence of absolute principles in contentious moral issues such as abortion, euthanasia and various complex bio-ethical dilemmas. As a result, other important matters of social justice whether domestic or foreign – and for Australians the

---

[24] Bibliography – General (East Timor): Gunn, G.C. 1997, pp163-4, 198-200; for further detail see Bibliography – Ch3: Tiffen, R. 2001.

[25] See: Thatcher, P.1992, 'Timorese Refugees in Australia - How, When and Who'. Paper to Seminar of the Centre for Migrant and Intercultural Studies, Monash University, June 19th.

[26] See: *East Timor in Transition 1998-2000,* DFAT, Canberra, July 2001.

[27] Bibliography – Ch8: O'Farrell, P. 1977; Campion, E. 1987.

[28] See: 'New Deal', by Roy Eccleston, The Weekend Australian Focus, May 2-3, 1998.

welfare of the East Timorese is both – had to compete for the attention of the Catholic community.

There were also challenges arising from within the national Church. Fifty per cent of the 2.5 million immigrants who arrived in Australia after the Second World War were Catholics. Many of them were poor, and all were in need of the Church's ministrations not least in the field of education. With vigorous Catholic traditions of their own they were to prove an important factor in diminishing the strongly Irish character of the Australian Church which had developed during the latter part of the 19th century (despite the fact that by then one in four Catholics had been Australian born).[29] The Church's cohesiveness was severely tested and, having to strain its resources to meet basic demands, it tended to pragmatism with little opportunity for reflection on the nature and manner of its mission.

Moreover the Church was attending to the far-reaching implications of the Second Vatican Council (1962-5) and experiencing a time of considerable confusion and disarray in its efforts to respond appropriately.[30] Apathy had characterised the greater part of the Australian Catholic laity from earliest times. The strong influence of Irish Catholicism had persisted until the 1960s and had not helped to overcome this demeanour. Absolute episcopal power, clerical domination, lay subservience, and the separation of religion ('a private matter') from public affairs was a common feature. Earlier efforts to integrate the Church into Australian society had failed and the community had settled into a comfortable isolationism - from which it was now to be wrested.[31] Vatican II called for the development of new relationships - within the Church, with other Christian communities, with other religions, and with the world at large - and stimulated wide-ranging intellectual debate within the Australian Church, as elsewhere. In Australia a particularly important subject of dispute was the locus and manner of exercising authority in the Church, and the relationship between religion and politics - in particular the appropriate manner in which to effect the Church's Social Doctrine. Unfortunately, rising printing costs caused the cessation of a number of popular Catholic publications which might have assisted in the dissemination of information and encouraged more open discussion of sensitive issues.

In the aftermath of the Council there was a significant drop in the number of priests and religious in Australia as fewer felt called to such a life and many others withdrew from it. The number attending Sunday Mass (and the income generated thereby) was also to fall significantly after Vatican II. On the other hand, the involvement of the Australian Church in relief and development operations overseas which had begun after World War II was stimulated by the Council and by the recent Papal Social Encyclicals. Australian Catholic Relief (ACR), a lay initiative in Adelaide in the early 1960s, launched an annual Lenten Appeal - 'Project Compassion' - which became a considerable national Catholic effort funding many projects. ACR was to have a significant role regarding East Timorese welfare, as will be elaborated. There was also a positive aspect to the withdrawals from the priesthood and religious congregations – and to the disengagement of so many religious from Catholic schools. Other areas of the Church's work were to benefit from the influx of such capable men and women. This included its response to situations of social injustice – such as the plight of the people of East Timor.

---

[29] e.g. Large groups of Lebanese Catholics who cherished their own heritage; 350,000 Italians whose style of Catholic practice contrasted with those raised in the imported Irish tradition; 100,000 Vietnamese Catholics arrived in the 1970s with an oriental interpretation.

[30] See Bibliography – General (Theology): 'The Effect of the Council on World Catholicism: Australia and New Zealand', Isichei, E. in Hastings, A. 1991.

[31] Bibliography – Ch8: O'Farrell, P. 1977, op.cit.Ch.4.

Divisions within the Church

There were serious divisions within the ecclesial community which were to make a coherent and unified response to the East Timor issue very difficult. These contentions had their roots in the history of the Catholic Church in Australia, but especially in events within its recent past to which it is necessary to give preliminary attention.

A certain level of uniformity in the Australian Church had been brought about by its hibernicisation but the bishops had remained assertively autonomous in their own dioceses. Furthermore, the Vatican option in favour of provincial seminaries rather than a national institution had reinforced the competitiveness between states and capital cities which had already emerged and which was to become especially significant in respect of the rivalry between Melbourne (Victoria) and Sydney (New South Wales). In Melbourne the formidable Dr.Mannix (archbishop from 1913-63) had promoted Catholic intellectual life, afforded a remarkable autonomy to the lay apostolate, and encouraged lay engagement with Catholic Social Doctrine. In contrast, Cardinal Moran (1884-1911) and his successors in Sydney (Kelly from 1911, and Australian-born Gilroy from 1940) were suspicious of or uninterested in matters intellectual and generally sustained the clerical domination characteristic of the imported Irish Church. These factors lay beneath the damaging controversies which were to occur in the 1950s and which were to persist for years afterwards and significantly affect the Catholic response to the East Timor issue.

In the 1930s the Spanish Civil War had aroused anxiety among Australian Catholics about world affairs, in particular the perceived menace of Communism to the nation as a whole and for the threat it posed to the institutions and life of the Catholic Church. This led the Australian hierarchy at their 4th Plenary Council in 1937 to set up a National Secretariat of Catholic Action. They appointed Bob Santamaria as one of two full-time lay administrators and several practical initiatives were soon underway, including annual Social Justice Statements drafted for the Bishops Conference by Santamaria himself.[32] In due course Santamaria asked the bishops for moral and financial support to establish the Catholic Social Studies Movement (CSSM - usually referred to as 'The Movement'). Its aim was to contend with Communism by becoming assertive in the Australian Trades Unions and through them upon the Australian Labor Party (ALP). CSSM became sensitive to all signs of 'leftward leaning' and, after the Communists seized power in China in 1949, addressed itself to the matter of Australian foreign and defence policies and became critical of the positions adopted by Labor leader Dr.Evatt. Concerned about his own political future, Evatt claimed (in 1954) that the Catholic Church (via the Movement) was plotting control of the Labor Party and of future Australian government. This blatant appeal to sectarian sentiment caused a political explosion. It effected the re-election of Evatt, but was to lead to a split in the Labor Party that kept it out of office for twenty years. Santamaria played a significant role in the immediate creation of the Democratic Labor Party for those disaffected with the ALP. With some success he called his fellow believers to join him in order to fulfil their religious obligation to put Catholic Social Doctrine into practice.

This issue led to profound and lasting divisions within the Church as a whole. In the first instance the disagreement had been over how best to fight Communism - from within or from outside the ALP. But other concerns related to the way in which the Church should operate in an increasingly secular society, and with whom final authority rested. Santamaria's attempt to change the existing social order by an assertion of the principles of Catholic Social Doctrine was rejected by many other Catholics who regarded such a programme as amounting to an inappropriate religious imperialism. Some of the hierarchy were also ill at ease with the degree of autonomy Santamaria claimed as proper for what he understood to be a lay initiative in the lay domain. At the deepest level the conflict was one between a reforming sect (the

---

[32] Bibliography – Ch8: Hogan, M. (ed), 1990.

Movement) and a conservative Church anxious to become integrated into society. The bishops, with the rest of the Church in Australia, were split, on roughly geographical lines: Victoria (Melbourne), Tasmania and Western Australia opposed by New South Wales (Sydney), Queensland and South Australia. Concerned over the very public divisions among the Australian bishops, Rome adjudicated that CSSM should confine itself to spiritual and moral formation while reiterating the obligation upon the laity to act within trades unions and the political arena to promote Catholic doctrine and combat Communism. Santamaria judged this Roman prescription to be self-contradictory and certainly unhelpful to his project. He determined that in order to act effectively it was necessary to establish an entirely lay organisation which would bring Catholic teaching to bear but not be subject to episcopal authority or dependent upon Church support, be that moral or financial. Accordingly, in December 1957 he established the National Civic Council (NCC) to take up the fight against Communism and to urge the adoption of Catholic principles for the benefit of Australian society. This was to be done via Catholic membership of public organisations, use of the media, and in the halls of academe.[33] But the legacy of acrimony and disunity persisted within the Church at all levels and, along with the activity of the NCC, was to have a direct and considerable influence upon the reaction of Catholics to the events taking place in East Timor.

Divergent views on policy

As an institution the Church in Australia cannot be said to have had a coherent and unified policy in respect of the people of East Timor at any stage. The bishops themselves had different viewpoints, and various perceptions were evident within the ecclesiastical agencies that addressed the matter on their behalf or independently of them, and among the laity as a whole. Thus segments within the Church aligned with Australian government policy, some remained idle, while others were highly committed to a just and peaceful resolution of the issue.

There was a general concern within the Catholic community to maintain positive relations with the government – it was felt that the Church's contribution to the resolution of social issues must be exercised judiciously if it was to be effective at all. The Church existed in a secular setting, and there were many Catholics who, for precisely this reason, considered it imprudent for the Church to press its perceived moral authority too strongly. Thus, determining the most appropriate response to the East Timorese plight proved problematical. Was it best to 'make a noise' or pursue 'gentle diplomacy'? How could a non-partisan disposition be sustained while giving practical support to the needy through humanitarian aid and development projects? Was it possible to become engaged in the issue without being ideologically drawn, or involved in day to day political struggles? Could an effective moral lead be given through statements of principle alone?[34]

Events in East Timor became the concern of Australians generally and of Catholics in particular when the political revolution in Portugal in 1974 aroused anxiety about the character of the regime which would develop both there and in the former Portuguese colony three hundred miles to the north of Darwin. The left-leaning disposition of the transitional government in Lisbon disturbed the anti-Communist constituency marshalled by Bob Santamaria whose accounts of the situation developing in the metropole and beyond were disseminated via the journal of his National Civic Council, *News Weekly*.[35] When East

---

[33] See Bibliography – Ch8: O'Farrell, P.1977, op.cit. pp392-403; Campion, E. 1988, op.cit., pp165-170; Henderson, G. 1982; Santamaria, B.A.1997.

[34] Members of the hierarchy, officers of Church agencies, clergy and laity to the author - Darwin, Melbourne, Sydney, Canberra & Brisbane, August - September 1997.

[35] At this time *News Weekly* had a circulation of some 18,000 across the continent, a significant number in proportion to the overall population. /Note continues...

Timorese students returning from Lisbon brought a more extreme left-wing dimension to the FRETILIN party (albeit temporary and of limited penetration) this development was covered by *News Weekly* with the alarmist zeal born in the 'Movement' of the 1950s. Bishop Riberio's sentiments in respect of FRETILIN were grist for *News Weekly's* mill as were the arrival in Darwin of pro-UDT East Timorese refugees fleeing the civil war in August 1975. In due course the (mis)perceptions of the bishops of Atambua and of Kupang in West Timor, who (as already noted) were subject to Indonesian propaganda, also reached concerned Australian Catholics and held considerable sway with the Australian hierarchy - despite being challenged by officers of both Australian Catholic Relief and the Catholic Commission for Justice and Peace (CCJP).

Australian Catholic Relief

Between 1975 and 1994 ACR generated nearly half a million Australian dollars for East Timorese relief and rehabilitation work via its annual 'Project Compassion' and other special appeals. In later years ACR and its successor Caritas Australia concentrated on giving support to practical development projects in the territory. This included funding such projects, initially via Caritas Indonesia (LPPS) and subsequently via Caritas Dili when it was established, and also giving necessary management support by acting as a 'consultancy'. ACR/Caritas also engaged in the dissemination of information about the situation in East Timor, and in some discreet advocacy of the East Timorese cause especially via its sister organisations or other agencies engaged in related work.[36] Such practical emphasis and discretion had proved to be necessary in surmounting the difficulties that arose of which the following are some early examples.

In 1976, responding to the request of the Bishops Conference, ACR sought to provide relief supplies to the people of East Timor then in the throes of an invasion. The Indonesian regime presented many obstacles to this provision - mainly by stipulating that the aid be channelled through Indonesian organisations (and thereby exercising control over its distribution). In ACR's view the pro-Indonesia stance adopted by the Australian government was not helpful in this matter and the agency felt that Canberra should hold back from formally recognising the annexation and urge instead a valid act of Timorese political self-determination.[37] ACR was also concerned about allegations of the partisanship of some members of the Australian hierarchy that had been made by the bishop of Atambua,[38] and was determined to avoid even perceived bias. Despite such efforts ACR was castigated (along with CCJP) by former PM Gough Whitlam for circulating the warnings given by Mgr Costa Lopes of Dili late in 1981 about impending famine in East Timor.[39] Considerable publicity was given to this clash of views, and Bob Santamaria accused ACR of 'funding Communists'.[40] But the agency's chairman bishop John Gerry strongly defended ACR's action in making public the information it had 'received from reliable sources': it was 'a voice for the

---

Note continued/....
In 1974 articles concerning the spread of international Communism appeared regularly. In 1975 they began in respect of Portugal (February) and East Timor (March) and were to continue on a very regular basis with a considerable influence in and beyond the Church.

[36] Letters from ACR archives – copies on file with the author.
[37] National ACR Committee, Meeting Notes, Nov.1976 - copy on file.
[38] See: 'Notes prepared for the Episcopal Committee for Development and Peace/National Committee of ACR', by Wm.C.Byrne then ACR National Director, 9.3.1978 - ACR archives.
[39] Whitlam voiced his criticism to the Senate Standing Committee on Foreign Affairs and Defence on May 14th 1982 after a short visit to East Timor under the guidance of Indonesian authorities in March. ACR had made its own submission to the Committee on March 30th.
[40] Bishop John Gerry to the author, Brisbane Sept. 1997.

powerless'. He emphasised that in doing so ACR had 'not been motivated by any ideological consideration', sentiments echoed by then National Director Michael Whiteley.[41] But for some time thereafter ACR opted to give minimal coverage to its East Timor projects in its annual 'Project Compassion' information materials.

Shortly after the Santa Cruz Massacre (November 11th 1991) Michael Whiteley participated in a short visit to the territory. He subsequently reported on the atmosphere of repression, the possibility of limited local autonomy as a political solution, the serious economic plight of the native people, their poor health, the ineffective and inappropriate education provision, and the shortcomings of the local Church. The report was to lead to the development (jointly with LPPS) of Caritas Dili with the pledge of funds to assist with the training of local 'motivators', and proposals for collaborative effort with Australian government agencies to feed children and advance the training of teachers.[42] ACR would also continue to urge the Australian government to keep up its diplomatic pressure on Indonesia to pay heed to East Timorese human rights.[43]

In 1995 ACR reviewed its East Timor partnership. It resolved (in April 1996) to support individual human development projects via Caritas Dili and assist in the monitoring of the human rights situation from outside East Timor. It also decided to continue to further Australian-based advocacy and education on East Timor issues, encourage an interagency gathering of Catholic agencies from various countries which were attempting to support human development in East Timor; and explore opportunities for AusAID (i.e. government) funding. In July 1996 the agency changed its name to Caritas Australia (CA) to emphasise its links with *Caritas Internationalis*.[44]

CA avoided becoming identified with campaigning issues 'which would only inflame the Bishops Conference and enrage the government' and engaged in non-partisan practical projects.[45] The importance, in matters of social justice, of achieving positive working relationships with large commercial companies, now with considerable power and influence, was also emphasised. Significantly, there seems to have been no public criticism by CA of the Timor Gap Treaty – despite its illegality according to International Law[46] - or of the plans of Australian oil companies (among others) to exploit this maritime area's mineral resources. Nor did the operation of British Aerospace in Australia face any public challenge from this agency of the Church. However, officers of Caritas Australia did feel it necessary and appropriate to align with and encourage collaboration between those social agencies, pro-democracy movements, women's groups, and other associations of ordinary people who, acting together, could effect the desired socio-political reform in both Indonesia and East Timor. CA did not set its sights upon the earliest achievement of political Independence for

---

[41] Statement of bishop John Gerry, May 1982. Whiteley declared he was pleased that the publicity had resulted in further aid to East Timor. Documents, ACR archives.

[42] Michael Whiteley, ACR National Director, 'Report on Visit to East Timor December 15-17, 1991'. ACR archives, 2.1.92. Citations from the report in an article by Tom Hyland for The Age, 13.4.92 (in ETAN docs Vol 12 p52).

[43] e.g. On January 6th 1992 ACR Director M. Whiteley wrote to FM Gareth Evans expressing concern over the Military interrogation of Fr.Ricardo da Silva, Vicar General of Diocese of Dili and asking for the government to make representations to the Indonesian authorities.

[44] ACR established in East Timor a Rural Development Programme in partnership with Caritas Dili, and in Australia gave financial support to Christians in Solidarity with East Timor (CISET); the Mary McKillop Foundation for East Timorese (MMFET); and the East Timor Human Rights Centre (ETHRC), Melbourne. CI is the network of 146 autonomous Catholic aid and development agencies active in 194 countries around the world, e.g. CAFOD in the UK.

[45] Tom Storey, Caritas Australia Executive Director, to the author, Sydney Sept. 1997.

[46] See: Bibliography - General (East Timor): Krieger, H.1995, op.cit. Ch7 & 8; Bibliography – Ch3: CIIR/IPJET 1995, Ch12 &13.

East Timor for which it felt - with good reason - the people were ill prepared and which 'could prove to be an aggravation rather than a solution of their problems'. It was determined to 'encourage real dialogue between all concerned so that the most appropriate political arrangement should be arrived at steadily and with proper participation' - the position adopted also by bishop Belo.[47] With hindsight the wisdom of this course of action was evident. When the rapid events of 1999 made such aspirations obsolete, CA accepted the task of heading up the co-operation between sister agencies in the international Caritas network. It was also ready give whatever assistance it could to other non-governmental organisations seeking to serve the varied and pressing needs of the traumatised people of East Timor.

The Catholic Commission for Justice and Peace

In emulation of the Pontifical Commission for Justice and Peace the Australian hierarchy set up its own national organisation in 1972. In 1976 this became the Catholic Commission for Justice and Peace (CCJP) and spearheaded a renewed concern with social and political thinking in Church circles. But from the outset this lay-led organisation suffered from the conflicts within the Australian Church - the very decision to locate the Commission's headquarters in Sydney in preference to Melbourne suggested a desire on the part of some of the bishops for caution and close supervision.

The Liberal-Country coalition government of Malcolm Fraser did not take kindly to the social analysis and critique presented in CCJP's annual Social Justice Statements,[48] and Bob Santamaria and his NCC supporters were hypersensitive to the malevolent influence of Marxism that they perceived within the Commission's political commentary and policy recommendations.[49] They were joined by other Catholics influenced by the New Right theology exemplified by Michael Novak in the USA with its support of individual freedom and free enterprise.[50] Communist victories in Asia, especially in Vietnam where Australians had been militarily involved, reawakened the fears that had subsided in Catholic circles after the dissolution of the Movement in the late 1950s.

Some of the bishops (especially those influenced by the NCC) considered CCJP to be too public in its criticism and too political in its methods. Increasingly the hierarchy distanced themselves from the Social Justice Statements although this was not sufficient to obscure the evident public division among them over the line taken by CCJP on various issues.[51] A detailed chronology provided by the CCJP of its response to the East Timorese plight reveals its engagement in the issue from prior to the Indonesian invasion. In November 1975 the agency urged Foreign Minister Andrew Peacock to acknowledge the right of the inhabitants to determine their own social and economic development.[52] Thereafter the CCJP continually called for a genuine act of political self-determination by the East Timorese people. It also stressed the importance of effective humanitarian aid; drew attention to the plight of East Timorese refugees; and pointed to the crucial role of international observers and relief workers to monitor human rights abuses and provide humanitarian assistance. The CCJP made direct and public appeals to the Australian government which were strongly critical of its pro-Indonesia policies and biased reports, and called for a full impartial parliamentary inquiry into all aspects of the East Timor situation. It urged the United Nations to carry through its own resolutions in respect of East Timor, and for the government of Portugal to be

[47] John Scott Murphy, CA Public Policy & Advocacy Officer to the author, Sydney August 1997, and July 1999.

[48] e.g. against the 1979 Statement 'Beyond Unemployment'.
[49] e.g. against the 1980 Statement 'Poverty, Power and the Church'
[50] e.g. against the 1983 Statement 'Changing Australia'.
[51] Bibliography – Ch8: Hogan, M. (ed), 1992: Kerr, N. (ed), 1985.
[52] Bibliography – Ch8: CCJP 1987; a summary is given in CCJPD, 1993, pp60-61.

more assertive of Timorese rights.[53] CCJP publicised reports of other reputable agencies, endorsing their declarations concerning the illegality of the annexation and condemning the human rights violations being perpetrated in the territory.[54] The agency also presented its own submission on the situation in East Timor to the Senate Committee on Foreign Affairs and Defence.[55] The CCJP's effort culminated in its publication of 'East Timor: A Christian Reflection' (1987). This document attempted to widen the understanding of the Christian community in Australia of the extent of human suffering in the neighbouring territory and stressed that the responsibility to find a just and lasting solution was one shared by the Australian government and people.

However, the anxiety of the Australian hierarchy in respect of the CCJP's activity in general led to their commissioning in 1987 of the Nestor Report which recommended that they should take a more direct responsibility for justice and peace education, and it was decided not to renew the CCJP charter.[56] It has also been suggested that the Federation of Asian Bishops Conferences (FABC) - itself strongly influenced by the Indonesian Bishops Conference (MAWI) - had a part to play in the CCJP's suppression.[57] Some analysts have considered that the influence of the Vatican can also be discerned in this decision.[58] In any case, the sterling support for the East Timorese cause given by this agency ceased at that time, although its stance was later (after the Santa Cruz massacre) to be taken up by a few of the bishops.

In place of the CCJP the hierarchy set up a new body, the Bishops Conference Commission for Justice, Development and Peace (BCCJDP) with its subsidiary organisation, the Australian Catholic Social Justice Council (ACSJC), under their close supervision. Thereby they hoped also to avoid being identified with the 'left-wing'.

The Australian Catholic Social Justice Council

The Charter of the ACSJC (1992) clearly indicates that its mandate and purpose derive in the first instance from the Gospel (Luke 4:18-19 is cited) and then from the Social Doctrine of the Church. It begins with a quotation from the 1971 Synod of Bishops: 'Action on behalf of justice and participation in the transformation of the world fully appear to us as a constitutive dimension of the preaching of the Gospel'. Among the purposes of ACSJC included in its Charter are the following:

> To advise the Bishops Conference on the statements and actions necessary to promote the values of God's kingdom;
> To encourage Catholics to think and act in respect of their obligations in and to society;
> To offer a credible national Catholic voice on social justice issues and a contribution to their resolution; to provide research and educational materials to promote social justice and peace.

---

[53] Letter to UNSG Kurt Waldheim by Bishop William Murray (chairman) on behalf of CCJP 8.7.81, cited (with Lisbon letter) in Timor Information Service No 32, Sept/Oct 1981, p5.

[54] e.g. The Report (1982) published by CIIR, London; the Statement (1986) prepared by the Justice and Peace Commission of the Dutch Catholic Church in conjunction with several other European Justice and Peace Commissions.

[55] See: 'The Human Rights and Conditions of the People of East Timor', Report (1983) Senate Standing Committee on Foreign Affairs and Defence, Canberra.

[56] For an appraisal of the work and suppression of the CCJP see Bibliography – Ch8: Woolfe, T.M.1988; cf. Brennan, G. & Williams, J.K. (eds), 1984.

[57] Some Australian bishops asserted that MAWI had claimed CCJP's stance was making things difficult for the Indonesian Church. But Chris Sidoti (CCJP Secretary at the time, subsequently Australian High Commissioner for Human Rights) recalled that the Archbishop of Jakarta, Leo Soekoto, had told him that the Australian bishops' contact with MAWI had actually been very limited and that they lacked the information to draw such a conclusion. To the author, Sydney Sept.1997.

[58] e.g. Bishop Hilton Deakin to the author, Melbourne August 1997.

In fact the response of the Council to the East Timor issue was very limited.The first executive officer, Juan Federer, soon resigned over what he considered to be a lack of action by the Council.[59] His successor, Keith O'Neill, who had a background in Australian Defence Intelligence, tended to urge a 'discreet' style of operation and to have the highest hopes of co-operative ventures between the Australian and Indonesian governments. Thus ACSJC gained some satisfaction by its successful arrangement of part funding for the Dili Diocesan Justice and Peace Commission from AusAID. However, the effectiveness of this East Timor diocesan institution was severely limited by other factors such as an overwhelming case load, very limited human resources, and constant surveillance by Indonesian military intelligence. In 1992, ACSJC published an essay offering an astute critical analysis of the situation then prevailing in the country.[60] In due course it supported literacy schemes in East Timor - in particular by the publication and dissemination of a 'Beginner's Course' in Tetum-Praca, the *lingua franca* of East Timor.[61] Occasional articles on East Timor, mildly critical of the Indonesian rule there, appeared in the Council's news bulletin *Justice Trends* and also in the 1997 'Statement' for Social Justice Sunday (itself an institution of ACSJC). ACSJC also prepared materials for the commemorative liturgies that began to be organised annually in a number of dioceses following the Santa Cruz massacre. Considerable effort was put by ACSJC officers into negotiations lasting several years with Canberra and Jakarta for a formal visit of observation to East Timor by a small delegation from the agency.[62] Other Catholic organisations (and many Timorese) expressed to this author their considerable reservations and misgivings about the value and possible negative effects of such a visit. Finally it went ahead in 1998 producing a report (of which only the Australian and Indonesian governments and the United Nations received copies) as its only evident fruit. Human rights abuses were certainly of concern to ACSJC and weekly telephone calls were made to bishop Belo by chairman bishop William Brennan (who made several fraternal visits to his episcopal peer in East Timor) as an expression of solidarity and to check on the veracity of alleged violations. However, ACSJC did not publicly challenge the denial of the fundamental human right of the Timorese people (to political self-determination) which would have put it in a confrontational position *vis-a-vis* the Australian as well as the Indonesian government. Indeed its executive officer Keith O'Neill appeared to regard 'integration' as a *fait accompli* and in the long term best interests of the East Timorese: for him, 'reconciliation with Indonesia' was paramount. He seemed reassured by a copy of 'Guidelines' he had received from an Indonesian Commander which (in his view) indicated that, as a fruit of the ongoing military co-operation between *ABRI* and the Australian Defence Force, respect for human rights was now included in their men's code of practice.[63] O'Neill remarked to this author that what violations there were in East Timor would surely stop if the Resistance would only cease their disruptive activities! Likewise, bishop Kevin Manning (ACSJC secretary) opposed a Bill advanced by politician Garry Gibson for the closer monitoring of defence co-operation on the grounds that in respect of Indonesia 'the more co-operation there is, the more our [Australian] standards will be adopted'. In his view there had been 'many improvements in East Timor under Indonesian administration', 'the media had exaggerated the instances of human rights violations', and anti-Indonesian demonstrations were 'neither necessary nor helpful.'[64]

---

[59] Juan Federer, to the author, Darwin, August 1997.

[60] Biblography – Ch8:Hull, G., 1992.

[61] Hull, G. 1994, *Mai Kolia Tetun*, ACR & ACSJC, North Sydney.

[62] Comprising Bishops William Brennan (Chairman) and Kevin Manning (Secretary), Keith O'Neill (Executive Officer), and Dr. Geoffrey Hull (linguist).

[63] Biblography – Ch8: Dunidja, D. 1986.

[64] To the author, Paramatta, NSW, Sept. 1997.

Officers of other agencies acting for the Australian Bishops Conference were critical of ACSJC. They opined that the 'muted public role', the 'avoidance of politics' and the 'secrecy' which had characterised its approach to the East Timor issue virtually since its inception meant that in practice it was 'directionless' 'did very little', and 'had very little influence'.[65] Evidently there was some distance between Catholic organisations, even those operating from within the same building.

Responses of the Laity

The differences of viewpoint and action among the lay officers of the agencies of the Bishops Conference were of course to be found among the lay faithful at large. Their interest in the East Timor issue varied over time, in extent, and in expression and was affected by a number of considerations. Such factors included: the ratio of lay Catholics within the population as a whole; their dispersal over the continent; and whether the plight of the East Timorese and the events in East Timor seemed to impact in any way upon their own lives or contravene their personal or religious principles.

Concerns with regard to the threat of Communism arose at the time of the Portuguese revolution and were enhanced by the political instability in East Timor which soon ensued - but these anxieties, stirred in no small measure by Bob Santamaria's NCC, subsided after the Indonesian 'intervention'. Thereafter humanitarian concerns for East Timorese welfare were shared by many. For example the St.Vincent de Paul Society, a lay pastoral organisation spread throughout the continent, arranged the provision of relief supplies to East Timor and assisted refugees arriving in Australia. But relatively few lay persons persisted in calling for a UN-validated act of political self-determination - the majority tending to accept the federal government line that the best interests of the East Timorese lay in accepting their new status as Indonesia's '27th Province'. Lay energies were engaged in the provision of relief supplies, the funding of development projects, or (rather unproductive) attempts to arrange 'parish twinning'.

Like their compatriots, Catholics were anxious for Australia to maintain harmonious relationships with Indonesia which were highly pertinent to its own economic welfare. They were also concerned not to create difficulties for the Catholic Church in the archipelago, and initially they were ill at ease with the Lusitanian character of the then relatively small Catholic Church in East Timor. For historical reasons already noted many of the laity (perhaps the majority overall) tended to be of a conservative disposition or reliant on direction from the hierarchy. Such direction was in fact slow to develop and never achieved unanimity.

The most extensive coverage of the East Timor issue in the Australian Catholic media over the years was that provided by Bob Santamaria's *News Weekly*. An analysis of the articles in this magazine made by campaigner Pat Walsh in 1981 revealed that:

> At no stage was there any defence of the East Timorese right to self-determination...
> Almost all reporting was devoted to attempts to discredit critics of Indonesia and/or supporters of the East Timorese, or to discredit information critical of Indonesia...
> There was also sustained justification of events in Timor in terms of the importance of the need to counter a possible 'leftist' or 'communist-line' independent East Timor, and in respect of the importance of the Australian-Indonesian relationship.[66]

Walsh noted that Santamaria admitted to having close links with the CSIS in Jakarta - 'the most influential foreign policy making body associated with the Indonesian government'.[67] This author studied all issues of *News Weekly* archived at NCC headquarters in Melbourne for

---

[65] To the author, North Sydney, Sept. 1997, July 1999.
[66] Bibliography – Ch8: Walsh, P. 1981, p14-16.
[67] B.A.Santamaria, in The Australian 9.9.77, cited by Walsh, P. 1981 op.cit.p16.

the period 1974-1997 to discover little variation from that original position. However, the remarkable numerical growth of the Church in East Timor, continuing negative accounts of the situation by foreign visitors and Australian religious personnel to the territory, combined with the succession of asylum seekers bringing to Australia their own tales of oppression, caused a steady increase in lay concern. Pope John Paul II's pastoral visit to Australia (1986) was an occasion when the Timorese profile was raised fleetingly in Catholic circles[68] and coverage of the Papal Visit to East Timor in 1989 encouraged a greater interest among the laity for a time. In due course a disposition more sympathetic to the suffering of the people was in evidence in some other Catholic media outlets, including an increasing attention to the needs of those seeking asylum in Australia. But criticism of Canberra's position and support for East Timorese self-determination was limited and hesitant prior to the Santa Cruz massacre in 1991 and the award of the Nobel Peace Prize to bishop Belo in 1996. The tensions that preceded the UN ballot and its violent aftermath in 1999 were to generate more extensive and searching coverage but that was led by the secular Press.

As already noted, the Santa Cruz killings stimulated the emergence of a number of new non-governmental organisations supportive of the East Timorese cause with which individual Catholics associated themselves. Thus the East Timor International Support Centre (ETISC) based in Darwin was headed up by Juan Federer, former executive officer of ACSJC, and the East Timor Human Rights Centre (ETHRC) in Melbourne elected bishop Hilton Deakin as its chairman. However, the demeanour of some of the more radical campaigning groups created problems for Catholics by their concentration upon the single-issue of East Timorese welfare. For example, it was to the detriment of the good will of many in the Church in Darwin when leaders of a demonstrative group of pro-Timorese activists attempted to hijack an anti-euthanasia rally by intrusive heckling of participant bishop Ted Collins. Many Timorese living locally were also offended or alarmed by such actions which happened on more than one occasion.[69] But there were groups of Catholic activists, motivated by Gospel principles (such as members of Pax Christi, or groups affiliated to or inspired by Dorothy Day's Catholic Worker fellowship), who became increasingly engaged in bearing witness to their ideals in public demonstrations about East Timor's predicament. 'Prophetic acts' carried out by such lay Catholics alongside other committed Christians took various forms. There were protest marches castigating Australian Defence Force co-operation with the Indonesian Military or commercial enterprises seen as supportive of Jakarta's occupation and exploitation of East Timor. The production and sale of military aircraft to Indonesia (by BAe - Australia), or the exploration of the hydrocarbon deposits in the Timor Sea (by Australian oil companies) was overtly criticised by these groups (with little support from the institutional Church). Some public protests took the form of acts of 'civil disobedience', while others had a para-liturgical character. [70] Such actions were prepared for and supported by retreats, fasts, and nights of earnest prayer and took place in different parts of the continent from Perth to Brisbane. In addition, a continual stream of letters were sent to State and Federal officials and to the local

---

[68] Although the Timorese community in Australia did not gain special access to the Holy Father they drew the Pope's attention to their presence at various locations in his tour, which received some coverage in the local and regional and Catholic press (e.g. The Sunday Times [Western Australia] 30.11.86.

[69] Bishop Ted Collins, Fr.Luis Rey CMF – chaplain to the Timorese, the Anglican bishop of Darwin, and David Odling-Smee (of ETISC - an Anglican) to the author, Darwin Aug.1997.

[70] e.g. Campaigners in Brisbane interviewed by the author in Sept 1997 had during the previous 18 months held several candle-lit vigils, conducted a 'Funeral Liturgy' at Canungra military base and 'peaceful sit-ins' at Defence HQ, undertaken 'non-violent witness' outside Garuda Airlines, presided over a 'Liturgy of Deliverance' (exorcism) outside the Petroz Oil Company and organised the public burning of Australian/Indonesian military flags in protest over the Defence Pact signed by PM Keating and President Suharto.

and national Press challenging the policy pursued by successive governments. All such activities were greatly encouraged by the 1996 Nobel Peace Prize award to bishop Belo and Jose Ramos Horta. Opportunity for increasing lay involvement was also provided by the 'Commemorative Liturgies' organised by individual dioceses on the anniversaries of the Santa Cruz massacre, or of the Indonesian invasion on December 7th 1975, and associated with key events as they occurred in 1999.[71]

The various factors militating against a coherent and vigorous response by the Catholic laity in Australia were most evident to this author in Darwin. This is the Australian location most vulnerable to the intrusion of Communism from SE Asia, or to inundation by its peoples, and is also the nearest point to East Timor. The vast Northern Territory beyond the State capital has an overall population of only 150,000, two thirds of them resident in the environs of Darwin itself. The total number of Catholics in this whole region is 40,000, only 10% of whom were regarded by the clergy as 'practising' and who were predominantly 'conservative' in attitude. These folk had some concern for Timorese welfare but they were upset by the behaviour of a few radical activists (as noted above) and confused by the disunity evident among the refugees in their midst. Such intra-Timorese discord arose from persisting political party loyalties, the different priorities of successive generations of asylum seekers, and the pace at which, or methods by which, the exiled Timorese hoped a peaceful settlement might be achieved in their homeland.[72] Darwin had an increasingly cosmopolitan nature and this hardly facilitated an agreed course of action among its Catholic component, especially with Indonesians (Catholics among them) included among those taking up local residence or associated with the Consulate. Indeed the Consulate was located there precisely to encourage Australian-Indonesian economic co-operation and it was hoped that this would be of particular benefit to Darwin residents. It should also be reiterated that Australia had severe social problems of its own during the period under study, and a particularly important issue of justice confronting all the people (but especially Darwinians) who had come to settle in this land: their proper relationship with the Aborigines.[73] The attitude among lay Church leaders was sympathetic to the East Timorese plight but there was uncertainty as to how best to proceed and generally action tended to be discreet rather than overt.

Efforts of Australian Religious

There are three principal dimensions to the work of Australian religious orders for the East Timorese people to which only brief reference can be made here. Their members played an important role in the communication of accurate information about the East Timorese plight, challenging misconceptions and misrepresentations. Some did valuable work in preserving East Timorese culture, in particular the *lingua franca* - Tetun. Religious also headed up support for the welfare of East Timorese refugees in Australia, notably their right to asylum. Yet even within particular religious families conflicting positions were sometimes adopted.

For example, Fr.John Eddy *SJ* of the Australian National University and the Jesuit Research Centre in Canberra was a vigorous critic of CCJP's stance on East Timor although his views were not based on any personal investigation. In the period late 1976-early 1977 he directed letters of criticism to then chairman bishop Mulkearns of Ballarat (Victoria) denouncing as highly questionable the claims CCJP had made of widespread and indiscriminate killing of East Timorese by Indonesian forces. He also wrote to the secretary of

---

[71] e.g. Bishop Deakin presided at a requiem Mass in Melbourne on April 24th for all the East Timorese murdered in Dili by TNI-backed militias; and an ecumenical service for Forgiveness and Unity was hosted in St. Mary's Cathedral, Darwin on Ballot Day Aug.30th.

[72] Such disunity was commonly remarked upon to the author also in Melbourne and Sydney.

[73] Catholic Church commitment to this issue was considerable. See, e.g.: CCJP Statements 1978 'A Statement of Concern', and 1987 'A Just and Proper Settlement'.

the Australian Bishops Conference (bishop P.Dougherty) calling for an inquiry into CCJP's finances, *modus operandi* and relationship to ACR. He urged the withdrawal of episcopal sponsorship from the agency 'whose pronouncements...have created and fostered a divisive and destructive factionalism within the Australian Catholic community'.[74] In contrast, Fr.Mark Raper *SJ* had been a member of the Australian Council for Overseas Aid (ACFOA) mission to East Timor in 1975[75] and, in 1976, as Director of the Australian Asian Bureau, he castigated the government for having acted 'completely without morality on the East Timor issue'. His reports were among the first to reach the wider world and to challenge perceptions of the East Timor situation.[76] He exhorted Australians to 'press strongly for *a properly observed, active, free choice by the people*'. His critique included an attack on the allegations of Communist assertion that had been made with such tragic consequences for the East Timorese:

> Australia is ready to put sheer pragmatism before any principled consideration...
> Many Australians have slandered the East Timorese by calling them Communists...
> That was bad enough, but it was not so horrifying as what that slander was allowed to justify...Many people claimed, first, that they are Communists - which they are not. Then they said that because they are Communists killing them is justified...Even if they were Communists all people have the right to self-determination, whatever their political beliefs...[77]

From 1989 the Jesuits in Sydney headed up the administration of Christians in Solidarity with East Timor (CISET) - an ecumenical group working in support of the Timorese cause - until the Josephites took on this task in the person of Sr.Kath O'Connor *RSJ*. The Jesuit Refugee Service assisted East Timorese who had fled.

Fr.Pat Walsh *MSC* was first involved with Timorese refugees in Australia. He became a leading campaigner for their human rights to be respected and their welfare needs to be met also in their homeland. He continued his commitment (perhaps even more effectively) after withdrawing from the Missionaries of the Sacred Heart and returning to the lay state. He facilitated the action of a number of NGOs engaged with the East Timor issue and his many reports, papers and submissions (some of which are cited throughout this text) are too numerous to list in full.[78] They were notable for their objectivity and for their challenge of the Indonesian propaganda that was being so readily echoed by Australian government officials, by many in the mass media, and accepted too easily by members of the Catholic hierarchy and laity – and within his own and other religious congregations.

Some religious personnel visiting the country in later years gained a positive impression of the 'improvements' brought about by the Indonesian administration and urged that 'simplistic solutions' should not be proposed for a complex issue by identifying with particular Timorese political factions. However, even such reports as were appreciative of Indonesian achievements did not deny the repressive and exploitative nature of their regime in East Timor.[79] Also those religious congregations, such as the Canossians, who had

---

[74] Letter to ABC, 28.2.77, cited by Walsh, P. 1981, 'Australia's Support, etc.' op.cit.p20-21.

[75] 'Aid for Timor Appeal Launched', The Age, Melbourne 31.10.75.

[76] e.g. See Bibliography – General (East Timor): Dunn, J. 1996, op.cit. p283;and 'The Church in Indonesia: to speak or not to speak', IDOC International Bulletin No3, 1984.

[77] Catholic Weekly, 8.4.1976. The ABA under Raper's directorship also made a Submission to the Senate Standing Committee on Foreign Affairs and Defence 1981, op.cit.

[78] See Bibliographies – Ch5, 6, 7, 8, & 12. See Bibliography – General (East Timor): Retboll, T. 1984, for some of his shorter articles.

[79] 'Letter from Dili' by Fr.Bill Burt *SVD*, 3.8.1992, ACSJC files. Fr.Burt includes quotations from Indonesian press interviews with bishop Belo in which a strong critique of the regime's practices can be discerned beneath the Apostolic Administrator's careful acknowledgements.

endeavoured to avoid being perceived as having any political stance or intent 'for the sake of their future work in the territory and in the Indonesian archipelago', publicly supported the Australian hierarchy when they urged justice for East Timor: 'We have a duty to do that, without being afraid'.[80] This institution also undertook considerable work in Australia for the welfare of East Timorese refugees, especially in Brisbane and in Darwin.

The National Council of Major Religious Superiors of Australia (NCMSA) wrote in solidarity to bishop Belo in 1984. They called for 'radical alternative solutions' to the continuing crisis. They also urged a reconciliation that respected the East Timorese people and afforded them 'due participation in decisions affecting both their socio-political future and the economic, cultural and family affairs of daily life'.[81] In 1991 this Council made a public statement deploring the Santa Cruz massacre.[82]

Special mention should be made of the activity of the Sisters of the Josephite Congregation - the only Australian religious foundation - in the East Timorese cause.[83] Much of their work was undertaken discreetly and with considerable courage. Visits of observation were undertaken in East Timor, sometimes in co-operation with members of other religious institutes with whom confidential but comprehensive reports were produced on the prevailing situation in the country.[84] The Mary MacKillop Institute of East Timor Studies (MMIETS) was to the forefront in safeguarding the East Timorese cultural heritage especially through its efforts to preserve and strengthen the Tetun language.[85] This was a significant contribution to Timorese development, and 'it enhanced the Timorese sense of dignity and personal worth - and probably strengthened their spirit of resistance!'[86] In Australia itself, it was the Josephites who promoted the Sanctuary Movement from November 1995 'to stand by the [1360] East Timorese refugee applicants and to state our belief that Australia has a moral obligation to them'.[87] This movement gained support from many other religious congregations (predominantly those of women) and then from as many as ten thousand Catholic laity. In due course it became a significant 'communitarian action' by a wide range of East Timorese sympathisers across the entire continent, presenting a significant political challenge to the government's persistent attempt to off-load responsibility for the refugees' welfare upon Lisbon. Supporters participated in special liturgies and pledged to provide sanctuary to the refugees 'in a spirit of solidarity and moral obligation' should the government attempt to remove them to East Timor, Indonesia, or to Portugal. There were significant and positive legal developments on this issue although it remained unresolved by the time of East Timor's

---

[80] Sr. Anne Bosio, Canossian Superior (Darwin), cited in The Canberra Times 23 July 1994.

[81] Letter of NCMSA 21.2.1984 in CCJPD, 1993 op.cit.p23.

[82] Media Release – E.Timor: 'Australian Religious Leaders speak out for E Timor', 13.11.1991, Australian Conference of Leaders of Religious Institutes, National Centre for Religious, Annandale.

[83] Founded by Mary MacKillop (1812-1909), see Bibliography - Ch8: Modystack, W. 1982. Because of the Congregation's origin in their country Australian Catholics have a particular regard for, and responsiveness to, the work of these religious sisters.

[84] e.g. '[Confidential] Report on East Timor' 1995, Br. D.K.Courtney CFC, and Srs. Mary Byrne RSC and Colleen O'Brien SGS, ACR archives, N.Sydney; and see Bibliography – Ch8: CISET 1994.

[85] Documentation available from MMIETS, St.Mary's NSW. e.g. Letter: 'Inauguration of the MMI-ETS, 8th August 1994' by Sr.Josephine Mitchell, Administrator; 'Activities and Aims 1995/6/7, etc'; 'East Timor Visit June-July 1996 [Confidential] Report', by Srs. Josephine Mitchell, Susan Connolly, and Mr.Manuel Viegas; 'Language and Literacy in East Timor: the role of the MMIETS', Sr.J.Mitchell RSJ, VII Jornadas, Oporto University, July 1997.

[86] Sr.Josephine Mitchell, Institute Administrator, to the author, St. Mary's NSW, Sept. 1997.

[87] See: 'Statement of the Sanctuary Movement' 5.11.1995, CISET/UNIYA (East Timor Desk), Sydney; text of the original Josephite commitment signed by Congregational Leader Sr.Mary Cresp RSJ archived at Administration Centre, Mount St., North Sydney.

eventual transition to UN administration in the winter of 1999-2000.[88] The Sanctuary Movement received a mixed reaction from the hierarchy some of whom were supportive while others were patronising: 'the nuns are letting their hearts rule their heads'. There was also some opposition among the long-term East Timorese residents in Australia who felt the asylum seekers might put at risk their own security and stability in the country.[89] Nonetheless, the Sisters remained adamant:

> The hypocrisy of both the Labor and Liberal governments is clearly set out...
> The tragedy of the whole situation is not only the fate of refugees seeking asylum here, but the Australia we are portraying to the rest of the world and to our children and their future: a country without honour, compassion, fairness, integrity or justice. It is we, the people, who must take responsibility and stand up and say: 'Enough'. By our silence we are colluding with the government in its unjust and dishonourable deeds.[90]

During the 'Year of Crisis' the Josephites fearlessly continued their humanitarian activity in East Timor while urging the Australian government to end its 'betrayal' and take action 'in the spirit of ANZAC' to prevent further bloodshed.[91] The response of the national Catholic Church to the East Timorese plight as represented by such women could hardly have been more forthright:

> Our Foreign Minister and his tunnel-visioned master pirouette around the issue, snubbing the US military here, telling a few porkies there, pretending to be neutral, and always desperately trying to resuscitate the corpse of the 'civil war' and 'warring factions' deceit, so dear to the heart of the Javanese, despite incontrovertible evidence to the contrary.
> As we approach a fundamental decision on our identity, we can ill-afford to ignore the serious comment on our national character produced by our historical response to East Timor.[92]

Responses of the Hierarchy

Only two public Statements on the East Timor situation were made by the Australian Bishops Conference in the quarter century between the beginning of Portugal's decolonisation process after April 1974 and the withdrawal of the Indonesian administration in November 1999. The first, on 16th May 1976, pledged support to the Australian government to secure the admission of International Red Cross representatives and to 'any genuine efforts to provide relief to those in need as a result of the conflict'.[93] The bishops also promised to 'promote the sending of a relief shipment to the devastated area' but a year later these efforts were still being mostly frustrated by the conflict situation in the country and difficulties associated with gaining requisite permissions from the Indonesian and Australian governments.[94] The second Statement was made on 6th December 1991 in response to the Santa Cruz massacre. The bishops called for a 'credible and independent investigation by the United Nations into the recent tragic killings and other alleged human rights abuses in East

---

[88] The Federal Court decided in favour of one asylum seeker Jong Kim Koe on May 2 1997, raising hopes that this case would prove to be a precedent. Indonesian Foreign Minister Ali Alatas warned that this might lead to a new wave of arrivals in Australia, evoking old fears. 'Reject refugees or risk flood, Australia warned', Louise Williams, Sydney Morning Herald, 7.5.97.

[89] Sr.Kathleen O'Connor *RSJ*, leader of the movement, to the author, Sydney, Sept.1997.

[90] 'Honour sold out for trade', Kath O'Connor *RSJ*, Sydney Morning Herald, 13.11.97.

[91] 'Australians to send container of medical supplies to East Timor' AAP Newsfeed 19.3.99; 'Customs officials blocking release of Australian medical aid' LUSA 5.4.99; 'Nun's challenge to Downer: act now to stop Timor bloodshed', The Australian 12.4.99.

[92] 'East Timor: hard decisions must be faced' Sr.Susan Connelly *RSJ*, Letters, Sydney Morning Herald 12.8.99

[93] Motions of the Australian Episcopal Conference 16.5.76, archives AEC, Canberra.

[94] ACR Report to Members of the Australian Episcopal Conference on East Timor, 16.5.77.

Timor'. They also indicated their support for 'the Holy See's defence of the rights of all the Timorese to social peace, fundamental liberty, and their religious and cultural identity and human rights'.[95] There are several reasons for this sparse contribution to the public forum on the issue.

In previous history there had been very little contact between the relatively young Catholic Church in Australia and that of the former Portuguese colony in East Timor. It was only in 1976 that the Australian Church was transferred from the Vatican's missionary administration *Propaganda Fidei* to the Congregation for Bishops and entered the mainstream of the developed international Catholic world. The first religious contact between the Catholic Churches in Australia and East Timor was during the Second World War when Australian commandos requested the sacraments and when the first bishop of the Diocese of Dili, Dom Jaime Guilart, was consecrated in the seminary chapel at Manly (Sydney) in 1945. The next official liaison between the Churches (apart from the exchange of information necessary for the provision of humanitarian aid) was not until 1988. At that time the Australian Salesians responded to an appeal by the congregation's Provincial (S.Phillippines), Fr.Jose Carbonell, for their help in East Timor, a territory which by then had come under his jurisdiction. Although Mgr Costa Lopes toured Australia after his resignation as Dili Diocesan Apostolic Administrator in 1983 his speaking engagements were organised, not by the Australian hierarchy, but by NGOs committed to the Timorese cause (as were those of the Timorese priest Fr.Francisco Fernandes). The first official support from the hierarchy for such tours was that given to bishop Belo in 1993 and it was only in the 1990s that any Australian bishop went to East Timor.[96] This accounts for Belo's remarks to ABC Radio in the course of his visit to Australia:

> It is time the Australian Church do something, because during the Second World War many Timorese died for the Australian people - so now it is time to pay, to show the solidarity (sic). I think that the intervention of his Eminence the Cardinal is important.[97]

The influence of the Vatican was undoubtedly another factor. The Secretariat of State recommended to the Australian bishops that 'the question of East Timor be treated with discretion and prudence'[98] and successive Papal Envoys to Australia also indicated that the hierarchy 'should keep out of the East Timor issue as the Secretariat of State was handling matters'.[99] National Episcopal Conferences have a degree of independence but it is certain that the Australian bishops would have 'kept an eye on the Holy See'.[100] Furthermore, the Nuncio to Jakarta (Pietro Sambi) was very directive to the ACR delegation who met him in Bali (January 1993). He told them: 'It would be better for the Timorese to co-operate with

[95] Media Release 6.12.91, Catholic Bishops of Australia, archives AEC, Canberra - following previous Media Releases by bishop William Murray (Wollongong), then BCCJDP Chairman, and representations to the Australian Foreign Minister by bishop Brennan (Wagga Wagga), then Chairman of ACSJC.

[96] Bishop William Brennan made several visits as chairman of BCJPD, as did bishop Hilton Deakin, Auxiliary in Melbourne (but privately, to express solidarity with Belo). Cardinal Clancy visited in August 1996. In 1998 bishop Kevin Manning was in the ACSJC delegation.

[97] Interview with Anthony Balmain, ABC Radio, 17.12.1996. - ETAN docs Vol 26, p90-1.

[98] Letter from Archbishop Baitauto to Cardinal Freeman (Sydney) 26.1.82, ACR archives.

[99] Bishop John Gerry (Brisbane), Chair of ACR until 1988, to the author, Brisbane Sept.1997 with particular (but not exclusive) reference to Nuncio Barbarito.

[100] Dr.Michael Costigan (BCCJPD Executive Director) to the author, Sydney, Sept.1997. Bishop Kevin Manning (Chairman ACSJC) indicated to the author that 'Nuncio Brambilla will not approve the Church becoming involved in the affairs of another country' - Paramatta, Sept.1997. Nuncio Brambilla expressed disapproval over the arrest of bishop Deakin when participating in the APCET Conference in Kuala Lumpur in November 1996.

Indonesia and become part of the Republic, then their troubles would end'.[101] A change in the Vatican's attitude 'seemed discernible' after the visit to East Timor in February 1996 by the president of the Pontifical Council for Justice and Peace, Cardinal Roger Etchegaray.[102] The Cardinal declaimed that peace and justice were 'closely related' and that neither could be established without the other.[103] But even this did not seemingly effect a greater unanimity among the Australian bishops.[104]

Certainly the hierarchy were in receipt of a volume of information via their own agencies and other sources. But, in the earliest years especially, much that they received was contradictory owing to the effectiveness of Indonesian propaganda, Australian governmental bias, and the complicity of many in the media.[105] Thus in early December 1975 ACR Executive Director William Byrne sought to correct the misleading impression given to archbishop Knox and his successor archbishop Little (Melbourne) by letters from West Timor bishops Tillart (Atambua) and Manteiro (Kupang) which referred to the disruptive 'Communist activities' of FRETILIN. But archbishop Cahill (Canberra and Goulburn) dismissed Byrne's critique.[106] Only days later archbishop James Gleeson (Adelaide 1971-85, ACR Chairman) was joint signatory with bishop Mulkearns (CCJP Chairman) to a Statement calling for UN intervention in East Timor to end the fighting between Indonesian and Timorese forces and to provide for an genuine act of political self-determination. But within weeks archbishop Gleeson had to defend even the Church's humanitarian relief effort against criticism by the Knights of the Southern Cross, the largest national Catholic layman's organisation, on the grounds that this was, in their view, being supportive of FRETILIN and therefore politically partisan.

Such confusion still persisted by the time Mgr Costa Lopes' description of the situation and his warning of the likelihood of famine reached the Bishops Conference in 1981. As already noted, Costa Lopes' testimony was called into question by former Labor Prime Minister Gough Whitlam after a fleeting visit to the territory conducted by the Indonesian authorities. But it was also disputed by archbishop Baitauto in a letter to Cardinal Freeman of Sydney from the Vatican Secretariat of State.[107] Of course, the different accounts given by successive waves of East Timorese refugees with their various factional loyalties did not help clarify the situation and pastors who had a ministry to all Timorese - and Catholic Indonesian expatriates - endeavoured to remain 'non-partisan'.

The internal divisions within the Bishops Conference itself, already elaborated, made a coherent, unified and vigorous response all the more difficult. This is not to say that the bishops did not concern themselves with the East Timorese predicament, but that their concern tended to be expressed through their agencies (ACR, CCJP, ACSJC) and as individuals - variously. An example of the divergence of their response would be the contrast between that of Francis Carroll (Canberra-Goulburn, from 1983) who adopted the position of his predecessor (given above) and that of his auxiliary (from 1986) Pat Power. Bishop Power participated in demonstrations and vigils outside the Indonesian Embassy critical of Jakarta-

---

[101] Bishop Edmund Collins *MSC* to the author, Darwin August 1997.

[102] Bishop William Brennan (Chairman, BCCJPD) - telephone conversation with the author, Sydney/Wagga Wagga, Sept.1997.

[103] Cardinal Etchegaray, homily in Dili Feb 25th - Timor Link, CIIR London, March 1996.

[104] Bishop Kevin Manning (Chairman ACSJC) opined to the author that Etchegaray's speech in Dili had been 'inflammatory' - Paramatta NSW, Sept.1997.

[105] For detail see Bibliography – General (East Timor): Gunn, G. 1994, op.cit., p135-140.

[106] Letter from West Timor bishops to Cardinal Knox, 3.12.75 (four days prior to the invasion); Letter from Wm.Byrne to Archbishops Little and Cahill, 18.2.76;Letter from Archbishop Cahill to Wm.Byrne, 2.3.76; Statement of CCJP/ACR, 9.12.75 (two days after the invasion); Letter of KSC to Archbishop Gleeson, 16.3.76, Gleeson's reply to KSC, 23.3.76. ACR archives.

[107] Letter 26.1.82, copy on file with author.

Canberra policy in East Timor.[108] Meanwhile, bishop Ted Collins in Darwin (from 1986) actually cultivated relations with the Indonesian Consulate there in the hope of 'bringing a positive influence to bear'.[109] As noted already, there were also differing attitudes among the bishops regarding the Sanctuary Movement.[110] Another example of contrast would be that between the sympathy extended to the East Timorese refugees in Melbourne by archbishop Little (1974-96) and bishop Hilton Deakin (auxiliary in Melbourne from 1993). The archbishop gave the Timorese minimal attention and thereby conveyed the impression that their plight was not of significant importance. But bishop Deakin welcomed them into the Cathedral itself and from among the Australian hierarchy became perhaps their most outspoken advocate.[111] On the first anniversary of the Santa Cruz massacre he challenged the Australian government and people - and all who remained complicit in the East Timorese tragedy - with these words:

> If we confess the [freedoms and human] rights [we enjoy in this land] to be basic to people's well-being, or even to life itself, then denial of such rights should be given no shelter, either in political understandings and accommodations, or in the hidden depths of our own compromising minds.[112]

Bishop David Cremmin (Auxiliary in Sydney from 1974) spoke in similar vein about the Australian government's attitude towards East Timorese asylum seekers:

> We wish to state today that we abhor the gross injustices being inflicted on our East Timorese brothers and sisters who are seeking asylum in our country. We deplore hypocritical policies which shirk our responsibilities towards those who have been forced to flee and ask protection for their lives.[113]

Perhaps the wide-ranging response of the Australian hierarchy to the East Timor issue was summed up in the disposition of Edward Clancy (archbishop of Sydney 1983-2000, Cardinal of Australia from June 1988). Having had a limited interest in the Timorese plight prior to the Santa Cruz massacre and remaining doubtful over the influence the hierarchy would have upon Australian government policy (or even within the pluralist Catholic community) Cardinal Clancy uncharacteristically went out on a limb on their behalf:

> Sometimes it is hard to decide what is strictly a church matter and what is not - but it is a no-contest decision on East Timor. It's a matter of human rights and human rights concern all Christians.[114]

Cardinal Clancy spoke to the author (Sydney 1997) of the contrast between the 'cautious' Vatican disposition and the forthright comments of some of the Australian bishops as 'a creative tension'. On the second anniversary of the Santa Cruz massacre he preached on the 'mystery of suffering' and remarked that 'Christ does not teach us passively to accept and capitulate to all forms of suffering - especially that which comes from injustice and the denial

---

[108] e.g. At an ecumenical protest on Sunday 19th July 1998 which called *inter alia* for a referendum in East Timor under the auspices of the UN. The Declaration by (listed) Religious Leaders is archived on the ETRA web-site.

[109] Bishop Collins to the author, Darwin, August 1997.

[110] Archbishop Hickey (Perth, from 1991) was supportive; bishop David Cremmin (Auxiliary in Sydney) was a signatory; Cardinal Clancy (Sydney) had sympathy for the asylum seekers but reservations about the effectiveness of the Sanctuary Movement's approach.

[111] Emilia Pires, Timorese refugee and activist, to the author, Melbourne August 1997.

[112] Homily, St.Patrick's Cathedral, Melbourne, 11.11.1992.Text in CCJPD 1993, op.cit.p56.

[113] Homily, St. Mary's Cathedral, Sydney, 8.11.1997. Text: ETRA.

[114] 'Church V State: Clancy joins the Timor debate', Jenna Price, Canberra Times 23.7.1994.

of our human rights.' He emphasised: 'We must strive to secure justice and to claim God-given rights from those who oppress and persecute us.'[115] Convinced of the practical value of both quiet diplomacy and public pressure upon governments Cardinal Clancy engaged in discreet correspondence with Canberra. Interviewed on ABC Radio in July he also made a public appeal for an evaluation of the Australian government 'engagement' with Indonesia 'which certainly hasn't stopped the abuse of human rights. While such abuses continue I think it is the responsibility of the government to address the situation'. In 1996 he personally visited East Timor. Sensitive to the repercussions on the people of outspoken criticism of the local regime, he was nonetheless forthright in his observations to the Military Commander over the detrimental effects of the number and behaviour of the troops. After his return the *Sydney Morning Herald* (20th August) reported the Cardinal's denunciation of the oppression he had witnessed and published his call for a reappraisal of Australian government policy:

> There is a great deal of fear, mistrust and suspicion at all levels...plenty of informers, and personal freedoms are restricted and on occasion grossly violated...I suggest that we set aside political pragmatism and commercial self-interest and make a stand on principle and justice.

The Church in Australia - an evaluation

Within the Australian Catholic community there was certainly concern over the East Timorese plight from the outset, despite the many internal and external demands which pressed upon the Church. Efforts were always made to relieve the suffering of the people and to provide for their economic development, although these encountered a number of difficulties attributable to the Indonesian regime and the Australian government. At all levels within the Church there were those who expressed vigorous and even courageous solidarity with the East Timorese, recognising and responding to their predicament as an oppressed, marginalised and impoverished people. Such persons sometimes acted individually but most became associated with the activity of sympathetic agencies of the institutional Church or with non-governmental organisations whether these were faith-based or secular in motivation. Their response included a thorough investigation of the circumstances that actually prevailed in East Timor, often in person and at real physical risk. They endeavoured to communicate details of this situation through Church and secular media, but their accounts had to compete with those presented by many influential people who were complicit in the 'integration' project. Many sympathisers urged the East Timorese right to political participation and self-determination, and argued in defence of the people's resistance against an illegal, unjust and exploitative rule. They also sought to redress these injustices by trying to effect a change in those policies being pursued by government and commerce in Australia which were affording support to the Indonesian occupation. Various Church agencies applied the principle of 'subsidiarity' by enabling local development enterprises in East Timor. There were also those in all circles of Church life who responded to the difficulties faced by East Timorese refugees in Australia by helping to meet their practical needs and/or by charging the national government to accept its responsibility for their welfare. Spiritual fellowship with the East Timorese was acknowledged and given expression in public prayer.

However, culpable ignorance of the situation in East Timor was also evident every-where within the Church. There was a readiness to accept, and further disseminate, accounts that presented a positive description of the developments as being mainly beneficial to the in-digenous people. That such presentations derived from sources already sullied by self-interest or which were subject to political manipulation was overlooked or ignored. There was a wide-spread hesitancy to criticise national government policy. This attitude derived in part from an anti-Communist ideology or from economic self-interest that seemed impervious to contra-diction. Perception of the national advantages to be gained by Australian support of Indone-

---

[115] Homily, St.Mary's Cathedral, Sydney 12.11.1993, full text in CCJPD 1993, op.cit.p59.

sia's annexation of East Timor seemed to preclude or at least limit due attention being given by the Church as to how that incorporation contravened International Law. The exploitative arrangements agreed by the Indonesian and Australian governments regarding East Timor's maritime resources remained largely unchallenged. The Catholic media manifested some humanitarian concern for the East Timorese but cannot be said to have campaigned for their fundamental rights to be respected - in their native land, or as refugees in Australia - until very late in the day. Some influential media outlets were pre-occupied by anxieties over Communist assertion in the region that lacked any real foundation. Indeed, the defence of the Indonesian take-over in East Timor by some among the hierarchy, by individual members of religious congregations, and by some of the leading laity presented a major obstacle to the work of those within the Church who were trying to oppose it. Inhibitions over criticising the Australian government also arose from concern about the present and future welfare of the Church in Australia. Although the institution of the Church was not under any threat, there were many who felt that for it to retain the influence it had upon the social order any critique it might offer should be exercised with restraint.

In terms of the Church's continuation of the redeeming work of Christ evidence has been provided of how the Church in Australia did and did not act as *Pastor, Prophet, Disciple, Evangelist and Intercessor* on behalf of the East Timorese. Most if not all of the Australian Catholics who became engaged in the East Timor issue had a pastoral concern to improve the people's circumstances, defend their dignity, and promote their development. But some saw such an outcome principally as the fruit of accepting and supporting the Indonesian annexation – dulling the edge of the prophetical critique expressed by others who saw the illegal and brutal incorporation as the fundamental cause of East Timorese suffering. Some in the Church undertook a thorough investigation and analysis of the prevailing situation in East Timor, listened to the people, and questioned the policy of the secular authorities. But others believed too readily the accounts which ultimately derived from the Indonesian (or from a supportive Australian) government and accepted the *status quo* as the best that could be expected. Consideration was certainly given within the Australian Church as to how best the East Timorese might be 'set free'. But not all were willing to offer the people the support they needed to achieve the socio-political liberation they desired. Some could only subscribe to the promise of greater spiritual freedom that might be brought about through the provision of religious personnel to assist in the sacred ministry of the local Church. Liturgies were arranged with increasing regularity within various circles of Church life, all expressive of the mystical communion that pertains between members of the universal ecclesial community. Some of these encouraged Australian Catholics to be generous in the provision of humanitarian resources such as medicine, clothing, etc. In later years their content urged – at times strongly - a 'just resolution' of the East Timor issue and gave attention to the needs of the asylum seekers in Australia. But only the liturgies of the small radical activist groups overtly challenged the governmental and commercial 'powers' that were marshalled against the East Timorese poor and for whom the Church's Social Doctrine surely urged a 'preference'. Those created by the institutional Church generally avoided such a confrontation.

Although some explanations for the shortcomings of the Church's response have been provided these raise in turn the question of the extent to which the Social Doctrine of the Church can actually be applied in practice. In Australia it seemed that the secular setting and pluralist nature of the Catholic community, together with its internal divisions, prevailed against a forthright or even consistent application. No doubt the Church had many problems to contend with – in its own life, and in Australian society at large. Yet Catholics comprise some 25% of the Australian population, a significant proportion, so it is fair to ask whether any more should have been expected of the Church in response to the East Timorese plight.[116] The answers from within that Church varied depending upon the perspective of the respondent - some were fierce in their castigation, others were predictably defensive. To an outsider it is perplexing that more was not done to reach a common and consistent position and policy on an issue of significant national and regional importance as well as to the development of international relations based on the rule of law to which Australia is supposedly committed. In matters of such pertinence to Australian national integrity it is legitimate to expect that the Church would have played a more determined and up-front role. Why was it not possible, over a period of twenty-five years, for the Church in Australia to adopt a stance that derived from or harmonised with the principles of Social Doctrine – and one that was manifest and consistent in all its operations? It is particularly ironic that the Church agency which gave most prominence in its mission statement to the principles of Catholic Social Doctrine, namely the ACSJC, was the one which seemed to implement them the least in practice: a confrontational posture was apparently anathema.

Perhaps there is a more fundamental question deriving from the challenge of the Gospel itself, *viz* - to what extent was the Catholic community in Australia willing to *lay down its own life* for the Timorese cause? Among the range of personal and collective responses within the Church to the Timorese predicament - some admirable, some disappointing, some disgraceful - one appears outstanding. It was that of the Josephite Sisters, the one Religious community to have its own foundation in Australia. The ethos of this congregation seemed to this author expressive of the noblest Australian aspirations. Since its members were ready to forgo dignity and even liberty in Australia for the sake of the Timorese asylum-seekers - and to risk life itself in East Timor during the Year of Crisis and previously - they surely lived also according to the spirit of the Gospel. So theirs should be their voice that speaks such human judgement as can properly be made on the response of the Australian Church to the suffering of the Timorese people. About the disposition of the Australian government one representative of the Congregation commented on behalf of her fellows:

> An utter betrayal of the Australian spirit...ANZAC day is now a hollow experience... The Department of Foreign Affairs and Trade deals in fog and lies...
> The basic weakness of the government's position is its recognition of Indonesian sovereignty in East Timor: this is fundamentally wrong.

But criticism was then also immediately levelled at the institutional Church in Australia: 'The Church here needs faith like that of the Timorese. It is more anxious about the state of its buildings than it is about their suffering. It is more concerned with its own survival'.[117]

---

[116] Statistic provided by George Pell, archbishop of Melbourne (now archbishop of Sydney), in 'The Role of the Bishop in Promoting the Gospel of life', to Linacre Centre Conference, Cambridge, UK - BCEW Briefing Vol 30 No8, 13.9.2000, p16.

[117] Sr.Susan Connelly *RSJ* to the author, Mary MacKillop Institute for East Timorese Studies, St. Mary's NSW, Sept.1997.

CHAPTER NINE - THE CHURCH IN THE UNITED STATES: IGNORANCE AND INFLUENCE

Currently comprising some 23% of the overall population of the United States the Church in North America is arguably the most successful national Catholic Church in the world. But a number of factors affected the extent to which the Catholic community in the United States appreciated the situation suffered by the people of East Timor and the degree of influence that the Church could have upon developments regarding their welfare. The most important of these were the strategic concerns that determined the US government's foreign policy in the middle and latter half of the twentieth century, which had significant domestic repercussions, and the insularity of the American people.

Strategic Objectives of US Foreign Policy

By the end of the Second World War the United States had become the greatest economic, political and military power on the planet (and in history), a strength swiftly deployed in an all-out effort to serve 'national security' in terms of both defence and the provision of resources. This American project faced its greatest challenge in the growth, from its heartland in the Soviet Union, of international Communism - a confrontation that for the United States had both a foreign and a domestic dimension.[1] It found ideological support in the anti-Communist critique of Catholic Social Doctrine and the practical assistance of many fervent American Catholics both at home and overseas. However, the commitment to national security (and prosperity) preceded this overt confrontation and it continued after the Cold War had come to an end – with significant consequences for the East Timorese.

The basis for US foreign policy in SE Asia, already being crafted in the early years of World War II, was the 'need' for overall regional stability, i.e. an environment open to US capital penetration and exploitation.[2] With the Axis powers vanquished and the Allies in Europe exhausted, the United States was eager to take advantage of the extensive resources and commercial opportunities present in the region. Intervention in the former French Indo-china was the apogee of US military involvement but in terms of the overall strategy of maintaining SE Asia within Washington's sphere of influence it was Indonesia that was the centre-piece of the envisaged political-economic order. Thus the US was involved in the overthrow of Sukarno and in the elevation of General Suharto to the presidency in Jakarta. Defeat in Vietnam gave rise to a renewed isolationist posture in the United States and the Suharto regime's opposition to Communism became all the more important. His Administration also facilitated US capital penetration of Indonesia, and of other countries in ASEAN. Indonesia's support would likewise be appreciated by the United States government and big business cor-porations in assisting 'free trade' among the countries of the Pacific Rim. Compared to such geopolitical and macro-economic benefits to be derived from a positive relationship with In-donesia the plight of East Timor's population of less than a million was of small importance.

United States Foreign Policy and East Timor

The disposition of successive US governments had a critical effect upon events in and relating to East Timor, as did that of the US business community and mass media. There were

---

[1] See Bibliography – Ch9: Jenkins, P.1997; Oshinsky, D.M. 1983; Patterson, J.T.1996.

[2] See: Bibliography – General (East Timor): Gunn, G. 1994, Ch3; 'Indonesia's Importance to US Foreign Policy', Hearings: House Committee on Appropriations on Foreign Assistance, 1976; Bibliography – Ch1: 'Indonesia: Mass Extermination and the Consolidation of Authoritarian Power', Budiardjo, C. in George, A. (ed) 1991; Bibliography – Ch9: Ambrose, S.E. 1993; Selden, M. 1975, pp 15-33.

two dimensions to Washington's engagement in the issue – the passive or permissive, and the positively active.[3] The Central Intelligence Agency furnished the government with an abundance of information indicating Indonesia's intentions, motives and likely style of operation in East Timor.[4] Because of Jakarta's dependence on American military and economic aid Washington had the opportunity and the means to prevent the invasion but deliberately refrained, effectively giving Jakarta the 'green light'. Subsequently the United States gave *de facto* recognition to Indonesia's 'integration' of East Timor as its '27th Province' on the contentious grounds that this arrangement would ultimately be to the benefit of the indigenous people and that there was no feasible alternative.[5] This recognition was confirmed by Washington's willingness to conclude treaties with Indonesia that included the territory of East Timor. As noted already, the oil and natural gas reserves in the southern Timor Sea, and the deep-water submarine passage in the Ombai-Wetar Straits to the north of Timor island were of strategic commercial and military importance to the United States. But more fundamentally the United States was anxious to have Jakarta's co-operation in its capitalist project and to avail of Indonesia's material and human resources: 'We regard Indonesia as a friendly, non aligned nation – a nation we do a lot of business with'.[6] Support was also given by successive US Administrations to Indonesia through generous Development Aid (some specifically directed to projects in East Timor) and other economic assistance. Moreover, the Indonesian military were provided with substantial arms supplies - 90% of the weaponry used in the invasion of East Timor and further extensive resources readily provided thereafter whenever the efforts of *ABRI* at 'pacification' faltered.[7] Of decisive importance to the Indonesian military campaign was the provision of aircraft such as the anti-insurgency Bronco OV10s, and Skyhawks. Successive administrations evaded by dissemblance and subterfuge the determination of Congress that arms supplies to Indonesia should be only for the purposes of national defence.[8] The Indonesian Armed Forces were given access to training in the United States under

---

[3] Bibliography – General (E.Timor): esp. Krieger, H. 1995; Chomsky, N. 1978, 1979, 1982, 1996; Chomsky, N & Herman E.S. 1979; Gunn, G.C. 1994; Horta, J. 1987; 'The United States and East Timor', in Retboll, T. 1998, Ch15; 'East Timor: The United States, and International Responsibility' (Chomsky, N.) & 'US support for the Indonesian Military: Congressional Testimony', (Nairn, A.) in Tanter, R., Selden, M, & Shalom S.R. (eds) 2001, p127f, & p163f; 'The United States: From Complicity to Ambiguity', Scheiner, C. in Hainsworth P. & McCloskey, S. (eds) 2001, p117f.

[4] Liechty, C.P., [former CIA operations officer] 'How Indonesia engulfed East Timor', The Washington Post, 6.1.1992; cf. John Lyons, 'Indonesians lying over Dili, says ex CIA officer', Sydney Morning Herald, 8.2.1992 cf. Dan Southerland, 'US might have averted tragic Timor takeover', The Christian Science Monitor, 17.12.1980, p1f.

[5] See: State Dept Legal Adviser George Aldrich 'Statement before Subcommittee on International Organisations of the House Committee on International Relations, 19th July', State Dept Bulletin Washington DC 12.12.1977. Cited in Krieger, 1995 op.cit. p242.

[6] State Department official, Jan.1976, quoted in 'Aid to Indonesia doubled as US shrugs off Timor', The Australian 22.1.1976, cited in Bibliography – General (East Timor): Retboll, T.1980, pp85-6.

[7] Over $1.1 billion worth of weaponry was supplied to Indonesia by the US from 1975 – 1997. See Bibliography – Ch8: Hartung, W.D., & Washburn, J. 1997.

[8] See: US-RI Mutual Defence Agreement 1958 and subsequent provisions of the Foreign Assistance Act and Foreign Military Sales Act; Statement of G.H.Aldrich, Deputy Legal Adviser, Dept of State, Hearing before the Subcommittee on International Organisations of the Committee on International Relations, 19.7.77. in Krieger 1995, op.cit.p241-242. Evasive tactics by the Administration included: 1) Secretary of State Henry Kissinger justified arms sales to Indonesia by alleging that the Timorese Resistance constituted an assertion of international Communism which menaced Indonesian and therefore regional stability – see: 'Secret/Sensitive Memorandum of Conversation', The Nation (US), 18.12.1975 (Bibliography – General (E Timor) Gunn G. 1994, p125); Bibliography – Ch9: Hitchens, C. 2001.

(2) President Carter arranged for Jakarta to be supplied with Skyhawks through the agency of Israel (source: Noam Chomsky to the author, MIT Boston, 8th Sept.1998).

the (US) International Military Education and Training programme (IMET). The US also deployed its diplomatic strength, bringing its influence to bear at the United Nations and upon individual governments. Thus (Catholic) Daniel Patrick Moynihan, US envoy to the UN during the Ford administration, took pride in his ability to prevent effective UN action against US interests in general and on the issue of East Timor in particular.[9] Likewise, and at a critical period, Washington pressured the Fraser government in Canberra to keep Australian-Indonesian relations positive for the sake of 'Allied interests' in SE Asia.[10] Descriptions of the situation in East Timor biased in favour of Jakarta's rule were being presented to Congress well into the 1980s. This was despite the dreadful loss of life in the territory, the deprived circumstances of the great majority of native people, and the gross human rights abuses being perpetrated against them by the Indonesian Military.[11] Even after the Santa Cruz massacre (1991) the IMET programme was defended as 'increasing the professionalism of *ABRI*, and exposing trainees to democratic values and respect for human rights'.[12]

However, as evidence of gross maladministration in East Timor began to mount, the positive descriptions of Indonesian rule in the territory were increasingly questioned on Capitol Hill by Congressmen sympathetic to the Timorese cause.[13] They called for human rights issues to be raised with Jakarta by the US President and government representatives at every significant opportunity. The visit of Pope John Paul II to East Timor in 1989 (see Chapter 12) did much to raise concerns in Washington, and in 1990 the visit to East Timor of US Ambassador to Jakarta John Monjo was a further stimulus.[14] But such challenges as were presented by US officials to Jakarta were diminished in their effectiveness by the simultaneous effort of successive Administrations to sustain positive relations with Indonesia and to seal lucrative commercial deals.[15] Eventually (from the mid 1990s), *some* limitations were placed upon arms sales to the Indonesian Armed Forces and upon their access to the IMET programme in the United States.[16] In the meantime development aid to Indonesia and other economic help continued with only limited curtailment, the US supporting grants to Indonesia from the Inter-

---

[9] See Bibliography – Ch9: Moynihan, D.P. 1978. The passage was often cited by East Timor campaigners. However, by 1980 Moynihan was signing Senate appeals and by 1982 was expressing regret to his staff over what he did in 1975-6. In 1994 he urged East Timorese self-determination – see: Letter to ETAN US, 7.3.1994, ETAN Docs Vol 17, p103.

[10] 'Fraser given blunt warning at Washington talks: 'Don't anger Jakarta' – US protecting Indon channel for its N-subs', Michael Richardson, The Age, Melbourne, 3.8.1976. Cited in Retboll 1980, op.cit.p94-5, 98-9.

[11] e.g. Statement of H.S.Meyner, Report on Congressional Delegation Visit to East Timor 1977', Hearing before the Subcommittee on International Organisations of the Committee on International Relations, 95th Congress Session I, Washington DC 28.2.1977; 'Statement on the Situation in East Timor' by Ass.Sec.for E.Asian & Pacific Affairs J.H.Holdridge, before the Subcommittee on Asian & Pacific Affairs of the Committee on Foreign Affairs, House of Representatives, 14.9.1982. Full citations in Krieger, 1995, op.cit., pp 242-255, 313-315.

[12] e.g. 'Crisis in E Timor and US Policy toward RI', Statement of K.M.Quinn, Acting Assistant Secretary for East Asian & Pacific Affairs of the House Committee on Foreign Affairs, 6.3.1992. See: Krieger, op.cit., pp315-326.

[13] e.g. Senators Russell Feingold, Patrick Kennedy, Patrick Leahy and Claiborne Pell; Representatives Donald Fraser, Tom Harkin, Tony Hall, Chris Smith, Frank Wolf.

[14] For detail see: Bibliography – Ch2: Macmillan, A. 1992, Ch7; Pinto, C. 1995, pp115-118.

[15] e.g. (1). In 1982 President Reagan praised Indonesia's achievements to visiting President Suharto hoping to enhance US-RI economic and trade relations - 'Remarks at the Arrival Ceremony', 18.10.1982. See Bibliography – General (East Timor): Retboll, T.1984, p99f. (2) In 1994 President Clinton raised Human Rights issues with Suharto at the APEC meeting in Jakarta, but the same year $57 million weapons sales by US corporations to Indonesia had been approved by his Administration. The day after the APEC conference US energy giant Exxon signed a $35 billion deal with Indonesia.

[16] 'East Timor and the United States' Allan Nairn, New Politics, (Brooklyn, NY) 4.1.2000.

governmental Group on Indonesia, IMF and World Bank as well as providing its own substantial unilateral financial assistance.[17] Former US ambassadors to Indonesia persisted in their defence of Jakarta's rule in East Timor.[18] Only when Washington perceived Suharto as a liability to the US project in the region - and when his ousting did not bring political instability in Indonesia to an end - was pressure brought to bear upon Jakarta to settle the disruptive issue of East Timor.[19] This increased significantly during the violent aftermath of the plebiscite conducted by the UN in 1999 and included a total embargo on arms sales and denial of IMET to the Indonesian Military. As soon as order was restored in East Timor by INTERFET and the territory came under UN administration the US immediately sought to resume and defend its positive and extensive relations with Indonesia. But the prohibition on arms sales and IMET did remain in place.[20]

Clearly, the influence the Catholic Church in the United States could have upon the outcome of the East Timor issue would be considerably circumscribed by these governmental and corporate priorities. Moreover, the Church's understanding of the East Timorese plight was at first rather limited, as Dom Martinho Costa Lopes knew when he visited America and sought the support of the US bishops for his people in 1984. In a communication to the national hierarchy on June 12th 1984, publicised later that year in *Pro Mundi Vita*, he attributed this ignorance to 'the isolation of East Timor from the outside world' sustained by the Indonesian regime since its military incursion in December 1975. There were other important reasons besides, as will be elaborated. Dom Martinho drew attention to the Indonesian military's 'targeting' of the local Church 'in retaliation' for its efforts on behalf of the people's basic human rights but he felt it necessary to stress the root cause of his people's suffering. He reminded the bishops that the US State Department itself recognised that no internationally recognised act of political self-determination had yet been afforded to the East Timorese. 'Humanitarian aid would not solve the fundamental problem', he declared, 'war and misery will continue until genuine self-determination is carried out.'

The Response of the Catholic Church in the United States

There are therefore three important dimensions of the American Catholic Church's response to the suffering of the people of East Timor to which consideration should be given. First, the various factors that affected (negatively or positively) the understanding that the Catholic community had of the East Timorese plight. Second, the attention given on Capitol Hill to the concerns of the Church in respect of the East Timor issue. Third, the question as to whether, in its action on behalf of the people of East Timor, the Church attended only to the matter of providing very necessary humanitarian aid, or if it addressed as well the important issue of East Timorese human rights - including that of political self-determination. But first it is necessary to give a brief description of the relevant institutions of the Catholic Church in the United States including their relationship to one another.

The Institutional Church

The national Catholic Church consists of 195 Dioceses each under the direction of an archbishop or bishop who usually operate autonomously. During the historical period covered by this study the institutional edifice included the territorial episcopal conference known as

---

[17] e.g. In 1998 US assistance to Indonesia included $26 million in technical expertise for the Government; $1 billion in short-term trade financing through the Export-Import Bank; $400 million in credit guarantees through the US Dept of Agriculture; $105 million for humanitarian purposes.

[18] 'Indonesia's detractors see only a tragic record of violence, etc', US envoy to the UN Edward Masters (Carter Administration), in Bridge News, 19.12.1996; 'An Errant Nobel Peace Prize', Robert Barry (UN envoy 1992-95), in Washington Post, 29.10.1996.

[19] See: 'The Peace Process in E Timor', Tanter, R. 1997, Inside Indonesia, No 53, 1998.

[20] 'US Policy towards Indonesia and East Timor: a brief overview since the 1970s', by Jane Morse, Office of International Information Programs, US Dept of State 12.10.1999.

the National Conference of Catholic Bishops (NCCB) and the United States Catholic Conference (USCC). The NCCB emerged in response to the expectations of the Second Vatican Council decree *Christus Dominus* that bishops 'jointly exercise their pastoral office' (#38). The USCC was a civil corporation and operational secretariat through which the Bishops, in co-operation with other members of the Church, acted on a wider-than-ecclesiastical scale for the good of the Church and society in the United States (and beyond). These entities have now united to become the United States Conference of Catholic Bishops (USCCB). Within the USCCB are a number of Executive and Departmental Committees including the Committee on International Policy and the Department of Social Development and World Peace – which in turn has an Office of International Justice and Peace. There are also a number of 'Related Organisations' which include Catholic Relief Services (CRS) the official overseas relief and development agency of US Catholics founded by the Bishops in 1943 to assist the poor and disadvantaged outside the USA. CRS operations are funded partly from the proceeds of an annual collection and from Operation Rice Bowl, a Lenten programme that includes almsgiving from individuals, church/school groups, and foundations and corporations around the country. Significant assistance is also given to CRS from the federal government - provision of foodstuffs; defrayment of ocean freight costs; and grants for some emergency operations. The Vatican's *Pontificia Opera Missionaria della Propagazione della Fide* that supports the Church's missionary endeavour throughout the world has a national organisation in the United States entitled the Society for the Propagation of the Faith (SPOF). Each of these institutional entities was engaged in the issue of East Timor but the response of American Catholics was not limited to their activity.

Factors with a negative effect upon the response of the Church

Besides the strategic priorities of successive government administrations the fact that East Timor itself was never an actual *focus* of foreign policy (until the crisis of 1999) also limited the degree of popular knowledge of and reaction to events there. Powerful commercial corporations, especially those engaged in mineral and hydro-carbon exploitation and in arms production, were certainly involved in the decision-making process. These government/business priorities were given sympathetic treatment by the corporate institutions of mass communication that dominated public discourse in the United States.[21] There were indeed a number of editorials and articles in the national press which attended objectively to the East Timorese situation but the inevitable consequence of the isolation of East Timor achieved by the Indonesian regime was a dearth of information needed for any adequate coverage in the print media. Moreover, apart from some footage of the Papal visit in 1989, until the Santa Cruz massacre in 1991 there was a complete lack of television material. These realities significantly affected the understanding that Catholics, along with their fellow citizens, could have of the issue and so had a determinative effect upon the measure of their response.

After the traumatic experience of the American debacle in Vietnam the public mood in the United States was one of exhaustion and political isolationism. Certainly in respect of SE Asia there was no popular wish to become involved in local or regional issues that might prove costly on many counts. To an ill-informed American public the East Timor affair appeared in its early stages to have the hallmarks of another expansionist effort by Communist powers. It seemed preferable for this to be curtailed through the actions of another party, namely Indonesia. Catholics generally shared the national anti-Communist disposition even though Pope John XXIII, in his landmark encyclical *Mater et Magister* (1961), had adopted a more positive approach towards Communism and Communists than had his predecessors.

Events in the 'backyard' of Central America also engaged the attention of the public in the United States before that of the situation in remote Timor. This was especially true for

---

[21] See esp. Bibliography – General (East Timor), Chomsky, N; Bibliography – Ch3: Parenti, M.1993; Rubin, B. & Associates, 1977.

Catholics, many of whom were immigrant Latin Americans, whose missionary personnel provided ongoing and extensive information about the desperate situation that prevailed in Nicaragua, El Salvador, Guatemala, and elsewhere.

A 'linguistic brotherhood' was lacking in America for the East Timorese because there were no refugees from that country. Even the Portuguese immigrants were mostly located in Massachusetts and Rhode Island with their interest primarily engaged with events in Portugal itself rather than in East Timor during the early years of its trauma. Until the late 1980s no American missionaries were present in East Timor to convey first hand experience and evoke concern among the faithful back home in the States.

Moreover, unless directly affected, the great majority of American citizens tend not to give overmuch attention to what happens overseas or even beyond their own locality - despite the significant impact of United States foreign policy upon the world stage. In the context of such insularity, arousing interest in the issue of East Timor among Catholics – whose presence is unevenly spread across the continent - inevitably proved to be a difficult task.

Nonetheless, a significant number of Americans were involved in non-governmental organisations that responded to the East Timor issue. Many of these NGOs, some of which were based in other faith-communities, included Catholics in their ranks and also as executive officers.[22]

In any case, there were matters of serious social concern to attend to within the United States itself: racial tensions, increasing drug abuse, rising unemployment and growth in the numbers of the poor - especially as the 'Defence' expenditure of the Reagan administration exacted its toll from the national coffers. Even before this, in the years between 1979-83, there was a 25% increase in the number of US citizens classified as living below the poverty level – a total in excess of 35 million people.[23] This social phenomenon engaged the attention of the Church at all levels - in the provision of urgent social analysis and in practical support for the needy.[24] Inevitably this involvement affected the Church's capacity to respond to other issues - especially those regarded as 'remote'. Furthermore, the social justice activism in respect of particular situations overseas which had engaged the energies of some Church members in the late 1960s and early 1970s diminished thereafter for these reasons, and because of 'compassion fatigue' and the growth of individualism. Also it became increasingly recognised that the growth of globalisation impacted upon particular situations and that more radical responses were required to challenge corporate power.

During the 1960s-70s, as elsewhere in the affluent Western world, secularism, relativism and consumerism also impacted upon the life of the American Catholic community further affecting the pre-World War II cohesion and confidence and the capacity for concerted action. In general the wealthy looked away from justice issues, while the new middle classes were anxious not to risk the security they had achieved. There were also increasingly complex and challenging medico-moral issues that occupied the attention of hierarchy, congregations of

---

[22] E.g.
International campaigns such as Saferworld, Friends of the Earth, Human Rights Watch, etc. and national organisations such as Peace Action, Veterans for Peace, Visions in Action, Foreign Bases Project, Americans for Democratic Action, War Resisters League, etc. The East Timor Action Network established in 1991 was to become one of the most effective pressure groups. Religious organisations included: Pax Christi (US), Network (National Catholic Social Lobby), Episcopal Peace Fellowship, Common Global Ministries Board (UCC), East Timor Religious Outreach, Friends Committee on National Legislation (Quakers), Religious Action Center of Reform Judaism, Union of American Hebrew Congregations, Jews against Genocide, etc.

[23] Bibliography – Ch9: Jenkins, P. 1997, op.cit. pp 287, 293.

[24] Bibliography – Ch9: USCC 1986. In San Francisco in 1998 this author was informed that over 2000 meals *a day* were provided for the poor by just one inner city parish among others. New York City had 1000 emergency food programmes in 1997.

religious and the laity alike and gave rise to multiple 'communions of conscience' or divergent views among groups within the overall family of the Church.[25]

The Second Vatican Council stimulated a number of positive developments in the life of the Church but also had its negative repercussions. These were similar in many ways to those already outlined in respect of the Church in Australia. Religious ministry to overseas situations, which had always included the supply of humanitarian aid, began to incorporate social analysis, the promotion of justice and the defence of human rights – but there were many places competing with East Timor for attention. There was a sharp decline in the number of Diocesan priests, and of men and women joining religious congregations. This meant that the usual constraints upon the parochial clergy to give attention to their local responsibilities could only increase, along with the tendency of many pastors to concentrate on the internal affairs of the institutional Church including administrative and liturgical concerns. Activism in social justice issues is always problematical for those who must minister to a cross section of the community, and with vocations increasingly deriving from the middle class a management perspective which sought to avoid 'rocking the boat' became inevitable. The decrease in men and women belonging to congregations of religious likewise diminished the range of tasks to which they could attend (creating particular problems in the maintenance of the system of Catholic education. The loss of personnel, and the rise in the median age of those remaining (to 60 plus years by the 1990s) detracted from the resources and energy they could bring to issues of social justice. However, it also meant that their action became more focused and that mature judgements were made by these men and women who were rich in experience. The East Timor situation came to be included in those addressed by their members, present and previous alike, as will be seen. But, at the same time, internal issues of justice – such as the proper role of women in the Church – assumed a new importance. Various external concerns such as welfare cuts and unjust aspects of the process of receiving immigrants into the United States also had greater immediacy than the issue of remote East Timor which lacked a direct US connection obvious to the general public.

In the years following Vatican II perhaps only a third of American lay Catholics could be described as highly committed but with 60 million members overall the Church constituted the country's biggest religious body so this core still amounted to a politically significant group.[26] Social justice issues, at one time associated more with special groups such as the Catholic Worker movement founded by Dorothy Day, steadily became 'mainstream' concerns within the Catholic community. However, they were still not regarded as a *constitutive* part of parish life and, apart from appeals for financial contributions to particular needy causes, could easily be marginalised or overlooked altogether. Despite an increase in adult catechesis after Vatican II, ignorance of the Scriptures and of Catholic Social Doctrine remained widespread, and the motivation for social justice activism was thus diminished. For many Catholic laity, participation in Sunday Liturgies did not connect with such Gospel imperatives. Moreover, as poverty increased in the United States itself domestic issues began to outnumber the international concerns to which diocesan and parish 'Offices of Justice and Peace' could give their attention. With an increase in the numbers of elderly people, 'care giving' became a major social phenomenon, and those committed to such service had correspondingly less time for any other cause. Although a significant migration of Asian Catholics to the United States (from the Philippines, Samoa, Korea and Vietnam) had taken place after World War II these people were also understandably preoccupied with their own needs, and for them likewise the problems facing the East Timorese were very distant.

The huge territory in which the American Catholic Church lives and the autonomous character of its one hundred and ninety-five Dioceses were also factors that militated against co-ordinated action. Far from being a totalitarian monolith the Church in the United States is

[25] For more detail see Bibliography – Ch9: Morris, C.R. 1997, Ch 2 and 6.
[26] See Bibliography – Ch9: Morris, C.R. 1997 op.cit. Part III 'Crisis'.

actually one of the most decentralised large organisations in the country. But its sheer size, dynamism, and relative wealth has also meant that the influence of the Vatican upon the activities of American Bishops with regard to both domestic and foreign affairs has always been limited.[27] It is therefore thought unlikely that the Papal Envoy to the United States exercised any restraining influence upon the American episcopate in respect of the East Timor issue.[28] This is not to say that the bishops' posture on matters of social justice generally was unaffected by Vatican policies, a matter with implications for the status afforded to its official Social Doctrine within the Church itself.[29]

Factors with a positive effect upon the response of the Church

The most important positive influence upon the Church's response to the East Timorese plight was the dedication of a number of key individuals whose contribution cannot be overstated.

Dom Martinho Costa Lopes, former Apostolic Administrator to the East Timor diocese of Dili, was one such person. His 1984 communication to the US Bishops Committee for Social Development and Peace has been cited above and (more fully) in Chapter 5. He made an impact upon key USCC staff such as Ed Doherty, and met with Cardinal John O'Connor in 1984 and again in 1986. In 1990, not long before his miserable death in Lisbon, he sent to the American Bishops Conference a crucifix carved in precious Timorese sandalwood as a tangible plea for their continued concern for his people.[30] In the intervening years he had made his own efforts to enhance the US media's appreciation of the true situation in his homeland, approached the State Department and appealed to President Reagan[31] – but these efforts were not to be as fruitful as his contact with NCCB-USCC personnel.

The persistent advocacy of the East Timorese cause by Fr.Reinaldo Cardoso, the former Portuguese missionary to East Timor who had come to minister to his compatriots in Rhode Island was most important. To him can be attributed the 'breaking open' of the East Timor issue in the United States as a whole, as well as in the Catholic Church. He was an invaluable link between the Catholic Church in East Timor and Church and secular institutions in the United States. Because he had served in East Timor for twelve years (1960-72) and considered this time to be the most significant years of his ministry, after Indonesia's 1975 invasion he pursued contacts with his former colleagues like no other, tirelessly bringing information to the outside world. Members of the East Timor Church trusted him like almost no one else. At first his efforts were focused on appeals in parishes, gathering signatures for petitions to Congress and to the government of Portugal. When these made little headway he changed strategy and began to make direct contact with officials at the State Department and with Congressmen on Capitol Hill or in their constituencies. He entered into close association with Arnold Kohen who was already engaged in the East Timorese cause. This collaboration

[27] See Morris, C.R. 1997, op.cit. Part 1 Ch4, 5; Part 2, Ch 6, 9; Part 3, Ch13.

[28] 'The welfare of the American Church in its many dioceses leaves the Nuncio with little time to concern himself with any actions of the Bishops in respect of East Timor' – Bishop Wm.McCormack, SPOF, to the author, New York, 2.9.98.
'The Nuncio's influence upon the hierarchy's response to the East Timor issue has been only positive' – Thomas Quigley, Adviser on Foreign Affairs USCC Office of International Justice & Peace, to the author, Washington 25.8.98.

[29] 'Recent tendencies by Rome towards disciplinary action are enervating and latter-day appointments of 'conservative' candidates to the episcopacy result in most bishops refraining from engagement in public activism for any cause - even when/if they permit their clergy to be so involved.' – sentiments of various lay Catholics and consecrated religious expressed to the author, USA Sept.1998.

[30] Bibliography – General (East Timor): Kohen, A. 1999, p152.

[31] e.g. Costa Lopes wrote to President Reagan and to the New York Times in 1985. In 1986 he raised the issue with staffers of the House Committee on Foreign Affairs to be told he was 'out of luck'. Bibliography – Ch5: Lennox, R. 2000, p216.

was instrumental in promoting Hearings on the East Timor situation in the Senate and the House of Representatives. It was with Cardoso's help that the testimony to Congress by East Timorese priests Leonetto do Rego (1979) and Francisco Fernandes (1980) was arranged, arousing significant media interest. In 1989 he was again able to facilitate informative reports on the prevailing situation in East Timor by Timorese priests Leon da Costa and Domingos da Cunha in person. Thereafter the quality and range of the ongoing information he was able to communicate through intermediaries about events in East Timor to key persons in the US government and Catholic Church steadily increased. The assistance of Fr.Cardoso was also of crucial importance for US investigative journalists such as Allan Nairn and Amy Goodman who were to witness the Santa Cruz Massacre – about which he gathered significant information that saved many lives. This event proved to be a watershed in American national awareness of the East Timorese plight as it did in other countries around the world. It was he who convinced Bishop Belo to make his first visit to the USA in 1993 to address a meeting of the US Catholic Bishops, which had the greatest impact until that date to draw the East Timor issue toward their attention. For the sake of effectiveness, and for the welfare of the Timorese themselves, much of Fr.Cardoso's work was necessarily discreet and will probably never be fully appreciated.[32]

The importance of Arnold Kohen's engagement in the East Timorese cause is widely recognised and applauded by the international NGO community. Mgr Costa Lopes observed that the Church-sponsored organisation headed up by Kohen – the East Timor Research Project - 'played a highly significant role in bringing news of East Timor's plight to the attention of many in the United States, as well as to non-governmental agencies and the media'.[33] His collaboration with Fr.Cardoso was to bring him into a special relationship with the American Bishops Conference for whom he became a consultant on the East Timor issue supplying not only factual information but also sound advice on the timing and manner of any interventions by the Bishops Conference. Staff of the USCC interviewed by the author (Washington and New York, September 1998) were unanimous in their recognition that Kohen's knowledge and tenacity were of crucial importance in the stirring of concern within the Catholic Church, and more widely. From 1979 onwards a chief focus of his attention was work with Congress in respect of the East Timorese plight. It was he who supplied Noam Chomsky with the information the scholar deployed so effectively in various national and international forums, and in turn Kohen was put in touch by Chomsky with the Maryknoll Missioners who were to take up the East Timor cause with a will. Kohen won the support of Representative Tony Hall who proved to be a staunch advocate of Timorese welfare over many years, and several other Congressmen. Kohen's commitment to East Timorese welfare was able to gain the confidence of bishop Belo whose biographer he became. In 1993, in collaboration with Fr.Cardoso, he was able to arrange for Belo to spend some time in the United States, during which the bishop was able to meet with Congressional aides as well as with the US hierarchy including Cardinal O'Connor. There was no media coverage of this visit – it was deliberately avoided as at that time it would have caused considerable trouble for the Bishop.

Belo was a significant influence upon the Catholic Church's response. He made a very positive impression upon both ecclesiastical and government officials with his balanced opinions, his common sense, his humanity and compassion, and they recognised the support he had won in the Catholic Church world-wide. The bishops were particularly moved by the evident quality of Belo's pastoral relationship with his people. In 1995 he made a second visit to the USA and addressed the USCC Committee for International Policy (CIP), cannily alluding in his appeal to the comparable oppression endured by the Polish and Irish forebears of some of the bishops. Belo's courage and charisma gained the attention of the US media and

---

[32] Fr.Cardoso, Rhode Island, and A.Kohen, Washington DC, Aug-Sept.'98, to the author.

[33] 'Message to church and humanitarian agencies and persons of good will', October 1989. Copy on file. In 1994 the ET Research Project was renamed 'The Humanitarian Project'.

his receipt of the Nobel Peace Prize in 1996 raised the profile of the East Timor issue to new heights in the country. In 1997 he was to make a further visit during which he addressed the Kansas City meeting of NCCB and met with young Catholics in Boston.

Within the institutional structures of the US Church there were staffers who planted seeds or drove home concerns on the East Timor issue. Among them was Ed Doherty, a former US diplomat who was very active in this respect within the Justice and Peace Office of the CIP between 1979 – 1986 when he retired. He alerted the State Department, Congress, the news media, and grass roots Church constituencies as well as, and principally, the American bishops themselves. Fr.Bill Lewers *CSC* who was the Director of the CIP Justice and Peace Office between 1979-89 also urged that attention be given to the situation in East Timor.

The Catholic Institute of International Relations in London was another important influence upon the NCCB-USCC. Their well-informed personnel and published reports contributed to the understanding of the East Timor issue in Church circles and beyond in the United States, as they did in Australia and elsewhere around the globe.

The status afforded by US officialdom to the views of the Catholic Church[34]

There is no direct link between the institution of the Catholic Church and Congress but the USCCB has a significant influence upon Government policy and there is considerable respect for the stance taken by the Church on particular issues – including East Timor.[35] This is because the Catholic Church is the largest Christian denomination in the United States and cuts across political boundaries, and because its spokespersons are generally regarded as representative of their constituency. The Church's official pronouncements draw serious attention and carry considerable moral authority. At the very least they provoke discussion. Pope John Paul II is widely admired. Catholics are perceived as distinctively more concerned than some other churches about social justice issues in general, and even those who might not agree with them hold USCCB statements in some regard. A key factor is the refusal of Catholic leadership to join with extreme wings on issues or to be over-identified with particular organisations of activists. Consideration must now be given as to whether this respected status was fully exploited with regard to East Timorese welfare. The question must also be faced as to whether, besides providing the East Timorese people with humanitarian aid, the Church in the United States attended to their human rights and addressed the issue of their political self-determination.

Catholic Relief Services

The engagement of Catholic Relief Services (CRS) in East Timor falls into two distinct periods: from its first admission into the territory by the Indonesian authorities in September 1979 until 1994, and thereafter.

The first period was characterised by considerable ambiguity. CRS aid reached East Timor via Indonesian channels and was used for the maintenance of structures of oppression. Although the programme was efficiently conducted it was not a church operation, nor that of a voluntary independent agency. CRS worked as a subcontractor to the US government implementing a government-to-government programme on governmental terms:

---

[34] Appraisal derives from interviews conducted by the author with various staff of USCC, with Arnold Kohen (Washington DC, Aug.1998), with Maryknoll Missioner Fr.Ed Killackey (Washington DC, 26th Aug.1998), and staffers Joseph Reis, Bob Zachritz, and Linda Rotblatt representing respectively Representatives Chris Smith and Tony Hall, and Senator Russell Feingold, (Capitol Hill, August 27th 1998).

[35] E.g. US Government policy in Central America, the Landmines Campaign, Third World debt relief, international religious freedom, etc.

Essentially the programme is an exercise in American foreign policy the purpose of which is to secure and complete Indonesian take-over of an unwilling East Timor...

The bulk of the aid is coming from the US government...and CRS is working through the Indonesian government in East Timor, not the local church or any other agency...

CRS co-operation with the US and Indonesian government has extended even to the point of adopting without question their distorted analysis of the situation in East Timor...and [by] concentrating its efforts on 150 'resettlement sites'...which represent the first stages of an Indonesian re-structuring of East Timorese society...these centres are both the products of Indonesia's military subjugation of Timor and the means of furthering that process.[36]

Although CRS officials sought to convey otherwise, the engagement of CRS in East Timor initially took place without the consultation that would have been appropriate with USCC, or with the Vatican or with the Indonesian Bishops Conference, and was entrusted to the director of the CRS Indonesia programme. Despite its vaunted a-politicism, CRS collaboration with the Indonesian government locked it into Jakarta's position on East Timor. This it defended using the very same arguments and steadfastly avoiding the issue of self-determination – and even ongoing human rights abuses such as extra-judicial executions, political arrests, ill-treatment of prisoners, etc.[37] The CRS representative in East Timor dismissed the warnings by Mgr Costa Lopes of impending famine as without foundation although a colleague had described the malnutrition as 'like Biafra and the Thai camps' (in 1979).[38] Nor was there much sign of co-operation on the part of CRS in New York with the USCC Office of International Justice and Peace, or evidence of commitment to participation in the Congressional Hearings on East Timor.[39] The negative effects of CRS accounts of the situation in East Timor during this first period upon the US media – and therefore the general public, including Catholics – cannot be overstated.[40] CRS had direct access to Catholic parishes through its diocesan contacts whose fund-raising publicity disseminated the same positive evaluation of its work in East Timor. The silence of the agency on human rights violations in the territory and the ambiguity of its position was commented upon in the national Catholic press.[41]

In 1988 the US staffers of CRS left East Timor and handed direction of its projects over to local people working for the Catholic Church. To some extent this change of mode pointed towards the second stage in CRS engagement that got underway when Ken Hackett took over as director in 1994. Besides its previous concerns of relief and development, issues of justice and peace entered upon the CRS agenda and it became more engaged in advocacy of particular causes and also in entrusting management responsibility to local inhabitants. In East Timor's 'Year of Crisis' CRS endeavoured to support efforts at intra-Timorese reconciliation prior to the UN plebiscite[42], and subsequently became engaged in 'peace building' initiatives with the Diocese of Dili Justice and Peace Commission. The current ties between CRS and

---

[36] Bibliography – Ch8: Walsh, P.1980 (2) Development Dossier, No 1 (July), Australian Council for Overseas Aid (ACFOA), Canberra.

[37] Bibliography – Ch6: Walsh, P. 1980 (1) 'Notes on the East Timor Issue' and (2) Development Dossier No1, op.cit. editorial p 3, and 'The Politics of Aid to East Timor' p16-21. See also Bibliography – General (East Timor): Dunn, J. 1996 op.cit. p291-2; and CRS' own documents – e.g. 'Project Proposal: ETADEP' 29 July 1981, copy on file.

[38] Statement from Patrick C. Johns, CRS representative in East Timor, in the form of a letter to Bishop E. B. Broderick, Executive Director of CRS, New York (Feb.1982). Copy on file.

[39] Bibliography – Ch6: Walsh, P. 1980 (1), op.cit.

[40] Arnold Kohen to the author, Washington DC August 1998.

[41] See: 'Church leaders roles critical in East Timor as Indonesia continues siege'; 'British rights group charges CRS in Timor food aid fraud', Steve Askin, National Catholic Reporter, Washington, 7.5.82 and 28.5.82.

[42] 'Violence may delay [ ] ballot, etc', Atika Shubert, Catholic News Service (Dili), 19.7.1999.

the CIP Office of Justice and Peace are close and constantly exercised. However, CRS still remains financially beholden to the US government.

The Society for the Propagation of the Faith (SPOF)

The *Pontificia Opera Missionaria della Propagazione della Fide*, titled 'Society' in the US Church, is primarily engaged – as elsewhere - in generating financial support for purely religious development. The SPOF assistance to Church institutions and enterprises in East Timor included grants to the dioceses of Dili and Baucau. It is not the function of the APF to deal with political matters which are the responsibility of the Vatican Secretariat and the SPOF organisation did not on that account directly address the question of East Timorese political self-determination. As explained to the author on behalf of the Society by bishop William McCormack, the matter of self-determination should not be envisaged as a 'moral absolute' that the Church should defend as a matter of principle. However, it was considered that East Timor's claim in this respect 'was being properly pursued within the ongoing UN process' and concern was certainly expressed by SPOF over human rights violations in East Timor.[43]

The National Conference of Catholic Bishops–United States Catholic Conference

There are several dimensions to the response of the NCCB-USCC and of its individual members. There were the public Statements - which were few but of considerable importance. There was discreet advocacy including confidential correspondence and private meetings which was also of great importance but because of its very nature is not known by the general public. There were also more general recommendations made by the Bishops Conference that had their application, and some general policies that impinged upon the East Timor issue.

The first public Statement regarding East Timor was made in 1985. Bishop Francis Murphy, auxiliary in Baltimore, representing the Conference at the launch of an Amnesty International Report on East Timor, called for a full Congressional Hearing on Amnesty's allegations. 'We need to break down the walls of silence about that forgotten place', he declared.[44] In their next Statement on 25th March 1987 the Conference acknowledged that 'in recent years' the East Timor issue had 'begun to receive the attention it deserves' but that this 'had not yet been translated into action needed to right the wrongs which continued to this day'. The concerns already expressed by Pope John Paul II in 1984 to the Indonesian Ambassador to the Holy See, and by Bishops Conferences - and Justice and Peace Commissions - in Europe, Canada and Japan were noted. The Statement made blunt reference to 'the brutal invasion and take-over by Indonesia' and to the appalling loss of life during 'the armed conflict that persists in the territory'. It urged that 'a serious effort to bring a just and authentic peace to East Timor should be made' and called for 'freedom of expression' to be afforded to the local Catholic Church. Quoting from the Second Vatican Council's decree *Gaudium et Spes* (par.87) the Conference was critical of the birth control measures enforced by the Indonesian administration which had taken on 'the character of genocide' in East Timor. It was recommended that the 'East Timor tragedy be highlighted whenever possible' and the Conference called for 'appropriate representation' by the US government which 'could influence that of Indonesia to take measures that would help bring a just and authentic peace to the territory'. The view was expressed that the 'friendly relations' between the US government and that of Indonesia which included 'much economic and military assistance' gave Washington the 'right to raise these issues' with Jakarta.[45] A comprehensive policy Statement was issued by

---

[43] Bishop McCormack to the author, New York, 2nd Sept.1998.

[44] Cited in *Tapol* Bulletin No. 71, Sept.1985, p 23; Timor Link, CIIR, 3.10.1985.

[45] For text see: Bibliography – Ch8: CCJPD 1993, pp27-8; and East Timor Link, CIIR London, 10.7.1987, p5.

the USCC Administrative Board in 1987 which was circulated widely in the United States and abroad. A further Statement was made in 1991 when the Conference called upon the US government to denounce the massacre in the Santa Cruz cemetery which was 'a gross violation of the most fundamental right, that of life itself'. In 1994 another policy Statement was issued expressing solidarity with the Church and people in East Timor and castigating the 'genocidal policies' and 'abusive, harsh and often violent treatment' of the Timorese by 'their Indonesian military overseers'. Reference was made to the Santa Cruz massacre, and admiration expressed over the 'bravery of the people...and their determination to preserve their culture against overwhelming odds'. The Conference acknowledged the 'special bond we feel with them that comes from our shared Catholic faith' which had by then been adopted 'by over 90%' of the people. The view was that that a mechanism to resolve the issue, namely the tripartite meetings sponsored by the UN, was already in place and should be reinvigorated. It was recognised that there were 'different proposals among the people for resolving the region's status' but it was argued that the partnership between the US and Indonesian governments should give rise to 'new initiatives...to encourage both the resolution of the political crisis and full compliance on issues of human rights'. The Statement concluded by calling upon American Catholics to 'pray for the well-being of our Timorese brothers and sisters'.[46] In this communication the Conference came as close as possible to urging an authentic act of self-determination without prescribing or even recommending the means for such a process which might have invited the charge of 'political partisanship' or of an 'inappropriate interference' in political matters.

The award of the Nobel Peace Prize in October 1996 to co-laureate bishop Belo evoked words of congratulation from the Conference and a brief summary of the action that had been taken to date in solidarity with him and his long-suffering people.[47]

In 1999, East Timor's 'year of crisis', there was a sequence of very strong-worded communications from the USCC. In June the Conference expressed dismay at the violent intimidation 'fomented by army elements' that preceded the UN plebiscite. They called for 'decisive action by parts of the international community' and for 'greater diplomatic pressure to be applied immediately and urgently by the United States especially'. Washington was 'respectfully urged to act decisively to take the necessary steps, including consideration of maintaining a resident diplomatic presence in the territory throughout this period'.[48] On September 7th archbishop Theodore McCarrick declared on behalf of the Conference that:

> Our worst fears have been realised...the population is being terrorised by anti-independence militias reportedly with the support, or at least acquiescence of the Indonesian military and police. It is vital that our government use strong and effective pressure to convince the Indonesian government to meet its responsibilities to stop the violence and ensure that the wishes of the East Timorese are respected. If Indonesia is not willing or able immediately to fulfil its responsibilities...then the United States should support the prompt deployment of a UN peacekeeping force to establish order, protect the innocent, and ensure a peaceful transition to independence.

On September 15th the Conference welcomed the agreement of the Indonesian government to allow the entry of an international military force to secure and maintain peace but 'in view of the recent history of broken promises' this was with 'a certain scepticism that the violence will be stopped immediately'. In such circumstances:

---

[46] Statement: bishop Daniel P.Reilly, Chairman Committee on International Policy (CIP), USCC, Washington DC, 26 July 1994.

[47] Statement of bishop Daniel P.Reilly, Chairman USCC CIP, 11.10.1996.

[48] Statement on East Timor, archbishop Theodore E. McCarrick, Chairman CIP, 10.6.1999.

Sustained pressure from the international community and especially from the United States ought to characterise all dealings with the Indonesian authorities...Peace must be secured and the expressed will of the vast majority of the people for a free and independent East Timor must be respected.

A further and more comprehensive Statement was issued on September 30[th.] In this the US government was urged to 'take a leadership role' among the international community in working with the Indonesian government to achieve a number of key objectives. These were stated to be the complete cessation of the violence against East Timorese wherever they were; full, free and safe access to East Timorese in all locations by humanitarian agencies; and the safe return home of the many thousands of East Timorese who had fled their homes or been deported in the mayhem. Other practical recommendations included the making available of resettlement options, and that governments and agencies make every effort to keep families together.

Besides these principal Statements of the NCCB-USCC there were other important communications on the issue of East Timor. On November 6th 1992, to mark the first anniversary of the Santa Cruz massacre, archbishop John Roach wrote as CIP Chairman to acting Secretary of State Eagleburger urging greater US attention to the plight of the Timorese and expressing Conference support for the US Congress decision to cut military training funds for Indonesia (IMET). Washington was requested to encourage the UN to monitor human rights in East Timor and to take further steps 'to resolve *the central question of East Timor's political status*'. On February 2nd 1994 archbishop Daniel Reilly brought to the attention of Winston Lord, Assistant Secretary for East Asian and Pacific Affairs, the difficulties being experienced over the renewal of their visas by three dedicated Salesian missionaries in East Timor, Frs Eugenio Locatelli, Andres Calleja and Joao de Deus Pires. He took the opportunity to express concern over the continuing human rights violations in the territory. On October 24th 1995, at the time of the 50th anniversary of the founding of the United Nations - and in advance of a scheduled meeting between Presidents Clinton and Suharto - he wrote to Anthony Lake, National Security Adviser. Expressing concern about 'the rising tensions and violence...and reliable reports of torture and severe beatings meted out upon people in detention' in East Timor, he continued:

> It is urgent that the United States convey our desire that human rights be respected...and that the Indonesian leaders take concrete steps to restrain the security forces and the military... It would be fitting if the United States were to provide added backing for UN efforts to promote dialogue...such as might lead ultimately to measures acceptable to all parties.

Archbishop McCarrick wrote to President Clinton on May 29th 1997 requesting that he find time, if possible, for a 'private and off-the record meeting' with bishop Belo who was to be the guest of the NCCB Spring Assembly. When B.J.Habibie succeeded to the Indonesian Presidency in 1998, archbishop McCarrick wrote on behalf of the CIP to Secretary of State Madeleine Albright. He called for the United States 'to press anew for a speedy resolution of the East Timor status question, that, with the good offices of the United Nations, must be based *on the freely expressed wishes of the people of East Timor*'. He also urged that the US 'advocate an immediate reduction of the Indonesian military presence in East Timor, the release of political prisoners, the guarantee of freedom of speech and assembly, and an end to abuses of people's human rights'.[49]

---

[49] Letter to Hon. Madeleine Albright, Secretary of State, from archbishop Theodore E.McCarrick, Chairman CIP, USCC, 5th June 1998 – (author's italics).

In 1999, the year of crisis, besides the public Statements cited above, archbishop McCarrick wrote to Defence Department Secretary Cohen about the escalating violence being provoked by the 'militias' in the territory prior to the UN ballot. He expressed the bishops' view that 'the United States should do far more to exert its influence on Jakarta'.[50] When the referendum was followed by widespread violence bishop Joseph Fiorenza, president of the NCCB-USCC, wrote to President Clinton condemning the atrocities and calling for the immediate deployment of peacekeeping forces in the territory.[51] This letter was read aloud in St. Patrick's Cathedral New York on the express orders of Cardinal O'Connor – its tone is one of absolute outrage:

> We have been shocked, dismayed and deeply disturbed by the brutality unleashed against the defenceless people of East Timor by the Indonesian security forces and militias...
>
> This has been a week of unmitigated terror throughout the territory, a week of cold-blooded murder, or arson and plunder, of forced removal of thousands upon thousands of innocent people whose only mistake was to trust the international community while freely casting their ballots in favour of self-determination.
> It has been a week of broken promises and false assurances by the Indonesian government, and of temporising by the rest of the world community, including our own government. We have been overly concerned not to offend the Indonesian authorities who, by all accounts, are themselves unable to control the murderous bands in East Timor, but have been fully successful in preventing the essential deployment of an international peace keeping force.
>
> The Catholic Church in particular is experiencing a bloody persecution. ...[ ] Not only is East Timor experiencing human rights violations on a massive scale, it is also undergoing a brutal and systematic religious persecution...
>
> Mr President, this must end, and end immediately. A peacekeeping force must be sent to the region, with or without the acquiescence of Jakarta. [ ] An effort to come to the aid of the people of East Timor need not be an intrusion into a nation's internal affairs but a response to the will of the population...
>
> Together with the Holy See, the Bishops of the United States call for the immediate adoption by the United Nations of a resolution calling for the creation of an international peacekeeping force, and urge the United States to exercise strong leadership in securing that result.
> I pray that you will be guided to take the actions necessary to save the lives of the suffering people of East Timor who, by committing themselves to the democratic process, placed their trust in the great democracies of the world. We cannot betray them.

From such Statements and other communications it is quite evident that the hierarchy in the United States were seriously concerned about the continual violation of human rights in East Timor; and were convinced of the importance of Timorese participation in the determination of their own affairs. They were of the view that 'for social progress in East Timor there needed to be structures in place for political development'.[52] Some individual bishops became particularly supportive of the East Timor cause, for example John McCarthy (Austin, Texas), Thomas Gumbleton (Detroit), and John Cummins (Oakland, California) - who visited East Timor in 1990. Cardinal O'Connor demonstrated a special personal concern for East Timor,

---

[50] Letter to Hon.William.S.Cohen, Secretary Department of Defense, from archbishop Theodore E. McCarrick, Chairman International Policy Committee, USCC, 21 April 1999.

[51] Letter to President W.J.Clinton, 9th Sept 1999, from archbishop Joseph Fiorenza, President of the NCCB-USCC. Cf 'Call for peacekeeping troops in E Timor', S.Steele, Catholic New York, 16.9.99.

[52] Bishop William McCormack, for SPOF to the author, New York 2nd Sept.1998. The special support given to bishop Belo by archbishop McCarrick (Newark) and Cardinal Bernard Law (Boston) amongst others is remarked by Kohen, A. 1999, op.cit., p250.

meeting with each of the Apostolic Administrators of the East Timor Diocese of Dili on more than one occasion. As early as 1985 he wrote a letter of solidarity to bishop Belo, then only recently appointed as Apostolic Administrator. Later on he was to make Belo a promise that he would immediately contact the State Department on the bishop's behalf if ever Belo were in serious trouble, a pledge that was fulfilled.[53] In 1999 he met with a delegation of East Timorese in New York, telephoned religious sisters in East Timor to assure them of the US Church's concern for their plight, and appealed for support from American Catholics for donations towards emergency relief.[54] There is no doubt that the concern of the Cardinal over the welfare of the East Timorese was an important influence upon former National Security Adviser William P.Clark (Reagan Administration) to become engaged in the issue as the crisis peaked. A Catholic himself, Clark was influential not only within the faith community to which he belonged but also in political circles - despite the fact that by then he had been retired from government service in foreign policy areas for over fifteen years. Once appraised of the critical situation pertaining in East Timor in early September 1999 Clark worked assiduously with numerous Republicans, Catholic and otherwise during what was a crucial period. These efforts resulted in further pressure being brought to bear upon President Clinton to take positive action.[55]

But Cardinal O'Connor's influence upon the East Timor issue was broader than this. He continually asked questions about the 'moral dimension' of US government policy in general – 'an emphasis which cut through ideology and 'political spin' and focused on people, especially the poor and our solidarity with them. For him social justice was a moral issue that should be unaffected by political affiliations'.[56] Also important was the perspective of the 'community of conscience' adopted and promoted by Chicago's Cardinal Joseph Bernardin. For him the Church's mark of 'universality' meant that its members had a responsibility for others. He also used the image of the 'seamless garment' to emphasise that many disparate concerns – abortion, the death penalty, nuclear testing, third world poverty, racial justice - were all 'life issues'. This provided an important umbrella for activism on all counts, including that on behalf of East Timor, and brought diverse campaigners into greater unity of purpose.

Such general recommendations and policy directives included the NCCB-USCC publication in 1986 of a very significant pastoral letter on the national economy entitled 'Economic Justice for All' (cited above). This drew attention to the impact of US policies upon other nations and the powerful influence the US had in multilateral institutions such as the International Monetary Fund and World Bank, as well as the United Nations (par.13). The investment of resources in the weapons industry, and arms sales, were remarked upon as a drain on the national economy and as a contributing factor to political instability in other parts of the world (par.20, 288). US business and financial enterprises were described as helping 'to determine the justice or injustice of the world economy' (p.116). In sections on Poverty and Economic Inequality (par.170, 183) the bishops expressed the moral imperative of attending to the poor as a preferential option - both in the United States itself and in respect of other nations:

> We have to go beyond economic gain and national security as a starting point for policy dialogue. (par.260, cf. par.262)

---

[53] Arnold Kohen to the author, Washington DC, August 1998.

[54] 'East Timorese appeal to Cardinal O'Connor in Struggle', and 'Cardinal phones nuns in East Timor making pledge of support in crisis', S.Steele, Catholic New York, 20.5.99, and 23.9.99; 'Cardinal calls for Catholic solidarity, etc', Catholic Medical Mission Board, 25.9.99.

[55] Arnold Kohen, in email correspondence with the author, and see his article 'Under the Gun' in Columbia (Periodical of the Knights of Columbus) April 2000 Vol LXXX, No4, p.7.

[56] George Horton, Archdiocese of New York, for Cardinal O'Connor, to the author, New York 2.9.1999.

They were critical of the fact that 'our bilateral aid has become increasingly militarised and security related in recent years' (par 265) and urged that the country's economic relationships should be guided by policies that serve human dignity and justice:

> We must expand our understanding of the moral responsibility of citizens to serve the Common Good of the entire planet. (par.322)

The document drew particular attention to the importance of responsible investment by individual Christians and church institutions (par 354), a matter to which more consideration is given below. The Pastoral Letter also emphasised that the Church's call to a mission of 'servanthood' required that the practice of charity do more than alleviate misery:

> It should probe the meaning of suffering and provoke a response that seeks to remedy causes. True charity leads to advocacy. (par.356)

These principles, rooted in Catholic Social Doctrine, clearly had implications in the specific respect of the policies of US government and commerce which had impacted so extensively upon SE Asia including Indonesia and East Timor – and indeed for the Church's own response to the situation in that troubled territory. Interestingly, it seems that from this time onwards that the concern of the Bishops for the situation in East Timor was more publicly manifest than it been hitherto. Nonetheless, the Pastoral Letter caused no little controversy, and among its critics was right wing Catholic theologian Michael Novak who pointed up the potential of corporations to be 'instruments of redemption, humane purposes and values...bearers of God's grace' as much as 'obstacles to salvation'.[57]

As indicated already, in the United States Catholic community the Social Doctrine of the Church is effected through the individual and collective efforts of the hierarchy and through the organisational structure of the USCC. The public policy position of the USCC in respect of East Timor was twofold. First, to urge the US government to press Indonesia on the human rights issues affecting the people of East Timor. This was done both by encouraging Congressional letters to the US President before various scheduled meetings with Indonesian President Suharto (and his successors)[58], and by supporting the suspension of US military aid (IMET) to Indonesia.[59] Second, to encourage the UN to pursue ever more vigorously the mandated talks between Portugal and Indonesia on the political status of East Timor. In addition the USCC maintained a supportive relationship with bishop Belo and took other actions as appropriate.[60]

From 1987 onwards the USCC engaged in correspondence with Congressmen, the State Department, the Defence Department, and with the Indonesian ambassador to the United States. Its officials sought to appraise the general public of the USCC stance via communications to the mass media on the occasion of the principal Bishops' Statements or letters. Action Alerts and Updates on the situation on East Timor were regularly sent out to contacts in all the Dioceses of the US Catholic Church, including recommendations that actions being undertaken by Senators and Representatives sympathetic to the East Timor cause be supported.[61]

---

[57] Bibliography – Ch9: Novak, M. 1990, p60.

[58] E.g. via 'Action Alerts' on June 1993, prior to G-7 meeting in Tokyo; October 1993, prior to APEC meeting in Seattle; October 1994, prior to APEC meeting in Jakarta; October 1995, prior to the visit of President Suharto to Washington.

[59] E.g. Letters from Drew Christiansen *SJ*, Director CIP Office of Justice & Peace to Rep.Nita Lowey, & Rep.Frank R.Wolf June 23, 1995; to Rep. Jack Reed, June 4, 1996.

[60] Tom Quigley, USCC Office for International Justice & Peace, to the author, Washington 25.8.1998.

[61] E.g. Updates/Action Alerts were disseminated in June and October 1993, October 1994 and 1995, Feb.1996, 1997 and 1998, July 1998 and 1999, August 1999, Sept.1999, Feb. 2000 and 2001, etc.

'A tardy and limited response'?

Despite this vigorous and extensive activity the NCCB-USCC was criticised for the tardiness and limited scope of its response. Such criticism was sometimes voiced within the Catholic community itself, and ignorance of the commitment of the US Catholic Church to East Timorese welfare remained widespread – even among NGOs active in that cause, within the National Council of Churches, and on the part of some expatriate East Timorese. Some Congress staffers on Capitol Hill remarked to the author in 1998 that 'the Catholic Church was not as expert in lobbying as the Jewish community'. Bishop Belo, however, was appreciative of the effort being made and declared: 'No link is more important for us than that of my brother bishops in the United States'.[62] This remark was not merely diplomatic, and those persons in a position to know more of the inside story considered the NCCB-USCC response to have been 'reasonably considerable' bearing in mind the other issues which had greater immediacy for the Catholic community as a whole.[63] In any case the institutions and activities of the Catholic Church are nowhere limited to that of national Bishops Conferences and their agencies.

The contribution of US Religious Congregations

The work undertaken in respect of East Timor welfare by congregations of religious in the United States was of no small significance despite the fact that their presence in the occupied territory was very limited both in time and in numbers of personnel. In respect of individual families of religious it is only possible here to present a brief description of two responses but it is important to highlight a particular policy that was adopted by many such congregations and which was to have significant repercussions within the US Church as a whole.

One family of religious in America who took up the East Timor cause was the Franciscans. Two examples of their efforts must suffice. In California particularly, the Franciscans had become identified with social justice issues following the Second Vatican Council, the decrees of which – along with the principles of the Jocist Movement of Cardinal Cardijn in Belgium - provided the basis for their practical commitment. They became involved in various matters such as Hispanic welfare, the rights of farm workers, and the Church's work for the poor in Central America before turning their attention to the East Timorese plight. In San Francisco some of them participated in protests outside the Indonesian Consulate.[64] Nationally they disseminated to a wide readership the monthly international Franciscan publication 'Messenger of St. Anthony' which was to feature regular well-informed and analytical articles, many by Arnold Kohen, on the developing situation in East Timor.

Another Congregation that became active on behalf of the East Timorese was the Maryknoll Missionary Society, founded in the United States in 1911 and held in especially high regard by Americans although its membership of both men and women, which includes a lay Association and 'Affiliates', is international. The Society has always taken up issues of social justice, gaining an (undeserved) reputation for 'left-wing' sympathies among right wing elements in the United States government.[65] Following an appeal to religious congregations by bishop Belo in 1987 for assistance with the pastoral ministry in East Timor the Maryknoll Society provided several personnel[66] initially from its mission in Indonesia, who undertook

[62] Address to International Policy Meeting, USCC, 8th June 1995.

[63] Arnold Kohen to the author, Washington DC, 25th August 1998.

[64] Fr.Louis Vitale, *OFM*, to the author, San Francisco, 15th Sept.1998.

[65] Fr.Ed Killackey MM, Fr.Pete Ruggere MM, and other fraternal colleagues to the author in Washington/New York, Aug-Sept.1998; Joseph Reis, for Rep. Chris Smith, Capitol Hill, 27th August 1998.

[66] Author's interviews with Maryknoll Sisters D.McGowan, N.Maulawin, H.Lum, at Ossining, NY, 31.8.98, and with a Maryknoll Sister at Aileu, East Timor, Sept.1995.

local parish work with a particular care of youth. Their presence in the territory facilitated the dissemination of reliable current information about the situation prevailing there, some of which could be published in the society's magazines - which have a wide circulation. In fact, articles on East Timor had featured in these publications regularly from April 1977.[67] More recently, Maryknoll Missioners also promoted the East Timor cause through the Society's web site and by participating in NGO and Church/Inter-church forums, communicating the analysis and action alerts which emerged from such consultations.[68]

The national Conferences of Major Religious Superiors included East Timor in the justice and peace issues to which they drew attention.[69] Collectively the members of religious congregations established, in 1974, the Inter Community Centre on Justice and Peace (ICCJP). This forty-member coalition included the East Timor issue among various problematic situations to which it gave attention, disseminating its own Action Alerts on the subject. Women's congregations predominate in the CICJP, as they did at first in the Coalition for Responsible Investment (CRI), an important policy initiative that was subsequently taken up by most (not all) diocesan administrations nation-wide. The particular relevance for the Indonesia/East Timor issue was that the codes of ethics (now widely adopted) precluded investment in the arms industry. In respect of other commercial enterprises effort was made to have Church institutions represented at stockholders meetings where appropriate comment can be passed on the justice, economic and other, of company policy. The Maryknoll Society, among others, also supports the Churches Centre for Corporate Responsibility (CCCR), an ecumenical association, and religious congregations (especially those of women) make an important contribution to the Interfaith Centre for Corporate Responsibility (ICCR).[70]

The response within Dioceses – Parishes and Schools

Dioceses - and parishes and schools - were provided by the USCC with some information on the East Timor issue together with recommendations for practical action. As indicated already, each diocese is autonomous and determines its own priorities, as do their constituent parishes (and schools). Some undertook the recommended action[71], and many published the USCC material in their newspapers and bulletins - but always other situations of grave need competed for the limited space available. Diminishing numbers of diocesan clergy, their personal dispositions, and the wide range of matters demanding both their attention and that of their parishioners certainly affected the response given to the Timorese plight as has been noted above. There were places where significant action was taken, but a more detailed investigation than is possible here is required for a fair account to be given.

One responsive parish was St.Paul's in Boston where a youth group took the initiative. Their project involved an important ministry of awareness-raising especially (but not only) among their peers in other parishes besides their own - and in Catholic schools - and engaged the energies of many hundreds of young people in a prayer-based activism. Their campaign included lobbying at the White House and at the Indonesian Embassy in Washington, and they

---

[67] Maryknoll NewsNotes has a circulation of some 700,000. Articles on East Timor appeared on the following dates: April 77; Nov 78; Nov 80; Sept 82; Nov 82; Jan 84; Sept 84; May 85; March 91; Jan 92; Nov 92; May 93; July 93; July 94; Sept 94; Nov 94; June 96; Sept 96; Jan 98; Nov 99; March 2000; May 2000; etc.

[68] Maryknollers contributed to the deliberations on East Timor within the National Council of Churches, and featured the Action Alerts of *inter alia* the East Timor Action Network.

[69] e.g. As co-signatory to an NGO letter of support (14.4.97) for the Indonesia Military Assistance Accountability Bill (HR 1132) introduced by Patrick Kennedy in March 1997.

[70] Sr.Christine Mulready *CSJ*, for the Intercommunity Centre on Justice and Peace, at the Offices of the Archdiocese of New York to the author, New York 2.9.1998.

[71] e.g. Dioceses of Little Rock (Arkansas); Honolulu (Hawaii); Oakland (California); Memphis (Tennessee); Boise (Idaho); Rockville Centre (New York); Springfield (Illinois). Copies of correspondence between 1990-93 on file. The geographical spread is noteworthy.

added their voices to those critical of the accommodation being afforded to Indonesian commercial companies by the State of Massachusetts. But the most distinctive feature of their action was its emphasis on spiritual bonding with the youth of East Timor through the establishment of a network of 'Prayer Friends', and on 'the need for the radical power of the Holy Spirit to combat the radical evil present in East Timor'.[72] Bishop Belo encouraged these emphases when he met with the young people during a short visit to Boston in 1997.

A Catholic High School in San Francisco that included the East Timorese plight in its Religious Education curriculum did so within the context of a course on the subject of genocide.[73] The students' participation found liturgical expression and also bore fruit in organised protests at the Indonesian Consulate, and in due course to activism at various Universities attended by those who graduated to higher studies. The scholars responded earnestly to the Gospel ideals conveyed in the RE programme, but a number of their parents lodged objections to the subject matter of the course and queried its objectivity. Consideration of the issue remained within the Religious Department only and was not taken up in others as it might have been, despite the fact that the school was a Jesuit foundation.

Another noteworthy engagement in the East Timor cause on the part of the laity was that of some communities of the Catholic Worker movement, for example in Washington and New York. These associated their efforts with those of members of Plowshares and Kairos groups, and with the East Timor Action Network, and were involved in awareness-raising and peaceful demonstrations outside the Indonesian Embassy or Consulate. Their own evaluation of their work was that 'although a tight core maintained a prophetic witness the protests fell for the most part on deaf ears'.[74] At the time of the post-referendum violence in East Timor in September 1999 members maintained a prayer vigil outside the Indonesian Consulate in Manhattan and afterwards a Mass for peace was celebrated at the Catholic Worker house on lower East Side by the renowned Jesuit activist, Fr.Daniel Berrigan.[75]

The Church in the United States – an evaluation

There was a response to the East Timorese plight at every level in the US Catholic Church although this took time to develop due to a number of important socio-political factors including current pastoral demands within the Church itself.

The principal obstacle faced by the Church was the strategic priority of 'national security' as perceived by successive US federal governments. This was strongly challenged on the basis of Catholic Social Doctrine, but the anti-Communist element of this same Doctrine had also given support to government policy both foreign and domestic. The actions of Daniel Moynihan, the (Catholic) American ambassador to the United Nations, in single-minded pursuit of US interests (disregarding the provisions of International Law) had had very negative consequences for the East Timorese cause at the time of the Indonesian invasion and occupation. The over-identification with the Jakarta project by one of the Church's own agencies in East Timor (CRS) in the early years of the occupation was also very regrettable. This ambiguity was certainly a contributory factor to the delay by the US Church as a whole in addressing the widespread and fundamental human rights violations perpetrated against the East Timorese people.

Although detailed information on the situation in East Timor was lacking at first or given biased/inadequate coverage in the national media, the Church, through its own network of contacts, had better access than other institutions to the facts – an advantage perhaps not fully exploited. Expert commentary and analysis was disseminated by some Catholic publica-

---

[72] Bob and (son) Simon Dolittle, youth leaders, to author, Boston/Washington, 28.8 & 9.9.98.
[73] St.Ignatius High School, San Francisco. RE project described by the head of department, Jim McGarry to the author, San Francisco, 16th September 1998.
[74] Elmer Maas, CW New York, telephone conversation with the author, New York 3.9.1998.
[75] 'New Yorkers call for peacekeeping troops', Stephen Steele, Catholic New York, 16.9.99.

tions, notably those of certain religious congregations, but in both these and diocesan outlets the East Timor issue had to compete with the demands of other urgent causes that, it was felt, had more pertinence for the national Catholic community. However, as the Timorese predicament became better understood, the momentum of the Church's action in their defence gathered pace and expressions of solidarity increased in number, range, and effectiveness.

Bearing in mind the many other concerns – internal, and national, as well as overseas – that pressed upon it, the Church in the United States may be reasonably considered to have given due preference to the poor of East Timor. In due course the US Catholic agencies were to entrust the inhabitants of East Timor with the management of the Church's relief and development work in the territory in proper accord with the principle of subsidiarity. Church leaders and agencies also recognised and challenged the structural injustices from which the East Timorese people suffered and moved from the provision only of humanitarian relief to the advocacy of their human rights including the right to genuine political participation and an authentic act of political self-determination. However, the provisions of International Law in this respect did not appear to be fully deployed to this end in citation by the Church authorities, even allowing for the difficulties of interpretation and application. Public action in the East Timorese cause on the part of the American Church would not have put its work in the United States (or elsewhere) in any real jeopardy and a more public engagement with the issue may well have generated greater support nation-wide for the East Timor cause. But the Church authorities had to be sensitive to the repercussions such action might have for the people in East Timor (and upon the welfare of the Catholic community in Indonesia), and responded to guidance from the local Church leadership. Bearing in mind the substantial impact of the activities of the NCCB-USCC that were carried out over the years it appears evident that more lobbying in Congress and government circles would have further benefited the East Timorese cause. This fact also has implications for the effective application of Catholic Social Doctrine with regard to other issues - at least in the United States and in comparable democracies.

In terms of its continuation of Christ's own mission in the world the US Church's response to the needs of the East Timorese people had both strengths and shortcomings.

Humanitarian relief and development aid was provided to East Timor in generous measure from 1979 onwards, although its association with the Indonesian project compromised this activity. Missionary personnel from the United States assisted with the Church's pastoral work in East Timor, but they were very few in numbers.

The policies of Washington that impacted upon East Timorese welfare were prophetically challenged at all levels and in all circles of Church life from the national Conference to local groups of activists. Advocacy of human rights and social justice was urged as an essential dimension of discipleship or 'servanthood' and Catholics were also numbered among the members of other faith-based and secular non-governmental organisations promoting the East Timorese cause. But there was some initial inconsistency among the principal Catholic agencies in respect of their reaction to American and Indonesian governmental policies.

Despite the Vatican's official teaching, the realisation that action for social justice was a *constitutive* part of communal Catholic life was limited in its extent. Familiarity with both the Scriptures and the Social Doctrine of the Church was clearly lacking among the Catholic faithful. Many of those attending the parish liturgy evidently did not make the connection between its celebration and the Gospel mandate to 'proclaim liberty to captives and set the downtrodden free' – at least in respect of East Timor. Yet there was a growing commitment to the promotion of 'Corporate Responsibility', and the Pastoral Letter 'Economic Justice for All' had widespread impact. However, overt criticism by the institutional Church of the national policy of arms sales to Indonesia was very limited. Moreover, little attention seems to have been given to the interest of American oil companies in the exploitation of the mineral resources of the Timor Gap. These were matters that surely had an influence upon the government's disposition towards Jakarta yet they do not feature significantly in the US Church's response to the East Timorese plight.

A sense of communion with fellow Catholics in East Timor motivated concern and action within the community of the faithful, and prayer for Timorese welfare was generally urged by Church leaders. But the creation of specific liturgies or prayer services on behalf of the East Timorese people - and participation in such events - was given greater attention by activist groups (of all ages) and other Christian denominations than by the official agencies of the Church and in local pastoral planning. This was in some contrast to the practice of the Church in Australia and no doubt was related to the lack of an East Timorese component within American society. The result was that the opportunity for public witness to the East Timorese plight and advocacy of their cause was less than it might have been. Maybe the generally discreet style of the US Church's operation in the matter had the negative effect of diminishing its impact upon the general public the majority of whom remained insular in their disposition and for most of the time largely unaware of the East Timor issue and of the United States involvement in it.

Be that as it may, the intervention of the US Catholic Church, along with its counterparts elsewhere, was of crucial importance. In 1999, referring to the vigorous activity of the hierarchy, Church agencies and leading members of the laity that year, Arnold Kohen declared: 'If I could use one word to explain what changed US policy towards East Timor it would be 'Catholic''.[76] Serious inquiry into the work on behalf of the East Timorese carried out within the Catholic community by various dedicated persons and groups - especially members of the National Conference of Catholic Bishops and the United States Catholic Conference, and those who acted as their consultants and advisers – is revealing. It shows that these efforts, for the most part conducted in a necessarily discreet manner, began in some measure at the very outset of the Timorese agony and were to persist and expand over many years. They were to give legitimacy and significance to the East Timorese cause at the highest levels in American society. They provided the foundational awareness and concern within the US Congress - and more widely in the country - on which NGOs that began their campaigning after the Santa Cruz massacre had roused public consciousness of the Timorese plight were able to build. Without the commitment and co-operation within the Catholic Church across the world, and without the significant and fruitful contacts established over many years between the national Catholic Church and the State in America, the undoubted achievements of such activists in promoting East Timorese welfare latterly would not have been possible.

In late August 1999, a delegation from the NCCB-USCC including archbishop Theodore McCarrick and bishop John Cummins was in Vietnam and slated to go on from there to East Timor. Because of scheduling difficulties the bishops felt obliged to cancel their intended visit but USCC Asia-policy adviser Tom Quigley travelled to Dili in full knowledge of the perilous situation there. Then close to seventy years of age Quigley was in bishop Belo's house overnight as the militia assault grew in intensity and menace. On his return to Washington his experience enabled him to draft the passionate communications (cited above) which were issued by the US bishops between September 9th – 15th. Quigley's readiness to *lay down his life* for the sake of the long-suffering Timorese was a truly crucial element in the contribution made by the US Catholic Church towards evoking the positive action by the Clinton Administration on behalf of the beleaguered Timorese that was soon to follow.[77]

---

[76] 'Catholics made US intervene over war', Sean Steel, The Universe (UK), 9.4.2000.

[77] See: 'East Timorese bishop threatened by pro-Indonesia militias', Stephen Steele, Catholic News Service, New York, 25th August 1999; 'Timor violence touches a noted prelate', Gustav Niebuhr, Religion Journal, New York Times, Sept 8/9th 1999; 'Under the Gun', Arnold Kohen, Columbia, April 2000, Vol LXXX No.4, p7.

CHAPTER TEN - THE CHURCH IN JAPAN:
THE STRIVINGS OF A MINORITY

Solidarity for Justice

Late in 1986 the exiled Apostolic Administrator of East Timor, Dom Martinho da Costa Lopes, addressed a conference in Japan arranged by a small citizens' group[1] which had entered into solidarity with the East Timorese in their struggle for justice:

> I am trying to make all the governments of the world, and the people of the world, sensitive to our right to fight for justice. As long as we are alive, we have hope. God is in heaven looking down on us. We have no money - our force is only reason, justice and God.[2]

In the audience was the Catholic Bishop of Nagoya, Aloysius Nobuo Soma, Chairman since 1974 of the Japanese Catholic Council for Justice and Peace (JCCJP). He was moved by Dom Martinho's appeal and subsequently encouraged the response to the East Timorese plight already arising from within the relatively small community of Japanese Catholics.

Japan's domestic circumstances and international relations, especially with its regional neighbours, affected its posture towards East Timor and had direct consequences for the Timorese people. They impacted also upon the efforts made on the Timorese behalf by the Catholic community in Japan. The Japanese reaction to the East Timor issue, and the attitude of the Catholic Church, had roots in Japan's history - especially that of the period following World War II.[3]

Consequences of History

The first Western contact with Japan was by the Portuguese at Nagasaki in 1543, and the Catholic Church arrived in the person of St. Francis Xavier who reached Kyushu island in 1549. There was initial success in religious conversions - 150,000 by 1580 - but alarm at Christian missionary influence and the expansionist policies of the European nations led to opposition from the Tokugawa shogunate. Increasing repression followed which culminated in 1597 with the martyrdom by crucifixion of 26 Japanese and European Christians (and an East Timorese companion). Christianity was banned in Japan in 1626 and suppression of the Church continued for over 200 years until 1867. Catholicism survived clandestinely in the Nagasaki area but deep understanding of the faith was largely lost. There were new beginnings for the Church in Japan at the end of the 19th C. The Meiji Restoration (1868-1912) reversed the isolationist policies of the Tokugawa regime and openness to the outside world included new access for Christian missionaries of all denominations.

The new political posture revealed Japan's backwardness in science and technology and the importance of engaging with other nations. During the 1930s the militarists gained control of Japan's government. They abandoned the policy that had been pursued after World War I of seeking economic security through reliance on international trade and a peaceful world order (by participation in the League of Nations) and replaced it by one of imperial expansion. The 'Greater East Asia Co-Prosperity Sphere' that was promoted effectively amounted to the invasion, occupation, and exploitation of neighbouring territories under the guise of liberating them from Western colonial rule. Japan occupied East Timor in 1942 and its troops were responsible for great loss of life and physical destruction. No formal apologies

---

[1] Viz. The first East Timor solidarity group in Japan, founded by Jean Inglis, Kiyoko Furusawa and Akihito Matsuno.

[2] Bibliography – Ch5: Lennox, R. 2000, pp217-218.

[3] See: Bibliography - Ch.10, *passim*.

or reparations were ever made to the East Timorese. Solidarity groups in Japan and elsewhere, including those within the Catholic Church, have drawn attention to this unpaid moral debt.[4]

The post-war occupation of Japan by the Allies was dominated by the USA and developed into a firm alliance strengthened by a Security Treaty in 1951.[5] The US embraced Japan as an ally in the war against Communism and this led to an anti-Communist purge within Japan and was a factor in Japan's disposition regarding the Communist world. However, Japan did not share the ideological dogmatism of the United States, and the Japanese recognised their cultural kinship with other Asian peoples and the advantages to be gained from positive relations with their regional neighbours. Japan's economic recovery became the first priority of the national government after the Allied occupation ended in 1952. Japan re-established relations with the outside world becoming a member of the United Nations in 1956, and by the mid-1960s had become a major industrialised power and the largest or second largest trading partner of almost every country in East Asia and the West Pacific. The War Reparations negotiated by Japan with regional neighbours drew Japan back into SE Asia and took forms that ultimately benefited the Japanese economy (especially its big business corporations) and brought Japan into an economic strength second only to that of the United States. This led in turn to heightened expectations of Japan on the part of the international community, and the participation by Japan in international bodies convened to contribute to worldwide economic and political welfare.[6] By these means Tokyo sought to overcome the lingering hostility of some regional neighbours and to foster a peaceful world order. It was hoped that success would facilitate international trade - and permit the vast exchange of goods the Japanese nation of 122 million people needs to survive on their narrow and unprovided islands. Economic security – recognised as dependent on good international relations – has therefore been the prime concern for the Japanese government. From 1980 a 'Comprehensive National Security Policy' formally included as components both vigorous diplomacy with and generous Overseas Development Aid (ODA) to strategically important countries among which Indonesia has been most highly rated.[7]

The Relationship between Japan and Indonesia

There had been a tradition of cultural and commercial intercourse between Japan and Indonesia before the militarist government of the 1930s came to regard the extensive archipelago as an essential member of the Asian economic bloc it entitled the 'Co-Prosperity Sphere'. The Japanese occupation of Indonesia from 1942-45 brought the two countries closer together, and the bond between peoples with a strong community of interest persists to this day.[8] During the Sukarno presidency bilateral trade increased steadily and the respective national interests were considered to be complementary despite the ideological differences between the regimes. Access to the sea and air passages of the Indonesian archipelago is crucial for Japan - 70% of the nations' oil supplies and 40% of its trade flows through the Straits of Malacca alone. A number of factors impelled the prioritising of positive relations between Tokyo and Jakarta. These included: the natural resources to be found upon and between the wide spread of Indonesian islands; the huge market provided for Japanese manufactures by the Republic's

---

[4] e.g. Shohachi Iwamura, address to UN 1987; Media Release 'Japan and War Crimes – past and present', Australian Coalition for a Free East Timor 15.8.1995, in ETAN Docs Vol 39, 1995.

[5] Revised 1960 this expects Japan to provide for US military bases on its territory, and to support the major goals of US foreign/security policy in return for US military protection.

[6] e.g. The Organisation for Development & Co-operation (OECD) from 1964; ASEAN after its formation in 1967; and within the forum for Asia-Pacific Economic Co-operation (APEC), and to the multilateral security dialogue of the ASEAN Regional Forum (ARF) since 1994.

[7] See Bibliography – Ch10: 'Japan's Aid Diplomacy, etc', Juichi Inada, in Newland, K. (ed) 1990, pp113, 118; 'Bolstering the new order, etc', Kingston, J., in Koppel & Orr, 1993, p42 and p351.

[8] There are large numbers of Indonesia specialists in Japan, and there is mutual access to high levels of government and to corporate decision makers.

200 million people; and the opportunities for profitable investment which became accessible with the pro-Western administration of Suharto.[9] Such a policy was bolstered still further by the desirability (on grounds of security) of continuing the special relationship with Washington - which also took great interest in Indonesia and did all it could to develop a profitable alliance, as noted already.

In the 1970s Japan suffered several shocks which further encouraged the fostering of mutually beneficial relations with Indonesia. The quadrupling of the cost of oil by the Organisation of Petroleum Exporting Countries (OPEC) brought home to Tokyo the nation's vulnerability in respect of essential supplies – imported oil representing 60% of Japan's energy requirements. Access for such provision from the Middle East via the Straits of Malacca had to be assured, and additional supplies from Indonesia's own mineral deposits became all the more important. In the same period the Nixon administration in the United States took various actions which impacted upon Japan's sense of economic security.[10] As a consequence Tokyo came to regard too much reliance on relations with the US as unwise and was anxious to develop regional and global relations independently of Washington. Positive association with Jakarta became of even more critical importance and so Japan's aid to Indonesia continued to be the most generous of its disbursements under the ODA commitment. This was regardless of the Suharto regime's abysmal human rights record and the engagement of Indonesian military forces in both internal repression and external aggression. Neither did official acceptance of principled guidelines for such disbursement effect any noticeable restraint.[11]

Japan and East Timor[12]

It was in this period of Japan's particularly serious economic vulnerability that Indonesia invaded and occupied East Timor (1975). Japan supported the first Security Council Resolution in December that year which condemned the annexation of East Timor, but thereafter took the view that criticism of Indonesia would not of itself contribute to a solution of the issue (and would be detrimental to Japan's interests). For this reason Tokyo opposed further action on UN Security Council Resolution 389 (1976) which required Indonesian withdrawal from the territory and an authentic act of political self-determination by the East Timorese people, arguing that progress in such matters was well underway.[13] In the UN General Assembly from 1975-82 Japan also consistently opposed the resolutions for action against

---

[9] By the beginning of the 1970s Japan was Indonesia's principal trading partner, and by the 1980s Japanese investment in Indonesia was by far the largest in comparison with American or European, or with Japanese investments in any other countries of the region. Japan promoted the economic welfare of Indonesia via the Inter-governmental Group for Indonesia (IGGI) from 1967, and the Consultative Group for Indonesia (CGI) from 1992.

[10] Washington abandoned the gold standard on which international monetary practices had been founded since the Bretton Woods agreements of 1944; threatened an embargo on soybean exports to Japan; and entered into a rapprochement with Peking.

[11] e.g.

1) PM Toshiki Kaifu address to the Diet 'On Japan's ODA in Relation to Military Expenditures and Other Matters of the Developing Countries' (April 1990);

2) ODA Guidelines (April 1991) emphasised the pertinence of recipient country performance on democratisation and human rights, their reduction of military expenditures and of participation in arms trading, and their commitment to market-oriented economic policies.

[12] Further information see Bibliography – General (East Timor): Krieger, H. 1995 Index; Gunn, G.C. 1997, Ch7; Bibliography – Ch10: Furusawa, K. & Matsuno, A. 1993.

[13] See 'Extracts from Debates of UNSC regarding Res 389 (1976)', in Krieger, H. 1995.op.cit. pp108-9, 113-114.

In his memoirs, the Japanese Ambassador to the UN Shizuo Saito gives himself credit for mobilising 'understanding' for Indonesia among Asian countries where Japan played a diplomatic 'leadership role'.

Indonesia. In this forum Tokyo argued that Jakarta's policy of incorporation of the territory was in the 'best interests' of the East Timorese people and was therefore 'in accordance' with the UN Charter and with GA Resolution 1514 (XV) - the Declaration on Granting of Independence to Colonial Countries and Peoples. Tokyo was evidently willing to accept the Indonesian political manipulation in East Timor as a genuine expression of the popular will.[14] Besides such vigorous diplomatic activity, Tokyo also confirmed its acknowledgement of Indonesian sovereignty in East Timor by entering into various Treaties with Jakarta that included the occupied territory in their provisions, and by its huge ODA support for Indonesia.[15]

It is important to note that the Diet has comparatively little influence on government policy in respect of ODA (unlike the US Congress). The Ministry of Foreign Affairs (MOFA) and Ministry of Finance (MOF) carry most weight in its creation and management. MOFA and MOF are in their turn much influenced by the large Japanese Corporations which have substantial investments in Indonesia and which commit extensive human resources to the development of local projects in the archipelago. These enterprises have proved to be of benefit to Japan's diplomatic relationships with Indonesia and also to support Japan's economic well being. So it was that, even after the Santa Cruz massacre in 1991, when almost half the members of the Diet signed a petition criticising the Indonesian military's actions, the long-ruling Liberal Democratic Party (LDP) proved impervious to criticism of its consistent support for the Suharto regime. It was beholden to the interests of Japan's large commercial corporations.

In 1993 Japan voted in favour of 'no-action' in respect of the East Timor issue at the 53rd Session of the UN Commission on Human Rights on the grounds that the proposed action would 'embarrass' Indonesia and inhibit any process of international mediation. This posture arose not only out of concern for good relations with Jakarta, but also from the lack of a co-ordinated policy between government departments in Japan on human rights issues. The Japanese justice ministry also places obstacles in the way of any binding international procedure or protocol that it perceives as a threat to Japan's own judicial sovereignty.[16] Within academic circles most Indonesianists in Japan tended to avoid the East Timor issue lest they be denied access to Indonesia for their wider research purposes.

However, a Parliamentary support group, the Diet Forum for East Timor, was established in 1986 and slowly increased in number, its influence expanding somewhat after 1993 with the advent of the reform government of Morihiro Hosokawa.[17] In 1995, at the APEC summit held in Osaka, Foreign Minister Yohei Kohno informed his Indonesian counterpart Ali Alatas that henceforth Japan would support the UN mediation efforts in East Timor, and Tokyo provided US$100,000 to assist the All-Inclusive Intra-Timorese Dialogue promoted by the UN Secretary General. Nonetheless, Japanese officials continued to avoid criticism of In-

---

[14] See 'Extracts from UN General Assembly Debates and Meetings of the 4th Committee', Bibliography – General (East Timor): Krieger, H. 1995, op.cit.

[15] In 1990 Japan's aid package to Indonesia totalled $1.81 billion, including $110 million in grants and technical assistance; $1 billion for infrastructure development; and $700m in the form of 'special assistance' to alleviate balance of payments pressures (Koppel & Orr 1993, op.cit.p42). Treaties with Indonesia cited in Krieger, 1995, op.cit. pp292, 297.

[16] See: 'Tokyo's Cautious Diplomacy', Akihisa Matsuno, Timor Link, July 1997, p7.

[17] See: Summary account of the efforts of the Diet Forum for East Timor by its Convenor, Tomiko Okazaki to the International Symposium for the Peaceful Settlement in East Timor, Bangkok, March 1998. e.g. Members of the Forum visited East Timor in August 1994; (unsuccessfully) lobbied PM Hashimoto to raise the E Timor issue with Suharto in Jakarta in January 1997 and in Canada in November 1997; called upon UNHRC Mary Robinson to urge Japan to promote peace in E Timor (Letter January 23rd, 1998); etc. However, only ten members of the Forum were 'active' (in 1998) out of a membership which numbered but 40 (out of 700) representatives of the Diet – Fr.Stefani Renato to the author, Tokyo 22.4.98.

donesia and even provided diplomatic support for Jakarta's policies.[18] When East Timorese Nobel Laureate Jose Ramos Horta visited Japan in January 1997 both Prime Minister Ryutaro Hashimoto and Foreign Minister Yukihiko Ikeda pleaded pressing engagements to avoid meeting him.[19]

During East Timor's Year of Crisis (1999) the Japanese Defence Agency accepted more than the usual number of Indonesian soldiers for military training.[20] Although Tokyo formally indicated in various ways its support for the UN-organised 'popular consultation' these did not include a positive response to the UN request for the provision of civilian police.[21] After the ballot Japan called for the result to be respected 'by all parties' and for Indonesia to fulfil its pledge to 'uphold security'.[22] However, despite the conspicuous failure (indeed, obstruction) of both *TNI* and the Indonesian Police Force in that respect, the withdrawal or reduction of ODA to the regime in Jakarta was never seriously considered at any time.[23] On the contrary, Japan warned the international community that cutting off aid to Indonesia (including IMF and World Bank loans) could destabilise Indonesia's economy and affect Asia's fragile economic recovery.[24] Nor did the government attempt to make any revisions to the strict laws relating to the deployment of the national Self-Defence Force which would permit their participation in INTERFET or with the UN Peace Keepers who succeeded the coalition contingent.[25] Tokyo did provide US$2 million to help meet the needs of East Timorese refugees and $100 million to help UN peacekeepers establish and maintain order in East Timor, and was generous in its contribution to the Trust Fund established for the reconstruction of East Timor (TFET).[26] Such actions (along with other humanitarian contributions towards education and human resource development) continued in the following year.[27] They were entirely consistent with the government's fundamental priority of supporting regional harmony - and thereby safeguarding the economic welfare of Japan. The Church in Japan was faced with this inflexible policy.

---

[18] See: 'Japan's Political Ties with Asia', editorial AsiaWeek, 26.1.1997; 'Tokyo's Cautious Diplomacy', Akihisa Matsuno, Timor Link, July 1997, p7.

[19] 'Japan's Dilemma: Talk to Horta or not', Jean Inglis, *Asahi Shumbun*, 23.12.96; 'Horta Activity in Japan' and 'Japan's East Timor Policy', Kyodo, 6.1.97; 'East Timor Activist Asks Japan's Influence', Koichi Iitake, Asahi Evening News (on-line), 7.1.97; Horta's speech in Sendai 'What should be the human existence in our time?' (East Timor Relief Association, Australia) - copy on file.

[20] 'Stop accepting Indonesian soldiers in the Defence Academy' – Press Release, Free East Timor Japan Coalition, 2.3.1999.

[21] Japanese Government Statement on the East Timor Issue, 15.3.1999; 'Japan Mission to visit E Timor May 14-22', Indonesian News, 13.5.1999.

[22] 'Japan calls for Indonesia action on E Timor strife', Reuters, Tokyo, 6.9.99.

[23] 'As Top Donor, Tokyo asked to lean on Jakarta', Suvendrini Kakuchi, IPS,Tokyo 7.9.99.

[24] *PM* Keizo Obuchi, at APEC, New Zealand, Sept.1999; 'Japan not studying change in aid policy towards Indonesia', Dow Jones Newswires, Auckland, NZ, 12.9.99; Japan pledges continued support for Indonesia', AFP Tokyo, 13.10.99.

[25] 'Japan to revise law and allow troops to join E Timor force?', AFP, Tokyo 17.9.99. The Constitution established during the allied occupation of Japan limits overseas deployment of the SDF to medical and humanitarian support - in reaction to Japan's pre-war militarism and its regional aggression before and during World War II. This policy was relaxed a little in 2002.

[26] 'Japan gives 100 million dollars to UN force in Timor', AFP Tokyo, 13.10.99; 'Japan to send aid flights to West Timor', AFP Tokyo, 19.11.99; 'Japan 100 million dollars of aid to East Timor' AFP Tokyo, 16.12.99.

[27] 'Japan opens Diplomatic Mission in Dili', LUSA, 13.3.00; 'Japan grants $27.5m to E Timor to fix infrastructure', Kyodo, Jakarta 14.7.00; 'Japan rebuilding schools in Timor', Indonesian Observer, Jakarta 30.7.00; 'Training Human Resources in East Timor', Ministry of Foreign Affairs Press Conference, Tokyo, 1.12.2000.

The Domestic Situation in Japan

The domestic situation in which the Church in Japan is lodged was also far from conducive to action in solidarity with the East Timorese. The straitened economic circumstances that pertained immediately after the Second World War gave way to a period of high-speed growth (1955-74) and subsequently to one of general affluence (1974-89). This 'economic miracle' led to an ethos of consumerism, materialism, and even hedonism. But the era of affluence was also one of insecurity. A number of international factors conducive to growth in 1950s[28] disappeared in the 1970s and there was friction with the United States, Japan's chief trading partner. The resultant unease and uncertainty made Japanese society become more contentious and fragmented, and to a pre-occupation with private concerns on the part of individuals, families, interest groups, or businesses, and a corresponding lack of attention to the needs of the poor and oppressed. Such people included immigrants from Korea, short-term migrant workers from various East Asian countries, and the *Buraku* - the traditional outcastes of Japanese society. Social injustices being suffered by people in other countries could attract even less interest. Moreover, the post-war education system in Japan was very prescribed until quite recently, giving little scope for questioning the *status quo*, encouraging a dependence on authority in decision-making, and generally directed at preparing large numbers of young people for life-long participation in one of the great commercial corporations. Another pertinent factor is the cultural isolation consequent upon the unique character of the Japanese language that contributes (along with the very tight control over immigration) to the insularity of many Japanese and their consequent limited ability to bring their influence to bear upon the international policies of other countries.[29] The majority of Japanese remain socially unaware – even of the situation in Japan itself – and have materialistic priorities. Nonetheless, some citizens groups came into existence, critical of Government policies both at home and abroad, and (from 1986) a number of these took up the East Timorese cause, in due course coming under the umbrella of the Japan East Timor Coalition (JETC).[30] The period 1989-1995 was a troubled one. Economic uncertainty generated political instability, and disparities in wealth and income fed a general social malaise. Japanese families experienced the anxieties that had already come upon their American, German, and English counterparts: job security, school leaver unemployment, maintaining their standard of living. In 1998 an economic crisis in Japan exacerbated an already difficult situation.

In such a distracting, depressing and debilitating ethos the religious beliefs which are present in a national culture might yet prove to be a stimulus to action by their adherents on behalf of the oppressed and deprived - were this the thrust of their message. But the old religions of Japan and popular modern-day cults tend not to engage their members in issues of social justice either at home or abroad.[31] Christians altogether comprise *less than 2%* of the modern day population in Japan, and Christianity is regarded as a 'foreign' religion, its theology largely dismissed. Christians are respected for their moral principles and are among the best-educated and leading elements of society with an influence greater than their numbers would suggest. In the relatively short period of its re-establishment in Japan (from the last quarter of the 19th century) the Christian community has engaged in various works of social service - for the underprivileged and the sick, and in education. However, it cannot be claimed

---

[28] *Viz.* Secure access to low-cost raw materials; currency exchange rate stability; open world markets; and a booming international demand for Japanese goods.
[29] Comments made to the author by several interviewees. See also Report (January 2000) of an Advisory Commission established by *PM* Keizo Obuchi - summarised in 'Dare to be Different, Japanese are Urged', by Jonathan Watts, The Guardian UK, 19.1.2000.
[30] About 40 groups nationwide, 13 active in major cities – founders of JETC Jean Inglis (Hiroshima), Kyoko Furusawa (Tokyo), Akihita Matsuno (Kyoto), to the author, April 1998.
[31] See Bibliography – Ch10: Reischauer, E.O. 1997, pp203-215; Davis, Winston B. 1992; Reader, I. 1991.

that the local Christian communities have been outstanding for their engagement in furthering social justice in Japan, still less overseas.

The Catholic Community in Japan[32]

Numerically the Catholic community is small, comprising about 0.03% of the overall population in Japan (i.e. 450,000 out of 122 million people in 1996)[33]. The faithful from Nagasaki (where lie the Church's historical origins and where its early martyrs met their deaths) appear to be a dominant group. Nagasaki Catholics are widespread throughout the country and tend to disseminate a devotional, inward-looking and conservative expression of Catholicism, one not given to action on social issues.

In the immediate Post World War II period a significant number of conversions to the faith were at least partially motivated by the access this provided to gifts donated by the American Catholics. In more recent times converts have been mainly middle class women whose economic security facilitates their attendance at the lengthy course of instruction. Such persons tend not to challenge the present social order. Catholic schools have been heavily dependent upon government subsidy and unable to veer away from the prescribed curriculum. Besides, parental expectation for the most part is for children to be taught 'how to behave' - which is regarded as more to do with personal and social discipline than the content of religious belief. In such an environment it is difficult to evoke a response to issues of justice and liberation.

Like their compatriots Japanese Catholics are subliminally influenced by Confucianism – in particular the notions of cosmic harmony and of hierarchical order in society. This evokes among them a desire for keeping the peace, for non-confrontational behaviour, and gives rise to dependence upon their religious leaders for guidance in significant matters. There is also an emphasis on the right handling of particular relationships rather than adherence to universal principles. This gives rise to a relativist evaluation of issues and to a reticence about becoming involved in the problems of other people. An indication of this frame of mind is the disposition of editors in both the secular and Catholic Press, some of whom refrain from publishing items on contentious social justice issues. Because of the importance placed on good relations with Indonesia by both government and commerce in Japan, this included East Timor. Furthermore, as the bishops have considerable control over the content of diocesan newspapers in Japan, coverage of East Timor in Catholic media outlets was dependent upon the episcopal attitude - which was not always sympathetic.[34]

The Catholic community in Japan clearly has limited human resources but it seems to be well provided for financially. Its members are generous with their donations to needy causes but do not in general engage in the energetic practice of a 'Social Gospel' although this has been promulgated.[35] Nor is it the case that Japanese Catholics have been unaware of the East Timorese predicament in particular. But such social awareness and action has tended to be on the part of a minority within a Church that is already very much a minority group in Japanese society. As already intimated, the leadership given to the Catholic community by the hierarchy is a particularly pertinent factor in the Japanese context.

[32] For history of RC Church in Japan see: Bibliography Ch 10. For information on the contemporary RC Church in Japan see Bibliography – Ch10: CBCJ 1998; updated at CBCJ Internet web site.

[33] Bibliography – Ch10: CBCJ, July 1997.

[34] Comments made by several interviewees to the author, including Fr.Stefani Renato, and Kimoko Tsuzaki of the Japanese 'Catholic Weekly' (Tokyo, 24.4.1998).

[35] See Bibliography – Ch10: JCCJP; Yamada, N.K. 1994, and 'Witness to the Social Dimension of the Gospel – Answers to 15 Questions', in JCCJP Justice & Peace Pamphlet Series.

The Institutional Church in Japan

The major post War concern of the bishops in respect of the relationship between religion and politics in Japan was to sustain the Constitutional separation of Church and State against efforts to restore State Shinto rites.[36] The anxieties of the bishops arose from memories of the disastrous alliance between the military, state and religion that had engendered Japanese aggression in East and SE Asia during the 1930s and into World War II. They were also worried about the detrimental effects upon the already weak position of the Japanese Catholic Church that might be consequential upon the government giving special regard to contemporary expressions of the indigenous religion.

Responding to the stipulations of the Second Vatican Council the Catholic Bishops Conference of Japan (CBCJ) was formed in 1966 and among various institutions it created was the agency 'Caritas Japan', set up in 1969 to assist the poor and needy at home and abroad, especially in undeveloped countries. Inspired by Pope Paul VI's establishment of the Pontifical Council for Justice and Peace in 1967, the Bishops Conference in due course officially recognised their own Bishops Commission for Justice and Peace (1970) and facilitated the formation of an independent lay persons' justice and peace Commission. In 1974 this two-tier structure was re-launched as one entity, the Japanese Catholic Council for Justice and Peace (JCCJP). Since that year justice and peace committees have been established in most districts of Japan. However, the first national meeting of the Council did not take place until November 1975, a matter of days before the Indonesian invasion of East Timor.

The Papal Visit to Japan in 1981 stimulated the formulation of 'Basic Policies and Priorities of the Catholic Church in Japan' (June 1984), a Statement of the Bishops Conference that emphasised the missionary vocation of the Church in contemporary society.[37] It is noteworthy that included as 'basic policy' was a 'proclamation of the Gospel that should change present society into a culture that respects all and everyone'. But the same document also acknowledged the lack of unity within the Catholic Church in Japan, and called for the organisation in 1987 of a national convention of bishops, priests, religious and faithful to promote a co-ordinated evangelisation. Among the episcopate were some bishops[38] who saw a need for greater 'openness to Japanese society and to the world beyond Japan', a spirit which prevailed at the 'First National Incentive Convention for Evangelisation' (NICE I) when it was duly held. Responding to this meeting the Bishops Conference urged the Church to 'participate in society and become a community that shares with people and in their sufferings':

> Led by the Spirit we shall renew efforts to live the faith on the basis of life's realities and to evangelise in response to societal needs. We want to do so in solidarity with those experiencing pains and sufferings due to societal conditions. These suffering brothers and sisters of ours are loved by God and we should strive to make their plight our concern. ...

> Let us join hands with our fellow Asians and with all people of good will so that we can bring about an 'Open Church' that will not disappoint those who put their hopes in the Gospel in today's world.[39]

A second such gathering was prepared, but when NICE II took place in 1993 the direction given by the majority of the bishops resulted in a reversion to the former inward-looking disposition of the Church in Japan, and the convention concentrated on the welfare of 'the family'.

---

[36] For detail see: 'The Catholic Church in Japan Today, para. 6: Politics and Religion' at the CBCJ Internet web site, op.cit.

[37] See: Bibliography – Ch10: CBCJ 1996, 'Basic Policies and Priorities' , op.cit.

[38] Notably, Bishop Soma (Nagoya Diocese) and Bishop Hameo (Yokohama Diocese) successive chairmen of the JCCJP and the most active bishops in the East Timorese cause.

[39] Bibliography – Ch10: CBCJ 1987, 'Let us Live Together in Joy'.

Another significant general Statement of the Bishops Conference expressing a 'Social Gospel' was the 'Resolution for Peace' on the fiftieth anniversary of the end of World War II. Addressing their document to the faithful, priests and religious, the bishops repented of the support given by the Catholic Church to the militarist regime which had led the nation into World War II. They then appealed for Christians to become reliable 'workers for peace' in the world by 'living up to and spreading the Gospel of Christ'. Citation was made of Pope John Paul II's exhortation in his encyclical '*Tertio Millennio Adveniente*' that every member of the Church should 'purify themselves of the mistakes of the past – unfaithfulness, lack of consistency, slowness to act, and all the rest'. The Episcopal Conference then urged 'not only Catholics, but all people of good will, to work for a peace based on the harmony of love, truth, justice and liberty in the light of the Gospel.'[40]

A number of Committees and Commissions of the Conference have addressed some specific issues of social justice [41] - indicating a degree of sympathy with those who suffer and some desire to relate the Church's Social Doctrine to such situations.

However, commentators within the Church community in Japan as well as outside it have opined that most of the bishops appear to have been content with such general exhortations and to have avoided making concrete decisions, 'pronouncing from above and apart'.[42] It was remarked that the majority of the bishops were reticent about publicly identifying either as individuals or collectively with the poor and the marginalised. Such a posture, widely observed, suggests that these bishops are pre-occupied with what they perceive to be the vulnerability of the Church in Japan (or of themselves personally) and are therefore unwilling to 'rock the boat' by criticising government policies. Such a disposition certainly had repercussions within an ecclesial community already inclined to regard religion as a 'private' matter, to be introspective in Church concerns, and to adopt a low profile in public affairs.

The Response of the Church in Japan to the East Timorese Cause

The Bishops Conference

Throughout the years of Indonesia's occupation of East Timor the Bishops Conference of Japan only made two public statements expressing their concern about the situation, both in the form of letters to their peers.

In December 1991, following the Santa Cruz massacre, a 'Letter of Condolence' was addressed to Bishop Belo. In this the Conference expressed their wish 'that [the] right of self-determination which is a right of every nation and one that is guaranteed by the UN Charter and the Universal Declaration of Human Rights should be given back to the East Timorese through appropriate ways and means'. The bishops supported Belo's call for a referendum and urged the UN Secretary General to undertake 'a thorough investigation of the incident and do its best to find a total solution to the East Timor problem'.[43]

In between the two letters bishop Belo was invited (in 1993) to address the Japanese Episcopate. However, the Bishops Conference was anxious lest such an arrangement might appear to the Japanese and Indonesian governments and to the Indonesian Bishops Conference as intrusive or even provocative. Such fears are indicative of their concern for 'harmony' (and

---

[40] Bibliography –Ch10: CBCJ 1998 op.cit.

[41] e.g. Discrimination against the *Buraku* people, the abolition of nuclear weapons, disabled persons, Vietnamese and other refugees, Filipino and other migrant workers, Registration of Aliens (notably of Koreans), peace education, environmental issues, research on human cloning, etc. See: CBCJ 1998, op.cit. and CBCJ internet web site op.cit.

[42] Various interlocutors - within agencies of the Bishops Conference, within the Catholic Press, members of NGOs (Catholic and secular) - to the author, Japan, April 1998.

[43] 'Letter of Condolence to Bishop Belo regarding the Massacre of the East Timorese, etc', CBCJ 12.12.1991 (cited in Bibliography – Ch8: CCJPD 1993, p53).

of the lasting and pervasive influence of Confucianism in Japanese society). Accordingly, Belo was invited to Japan by bishops Stephen Fumio Kameo and Peter Okada Takeo who had special responsibility for the Japanese Catholic Council for Justice and Peace. Such a personal encounter of the Conference with the Apostolic Administrator of Dili might well have made a significant difference to the institutional response, but unfortunately the circumstances then prevailing in East Timor prevented Belo from taking up the invitation. His failure to do so lost him sympathy among some of the Japanese bishops who were insensitive to the pressures he was under.

During East Timor's Year of Crisis (1999) the Conference addressed a 'Letter of Solidarity' to bishops Belo and Nascimento. In their message the bishops declared that they only 'came to know of the tragedy of East Timor when Mgr Martinho da Costa Lopes visited Japan (in 1986) to appeal on behalf of his people'. They went on to acknowledge also that 'much of the blame for the present situation' lay with 'the international community' and that Japan – 'as the biggest donor of economic assistance to Indonesia' was 'particularly culpable'. They promised prayers 'that the Lord be with every individual of East Timor to protect him or her from all evil and lead the whole population to true peace and freedom.' And they pledged to 'do everything in their power to assist in the creation of a suitable atmosphere in which to hold the coming vote...by appealing to as many national and international organisations as possible'.[44] An evidence of the fulfilment of that pledge was their sending of a letter to UN Secretary General Kofi Annan (copied to the Indonesian Ambassador in Tokyo) in which the bishops urged renewed efforts (on the part of the Secretary General) to facilitate a peaceful plebiscite in East Timor.[45] From this response it must be concluded that the awareness, condolence and solidarity of the Conference and of the majority of individual Japanese bishops in respect of the East Timorese plight were very limited, and very late in the day.

The Japanese Catholic Council for Justice and Peace
        The Catholic Council for Justice and Peace (JCCJP) roots its effort in the declaration of the Synod of Bishops (1971) that 'action on behalf of justice and participation in the transformation of the world are a constitutive dimension of [...] the Church's mission for the redemption of the human race and its liberation from every oppressive situation'.[46] The Council cites the Synod's declaration that the Church's action 'is to be directed *above all* at those men and nations which because of various forms of oppression and because of the present character of our society are silent, indeed voiceless, victims of injustice'.

        An indication of the Council's willingness to question government policy is provided by their Declaration to mark the 50th anniversary of the end of World War II. The document remarks on the 'economic invasion' that had been pursued by Japan in SE Asia since 1945. It points out that 'being in support of Japanese interests in the Asia-Pacific region and of multinational companies' profits...is repeating the mistakes Japan made in the past' (i.e. during the era of imperialist aggression).[47] Council action on behalf of the poor and marginalised in Japan itself has been very evident (see Note 41 above), and there was (and is) continual activity in respect of the East Timor issue.

        In June 1984 (that is, before Dom Martinho's visit to Japan), the bishops of the Council wrote to the Prime Minister of Portugal to encourage him to work for the self-

---

[44] 'Letter of solidarity to Bishop Belo and Bishop Nascimento of East Timor from the bishops of Japan', CBCJ, 20.6.1999.

[45] *Viz.* To provide international civilian police for East Timor; call upon Indonesia to disarm its military forces and their proxy militias, and (failing such an outcome) to set up a UN Peace Keeping Operation in the territory. CBCJ, 20.6.1999.

[46] 'The Establishment of the JCCJP', JCCJP, Tokyo.

[47] Bibliography – Ch10: CCJP 1998, 'Towards a New Beginning: A Declaration from the JCCJP on the Occasion of the 50th Anniversary of the End of World War II'.

determination of the East Timorese. The letter cited the resolution of the 1983 Session of the UN Human Rights Commission affirming their 'inalienable right to such an opportunity in accordance with GA Resolution 1514 (XV)'.[48] In November 1991 Fr. Stefani Renato agreed to travel to Dili on behalf of the Council to observe the meeting being planned between East Timorese and the delegation of Portuguese parliamentarians, personally witnessing the Santa Cruz massacre. Following this tragic event the Council secretariat addressed a letter 'to all the committees for justice and peace around the world'. They urged an appeal for a positive response from the United Nations and from the government of Indonesia to bishop Belo's call for a referendum of the East Timorese wishes regarding their political status. Significantly this letter remarked that 'until now it has been considered as taboo to take up the East Timor issue within the Church, but precisely because of this the East Timorese Church has been suffering immensely, feeling that they have been *ignored by the churches* in other countries'.[49] The Council also wrote to the UN Secretary General's envoy Amos Wako (sent to discover the truth of the matter in East Timor). In this they conveyed their concerns and indicated that the Council 'had been working on this issue for many years...and that several members had been [to the territory] to investigate the real situation'.[50] Stephen Hameo, bishop of the Diocese of Yokohama, then executive chairman of the FABC Office for Human Development, was among such visitors to East Timor (in July 1992). In the same year appeals for a just resolution of the issue were also made to the Japanese ambassador to the United Nations; to the Indonesian Ambassador in Tokyo; and to President Suharto in Jakarta.[51] The general repression in East Timor and the arrest of Xanana Gusmao in November 1992 were also protested to UN Secretary General Boutros Boutros Ghali, President Suharto, and to Cardinal Roger Etchegaray of the Pontifical Commission *Justitia et Pax* to whom appeal was made for help from the Vatican Nuncio in Jakarta (Mgr Canalini).[52] Further correspondence was addressed to the Dutch ambassador to Japan (December 1995), to Prime Minister Matahir Mohammad of Malaysia (November 1996), to President Suharto and to (Commander of Indonesian Armed Forces) General Feisal Tanjung (December 1996), to Indonesian Foreign Minister Ali Alatas (July 1997), and to the Austrian Federal Chancellor and Austrian ambassador in Tokyo (November/December 1997).[53]

From this it would appear that an immediate response was made by the JCCJP to every publicised incident involving the welfare of East Timorese. These letters also indicate that cultural *mores* and concern for the welfare of the Church in Japan did not inhibit the JCCJP, their representatives, or members of district justice and peace committees from making prophetic appeals to a variety of national and international leaders (including the Vatican). One of the most unequivocal was that made by JCCJP President bishop Niakeo Okada to the UN Special Committee on Decolonisation in July 1996. The following citation from the Statement is indicative of the general character of the Council's response to the East Timorese plight:

> Our Council has been making its statement every year at this forum since 1989.....We receive daily detailed information coming directly from East Timor on human rights violations...of such harrowing nature that we are driven to renewed joint endeavours...
> International Society, which has for so long ignored the tragedy of the Timorese people, must call upon the aggressor Indonesia to stop their acts of terror....

---

[48] Full text of Letter (19.6.1984) in Bibliography – Ch8: CCJPD 1993, p21.

[49] Letter, JCCJP, 20.1.1992 - author's emphasis.

[50] Letter, JCCJP, 6.2.1992.

[51] Letters, JCCJP dated 27.2.92; 28.9.92; and 27.9.92 respectively.

[52] Letters, JCCJP dated 23.11.92; 23.11.92; and 8.12.92 respectively.

[53] Letters, JCCJP concerning, respectively: East Timorese protests in Jakarta (19.12.95); disruption to the second APCET Conference in Kuala Lumpur (22.11.96); calling for an internationally acceptable solution to East Timor issue (13.12.96); the arrest of Timorese resistance leader David Alex (1.7.97); Timorese seeking asylum in the Austrian embassy Jakarta (19.11.97 & 3.12.97).

The United Nations and related countries must recognise that they have allowed the Indonesian Government to continue their invasion and cruel oppression over a long period of 20 years...Many countries have closed their eyes to this invasion in violation of International Law, and numerous violations of human rights resulting therefrom, and looked only at profits which come from trade with Indonesia.

The responsibility of our country, Japan, is also very big. Our country has 'Guidelines for Government Official Development Assistance (ODA)' which state [that in] providing assistance, attention will be paid to the democratisation and human rights conditions of liberty in the recipient country...Although Indonesia is the biggest recipient of Japanese ODA, this clause has never been applied to Indonesia....

As a member of a country which has allowed the invasion of East Timor by Indonesia for 20 years, and as a member of a human rights organisation of that country, I wish to ask forgiveness from the bottom of my heart and promise that we will strengthen our effort to assist you...[54]

With the accession of B.J.Habibie to the Indonesian presidency in 1998 the JCCJP became even more forthright. Council president bishop Paul Yoshinao Otsuka of Kyoto Diocese, in a Statement to the UN Decolonisation Committee, declared that the resignation of Suharto 'gave those of us who have been seeking a fair resolution of the East Timor question great joy since he had been responsible for outstanding violations of human rights in East Timor'. He went on to call for the 'immediate withdrawal of the Indonesian army from East Timor and the implementation of UN resolutions requiring self-determination of the East Timorese people'.[55] At the same UN Committee a year later, in the midst of the Timorese crisis, bishop Otsuka was critical of the flawed peace process which 'had offered no participation to the Timorese themselves'. He also pointed to the shortcomings of the New York Agreement (5th May 1999) which evidently regarded the Indonesian army as 'a neutral party' and had entrusted it with providing security for the popular consultation. The bishop lamented the fact that 'the cries of the East Timorese – which have reached our ears from the very beginning of the issue - have been ignored by the international community with the exception of small NGOs in different parts of the world'. He then repeated the points recently made by the Japanese Bishops Conference in their letter to UNSG Kofi Annan (cited above). In September that year, as the crisis peaked in East Timor, the JCCJP associated itself with a 'Joint Statement of Japanese Citizens and NGOs on the Current Situation in East Timor'. This deplored the violence orchestrated by 'the Indonesian military establishment' and urged Jakarta to request immediate intervention by the United Nations 'to restore and ensure public peace'.[56] Such direct association with non-Church solidarity groups in Japan continued and included criticism of Japan's support for 'the authoritarian government of Indonesia through the CGI' urging that aid to Jakarta be conditional upon full co-operation with the post-ballot UN Resolutions in respect of East Timorese welfare.[57]

[54] Statement of JCCJP to the Special Committee on Decolonisation by bishop Niakeo Okada, President JCCJP, 15.7.1996. JCCJP, Tokyo.

[55] 'Japanese Bishop tells UN to heed Belo', The Irish Catholic, 28.7.1998.

[56] 'Joint Statement of Japanese Citizens and NGOs on the Current Situation in E.Timor' to President B.J.Habibie, FM Ali Alatas, and State Secretary Muladi by Asia-Japan Women's Resource Centre, Pacific Asia Resource Centre, Network for Indonesian Democracy, Japan (NINDJA), and JCCJP. Disseminated by Pacific Asia Resource Centre, Tokyo.

[57] 'Japanese NGOs Letter to World Bank', 10.10.2000, Disseminated by NINDJA for several organisations including JETC, ODA Reform Network, Japan NGO Network on Indonesia, etc.

Caritas Japan

Established by the bishops Conference in 1969 this agency is engaged only in humanitarian assistance, i.e. not in advocacy, human resource training etc. as are some of its (larger) sister agencies in other countries (e.g. Caritas Australia, and CAFOD UK). Funds are mainly generated via an annual Lenten Campaign in Catholic parishes (Y100 million annually). It receives no government grants. Contacts with Caritas in other nations enables a degree of supervision of some of the projects that it supports in some countries around the world. Funds began to be provided for projects in East Timor following the visit to Japan of Mgr Costa Lopes in 1986. These have included such items as the provision of local water supplies in the Oecussi enclave, school materials for use at Suai, emergency foodstuffs and medicines to Baucau in time of drought, etc. A 'screening committee' of local and Japanese church leaders examined applications for support, but the very limited human resources of Caritas Japan prevailed against members of staff making visits to evaluate progress, and reports were rarely forthcoming from the recipients. For the same reason Caritas Japan did not participate in international gatherings of NGOs addressing the East Timor issue. As Hideo Nosaka, Director of Caritas Japan, explained to the author (Tokyo, April 1998), only minimal information about the situation in East Timor could therefore be provided to those parishes that contributed to the Lenten fund-raising effort.

Japanese Catholic Solidarity Groups

A number of groups acting in solidarity with the East Timorese came into existence independently of the Bishops Conference and its agencies, and there were some highly committed individuals. One such person was Sr. Monika Nakamura *ACI*, a member of staff in the JCCJP Office who was entrusted with the East Timor file. With the support of her religious congregation, the Handmaids of the Sacred Heart of Jesus, Sr. Monika personally visited East Timor on more than one occasion, produced and disseminated an East Timor News leaflet to parishes and religious houses, thereby generating Y40,000 annually for East Timorese welfare. Funds towards the support of Timorese in exile and in higher education, and to those in most need in the mountains of East Timor, were raised by bulk sales of port wine. This energetic religious sister provided information and encouragement to solidarity groups across the country, Catholic and secular alike, assisting with the arrangements made by the Japanese Coalition for East Timor of an annual 'Speaking Tour' by East Timorese or their international supporters.[58] One of the largest of these groups was the Association of Japanese Catholics in Solidarity with East Timor through which many parishes and religious congregations supported the Timorese cause. A Catholic network paralleled the secular Citizens Groups, mostly with a non-political emphasis, many of them started by individual parish priests. In April 1998 the author was able to meet with several of them.

For example, in Sendai a Justice and Peace Convention composed of Catholic and Citizens groups developed after the visit to this locality by Mgr Costa Lopes in 1986. In Shimonoseki an East Timor support group was active from 1990 onwards (under the inspiration of the local Parish Priest Fr.Hitashi Hayashi *SJ* who had himself visited Timor several times). They engaged in awareness-raising, fund-raising for projects in East Timor, and political activity such as letters and other forms of protest regarding national government policy. In Kyoto Catholic youth sustained an effort to provide water buffalo for East Timorese farmers from 1990 onwards. They were encouraged by their chaplain, Fr.Sebastian Yanagimoto, who himself travelled every year to and around East Timor gathering information and taking photographs used in the making of calendars as part of the fund-raising campaign. Students of the Salesian College in Tokyo assisted their tutor Fr.Julian Sloyter *SDB* in various technical proj-

---

[58] The author's research trip to Japan was facilitated by Sr.Monika who also translated into Japanese various publications on East Timor by CIIR (London).

ects in East Timor from 1987 onwards. These included the construction of an irrigation canal in the Baucau-Laga area, electrical installations at Salesian educational institutions in Comoro, Fatumaca and Fuiloro, and the transporting of medical resources including microscopes and X-ray equipment. In Nagano a Franciscan priest, Takashi Ito, and a non-Christian friend Hirokazu Kawasaki, initiated the Shinshu Group for East Timor which supported traditional Timorese farming techniques and drew attention to the damaging effects of the imposition of western agricultural methods. Although regarded as a non-religious NGO a significant proportion of the Shinshu Group activists were Catholics. In July 1991 a remarkable member of the Sisters of the Visitation, an indigenous Japanese religious congregation for women, Dr.Yoshie Kamezaki (Sr. Noemi *SV*), established - at the age of 70 years - the Japanese Medical Mission in East Timor. Visiting remote villages of East Timor each year from then on this redoubtable woman was given financial support by her own religious community, and practical assistance by other volunteer medical professionals and students. In due course these efforts led to the establishment (in 1998) of the Alliance of Friends for Medical Care in East Timor (AFMET) to facilitate a Primary Health Care Referral Centre. The Catholics of Nagasaki became engaged in the East Timor issue partly through the extraordinary and courageous enterprise of Sr. Noemi and in 1995 hosted the annual 'Speaking Tour'. For Nagasaki Catholics the suffering of the East Timorese evoked the martyrdom of their own early history. By 1997 even such a traditionally conservative Catholic community was willing to promote a local exhibition in defence of the human rights and freedom of the East Timorese people, staged by the Nagasaki Solidarity Committee for East Timor. Yet a Justice and Peace Commission was never established in that diocese!

Some of those who were involved personally in ongoing projects in East Timor sought to avoid political action so as not to jeopardise the valuable humanitarian work they were undertaking. Others felt it necessary to associate with secular groups in political protest at Japanese and Indonesian government policies that were the cause of the East Timorese plight. Several discovered that their names had been added to the Indonesian Immigration Authorities 'black list' of 'undesirables'. There is no doubt that all of those who visited East Timor on a regular basis took considerable personal risks for the sake of East Timorese welfare - in the true spirit of the Gospel. A number felt constrained to express to this author their disappointment at the lack of support they had received in their various efforts from the Japanese hierarchy, and from the parochial clergy (some of whom did not appear to them to 'identify with the poor'). They were also distressed by the attitude of 'too many lay Catholics who were preoccupied with material success and security'. 'In the Japanese Catholic Church', they lamented, 'the Gospel is not understood'.

Bishop Soma of Nagano - an inspiration

There is no doubt that both Catholic and secular activists in the Timorese cause – in Japan and much further afield – found inspiration in the commitment to social justice of diocesan bishop Aloysius Nobua Soma of Nagano. Born in 1916 and consecrated bishop in September 1969 bishop Soma was Chairman of JCCJP from 1974 (and President after his retirement). He had a significant and positive influence in promoting solidarity with various poor and marginalised groups in Japan and elsewhere including (and especially) the suffering people of East Timor.

In an extensive, courteous and frank correspondence bishop Soma called for all the fundamental human rights of the East Timorese people to be respected. In particular he continually appealed for greater sympathy with their legitimate aspirations for political self-determination. Letters on these matters were addressed *inter alia* to the Federation of Asian Bishops Conferences (1989), the Indonesian Bishops Conference (1989), successive UN Secretary Generals, Pax Christi International (1991), and Pope John Paul II (1995). A particularly significant effort was his appeal in 1989 to the 5 cardinals, 32 archbishops, 77 bishops and 1359 other Church leaders of the Asia-Pacific region evoking support for bishop Belo's request to UN Secretary General Peres de Cuellar for an authentic plebiscite in East Timor.[59] Another was his 'urgent appeal for solidarity with our suffering brothers and sisters in East Timor' addressed jointly with bishop Hilton Deakin (Australia) and bishop Gabriel Garol (Philippines) to a number of Indonesian Christian institutions. These included the Catholic Conference of Bishops and the Protestant Bishops Council and their agencies, and the Federation of Religious Orders (1996). The letter exhorted them all to call upon President Suharto and Armed Forces Commander Feisal Tanjung to effect a peaceful and a just settlement of the East Timor issue. [60]

Bishop Soma's activity was not limited to the writing of letters. He made a personal Statement to the UN Decolonisation Committee in New York in August 1989. In this his forthright advocacy of East Timorese human rights included an expression of his regret for 'the close commercial partnership between Indonesia and Japan' and 'the fact that part of Japanese financial aid to Indonesia is spent to oppress the Timorese movement for freedom and peace'.[61] He personally visited East Timor in 1993 and addressed his words of solidarity and faith to the assembled crowds in their native Tetum.[62] In 1994 he contributed words of exhortation to the first meeting of the Asia Pacific Coalition for East Timor (APCET) in Manila.[63] He also attended the VI Symposium on East Timor of Oporto University in Portugal where he castigated the betrayal by the Indonesian regime in East Timor of 'the founding principles of the Republic (*Pancasila*), International Law, and the spirit and ideals of the United Nations'.[64] Such activities brought upon bishop Soma the disfavour of Jakarta – as was indicated by his being prevented from attending the inauguration of the rebuilt seminary in Dili in 1995,[65] and by his deportation from Malaysia along with other activists participating in the second APCET meeting in Kuala Lumpur in 1996. When he died in October 1997 there were many tributes from the solidarity movement within and far beyond Japan. The APCET co-ordinator, Gus Miclat, expressed the sentiments of many when he wrote:

> Bishop Soma was the epitome of a humble and dedicated warrior for peace. In spite of the tremendous odds and pressures that his advocacies reaped, and the onslaught of old age, he never buckled...Such was the energy exuded by bishop Soma, a room could be his cathedral. Move on, our beloved bishop. We have been honoured and we will always be honoured to have been touched by you.[66]

The Church in Japan – an evaluation

Support for the East Timorese cause arose within all levels or circles of the Japanese Church, but fully pervaded none of them. Even prayer for a just and peaceful resolution of the issue, though promised by the Bishops Conference in their letters to bishop Belo, did not appear to become a factor common to all groups or in all localities of the Catholic community. This suggests that a sense of spiritual communion with suffering members of the mystical body in East Timor was somewhat lacking, as well as a common obedience to the Gospel imperative as interpreted in the Church's Social Doctrine. Although the political influence of the

---

[59] See Bibliography – Ch8: CCJPD 1993 op.cit. p35f.
[60] 'Appeal for Solidarity, etc' December 1996. Copy on file.
[61] Text in CCJPD, 1993, op.cit, p36f. In 1994 bishop Soma (then retired) addressed the UN Decolonisation Committee via his representative Kan Akatani. [Text: Indonesia Publications, email > apakabar@igc.apc.org <].
[62] Text of Bishop Soma's homily (13.2.93) on file with the author.
[63] Full text in 'Report from APCET – Bishop Aloysius Nabuo Soma', June 1994, ETAN (New York), p21.
[64] 'Role of the Asia-Pacific Church and of Japan in the Issue of East Timor', Aloysius Soma, VI Symposium on Timor, Oporto University, Portugal, October 5th, 1994.
[65] For further detail see Bibliography - General (East Timor): ETAN docs, Vol 41-2, p61f.
[66] Copy on file with the author.

Church upon the government was limited by the size of its constituency there were Catholics (and other Christians) in the higher echelons of society. Evidently many in the ecclesiastical leadership were anxious with regard to the security of the Church itself in Japan. This made them hesitant to challenge government policies, an inhibition already present because of the national cultural heritage and because of Japan's perennially precarious economic situation.

Certainly there were those who faithfully responded to the Church's Social Doctrine in respect of the East Timorese (and other oppressed, marginalised and impoverished people). Indeed, it seems that action with regard to various issues of social justice was commonly undertaken by the same people throughout the Japanese Church – while others, at all levels, were engaged in none. The activists among the hierarchy, clergy, religious and laity urged respect for Timorese human rights whenever opportune, in collaboration with secular organisations committed to the same cause, and often at personal risk. They challenged the government's ODA policy – and thereby the power and priorities of the Japanese business Corporations. They called for the principles of International Law to be respected in practice. They had greater impact than might have been anticipated from such a numerically small group.

But too many others distanced themselves from the situation in East Timor, and other issues of social justice, either by remaining content with general exhortations or by allowing themselves to become pre-occupied with personal affairs (be they secular or religious). The limited influence of the Catholic Media was not only diminished by a general reticence with regard to expressing criticism of the government (and of the policies of the powerful Corporations) but was further circumscribed by the various anxieties of the majority of bishops. Those who were sympathetic to the promotion of a just and peaceful settlement in East Timor gave scope to the initiatives of their subordinates and provided them with support when it was called for. But some people whose sympathies for the Timorese predicament were slight or non-existent actually put obstacles in the way of those willing to take up that burden of responsibility. The Catholic community in Japan, assembled in formal conventions, subscribed theoretically to certain basic policy priorities and objectives that indicated an awareness of the principles of social justice expounded by the Universal Church. Nonetheless, there was a wide range of responses in bringing these principles into practical effect - in general, and in the particular case of the issue of East Timor.

Again, if consideration is given to the matter of identification with the various dimensions of Christ's personal ministry of redemption, then shining examples can be discovered within the Japanese Church. It has been noted how among the bishops, the priests, the religious and the laity there were individuals who were committed *pastors, prophets, disciples, evangelists and intercessors* in respect of the people of East Timor. These members of the Church sought to improve the circumstances of the Timorese. They drew attention to the injustice of the situation prevailing in the territory that they had thoroughly investigated. They criticised governmental and other policies that were detrimental to the people of East Timor. They strove for East Timorese liberation, at least in political and economic terms. The opportunities for Japanese to contribute personally to the spiritual freedom and renewal of the East Timorese were limited because of a lack of personnel to spare as well as the minimal access afforded them to the occupied territory. Yet those with the will and the courage overcame such obstacles. It has been remarked already that these persons were ready to risk their lives for the sake of their suffering brothers and sisters in East Timor.

The question therefore arises once again as to the status that is given to the Social Doctrine of the Church within the Church itself. It seems that while some members of the Church are inspired and guided by it *'even to the cross'*, others (at every level or circle) can remain unmoved in terms of a practical response - or find reasons not to apply its principles to particular (usually contentious) issues. In Japan, as elsewhere, concern over the perceived welfare of the local Church itself provided one such reason. Another relevant factor might be that, in this Asian context, the very principles of that doctrine are alien in so far as they are derived from a Western (indeed, European) philosophical tradition. It could be asked whether the Social Doctrine of the Church might evoke a more positive and widely shared response in a location with a non-European heritage if its foundational Gospel precepts were married with appropriate oriental forms of thought. In such a case its principles would not appear as an entirely "foreign" concoction. It is beyond the scope of this present work to elaborate on ways in which this might be done although some suggestions are outlined in due course. But in any case, as observed, the problem lies as much in the readiness of the local Church to actually carry the principles into practice as it does in the nature of their source. It seems appropriate to conclude with the exhortation made by bishop Soma in his homily at Mass during the APCET gathering in Manila in 1994 and noted above. Based simply on the Gospel itself, and arising from his own deep faith, the words he spoke on that occasion inspired the efforts of many – including this author - to persevere in their efforts for justice in East Timor in solidarity with its long-suffering people:

> Blessed are those who work for justice. The people of East Timor are working for justice, fighting for their rights, and they are blessed. We can join their struggle. God is raising up people everywhere to work alongside the East Timorese. Those who work for East Timor are doing God's work. In 1989 bishop Belo wrote that the world has forgotten East Timor. Let us show that it is not true.

CHAPTER ELEVEN - THE CHURCH IN ENGLAND:
ACTION, INACTION, AND AMBIGUITY

An examination of the response within the Catholic Church in England and Wales to the plight of the East Timorese people reveals a curious mixture of effective action, notable areas of inactivity, and a certain ambiguity of posture. No doubt a significant factor in bringing this about was the attitude of the successive British governments in office during the years of the invasion, occupation, and eventual liberation of East Timor. The government disposition had roots in an earlier period of international relations and arose also from the contemporary exigencies of global politics and the national economy as perceived in Whitehall. Of itself it does not excuse any shortcomings on the part of the Church. Other explanations for the Church's response are to be found in the social circumstances that prevailed in the country during the years of Timorese suffering, and within the Church itself as it reacted to the challenges of the Second Vatican Council and to its changing milieu.

Historical Roots of Government Priorities
The principal aim of British planners for the post-World War II period was to exercise as much control as possible over the world's most economically important regions. In this, and in the adoption of an anti-Communist political posture, priorities in London mirrored those in Washington. Specifically, Indonesia was regarded by the Foreign Office as 'very important in peace, as a dollar earner, and as a sterling source of essential raw materials'.[1]

Having covertly co-operated with the United States in assisting General Suharto to gain power in Indonesia in 1965-6, Britain became a member of the Intergovernmental Group of Indonesia (IGGI) that was to provide massive financial assistance to the country under its new, pro-Western, regime. The British government, industry and commerce were prepared to acquiesce in the internally repressive and externally aggressive policies of the *Orde Baru* so as to benefit from political stability in Indonesia, and to exploit the country's vast mineral resources. In 1975 the Confederation of British Industries (CBI) reported 'the enormous potential of Indonesia to the foreign investor' and that the country enjoyed 'a favourable political climate'.[2] When, in the same year, Lisbon lurched to the Left and there was clear intimation that Indonesia intended to exploit the unstable political situation in East Timor and take over control of the half-island, the advice of the British Ambassador to Jakarta was only to be expected:

> The people of East Timor are in no condition to exercise their right to self-determination.... As seen from here, it is in Britain's interests for Indonesia to absorb the territory as soon as and as unobtrusively as possible; and that, if it comes to the crunch and there is a row in the United Nations, we should keep our heads down and avoid siding against Indonesia.[3]

This was precisely the posture that was adopted by Britain in that forum. Certainly the United Kingdom was a signatory to the unanimous Security Council Resolutions 384 (22.12.1975) and 389 (22.4.1976) which 'deplored' the intervention of Indonesian Armed Forces, and required both their withdrawal and a demonstration of respect for the East

---

[1] On Foreign Policy priorities see Foreign and Commonwealth Office, *Documents on British Foreign Policy Overseas* (HMSO London) Series 11, Vol. 11, p164-5; cf. Kennan, G.F. 'Current Trends, US Foreign Policy', PPS/23. *Foreign Relations of the US 1948*, Washington DC, Vol 1, Part 2, pp509ff; and Bibliography - Ch11.
[2] Cited by Curtis, M. 1993, see: 'The Primacy of Economic Interests' in <u>Timor Link</u> No 28, January 1994, p5-6.
[3] Sir John Archibald Ford, cable to London, July 1975. For full citation see: Bibliography – Ch8: Munster, G. & Walsh, R. 1980, p192.

Timorese right to self-determination. But in the General Assembly the British delegation abstained on every Resolution concerning the East Timor issue - from December 1975 until November 1982 when the matter was entrusted to the Secretary General.[4] Even the Santa Cruz Massacre had little effect on the posture of the British government, as will be noted below. London's policy only changed when Suharto was no longer deemed capable of ensuring the political stability in Indonesia that British and other Western economic interests required. The achievement of this stability was seen as being in no small measure dependent upon the satisfactory resolution of the East Timor issue - and so backing was given to interim Indonesian president Habibie's suggestion of a 'popular consultation' to determine once and for all the country's political status. The government had some concern about Timorese welfare but the relationship with Jakarta remained of paramount importance.

Britain, Indonesia and East Timor, 1975-1999

Nonetheless, it is to the credit of the British government that from the time of Indonesia's invasion of East Timor in 1975 to its withdrawal at the end of 1999 the Jakarta regime in the territory was never recognised by London as legitimate. The consistent position of Her Majesty's Government (HMG), adopted also by other countries in the European Union, was to expect an authentic act of political self-determination to be conducted in East Timor in accordance with UNGA Resolution 1514 (XV) [14th December, 1960]. Britain never expressed formal acceptance of Indonesian rule in East Timor either *de iure* (as did Australia) or *de facto* (as did the United States). The UK looked to Portugal and Indonesia to resolve the situation satisfactorily and its delegation pledged support to the efforts of the UN Secretary General in facilitating fruitful negotiations between these two states.[5] As noted, when a real opportunity for substantial progress in this matter arose in 1999 the British government backed the process both independently and in liaison with the EU. However, this principled position did not in any way hold Britain back from pursuing its interests with Indonesia and turning a blind eye to what was happening in East Timor. The UK embassy in Jakarta did everything it could to assist British industrial/commercial interests in Indonesia and the government itself provided substantial development aid and backed significant weapons sales to the Republic, even linking the two for a sustained period of time. These two aspects of government policy evoked the most vigorous castigation from its opponents, as is further elaborated below. The British government covered up the murder of the five Western journalists (including Englishmen Brian Peters and Malcolm Rennie) by Indonesian troops at Balibo in October 1975 for as long as was possible, despite persistent challenges from some non-governmental organisations.[6] In the early years of the occupation British journalists were discouraged by the Foreign Office from drawing attention to the human rights abuses being perpetrated by the Indonesian military in East Timor - so as not to 'rock the boat'.[7] East Timorese independence activists perceived

---

[4] For full texts of UNSC and UNGA Resolutions, and the voting pattern, see Bibliography – General (East Timor): Krieger, H. 1995, Ch.3, pp 53, 93, 123-133.

[5] e.g. Delegate Murray at UN Security Council debate on East Timor, 22.4.1976, see: Krieger, H. 1995, op.cit.p118; FCO SE Asia Desk head Burns to refugee Timorese priest Fr.Francisco Fernandes, July 1980, *Tapol* Bulletin No.40, p6; Delegate Maclay at UNGA 4th Committee debates, 15.11.1982, see: Krieger, H. 1995 op.cit p164; FCO Minister A.Goodlad, Statement to the House of Commons 10.2.1993, see: Krieger, H. 1995 op.cit. p302; etc.

[6] See: Dunn, J.1995, 'East Timor: The Balibo Incident in Perspective', Australian Centre for Independent Journalism, University of Technology, Sydney; Bibliography – General (East Timor): 'The Balibo Murders: Balibo and Beyond – the International Cover-up', Dowson, H., in Retboll, T. (ed) 1998. 'Chronology of a cover-up', by Hugh Dowson in Bulletin of the UN Association of Great Britain & Northern Ireland (Western Region), Jan-Feb 1997.

[7] See Bibliography –General (East Timor): Taylor, J. 1991, p83 and Note 14.

Britain to be 'the single worst obstructionist in promoting international action'.[8] The stance taken by Britain in various international forums, and its pursuit of economic benefits by sustaining a positive relationship with Indonesia, had the practical effect of affording legitimacy to the *Orde Baru*'s annexation of East Timor. Indeed, some analysts considered Britain's behaviour as even more cynical than that of Canberra or Washington because it was 'more subtle'. Yet it must also be noted that during its presidency of the European Union in 1998 the UK urged a Common Position on Arms Sales to Indonesia and also promoted and led an important visit of observation to East Timor by a troika of EU ambassadors.[9] In East Timor's Year of Crisis the British government acted quite positively, as will be summarised below. However, the prioritising of good relations with Jakarta gave rise to two major policies of successive administrations that had repercussions for East Timor: generous Development Aid and extensive Arms Sales to Indonesia.

Development Aid

Government aid to Indonesia was both multilateral (via the IGGI from 1967, and via the Consultative Group on Indonesia, CGI, formed after the Santa Cruz massacre in 1991) and unilateral (Overseas Development Aid, ODA). It was always substantial when compared with that given to other recipients, and was continued despite compelling evidence of gross human rights abuses by the Indonesian military in East Timor (and in Indonesia itself).[10] Aid to Indonesia was persistently justified on the grounds that it relieved poverty and was in support of Jakarta's 'sound economic policy.'[11] A Report by the National Audit Office in 1996 presented government aid policy as positively as possible but the inconsistencies between the government's stated criteria for Aid and its practice in respect of Indonesia was still discernible. It was evident that certain projects had been supported in order to win future arms sales rather than on their developmental merits.[12] Such criticisms had been levelled repeatedly both in and outside parliament.[13] When 'New Labour' came to power in 1997 the longstanding 'Aid and Trade' provision (which accounted for 50% of British Aid and, *inter alia*, directly linked ODA provision to arms sales), was terminated globally.[14] But major funding for a development project in East Timor was approved by the Department for International Develop-

---

[8] Independence spokesperson 1992 quoted by Mark Curtis in 'Touting for Terror', New Internationalist March 1994, p20-22; *Tapol* Bulletin 116, April 1993; Portuguese Assembly Plenary, 17.6.96; J.R Horta, 'One step to our dream of freedom', The Guardian 9.4.97.

[9] For a critique of the Common Position see: Timor Link No41 (Feb 1998) p6, and Supplement, CIIR London; Michael Crowley, 'EU acts on arms trade' in Amnesty, July/August 1998. For a critique of the troika visit to E Timor, see *Tapol* Report No.24, 7/98, *Tapol*, London.

[10] e.g. In 1984 alone British aid exceeded £28m, Indonesia being the sixth largest recipient and the largest outside the commonwealth (ODA figures). In Spring 1991 Douglas Hurd urged the EC to 'cut aid to countries that violate human rights', but after the Santa Cruz massacre in November that year HMG actually *increased* aid to the Suharto regime by 250% (to £81m), the largest percentage rise of any donor country (*Tapol* Bulletin 118, Aug.1993).

[11] Baroness Trumpington, House of Lords, July 16th 1992 (Kreiger op.cit. pp300-302); cf. Baroness Chalker, House of Lords, July 21st 1993 (Hansard).

[12] 'Aid to Indonesia', National Audit Office Report (HMSO 29.11.1996). Critique by MP Anne Clwyd (Press Release 29.11.96) reported by David Hencke, 'Indonesia aid "tied to arms sales"', The Guardian, 29.11.96; and *Tapol* Bulletin 137, p129.

[13] Critics included: Lord Avebury cited the 4th Geneva Convention article 146 (House of Lords debate 16.6.1992 - Krieger, H. 1995 op.cit. p300-302) and the government's own criteria (House of Lords debate 2.3.1994 - in ETAN Docs Vol 27, p93-4); Anne Clwyd MP (Lab), 'British Aid to Indonesia: The Continuing Scandal' A Report, (*Tapol* Bulletin 131:17,13); Barber, P., 1995, 'Partners in Repression: The Reality of British Aid to Indonesia', *Tapol*, London.

[14] 'Country Report – Indonesia', HMG Dept for International Development, Sept.2000, p6.

ment (DFID) in 1998 as part of its aid programme in Indonesia – again giving a mixed message in respect of the government's position on East Timor's political status.[15]

Arms Sales and Military Training

The extensive supply of military equipment by the UK to Indonesia is well documented.[16] A particular aspect of that provision was the sale of Hawk combat aircraft by British Aerospace (BAe, now BAE Systems) under government licence. Ministers in successive governments justified this policy on several grounds. It was maintained that Indonesia was entitled to purchase 'the means of national defence' and that HMG 'always stipulated that such arms were not to be used for the violation or suppression of human rights and fundamental freedoms' through either 'internal repression or external aggression'. The government claimed to be 'continually monitoring the human rights situation in East Timor and Indonesia'.[17] Officials admitted that there was no feasible way to control the end use of the equipment sold to Indonesia and that the regime had violated human rights in East Timor (and elsewhere) but always argued that in such matters Jakarta had made 'noticeable improvements'. The 'defence industry' was defended also on the basis of its contribution to Britain's national economy and by its provision of jobs to a sizeable work force.[18] Foreign sales were regarded as 'a tremendous national asset.'[19] Moreover, arms manufacturing was heavily subsidised and protected against customers defaulting on payment by the arrangements of the Export Credit Guarantees Department (ECGD). Britain also provided training to members of the Indonesian armed forces including its police officers throughout the period under study, the argument being urged that 'such training included an important human rights component' and would lead to an increased 'professionalism' on the part of the recipients.

Criticism of the government's policy and of the practices of the 'defence industry' was widespread. Some NGOs (such as *Tapol*, the Campaign against the Arms Trade, the World Development Movement, and *Pax Christi*) and some journalists such as John Pilger were particularly forthright.[20] Challenges were presented by individual Members within both Houses of Parliament and collectively outside of them by the Parliamentary Human Rights Group (PHRG) under the chairmanship of Lord Avebury. The PHRG also lobbied more generally on behalf of the East Timorese welfare. There was a broad-based popular concern about the matter of arms sales and activists included both secular and religiously motivated groups and individuals. As evidence mounted of the use of British-made equipment for repression in Indonesia itself the government's policy became increasingly untenable for any reason other than Britain's alleged economic benefit - and the arguments for this were unconvincing. Critics drew attention to the over-dependency of the national economy on the 'defence-industry'

---

[15] 'Britain funds development project in E Timor', DFID Press Release 27.3.1998.
[16] e.g.: 'The Supply of UK Military Equipment to Indonesia', Campaign against the Arms Trade (CAAT), London; 'UK Government Position' in *Indonesia: Arms Trade to a Military Regime*, European Network Against the Arms Trade (ENAAT) 1997, Amsterdam, p105f; 'Gambling on Genocide - Indonesia', in *Gunrunner's Gold*, 1995, World Development Movement (WDM), London.

[17] e.g. UK delegate George, UNGA Decolonisation Committee (1340), 12.8.88 (Krieger, H. 1995, op.cit. p170); Armed Services Minister A.Hamilton (Hansard 12.1.93); FO Min. A.Goodlad (BBC World Service 21.2.94); FO Min. G.Hoon (House of Commons 20.7.99).
[18] e.g.: House of Lords debates 14.1.1992, 21.6.1992 (Hansard), 16.7.1992 (Krieger, H. 1995 op.cit. p300-302); House of Commons – Questions: 10.2.1993; FO Minister D.Fatchett in 'Human Rights Annual Report', FCO 21.7.2000 – a summary of HMG role during the E Timor crisis 1999; this author's correspondence with the FCO from 1994-2000; etc.

[19] Ministry of Defence, Head of Exports, The Guardian, 6.9.1993.
[20] See: Bibliography – Ch11: Pilger, J. especially 1994, Ch VI p294f, and 1998 Ch II p115f and regular publications of CAAT and *Tapol* Bulletin.

and the subsidies that were required to maintain it.[21] They also pointed to the destabilising effect increased amounts of weaponry had in those recipient countries (such as Indonesia) where there was growing social tension. Campaigners including journalists criticised especially the transfer of Hawk combat aircraft referring to numerous sightings of these jets in an offensive (or at least an intimidating role) in East Timor from 1983 through to 1999.[22] The deliberate damage of one of these adaptable aircraft in its hangar at the BAe factory at Warton, Lancashire in January 1996 generated considerable publicity. This increased significantly when the perpetrators were later acquitted by the jury at Liverpool Crown Court who accepted the defendants' plea that they had been acting in obedience to 'a higher law', their purpose having been to 'prevent genocide in East Timor'.[23] The training of Indonesian military personnel in this country was opposed (e.g. in successive reports by Amnesty International) on the grounds that there was little evidence to show that the 'human rights component' had born any fruit in the subsequent behaviour of the participants. Nonetheless government policy continued largely unchanged even under the New Labour administration which took office in May 1997 claiming an 'ethical dimension to its foreign policy'.[24] Some effort was certainly made by officials to effect a tighter control over arms sales, but despite success in achieving a 'Common Position on Arms Sales in the EU' in May 1998, the new government found the termination of contracts already agreed to by its predecessor genuinely problematical. Differences of perspective between the Foreign Office, the Ministry of Defence, and the Department of Trade and Industry also contributed to these difficulties.[25]

The Year of Crisis

In 1999 Britain gave assistance to the 'popular consultation' proposed by president Habibie and was represented in the UN Security Council delegation sent to investigate the post-ballot situation. Foreign Secretary Cook mobilised international support for the creation and deployment of the International Force to establish security in the territory, and British Ghurkhas were a contingent of this military coalition. Sanctuary was afforded to Xanana Gusmao and significant funds were allocated towards humanitarian relief, reconstruction and development in East Timor. An embargo on arms sales to Indonesia was imposed unilaterally and in collaboration with the European Union from September until the end of 1999. Financial and diplomatic support was sustained into the following year to effect the repatriation of East Timorese deported by *TNI* to West Timor and elsewhere in Indonesia.[26]

---

[21] See, e.g., 'Arms sales worsen conditions for the people in Britain too', in 'Death For Sale: British Arms Sales and Developing Countries', CAAT ; WDM 1995, *Gunrunners Gold*, op.cit.

[22] Statement from J.Horta, from CNRM Lisbon, via BCET UK 16.11.1994, in ETAN Docs 1994, Vol 33 p110-111); UK journalist Hugh Shaughnessy, 12.11.1996 (ETAN Docs Vol 41 p37); in 1999 by many foreign observers (BBC Radio, via Reuters, London 31.8.99); etc.

[23] For detail see: Bibliography – Ch11: Pilger, J. 1998, Ch.V pp313ff; Bibliography – General (East Timor): 'Seeds of Hope – East Timor Ploughshares: Disarming the Hawks', Needham, A., Parker, J., & Wilson, J., in Hainsworth, P., & McClosky, S. (eds) 2001, pp85-93.

[24] See Bibliography – General (East Timor): 'New Labour, New Codes of Conduct? British Government Policy towards Indonesia and East Timor after the 1997 election', Hainsworth, P. in Hainsworth & McClosky (eds) 2001, op.cit, pp95-116.

[25] See: 'Indonesian arms deal undercuts Cook's line', David Hencke and John Aglionby, The Guardian, 9.10.97; 'Long Arms: why are we waiting for export control?' Editorial, The Guardian 23.1.01; 'Human Rights 1998', published jointly by FCO & DFID (HMSO 1998). Critique in 'Analysis - Human Rights', The Guardian, 22.4.98; Richard Norton-Taylor, 'Ethical arms policy in disarray', The Guardian 24.6.98 and 'Britain still arming repressive regimes', The Guardian, 4.11.99; 'MPs turn on Byers over Jakarta aid', David Hencke, The Guardian 16.8.99, and 'Fresh row on "secret" supply to Indonesia', The Guardian 17.9.99.

[26] See: 'British support for East Timor and its displaced people in 1999', FCO Factsheet, 19.1.2000; UNHRC 56th Session, Geneva 25.4.2000.

Critics drew attention to notable shortcomings in the government's disposition, principally to the ready acceptance of Indonesian assurances with regard to 'upholding security' during the referendum. They were dismayed that Hawk aircraft were transferred to Indonesia and invitations to attend an arms sales fair in Surrey were extended to Indonesian armed forces in the very midst of the extreme post ballot violence in East Timor. Campaigners castigated the concluding of the EU arms embargo on Indonesia in January 2000 - before the safe return of deportees from West Timor and the disbanding of the violent militias called for by UN Security Council Resolution 1272 (25.10.99). (Catholic) FO Minister John Battle justified the simultaneous raising of Britain's arms embargo with words that clearly indicated that the government's priorities had remained unchanged:

> Britain wants to underpin not undermine Indonesia... because of [the country's] great strategic importance, its potential as a huge market, and because we have long-standing and extensive interests there already.[27]

The political will to hold Indonesia to its commitments to the international community in respect of justice for the East Timorese steadily diminished thereafter.

The Catholic Church in England after Vatican II.[28]

Along with other mainstream Christian denominations the Catholic community was challenged by all the social changes which were taking place in the country. From the 1960s individualism and secularism became pervasive and, together with a growing anti-authoritarianism, reduced the influence of Church leaders. Moreover, while some people within the nation sank into a socio-economic 'underclass', the majority entered steadily into a somewhat precarious prosperity. For these different reasons most of the population were concerned with personal security not social justice in far-away lands. Furthermore, permissive social legislation (such as the legalisation of abortion and homosexual acts between consenting adults) and a succession of medico-moral issues engaged the energy of the Churches, either in opposition or in defence of such developments. There were also challenges to the Churches from within the world of religion – the growth of other 'fundamentalist' Christian communities mostly imported from America and of the adherents of traditional non-Christian faiths consequent upon immigration. 'New-age' cults became attractive to many. The decline in active Church participation was greater in England than elsewhere in the British Isles or in the United States, most closely resembling that which also took place in Australia

In addition, the Catholic Church was endeavouring to respond appropriately to the teachings of the Second Vatican Council. Comprising some four to five million adherents the Church in England and Wales contrasted with that in Ireland (or even in Scotland) in so far as it was a small minority in an overall population of some 50 million people. It was also more varied, cosmopolitan and racially mixed. This heterogeneity was a factor in the dissent and divisions that arose following the promulgation of the Council's decrees.

For example, the call to new ecumenical relations confused many stalwarts among the faithful, and the response to liturgical developments proved to be a debilitating distraction from issues of social order and much else besides. Catechetical renewal was also contentious, and the concern of the hierarchy to 'preserve the faith' disposed them to direct enormous financial and personal resources into the provision and maintenance of Catholic schools. Whatever the merits of such a policy it meant correspondingly less support was available for the

---

[27] 'Briefing by Minister of State J.Battle on his visit to Indonesia and East Timor' (FCO website), & 'UK sees no extension to Indonesia arms embargo', Reuters, London 13.1.2000; Speech to British Chamber of Commerce, Jakarta, 18.1.2000, cited in *Tapol* Bulletin 156, Jan/Feb 2000, p3. Personally Battle had shown active sympathy for the East Timorese plight.
[28] See: Bibliography - Ch 11: CBCEW; CIIR; CIS; Cumming, J. & Burns, F. (eds), 1980; Davie, G. 1994; Hastings, A. 1986; Hornsby-Smith, M. 1987, 2001.

development of adult formation and engagement in issues of justice and peace. The encyclical letter of Pope Paul VI, *Humanae Vitae*, on the issue of contraception, provoked a crisis of authority and disaffection within the Catholic community. An important consequence was a further reduction in the numbers of those exercising an ordained ministry within the Church, already diminishing for a variety of other reasons after the Council. The net result was an increase in the burden of work upon those who felt their vocation was to this form of service. It became necessary - as well as appropriate - to put effort into developing greater collaboration between clergy and the laity in pastoral ministry. All these matters tended to focus the attention of the Church upon its own internal life and its more immediate external relationships.

However, a National Pastoral Congress was convened in 1980 with the purpose of encouraging greater cohesion and various healthy developments in the life of the Church, and these included an engagement with a wide range of social justice issues. Three aspects of this Congress are noteworthy for the present study. First, that the pre-Congress discussion material included a raising of the subject of Britain's arms sales and overseas aid. Second, that the reports brought to the Congress from many Dioceses made specific reference to these matters:

> A more common mind emerges over arms sales. Several reports deplored the sale of weaponry to poor countries...
> Reports stressed that Britain's Aid should be a genuine effort to set things right: at present through being tied to purchase in Britain it is often more to the donor's benefit than to the recipient's... The Church should make itself aware of the actions of British companies in the Third World, encourage investments in socially useful schemes, and re-examine Church investment policy.[29]

The Chairpersons who presented the recommendations that emerged from the Justice sectors (domestic and overseas issues) 'felt compelled to place on record our failure to proclaim the Gospel of Jesus Christ in all its fullness in this land'. They lamented 'the lack of concern for international justice, and the failure to appreciate the urgency of these problems'. Significantly this confession was also addressed to 'our sisters and brothers in the Third World *whose sufferings and oppression we have in good part caused and are still causing*'.[30] A prayer was raised 'that God give us the grace to make an entirely new attempt to face up to the demands of the Gospel and to put them into practice in our lives'.[31] Justice Sector President Anne Forbes declared in her forthright presentation at the end of the Congress:

> The delegates were aware of the apathy that exists in many parts of the Catholic community towards these issues, so several practical recommendations on peace education were made... Furthermore the scale and irresponsibility of the arms trade was strongly criticised and a call for its reduction and eventual elimination had overwhelming support.[32]

The third feature of the Congress deserving attention here is the character of the eventual response to it that was made by the hierarchy of England and Wales.[33] The bishops began by reiterating the Vatican II decree *Gaudium et Spes* and then recalled the assertion by the Synod of Bishops (1971) that 'working for justice was a constitutive element of preaching the Gospel'. They noted 'the affirmation of this vision within the Congress'. But they then immediately elaborated on the *practical difficulties of applying gospel values*, 'honoured in the abstract', to 'specific situations'. Nonetheless they urged Catholics 'to work in whatever way is open to them for the necessary transformation of whatever structures and institutions prevent

---

[29] See: Bibliography – Ch11: CBCEW 1980, *Liverpool 1980: Official Report etc,* Sector G pp97-99.
[30] Author's italics
[31] op.cit. Sector G, Topics 4 and 5, pp272-289.
[32] op.cit. Sector G, Congress Report, p293.
[33] Bibliography – Ch11: CBCEW 1980, *The Easter People.*

people throughout the world from living fully human lives.' They also pledged themselves to 'keep in mind not only the need for a greater and more widespread understanding of the issues of justice...but also the need to find the right means for more effective action'. More specifically they repeated a previous declaration (first made in October 1978) of their concern for 'a realistic approach to the vital issue of arms control':

> We call on Her Majesty's Government...to examine uses of our industrial capacity so as to control and curtail the production and sale of armaments to other countries'.[34]

There were many complex issues of social justice to be addressed by the national Catholic community. In addition to a wide range of domestic problems there were distressed peoples overseas who called for attention. Response to such appeals was forthcoming although the involvement of the majority was limited to the donation of money. But the issue of East Timor was certainly not at the forefront of popular consciousness in England in the years that preceded the crisis of 1999. Before then only the Santa Cruz massacre in 1991 – its horrors vividly reported by British photojournalists Max Stahl and Steve Cox - had raised some awareness of the situation and stirred a concerned response.[35] Knowledge of events in East Timor was mostly limited to the membership of such organisations as were dedicated to the promotion of human rights and development. Indeed, it is probably the case that the great majority of the population had no idea where East Timor was - many being unsure even as to the location (and certainly of the significance) of Indonesia with which Britain's historical links had been fleeting or indirect. Although the sufferings of the East Timorese people were undoubtedly great during the invasion and first years of occupation by the Indonesian military the mass murder in Cambodia and the plight of the Vietnamese boat people were far better known in Britain. The small Timorese homeland was remote from these shores and there had been no historical association whatever with Britain. Until the mid-1990s the refugees from East Timor in England could be counted on one hand. Even the Catholic faith of their oppressed compatriots was not so widespread or as manifest at first as it was later to become. From 1975-1999 the attention of most British people was pre-occupied by foreign affairs more obviously pertinent to their interests – the Middle East, Northern Ireland, wars in the Falklands, the Gulf and the Balkans. There were also a series of pressing domestic issues such as fuel and stock market crises, industrial relations, unemployment, inter-racial tensions, etc. Moreover, the selection of matters meriting the concern of the British public was largely determined by the mass media, and newspaper articles on East Timor were a rare occurrence.[36]

These considerations raise the question as to the possibility of social justice for such small nations – and also point to the special obligation upon the Universal Church and its national components to speak up for the 'little people' in keeping with the principles of its Social Doctrine. In any case it was evidently necessary for general awareness to be raised as to the East Timorese agonies, and for a connection to be made with this country by drawing attention to the complicity of British government, industry and commerce in the ongoing Indonesian oppression of East Timor. It was also necessary for appropriate action to be urged within the Church community and by its leadership and their agencies.

---

[34] Bibliography – Ch11: CBCEW 1980, *Liverpool 1980*, op.cit. p378.

[35] (Catholic) Max Stahl's video recording was broadcast within hours by 'First Tuesday', Granada TV, Manchester; for Steve Cox's photographs see Bibliography – Ch2: Carey, P. & Cox, S. 1995.

[36] See Bibliography – Ch11: Lee, C. 2000, p463; and 'Making News – what drives the media agenda', interviews with leading journalists in TV and print media including John Pilger, John Snow, Dennis Rice, Daniel McGrory, John Downing, Julia Bicknell in Just Right (Jubilee Action, London), Summer 2001, p10-11.

The Response of the Catholic Church in England to the East Timorese cause
Besides noting the reaction of the hierarchy attention must also be given to the activity of the
agencies CIIR and CAFOD, and to the contribution of Religious Congregations, Catholic 'activists' and Church media outlets.

The Catholic Institute for International Relations

CIIR was founded by several leading Catholic laity in 1939 as 'The Sword of the
Spirit' with the objective of defeating Hitler's 'inhuman rejection of kinship and love' and to
'build a peace upon the new concept of the world as a global neighbourhood'.[37] After the war
its focus turned to advocacy and development, a combination that has continued ever since
and which gave rise to the organisation's current title.[38] Although not an agency of the
Bishop's Conference, CIIR received support from 'a significant group of bishops', including
some financial help. It has also been backed by the Conference of Religious and by Justice
and Peace groups within the Church. It has always adopted a discreet style of operation,
working mostly 'behind the scenes'.[39]
    The organisation began its attention to East Timor in the mid-1970s - that is, from the
very outset of the conflict. Although there then seemed little prospect of change to the situation in East Timor the board considered that there was a moral responsibility to continue in
solidarity with the East Timorese people. CIIR was to play an important role in the international response to their cause both within and beyond the Catholic Church. It has maintained a
comprehensive archive on all aspects of the East Timor issue, perhaps the most extensive in
the world – certainly outside Australia and Portugal. In successive publications CIIR presented a thorough and balanced analysis of the ongoing situation in East Timor and of the international response to it. These documents formed the basis of endeavours in other national
Catholic communities and provided substantial information to many secular groups and po-
litical-diplomatic leaders around the world who became advocates of the Timorese cause or
who were involved in development work in the territory.[40]
    CIIR facilitated the visit to England of East Timorese refugee Fr.Francisco Fernades in
1980. It was CIIR which hosted the former Apostolic Administrator Mgr Costa Lopes in 1983
when, exiled from his native country, he appealed to the Churches in Britain to press the UK
government to support the East Timorese right to political self-determination. A team of experts including a doctor, an agriculturalist, a lawyer and linguist – all with considerable local
knowledge - was assembled to visit the territory, an attempt frustrated by the Indonesian government. In June 1985 CIIR published 'The View of East Timor's Church' (a Statement of the
Dili diocesan clergy, quoted earlier) in *Timor Link*, a quarterly publication of analysis and advocacy which began that year and which continued until after Independence was declared in
2002.[41] Meetings with officials of the Foreign and Commonwealth Office were sustained over
the years of East Timor's occupation and subsequent liberation - in support of HMGs positive
efforts on behalf of the East Timorese people and in criticism of its complicity and compro-
mises with the Indonesian regime. CIIR convened and attended international conferences from
1985 onwards, issuing declarations 'on behalf of East Timor' at their conclusion.[42] Delegates
also represented the organisation at the annual meetings of the UN Decolonisation Committee

---

[37] For further detail see: 'Challenging injustice with the Sword of the Spirit', CIIR News, October
2000, p10-11, and the CIIR Internet website.
[38] 'Changing minds, changing lives: two departments – one strategy.' 'CIIR at a Glance', in CIIR Annual Review 1998-99, p2-3.
[39] 'Fighting a Global Battle against Injustice', interview by Paul Donovan with CIIR Director Ian Lin-
den, in The Universe, London 19.3.2000.
[40] See Bibliography – General (East Timor): CIIR 1985, 1992, 1996.
[41] See 'A voice for the voiceless', Archer, R. Timor Link August 2000, 50th issue anniversary edition.
[42] See Bibliography – Ch11: CIIR 1987, 1990; Bibliography – Ch8: 'Declaration on Behalf of East
Timor' (1985), in CCJDP 1993, p23-4.

right up until the last in respect of East Timor was held in July 2000.[43] In Britain CIIR facilitated and was always represented at the strategy meetings of the British Coalition for East Timor (BCET), a gathering of NGOs which approached the issue from different perspectives. CIIR's advocacy and analysis included a trenchant critique of Britain's arms export policy.[44]

During East Timor's year of crisis CIIR was present in the territory itself, contributing an expert team to observe the 'popular consultation' and was party to the Press Statement made by International Observer Missions.[45] This commended the courage of the East Timorese during this process, condemned the systematic intimidation which had been perpetrated by the *TNI*-backed militias, and called on the Indonesian government to effect the security to which it was pledged by the New York Agreement.[46] A Statement was also made by CIIR to the UN Human Rights Commission Special Session on East Timor (Sept 23-24) on the violence and intimidation preceding and in the aftermath of the plebiscite, and rejecting the allegations of 'ballot irregularities' by pro-autonomy forces.[47]. In October Jose Ramos Horta was guest speaker at CIIR's AGM, his own being perhaps the best testimony to the importance of CIIRs solidarity over the years: 'a beacon of integrity and ethics'.[48] Frequent strategy meetings were sustained until the end of that year including the preparation of 'advocacy points' for the World Bank Donor's Meeting in Tokyo in December. Under the UN Transitional Administration in East Timor CIIR established an office in Dili and began to play a major role in organising and working with East Timorese women on reconciliation and reconstruction in the country.[49] The organisation continues its work of analysis and advocacy.

The Catholic Agency for Overseas Development

It was also lay initiative that led to the establishment of Cafod, in this instance the National Board of Catholic Women. In 1961 they organised the first Family Fast Day and a year later the Bishops Conference officially set up the 'Catholic Fund for Overseas Development' to promote the Day and as a focus for the various small charitable efforts that were then taking place. The Conference maintains 'oversight' of Cafod's work, 'supporting it and trusting its professionalism'.[50] At the turn of the century Cafod was in partnership with over a thousand programmes world wide, and had become the English and Welsh arm of '*Caritas Internationalis*' (the global network of Catholic relief and development organisations). Re-titled the Catholic Agency for Overseas Development, it is a national and indeed a world leader among humanitarian agencies. Cafod engages in 'awareness raising' (educational programmes) through Catholic parishes and schools, and also in a discreet but very effective advocacy that is provided with reliable information gained first hand in the countries where it supports local development projects. It has assisted other *Caritas* organisations, is in liaison with various non-governmental organisations concerned with human rights and development, and regularly urges the British government to give due consideration to important aspects of contentious or critical overseas issues on which it can speak with authority.

---

[43] For the 1986 Statement (a typical example) see Bibliography – Ch8: CCJDP op.cit.p24-27. The final Petition to the Committee, July 5-7 2000, is archived at CIIR and on email conference: > east-timor@igc.apc.org <

[44] e.g. 'The true cost of selling arms', P.Eavis & A.McLean, CIIR News May/June 1997,p11.

[45] For details see Bibliography – Ch3: CIIR 1999. See also CIIR News, June, Sept. & Dec. 1999.

[46] Press Statement by International Observer Missions at the East Timorese Popular Consultation, Dili 1.9.99; CIIR Media Release 5.9.99.

[47] *CIIR Statement to the UN Commission on Human Rights Special Session on East Timor*, 23-24 September 1999.

[48] For an edited version of J.Ramos Horta's address, see: Timor Link, No48, Dec. 1999.

[49] See: 'CIIR to focus on women's role', by Catherine Scott, CIIR News, Nov.1999; 'CIIR UA: Women's Representation East Timor's Constituent Assembly – need for quotas', 7.2.2001.

[50] Francis McDonagh, 'Cafod Reporting', The Catholic Times, 9.9.99.

Cafod's involvement in the East Timor issue was (and remains) of significant importance. The agency provided some financial assistance to the work of CIIR, and also made funds available to the diocese of Dili via the *Caritas* network in Asia (Asia Partnership for Human Development - APHD). This was to pay the legal costs of people in prison in East Timor and provide welfare assistance to widows or to those in hiding. Cafod also supported the consultancy of Arnold Kohen (the 'East Timor Research Project') which was of such help in clarifying the East Timor affair for the United States Bishops Conference and its agencies. At first this was done via APHD, but when *Caritas Indonesia* advised the Partnership to withdraw from such international advocacy of the East Timorese cause - on the grounds that it 'raised futile hopes among the people'- Cafod assumed direct support for Kohen's work. It did this in collaboration with Western agencies such as CCODP (Canada), *Broederlijk Delen* and *Entraide et Fraternite* (Belgium). Cafod also funded the early meetings of the European 'Christian Coalition for East Timor' (CCET) which was facilitated by CIIR.

In 1989 the Indonesian regime felt confident of the success of its efforts at 'pacification' in East Timor and 'opened up' the territory to foreign visitors. Cafod availed of the opportunity this new disposition presented for investigation of the most pressing needs of the people and the determination of appropriate responses. Thereafter its field officer visited the territory annually and established enduring links with personnel of the local Catholic Church. From these close contacts among others there emerged a fund of detailed information which was presented in well-analysed and balanced confidential reports on the political context, socio-economic situation, and the important role of the Church. A number of practical projects were undertaken, and advocacy of the East Timorese cause could be pursued even more effectively in collaboration with other sympathetic organisations in England, Europe and further afield. Projects included helping to establish a central social development office in Dili (*Delsos*) by improving staff skills and providing equipment and agricultural support in the parish of Suai on the south coast (*Sadep*). Help was given towards treatment for tuberculosis and with the setting up of a diocesan radio station (*Radio Kamanek*) to provide education on health and agricultural issues. Besides giving financial support of several tens of thousands of pounds annually to these projects in the years after 1989 Cafod also made a number of smaller grants for emergency needs, channelled through bishop Belo, Parish priests or religious sisters and to be used at their discretion.[51]

In 1995 Cafod was instrumental in the establishment of the Dili diocesan Justice and Peace Commission. The following year, with the assistance of its regional offices in England and Wales, Cafod organised a collection of theological books to supply the library of the new seminary provision being established in the Diocese of Dili. In 1997 Cafod invited Bishop Belo to London to be the first speaker in their three-year series of 'Millennium Lectures'. The bishop availed of the opportunity to castigate British arms exports, especially to Indonesia, to implore greater control over such sales, and to thank 'all those who have - one way or another - taken practical action to bring about a reappraisal of arms manufacture and trade, and to question its morality'.[52] On the invitation of archbishop Kelly (then chairman of the Bishops Conference Department for International Affairs) Belo preached at a Mass held in the Catholic Cathedral in Liverpool the following day. On this occasion archbishop Kelly publicly promised to visit East Timor soon, 'in solidarity'- a pledge still to be fulfilled.

---

[51] Letter to the author from Olwyn Maynard, Projects Department/Asia, 12.4.1994; also discerned from the author's sight of confidential field reports 1990, conversations with Cafod field officers and the author's visit to *Delsos*, *Radio Kamanek*, and Suai Parish in 1995 and 1996.

[52] 'A Time for Justice', Millennium Lecture by Bishop Carlos Belo, Westminster Theatre, London June 7th, 1997. Full text in <u>Briefing</u>, 19th June 1997, CBCEW, p34-39.

Cafod's contacts with UK government officials in Britain and Indonesia was sometimes of critical importance in protecting East Timorese from serious, even fatal, harm.[53] Discreet advocacy was also undertaken in collaboration with other *Caritas* agencies (e.g. in Norway, Sweden, Australia), *Trocaire* (Eire), *CCFD* (France) and *Misereor* (Germany) that were engaged in a 'Donor's Forum' focusing on co-operation with development projects in East Timor.[54] In a related enterprise Cafod also arranged for East Timorese to attend journalism courses in England to enhance their skills in raising awareness of problems in East Timor.[55]

In 1999 Cafod committed additional funds to meet the developing crisis, working in partnership with *Caritas East Timor* which it had helped to establish and resource. Its advocacy included a letter to UN Secretary General Kofi Annan expressing concern about the 'symbiotic relationship' between *TNI* and the pro-Jakarta militias and urging the provision of an 'international security presence' to ensure a safe and 'credible ballot'.[56] A letter to UK Minister of State Geoffrey Hoon expressed Cafod's concern about the optimistic expectations that the international community had for impartiality on the part of the Indonesian security forces in East Timor.[57] As the pre-ballot violence increased, and its partners came under attack, Cafod urged the British government to demand the complete withdrawal of Indonesian troops.[58] When carnage and destruction ensued after the ballot result was publicised Cafod promoted fund raising 'to meet urgent needs and provide long term support to enable the people rebuild their shattered lives'[59], and quickly responded to the request of *Caritas Australia* to assist in managing a relief operation.[60] The agency also advocated an international arms embargo on Indonesia (and an indefinite embargo on arms sales by the UK), the establishment of an international Jubilee Reconstruction Fund for East Timor, and the creation of an International Criminal Tribunal for East Timor.[61] In its Annual Review for 1999 the agency was able to report:

> With its ten-year history of work in East Timor, Cafod was well placed to stand beside the Church and other local partners in East Timor. Emergency specialists went in to support the Timorese staff as they gradually returned from hiding, to build their capacity to deal with the long-term reconstruction of the country. The [national] Catholic community raised £100,000 for East Timor which, through Cafod, helped local people get access to shelter and food. In the UK Cafod campaigned vigorously for the deployment of an international peace-keeping force, presenting the interests of East Timor to government and international institutions and giving numerous media interviews. [62]

At the height of the crisis student leader Antero Benedito da Silva had written to Cafod: 'We would like to thank you as an organisation and as friends for your strong solidarity. You have enabled us to move across the rivers of hatred'. [63]

---

[53]   e.g. When Fr.Domingos Soares was in danger in January 1992 after his appearance in the Yorkshire TV documentary 'In Cold Blood' (1991) Cafod cabled the British Ambassador in Jakarta – email conference: > reg.easttimor < (9.9.92).

[54]   Confidential Minutes of Donor's Forum, 18.3.97.

[55]   'Words are the weapons for East Timorese', Nino Rodrigues in 'Cafod Reporting', The Catholic Times, 27.12.98.

[56]   Letter to UNSG 4.5.99, from Jim Simmons (International Division), Steve Alston (Asia Section).

[57]   Letter to Minister of State Geoffrey Hoon, from Steve Alston (Cafod Asia Section) 6.6.99.

[58]   Cafod Press Release 13.8.99.

[59]   Cafod full page tabloid newspaper advert September 1999. By the end of the month this appeal had generated £40,000, by November £100,000.

[60]   Letter to a concerned parish correspondent 4.10.99.

[61]   Cafod Policy Statement 21.9.99.

[62]   'Cafod is there in a Crisis and Beyond', Cafod Review 1999, p18-19.

[63]   Cafod Review 1999, op.cit.

Cafod continued to advocate the East Timorese cause and provide for development needs after Indonesia withdrew from the territory and the UN Transitional Administration was established and Independence eventually achieved.[64]

The Response of Religious Congregations

The 'Provincial' structure of institutions of religious men and women, even of the international missionary congregations, meant little direct involvement with the territory and people of East Timor by the religious residing in this country. But, as elsewhere in the world, the engagement of consecrated religious in issues of social justice has developed since the Second Vatican Council. The Conference of Major Religious Superiors (MRSC) set up its 'Social Justice Desk' in the late 1980s and since then has disseminated among its constituent communities updated information, recommendations for action, and appeals for prayer in respect of many overseas situations. These included East Timor, especially after the Santa Cruz massacre. The MRSC gave moral support to fellow religious working in the field, and participated in the awareness-raising and advocacy undertaken by CIIR, Cafod, and the British NGO coalition addressing the East Timor issue to which the agencies belonged (BCET). MRSC is not a funding organisation, but some individual communities or congregations contributed financial support to development initiatives in East Timor either through Cafod or via the internal structures of their own congregation.[65]

The Bishops Conference of England and Wales

The Bishops Conference of England and Wales (CBCEW) oversees the life of the Church in five Provinces comprising a total of 23 dioceses with Catholics approximating 12% of the national population.[66] Overseas issues come within the purview of the Conference's Department for International Affairs (DIA). The DIA Committee for Justice and Peace included East Timor among the subjects to which attention was given and was serviced by both CIIR and Cafod with information and advice. Several individual bishops came to have a particular involvement in the East Timor issue, and delegates from the Conference participated in the meetings of the Commission of Bishops Conferences of the European Community (COMECE) where the matter was also addressed.

The efforts of CIIR and Cafod meant that the Bishops Conference was in a position to know a good deal about the situation prevailing in East Timor from the outset of the Indonesian annexation of the territory. This would have included the plaintive appeal for solidarity made by the Religious of East Timor in 1981 (quoted at the beginning of this study) which was received and archived by CIIR and also published in England by the campaigning NGO *Tapol*.[67] However, the first public response of any member of the hierarchy to the East Timorese plight appears not to have been until *ten years later*. In October 1991 John Crowley, then auxiliary bishop in Westminster archdiocese and Chairman of Cafod, headed up the list of signatories to a letter to UN Secretary General Peres de Cuellar. The text appealed for

---

[64] e.g. 'East Timor needs help to rebuild'. Letter to the Editor, <u>The Times</u>, 30.8.2000; 'Cafod calls for economic sanctions against Indonesia if violence continues in West Timor', Press Release, 25.9.2000; Strategic Action Plan, Sept.2000; 'Statement on International Criminal Tribunal for East Timor', Press Release, 13.6.01.

[65] See archives MRSC Secretariat (Social Justice Desk), London. Examples include letters to UN Secretary General, UNHRC and UNHCR, constituency MPs, FCO, Indonesian Embassy, etc. Detailed information on the East Timorese plight was received by the Secretariat from fellow religious (based in other Provinces) who were working in Indonesia and East Timor.

[66] Statistics from *National Catholic Directory of England and Wales* (1994), published for CBCEW by Gabriel Communications, Manchester.

[67] *Tapol* Bulletin No53, September 1982, p10.

measures to be taken to safeguard those Timorese who would be interviewed by the planned Portuguese delegation.[68] Within days this expression of concern was followed by the declaration of 'sorrow and outrage' over the Santa Cruz massacre. This included an expression of 'solidarity' to 'our brother bishop Carlos Belo', and an appeal to the international community 'to seek urgently a just and lasting solution to the status of East Timor based on the free choice of the Timorese people'.[69] These sentiments were repeated in 1994 together with a further appeal to the British government 'to use its influence with the Indonesian authorities and to work with the UN to secure human rights and liberty for the people of East Timor as a matter of urgency'. The Catholic community were 'encouraged to pray for bishop Belo and his people at this time'. This statement followed a week-long visit to the territory by Victor Guazzelli, then bishop of East London, and Fr.Pat Davies of the CIJP secretariat. Bishop Belo was grateful for this expression of solidarity which, he felt, helped to safeguard East Timorese clergy.[70]

The award of the Nobel Peace Prize to bishop Belo and his compatriot Jose Ramos Horta in October 1996 was the occasion of the next Statement by the Conference. This was entitled 'In Praise of Bishop Belo' and expressed concern over the 'ongoing human rights violations in East Timor and the lack of real progress in UN the Tri-partite Talks and All-Inclusive Intra-Timorese Dialogue' being facilitated by the United Nations Secretary General. On this occasion the bishops urged the government of Indonesia 'to respect its obligations under International Law and take significant steps towards peace'. Inviting the Catholic community to pray for bishop Belo 'and all those working for these goals', the hierarchy also called on the British government, its EU partners and the UN:

> To press for the establishment of an effective UN human rights presence in East Timor...
> To encourage the parties to make real progress in the talks which were aimed at forging a just, comprehensive, internationally acceptable solution to the conflict which fully respects the legitimate aspirations of the Timorese people.[71]

As the Year of Crisis began, an article entitled 'Working for Justice', on the Church and the Arms Trade, by bishop David Konstant of the Diocese of Leeds (then Chairman of the Department for International Affairs), appeared in the Bishops Conference publication *Briefing*. Recalling Vatican teaching and that of the Church in England and Wales on this issue, bishop Konstant commended the positive developments that had been made. However, he felt obliged to assert:

> Much remains to be done...the vast majority of sales...are not subjected to moral scrutiny...It is still possible for weapons to be sold to regimes which violate international humanitarian law and problems with existing procedures (such as end use) remain. Much greater transparency needs to be built into the export of weapons.

Bishop Konstant also expressed concern over the extent of the government's support for arms sales through the Export Credit Guarantee system and suggested that this money might be better used to help arms manufacturers diversify into producing other 'more socially useful goods'. The article concluded:

---

[68] For text of letter see Bibliography – Ch8: CCJPD 1993 op.cit., p51.

[69] Statement 19.12.1991. DIA, CBCEW, in Briefing, Vol 21 No 24, p12 (Dec 19th) 1991.

[70] See: Briefing, 8.12.1994,p3; *cf*: 'Reflections on a Visit to East Timor' by bishop Guazzelli and Fr. Davies, on file with the author; 'English and Welsh Bishops' Visit', Timor Link, January 1995, p8

[71] Full text in Briefing, 19.12.1996.

The Church's fundamental concern remains the principle that the protection of individual worth and dignity must take precedence over the pursuit of profit and self-interest...
Profit should not determine policy. The sale of arms, however lucrative, does not represent an export triumph. It involves a tragic misuse of valuable resources.[72]

On April 30th that year Cardinal Hume sent a letter to bishop Belo expressing the solidarity of the Conference and assuring him of prayers. He declared that 'we are ready to do anything we can to help restore order, promote a just peace, and create conditions to satisfy the legitimate aspirations of the people of East Timor'.[73] In September, in the most strongly worded statement to date, bishop Konstant referred to the organised violence being perpetrated in East Timor as 'an injustice that cries out for action by the international community'. The text continued:

We cannot stand by and allow this violence to continue. We urge the British Government, the United Nations, the European Union, and all members of the international community, to bring all possible pressure to bear upon the Indonesian government...
There must be an immediate halt to all economic and military aid to Indonesia...
An international armed peace-keeping force must be sent in as soon as possible. The Indonesian government must be made aware that the international community will not tolerate savagery of the kind seen in East Timor since the [popular] consultation, and that the East Timorese people will not be abandoned. We appeal for prayers throughout England and Wales for Justice and Peace in East Timor.

These exhortations to prayer (and the additional appeals of Cardinal Hume) were not followed up by the dissemination of any materials to assist local churches, groups or individuals in the matter. Also there were few national or provincial liturgies arranged over all the years of Indonesian occupation in which the East Timorese people were specifically addressed and involved, and those that there were received limited pre-publicity.[74] This contrasts with the practice of the hierarchy and their agencies in Australia but is similar to that pertaining within the United States (as already described) and had much to do with the lack of a sizeable East Timorese constituency in Britain. However, religious houses included the welfare of the East Timorese in the spiritual efforts of their community as noted already, and Catholic activists around the country created their own prayer services, as will be seen.

In addition to these (very few) statements specifically referring to the developing situation in East Timor the Bishops Conference also published more general documents on social teaching which had relevant content. There are several examples to be noted.

The fiftieth anniversary of the United Nations 'Universal Declaration of Human Rights' was marked by some pertinent 'Reflections'.[75] This listed a number of rights (originally set out by Pope John XXIII in his encyclical *Pacem in Terris*, 1963) which were being violated *inter alia* by the Indonesian regime in East Timor. Citing Pope John Paul II's message in celebration of World Day of Peace that year the bishops also gave emphasis to the universality and indivisibility of human rights. This understanding was currently being challenged by the Suharto regime, defending its repressive policies by reference to cultural differences or so-called 'Asian values'.[76]

---

[72] 'Working for Justice', by bishop Konstant, Briefing 10.2.1999; cf. Bishop Konstant's homily for Mass at St. Aloysius Church, London, October 1999 (author's transcript on file).
[73] Cited in 'Cardinal joins calls for UN peacekeeping' [sic], M.Parry, The Universe, 9.5.1999.
[74] *Viz.* At the time of the Santa Cruz massacre (Westminster 1991), during the visit of bishop Belo (Liverpool 1997). CIIR, Cafod & Pax Christi (UK) arranged for the celebration of Masses for East Timorese on several occasions in St. Aloysius Church, London.
[75] See Bibliography – Ch11: CBCEW 1998, pp6-7.
[76] op.cit., pp19-20.

The lengthy Statement in election year 1997 entitled 'The Common Good' provides another example. This sought to re-present Catholic Social Doctrine for the current social context in England and Wales and was generally well received. However, its reference to the iniquities of British arms manufacture and exports was minimal – less than one sentence urging the application of the 'principle of solidarity' in a restriction on arms sales to poor countries.[77]

In 1999 the national delegation to the Commission of the Bishops Conferences of the European Community (COMECE) contributed to a Statement on the construction of peace in situations of conflict - much of which (as this author has observed) had direct application to the East Timorese issue, both before and after the Indonesian withdrawal.[78] The Statement drew particular attention to 'the dissemination of armaments of all kinds which is today undermining peace and stability in many regions of the world...encourages attempts at military solutions...creates a reciprocal armament dynamic...and facilitates many forms of domestic political repression'. The bishops of COMECE declared:

> It is imperative to convince political and economic partners in the field of arms production of the importance of restrictive standards for such exports, and to conclude binding agreements in this area as quickly as possible.[79]

However, the Conference's delegates do not appear to have specifically raised the issue of East Timor at the Commission, where the voice of the Portuguese hierarchy in advocating the Timorese cause was also a muted one, as noted already.

Cardinal Basil Hume seized a number of opportunities to encourage progress in the more restrictive control of arms sales. Following the publication in 1994 of the Vatican document 'The International Arms Trade – an Ethical Reflection' (and bishop Guazzelli's report of his visit to East Timor) the Cardinal arranged for the sale of the Westminster archdiocesan shareholdings in British Aerospace. In early 1995 he arranged a private seminar at Westminster at which senior Ministry of Defence officials were invited to sit with the Cardinal, Vatican Justice and Peace representatives, and other interested parties.[80] Cardinal Hume supported, and introduced, the campaign *Countering the Arms Trade – Churches Count the Cost* launched by the Council of Churches in Britain and Ireland in February 1996. He pointed out that in international relations 'economic self-interest and political opportunism too often prevail - and yet these have repeatedly failed, even on their own terms'. Recognising the complexity of the issue of arms manufacture and sales he nonetheless declared that there was no excuse for 'evading the rigorous moral evaluation which is always necessary'. On the 22nd Anniversary of the invasion of East Timor the Cardinal recalled the main points of bishop Belo's Millennium lecture 'A Time for Justice' and urged further progress in all the matters to which the bishop had then referred including further restriction of the arms trade – especially with Indonesia. Hume welcomed efforts to raise awareness of East Timor's situation and promote human development there, and urged prayer and support for the local Church.[81] Later that year he again made specific reference to the arms industry in an address to the Conference on Social and Moral Regeneration in which he examined several ethical responsibilities of business:

---

[77] Bibliography – Ch11: CBCEW 1997, paragraph 105.

[78] Bibliography – Ch11: COMECE 1999 (in CBCEW Briefing 14.4.99, p7-15). cf. Bibliography – Ch5: Smythe, P. 1999, pp99f.

[79] COMECE op.cit. paragraph 40 (Briefing, p14).

[80] 'MOD ready to act in Hawk deal' [sic], Greg Murphy, The Catholic Times, 22.1.95.

[81] Full text in Timor Link February 1998, p5.

Any sale or purchase of weapons must be justifiable in strict defence terms, and arms should not be sold when it is reasonably foreseeable that they may be used for internal repression or to violate human rights...Arms manufacturers have a moral obligation to assess...both the need for the purchase and its likely or possible end use... Likewise the Government, in deciding whether to grant an export licence, has its own moral judgement to make...

I am very pleased to see the recent agreement on a European Code of Conduct on arms exports which attempts to undercut [the disreputable] argument [in defence of an otherwise undesirable sale] that if we don't supply arms someone else will...

What we have here is an important and very welcome first step towards establishing rigorous international controls on arms sales.[82]

However, this attitude was not universal within the national Church as a whole where there was evident ambiguity regarding the morality of the 'defence industry'. There were two areas in which the actual practice within dioceses seemed to contradict the principles of Catholic Social Doctrine, *viz.* investment in and sponsorship by arms manufacturers. Moreover, two particular events - both concerning the British Aerospace factory at Warton in Lancashire – highlighted the fact that there were conflicting views about the arms industry still to be resolved within the wider Catholic community. These were the 'Ploughshares Action' in 1996, and question of the sale of Holy Family Church in 1998-99. These matters merit some further attention.

An Ambiguous Response

The damage caused to a 'Hawk' aircraft at the Warton factory in January 1996 by the five 'Ploughshares' women, and their subsequent acquittal by the jury at Liverpool Crown Court provoked considerable public debate.[83] Many Catholics were among those who both sympathised with and even extolled the women's action. Others were among those who were hesitant about the moral-legal justifications offered, or strongly critical of the women's law-breaking by their trespass and damage to property.[84]

In 1998 a proposal was made to negotiate a deal between BAe and the Diocese of Lancaster whereby the church of Holy Family parish in Warton would be demolished to improve access to the factory and a new one - to be built in another location - entirely funded by the arms manufacturer. Some parishioners were outraged at the proposal, many others were uneasy but hesitant about voicing criticism in view of BAe being the largest local employer. But others were in favour of what they regarded as a 'gift' to the parish. The Diocese entered into a lengthy dialogue with BAe arguing that the negotiations presented an opportunity for the Church to 'act prophetically in a positive way' by pressing its concerns about human rights violations in Indonesia and East Timor. Objectors to the dialogue considered this aspiration 'naïve' and the negotiation itself, regardless of its outcome, as a betrayal of Gospel values as enshrined in Catholic Social Doctrine. The Lancaster diocesan Faith and Justice Commission itself urged the utmost caution in respect of proceeding with the talks.[85] In the end, the Diocese did not take up the offer but the protraction of the whole affair was testament to the difficulties involved in the application of the general principles of the Church's Social Doctrine to

---

[82] Basil Hume: 'Ethics and institutions', at CSMR Conference, Newcastle, 23 June 1998.

[83] See e.g. 'BAe acquittal: the legal fallout', Bill Bowring, Timor Link, Oct.1996, p4-5; 'Four women's witness', C.Scott (CIIR), The Tablet 27.7.1996, p1001.
Catholics participated in a play 'A Hammer in the Hand' (by 'Theatre Wallop' Merseyside) which justified the damage by presenting the complicity of BAe in the oppression in East Timor.

[84] See 'Doves V Hawks – the 'Ploughshares Trial' by the author, Justice and Peace Bulletin, Diocese of Leeds, UK Summer 1996.

[85] Statement, Lancaster Diocesan Faith & Justice Commission, Autumn 1998.

specific cases.[86] These had, of course, already been underlined by the bishops in their response to the National Pastoral Congress in 1980, as noted above.

Within the Catholic press there were those who drew attention to the detrimental consequences of the arms industry upon the domestic economy as well as overseas, and the Movement for Christian Democracy, which engaged many Catholic parliamentarians, specifically addressed the matter of arms sales to Indonesia.[87] The Catholic activist group *Pax Christi* concentrated on this aspect of the Timorese issue providing 'Fact Sheets' and 'Biblical Reflections' on the arms trade as well as participating in demonstrations and sustaining critical correspondence with the Ministry of Defence, Department of Trade and Industry, and the Foreign Office.[88] Other local groups around the country participated in regional and national rallies critical of the Indonesian regime in East Timor that were organised by various NGOs and the coalition BCET. The Catholic Worker community in Liverpool provided assistance to Timorese refugees in England including accommodation and regular prayer for them and their compatriots, and raised popular awareness of the issue in the City. This group leafleted factory workers outside the BAe premises in Warton, arranged an East Timor photo exhibition in Liverpool Central Library, and promoted a formal 'bond of friendship' between the City and Dili.

Nonetheless, support was to be found within the Church community for both investment in and educational sponsorship by the arms industry. Although the Diocese of Westminster sold its shares in British Aerospace in December 1994 other dioceses around the country were slow to follow its lead. *Pax Christi* (UK) conducted a survey among diocesan financial secretaries in 1997 which revealed that, out of the 20 dioceses that responded to the inquiry, only five had a specific focus on excluding the arms industry from their investment portfolio. Another four expressed a commitment worded in general terms not to invest in companies 'whose activities conflicted with the mission of the church'. Notably, nine had no stated ethical policy at all, and two were awaiting the production of 'a national policy'.[89] Despite Cardinal Hume's plea that 'investors should look at other factors besides financial performance and quality of management'[90] some financial directors continued to argue that their prime moral and legal responsibility in investing diocesan funds was to 'ensure the maximum return'. In December 1997 Tony Bannister, financial administrator for bishop Konstant's own diocese of Leeds, wrote to the author quite explicitly:

> We do have an investment with British Aerospace. I personally do not share your view [sic] that BAe are responsible for the tragedy in East Timor anymore than the oil companies who supply aircraft fuel, the textile companies who supply clothing to the aircrew, or the pharmaceutical companies who provide medical care for military personnel. Surely the responsibility lies with the governments who give the orders to the military for their actions which result in the atrocities.

The general tardiness of the Churches in Britain in disinvesting in the arms industry was regretted by the co-ordinator of the Ecumenical Committee on Corporate Responsibility, ECCR. He suggested that the reason for the slow response might be that 'diocesan finance officers had developed fixed habits during earlier phases of their careers when the thirst for maximum profit was uppermost'. The Ethical Investment Research and Information Service

---

[86] Evident in letters on file with author and Catholic Press coverage e.g. The Universe, 11.10.98, 1.11.98, 8.11.98, 13.12.98, 10.1.98, 1.8.99; Catholic Herald, 15.1.99, 30.7.99; etc.

[87] e.g. 'Myths of the Arms Trade', Bruce Kent, The Tablet 16.8.97; 'Report on the Arms Trade', The Universe, Dec.1998; 'Britain must stand by ethical foreign policy', Paul Donovan, The Universe, 26.3.2000; etc.; and 'Arms Embargo Petition and Appeal', MCD, July 1998.

[88] cf. 'Christians face hard questions over arms', Pat Gaffney, The Universe, 18.6.2000.

[89] 'Responses to questions put to Roman Catholic Diocesan Financial Teams regarding Diocesan Ethical Investments Policy (Sept-Dec 1997). Pax Christi (UK), London.

[90] 'Ethics in institutions and the environment', in Briefing, 16.7.1998, op.cit.

(EIRIS) used by many dioceses (including Leeds) also held the view that 'the aim should be to ensure that investments were not held in firms whose operations clashed with Catholic principles'.[91]

In due course most Catholic dioceses withdrew their investments from arms manufacturers, but the persistent pressure from activist groups and individuals within and outside the Church had much to do with that.

As noted already, an impassioned plea in respect of these very matters (for ethical investments and tighter controls upon arms exports) had been made by some laity at the National Pastoral Congress in 1980 and had subsequently been acknowledged and re-iterated by the hierarchy in their considered response. But evidently the Church's Social Doctrine expressed in Vatican documents, and by the national hierarchy and its agencies, was not so compelling within the community of the Church as might have been desirable or expected.

Another indication of such discrepancy within the Church between principle and practice was the acceptance by Catholic schools of educational sponsorship provided by British Aerospace. The company promoted its educational programme (e.g. in *BAe Magazine*) as 'a gift for children'. The 'gift' included the provision of equipment and helpers for science and technology, working visits to factory sites, and guidance in making connections between academic studies and their application in industry. Job offers were made to promising participants. However, the compatibility of the work of such a company with that of a Catholic school institutionally committed to the promotion of the Church's Social Doctrine is highly questionable. Nonetheless, when the general secretary of *Pax Christi* aired such questions at a meeting of heads and school governors of Catholic schools in Hull, as a member of a panel which included staff from BAe, the response from the floor was 'emotional and at times heated':

> Some pointed out that a country has a right to self-defence and argued that therefore BAe's arms sales were legitimate. Others were disturbed about the implications for local industry at Brough if criticisms of BAe's work were accepted. A few were deeply concerned, as teachers and parents, about the message that the partnership would give their children and wanted nothing to do with it. [92]

Besides those present at the meeting it seemed that other Catholics in the country - including clergy - supported such a partnership between schools and arms manufacturers. A priest wrote:

> Is the sale of arms an absolute evil? .... The reality is that many religious and conscientious people work in the defence industry, supporting their families by developing and making products which can be used, as most things can, for good as well as evil. Partnerships between schools and such people cannot be all bad.[93]

Private correspondence entrusted to the author at about this time revealed that there were several instances of applicant teachers withdrawing from possible appointment to Catholic schools on discovering that such a partnership existed. Yet the head teachers and governors of these same schools had found the relationship acceptable, claiming that inquiries to ecclesiastical authorities had been reassuringly positive.

A letter from the author was addressed to bishop Konstant, the chairman of the hierarchy's International Affairs Department (following upon his forthright article 'Working for Justice' in early 1999 quoted above) bringing these significant discrepancies to his attention. It

---

[91] 'Catholic Church "half-hearted" over ethical investment', The Tablet, 24.1.98
[92] 'Defend our Pupils', Pat Gaffney, The Tablet, 27.2.99; 'Indoctrinate or bust', Pat Gaffney, Peace Matters, Spring 1999, p6-7.
[93] 'Defending the peace', Fr. William Joseph, letters page, The Tablet, 6.3.99

was written in the hope of encouraging greater unanimity and practical co-ordination within the national Church but evoked only the following brief reply:

> I note what you say about the apparent anomalies that there may be between theory and practice in matters arising from the social doctrine of the Church. As I am sure you are aware these matters are seldom quite as cut and dried as sometimes protagonists on either side might wish to present them.[94]

This answer can be interpreted positively as both pragmatic and in keeping with the general tenor of the hierarchy's reaction to the National Pastoral Congress. But it does not indicate any intention by the institutional Church in England and Wales to engage in addressing the (very real) discrepancies between principle and practice in the matters raised. It is ambiguous in character.

The Church in England and Wales – an evaluation

Overall the response to the East Timorese plight from within the Catholic Church in this part of the world was quite impressive, bearing in mind the lack of an obvious historical or geographical connection with the local people. Of course, this varied greatly around the country, from diocese to diocese. But the principles of Catholic Social Doctrine were pertinently expounded in all circles of Church life and solidarity with the suffering Timorese was (and is) expressed in many ways. Their right to resist oppression and be afforded the opportunity for an authentic act of political self-determination was advocated by agencies such as CIIR and Cafod enabling an appropriate response from the Bishops Conference. In their effective work in the territory, severely limited by prevailing political circumstances, Church agencies showed respect for the capacities of the indigenous people. The hierarchy, and the organisations they supervised or supported, together with the Catholic Press and many local groups and individuals active in the cause of East Timorese welfare, directly addressed the key linking issue of arms manufacture and export. Specifically, continually, and forthrightly they called for a moral evaluation of the arms industry, for diversification of its manufacturing potential, and in particular for greater control over its exports to Indonesia.

In terms of the Church's task of continuing the personal redeeming work of Jesus Christ in the world evidence has been provided of the efforts made by Church agencies and individuals to improve the circumstances of the Timorese people, at least by projects of social development. These also had spiritual fruits in so far as they enhanced the dignity of the people and increased their contact with the local church. Such pastoral care was accompanied by a prophetic advocacy that strove towards a re-ordering of their situation of injustice and a promotion of their human development in every respect – a 'speaking up' for 'the little people'. The analysis of the Timorese situation by agencies of the Church began as the invasion of their homeland was under preparation and persisted after they were liberated from Indonesian occupation. This assessment was of the highest standard and provided the basis of other national inquiries, appraisals and action around the world. A number of individuals from the national Church took some personal risk in venturing to that distant country and in overcoming the various human and topographical obstacles to internal travel. The purpose of their visits was to discover the real situation and the best ways in which to urge its improvement – and on their return the story of their experiences certainly encouraged further efforts within and outside the Church here for the East Timorese cause.

There were several shortcomings in the Church's response. The East Timorese did not win the attention they merited in accordance with the 'preferential option' urged by Catholic Social Doctrine - despite the fact that they were among the poorest, most oppressed, and most abandoned people in the world. Although work for social justice is supposedly a 'constitutive

---

[94] Bishop Konstant to the author, 19.2.1999.

dimension' of the Church's mission not every parish and only a proportion of the laity generally became engaged in such matters and fewer still specifically in the East Timor issue. There was inconsistency in attitudes towards the morality of arms manufacture and exports and serious discrepancy between the principles propounded and the actual practice within dioceses. Although the Catholic Press duly took up this matter, stirred by the activism of groups such as Pax Christi, little attention was given in Church media outlets to the practice of training Indonesian military personnel in Britain or to the propriety of Overseas Development Aid to Indonesia. Moreover, Catholic newspapers and periodicals were mostly late (post 1991) in lamenting the plight of the Timorese, following rather than leading the secular media - although there were some exceptional individual journalists (such as Max Stahl and Hugh O'Shaughnessy). Catholics were among those MPs and government Ministers who over the years prioritised good relations with Indonesia and they did not form a significant component of the Parliamentary Human Rights Group - although latterly those who had joined the Movement for Christian Democracy expressed their concerns about this liaison. High profile pro-Life campaigners (such as David Alton) and other individual Catholic MPs/Ministers (such as John Battle) became advocates of justice for the East Timorese as their struggle against Indonesian oppression reached its climax. The relatively principled position of the European Union on the Timor issue, and the supportive prescriptions of International Law were not fully exploited by the Bishops Conference either unilaterally or in collaboration with their peers at COMECE. Outside of the structures of consecrated religious men and women there seemed to be little co-ordinated stimulus to prayer for the people of East Timor and for those who worked on their behalf. The spiritual bond with fellow Catholics was recognised in theory but had a limited expression in practice.

Thus there was evidence of an earnest effort - among a somewhat diminished and disoriented community - to become outward looking and engaged in various issues of social justice. But a gap persisted between the principles of Catholic Social Doctrine as publicly declared, and their practice within the national Catholic family as a whole. The response of the Church in England and Wales to the issue of East Timor indicates the pertinence of Pope John Paul II's observation in his Encyclical *Centesimus Annus*:

> Today, more than ever, the Church is aware that her social message will gain credibility more immediately from the witness of actions than as a result of its internal logic and consistency.[95]

---

[95] *Centesimus Annus* (1991), Chapter VI, para 57.

CHAPTER TWELVE – THE RESPONSE OF THE VATICAN: VARIEGATED, VILIFIED, VALUABLE

Principles and Pragmatism

In 1989 a group of East Timorese students expressed strident criticism of what they perceived to be the Vatican's attitude to the plight of their compatriots:

> We strongly repudiate the indifference, the apathy, or the simple accommodation of the Catholic Church (both the Nunciature and the Vatican) and the ways it has disregarded, disgraced, and disowned the substance of our struggle for our liberation and the difference of our values and political independence...which may ultimately contribute to the subjugation and extermination of our people.[1]

Other analysts have also observed that - despite development of a coherent system of Social Doctrine - the actual response of Church officialdom to the situation in East Timor up to this point had lacked both vigour and consistency. Subsequently the Vatican demeanour appeared to become more sympathetic, but evidence of unequivocal support for the Timorese cause is sparse – even in the 'Year of Crisis'.[2]

The Vatican organisation has a number of levels or circles of operation and it is evident that these did not share the same priorities, and that even within them emphases shifted over time as personnel changed and circumstances developed in East Timor and internationally. The Vatican had to address a number of competing concerns and its response was pragmatic as much as it was principled. This gave rise to considerable confusion among observers and evoked forthright criticism from within East Timor and from various agencies and individuals sympathetic to the Timorese plight. Nonetheless, the contribution made by the Vatican towards a just resolution of the issue was considerable. Besides pronouncements and activity specifically to do with the East Timor situation, Vatican statements on related issues (e.g. the international arms trade, human rights, and development) had pertinence and impact.

The invasion of East Timor occurred during the pontificate of Paul VI, but the subsequent oppression of its people by the Indonesian military, and their eventual liberation from the Jakarta regime, mostly took place during that of his successor who undertook the Papal office in the autumn of 1978. Pope John Paul II's engagement in the Timorese cause was of significant importance and included a pastoral visit in October 1989.

The Vatican Secretariat of State adopted the position of the United Nations in respect of East Timor's political status, regarding it as a non-self-governing entity in the process of decolonisation. After the retirement of the Portuguese bishop Ribeiro from the diocese of Dili in 1977 the Vatican took direct responsibility for the affairs of the local Church via an Apostolic Administrator (Mgr Costa Lopes 1977-83, Mgr Carlos Belo thereafter). Secretaries of State (principally Cardinal Casaroli 1979-90, and then Cardinal Sodano) and their deputies had continually to bear in mind the welfare of the Church in Indonesia, and Church relations with other countries intimately involved in the whole affair, most notably Portugal but also Australia and elsewhere. Whatever their own disposition towards the issue might have been, the Vatican envoys to these countries were constrained by the policy of the Secretariat. The stance of the Papal Nuncios also had a bearing upon the response of the local Churches to the Timorese situation. The work of the Vatican Mission at the United Nations in New York had importance, and the Vatican envoy to the UN in Geneva also had a contribution to make.

---

[1] Letter, [East Timor] Association of Catholic Students to the Apostolic Nuncio, Jakarta, Feb. 23rd 1989.
[2] See Bibliography – General (East Timor): Kohen, A. 1999; Taylor, J. 1991, p152-157; Bibliography – Ch2: Budiardjo C. & Liem, S.L. 1984, 117-124; Bibliography – Ch5: Crowe, L. 1996; Federer, J. 1994.

A response to the needs of the people of East Timor was also forthcoming from two Pontifical Councils: the Commission *Justitia et Pax* (involved in advocacy on its behalf), and *Cor Unum* (which provided some financial support for the local church's pastoral efforts - as did the Pontifical Aid Societies)[3].

Valuable inside information on the East Timor situation and its repercussions elsewhere could be gained by the Vatican through various ecclesiastical structures of communication, although it must be recognised that such sources were not necessarily entirely objective in their appraisals. Nonetheless, Vatican interpretations and diplomatic assistance were highly respected and sought after at the United Nations and elsewhere.[4] Significantly, the long-suffering East Timorese were not alone in their efforts to secure Vatican backing - the contending national governments of Indonesia and Portugal also looked for, or claimed, the support of the Holy See for their policies in respect of the territory and its people.[5] Within the Vatican administration many other lesser diplomats and officials brought their influence to bear, with noticeable – if not always positive - effect.

Among the principled aspects of the Vatican response, and perhaps the most obvious, was its adherence to the position of the United Nations regarding East Timor's political status – a stance that was reiterated many times by the Secretariat of State, although not loudly declaimed. A direct consequence of that attitude was the Vatican's equally stolid refusal to countenance the inclusion of the diocese of Dili into the Indonesian Bishops Conference, despite every urging from the regime in Jakarta – and at one stage by the Indonesian bishops (and some laity) as well.[6] Arguments put forward ranged from those which urged that such an arrangement would greatly benefit both Church and people in East Timor to those which suggested that the FRETILIN administration and (subsequently) the ongoing organised Resistance in East Timor were Communist-inspired.[7] There were also thinly veiled threats regarding the future wellbeing of the Church in Indonesia.[8] But for the Vatican to have proceeded with such an incorporation would certainly have been interpreted as being supportive of the political annexation of East Timor, and not only by the Indonesian government. In the event the Holy See was generally successful in avoiding the partisanship that would have been widely perceived had it succumbed to such pressures, although there were occasional blunders as will be noted below.

---

[3] e.g. In 1994-5 US$120,000; in 1996-7 US$210,000 (*Rapporto, La Pontificia Cooperazione Missionaria e La Solidarieta' Tra Le Chiese*, International Secretariats of the Pontifical Missionary Societies: Propaganda Fide, St. Peter the Apostle, and Holy Childhood - Vatican).

[4] Tamrat Samuel, UN Official, to the author at the United Nations, New York 1998.

[5] e.g.
(1) In 1981 Indonesian Foreign Minister Mochtar Kusumaatmaja claimed that the Papal Nuncio to Jakarta Pablo Puente had expressed Vatican sentiments when he declared: 'integration was the best way to ensure the development and progress of East Timor.' (The Age, 25.11.81) – the Pontifical Council *Cor Unum*, and the Vatican Secretariat of State subsequently repudiated this claim (Timor Information Service No 34, Jan/Feb 1982).
(2) In 1996 Portugal's Prime Minister Guterres sought Vatican support in achieving progress within the Tri-partite dialogue with Indonesia under UN auspices. (*Diario de Noticias* 29.3.96) – citations in ETAN Documents Vo 43, Feb 1/ April 30, 1996, p101. There were many other instances over the years.

[6] See Ch.6 above. In 1981 the Indonesian Bishops Conference (*KWI*) urged the Vatican to adjust its policy. In 1986 the Indonesian Catholic Students Association called for East Timor to be incorporated into *KWI* (*Hidup* No4, Nov 25th 1986). Indonesian Catholic politician Frans Seda, favouring East Timor's integration, continually urged the incorporation of Dili diocese.

[7] See: The Age, Melbourne, 25.11.81; Timor Information Service No34 Jan/Feb; Walsh, P. 1982 'Church may hold key to Timor's future', National Outlook, Australia, Jan 1982, p13; Bibliography – Ch5: Crowe, L. 1996 op.cit. p136f; Federer, J. 1994 op.cit.p25.

[8] See Bibliography – Ch8: Hull.G. 1992, p12.

For the Vatican to have remained inflexible in this matter is all the more remarkable when it is recalled that positive relations with Indonesia were perceived as being of critical importance with regard to a number of the Vatican's strategic religious aspirations. These included further progress with the evangelisation of Indonesia (and thereby more widely in SE Asia as a whole), and a very real anxiety over the spread of Communism in the region. The Vatican, as well as Western governments, perceived the Suharto regime as an ally in the battle against Communism and as a bulwark in the defence of Christianity against a potentially aggressive Islam for reasons already noted.

After the invasion of East Timor and during all the years of its occupation the Holy See had humanitarian concerns for the welfare of the people. It might well have been easier for the Vatican to address these concerns by formally accepting Indonesian sovereignty, but again such acceptance was not forthcoming.

However, having such religious and humanitarian priorities also meant the Vatican was not as vigorous in its defence of East Timorese rights as it could have been, certainly in the earlier years of the occupation. The Holy See urged respect for East Timorese religious and cultural rights and defended their ethnic identity, but this was motivated at least in part by its desire for the inculturation - and thereby the growth - of the Church among the people (a religious aspiration). Critics opine that there is little obvious evidence of the Vatican being assertive or taking any diplomatic initiatives with regard to the fundamental question of East Timorese political self-determination.[9] They allege that such action was lacking despite Indonesia's blatant contravention of International Law by its armed invasion and by the manner of its subsequent annexation and rule of the territory. The Holy See seemed to them to have been concerned principally with being faithful to its 'transcendent' mission and with not appearing to favour one contender over another, or otherwise becoming involved in 'political affairs'.[10] In practice this attempted impartiality led to the perception that the Vatican was 'distancing' itself from the issue - which inevitably gave rise in turn to allegations of an irresponsible 'silence', and of outright complicity in the Indonesian aggression.[11] It can be argued that the Vatican was, at least, attentive to the conflicting points of view - to further progress in humanitarian provision for the suffering population, if for no other reason. However, the case can also be put that the Vatican had seemingly accepted the 'integration' of East Timor into Indonesia as a *fait accompli* and had come to regard the Resistance struggle as futile and dreams of future independence as unrealistic. Indeed, this view of the situation was expressed to the author (in 1995) by a significant number of clergy and religious who were working in the territory – Indonesians, foreign missionaries, and even a few native pastors.[12] The upshot was that the variety of remarks and actions by a whole range of Vatican representatives were widely regarded by outsiders as presenting very ambiguous signals overall and as offering a degree of comfort but not complete satisfaction to any party in the dispute. This ambivalence, and the uncertainty it provoked, served to encourage further lobbying of the Holy See by all concerned, and gave grounds for widespread criticism of

---

[9] See, e.g. *Pro Mundi Vita*, Dossier 4, 1984, p28 – echoed by various authors such as Taylor, J.1992, op.cit., Crowe, L, 1996, op.cit &c.

[10] Vatican II *Gaudium et Spes,* Part II, Ch IV, para 76; see also Part I Ch IV, and passim.

[11] e.g.

1) Statement of Religious in East Timor (1981) – cited in Introduction;

2) Jean-Pierre Catry, 1983, article 'The Silence of the Church' 28.5.83 (NGO *Pas e Possivel em Timor Leste*, Lisbon);

3) 'The international conspiracy of silence towards the tribulations of the East Timorese included the Vatican…which deferred to the Jakarta regime to protect its interests in Indonesia…Vatican efforts included coercion to convince the bishops in Dili to accept integration' (Federer, J.,1994, op.cit. pp 1, 18, 39 and *passim*).

[12] See: 'Church may hold key, etc', Pat Walsh, National Outlook, Jan.1982 op.cit.; 'Timor Time bomb ticks on', Desmond O'Grady, The Tablet, 1.6.1996, p724.

Vatican 'realpolitik': its 'cynicism' and 'sacrifice of principle for pragmatic realism'.[13] Officials were accused of being 'slippery'[14], 'cunning'[15] and of dismissing the East Timorese as expendable in their concern for the welfare of the Church in Indonesia and for progress towards the achievement of strategic religious objectives:

> It seems that the Vatican is willing to sacrifice a people... The connivance between the Vatican and the Indonesian government is noticeable... but in the long run this kind of politics will boomerang...
> It is wrong to think that by siding with the government the safety of the Indonesian Church will be assured. This is what is known as *realpolitik* - and as such it is devilish. ...
> It seems that the doctrine of the Church on social issues is only applicable in other places, while in the case of East Timor the Vatican is ready to force the local church into servility... Rome does not hear us![16]

Even Mgr Costa Lopes had felt that the East Timorese, 'the little ones', were being 'sacrificed for the big interests.' His successor bishop Belo often expressed disappointment at the Vatican response to the East Timorese plight and was confused and disturbed by the criticisms of his own spirited defence of East Timorese human rights which were conveyed to him by its officials: 'I don't understand Vatican policy... Surely the human person is more important than numbers.'[17].

However, three significant events catalysed a shift in the Vatican position to one that was more sensitive to the East Timorese plight, more supportive of their cause, and no longer intimating that integration offered them the most promising future. These were the Papal Visit in 1989, the Santa Cruz massacre in 1991, and the awarding of the Nobel Peace Prize to bishop Belo in 1996. Yet even in 1999, the year of East Timor's crisis, the Holy See's advocacy of the Timorese cause still manifested a somewhat ambiguous character.

The Secretariat of State

Cardinal Agostino Casaroli (d.1998) was Vatican Secretary of State from 1979 until his retirement in 1990. The Church's political line, he told the diplomatic corps in Rome in 1989, should generally be inspired by a spirit of impartiality and non-alignment, not swayed by pre-conceived sympathies, antipathies or ideologies. He added that this should not mean 'putting justice and injustice on the same footing.'[18] But it is difficult to accept that Casaroli's practical policies in respect of the East Timor issue managed to maintain the desirable features of impartiality and the promotion of justice that he had urged upon the diplomats.

As noted already, the position consistently adopted by the Secretariat and communicated through diplomatic channels to the Indonesian government was that the Vatican would not accept that East Timor was part of the Republic until this had been clearly demonstrated as the will of the people and/or the United Nations. Vatican concerns about the welfare of the Church in East Timor, and about respect for human rights were also conveyed to Jakarta.[19] But the Vatican gave no *public* support for the removal of the Indonesian administration from East Timor. Moreover, Casaroli (or his officials) prevented Mgr Costa

---

[13] Xanana Gusmao, interviewed by Pedro Sousa Pereira for Radio Macau, 26.1.1995 (Timor Link, March 1995, p4); Federer, J. 1994, op.cit. p18.

[14] Various foreign missionaries and East Timorese clergy to the author, East Timor 1995/96.

[15] Xanana Gusmao, 1989 (*Tapol* Bulletin 93, June 1989; Timor Link 18/19, 1989, p6)

[16] Deposition/Testimony of 'A Group of Laity in East Timor', prior to the Papal Visit 1989 (on file with the author). cf also Federer, J. 1994, op.cit. p39.

[17] Citations in Bibliography – General (East Timor): Kohen, A. 1999 op.cit. pp113, 175, 179, 199.

[18] Obituaries: 'A diplomatic progress by dialogue', M.Walsh, The Guardian, 10.6.1998; 'The diplomat who negotiated with the Communists', D.O'Grady, The Tablet, 13.6.1998, p791f.

[19] 'See Bibliography – Ch6: Walsh P. 1980.

Lopes from meeting with the Pope until after he had resigned as Apostolic Administrator and left the territory.[20] In 1986 the Vatican requested bishop Belo to meet secretly with Xanana Gusmao to propose the surrender of FALINTIL leaders in exchange for their safe conduct from East Timor. Gusmao's response indicated that 'Rome' had apparently not appreciated the extent of the Resistance to Indonesian rule: 'Are they going to remove all the Timorese from Timor?'[21] In 1989 the Portuguese press declared that the Secretary had expressed willingness to receive leaders of the East Timorese Resistance prior to the Papal Visit, and that a request on their part to meet with the Pope himself while he was in the territory would be considered. However, in 1991 Casaroli came under criticism in Portugal for refusing to forward to the United Nations Secretary General one hundred and eighty letters supporting the East Timorese call for self-determination. The bishop of Setubal had gathered these from as many high-ranking members of the hierarchy in Africa, Latin America, Canada and Europe.[22] In fact, the allegation was made that the Secretary of State 'tried to isolate the Pope' from the East Timor issue, and 'never presented him with the full picture'.[23]

Certainly a number of bureaucrats in the Secretariat seemed to have little patience with the vexing matter, or with the persisting attempts of the Apostolic Administrators in Dili to bring an end to the violations of human rights being perpetrated in the territory. Nor was bishop Belo's call for a referendum regarded favourably: the style of Papal diplomats is to avoid conflict and confrontation if at all possible.[24] The Papal Visit to East Timor in 1989 caused considerable nervousness in their ranks – some opposed it altogether - and revealed that the prime concern of many was with the welfare of the Church in Indonesia and its development in the wider region. The Papal emissary, Fr. Romano Tucci, urged the Timorese clergy to limit their expectations of the outcome: 'We are not going to sacrifice the whole of Christendom for 400,000 Catholics [in East Timor]!' This hyperbole upset many East Timorese and scandalised sympathetic foreign NGOs.[25] An official 'Note' disseminated after the Papal Visit to Portugal in 1990 referred to East Timor as the '27th Province of Indonesia' – a blunder repeated in 1997 which caused delight in Jakarta but outrage in Portugal and among East Timorese world-wide.[26] Allegations that Vatican officials filtered information from East Timor before it reached the Pope were common among the native pastors – the author heard them not only in the territory itself but from exiled clergy in Portugal, Australia and the United States. There is no doubt that General Benny Murdani and other Indonesian government officials such as Frans Seda sought to use their Catholic credentials to obstruct or to devalue the reports of Mgr Costa Lopes and bishop Belo within Vatican circles.[27] However, the Vatican was generally adept in keeping all parties 'on side', as was illustrated by the appointment of Mgr Belo as titular bishop of Lorium in 1988. The East Timorese felt honoured and 'noticed' by this arrangement which also pleased Indonesia because there was now a full bishop *in* Dili. Portugal was happy because the appointment of a bishop *of* Dili

---

[20] Catry, J.P., 'The Church of Silence, etc', op.cit.; Kohen, A. 1999 op.cit. p112.

[21] East Timor News (Lisbon), Memo No1/89, 5th May 1989; *Tapol* 93, June 1989, p1.

[22] *Expresso*, 21.8.1989; *Publico*, 14.9.1991. [Cited in *Factos e Documentos Vol 1,1991* (henceforth *F&D*) Assemblia de Republica, Lisbon, p200 & p513].

[23] Frs Reinaldo Cardoso and Domingos da Cunha, to the author, Rhode Island, USA 1998.

[24] 'Belo was cold-shouldered in Rome by Vatican officials' (Bishop Hilton Deakin to the author, Melbourne); 'Belo suffered from the suspicion of some elements in the Vatican' (Dr.M.Costigan ACSJC, to the author, Sydney) - Sept 1997; 'Vatican officials wanted Belo to stick to religion not "politics"', (Kohen, A.1999, op.cit. p1, & *passim*; Crowe, L. 1996, op.cit. p72).

[25] It was widely quoted, e.g. in the Deposition/Testimony of East Timorese Laity (cited above); East Timor News (Lisbon), Monthly Memo 5/89, 21.6.1989; Hull, G., 1992, op.cit.p12; Crowe, L.1996, op.cit.p136; Kohen, A. 1999, op.cit.p141; Taylor, J. 1991, op.cit.p156; etc.

[26] *Jornal de Noticias*, Lisbon, 15.5.1990 (*F&D*, op.cit., p441); *Kompas*, Jakarta, 9.1.1997, *Republika*, Jakarta, 11.1.1997, *Suara Pembuaran*, Jakarta, 9.1.1997, IPS (Jakarta, Rome)

[27] Kohen, A. 1999 op.cit. p153, 174, 179.

diocese was still dependent upon an internationally accepted settlement of the East Timor issue. But critics tended to regard this arrangement as yet another example of Vatican 'fence-sitting', 'ignoring the aspirations of the East Timorese people'.[28]

Belo's reception in the Secretariat continued to be less than welcoming during the administration of Casaroli's successor, Cardinal Angelo Sodano[29], although there were some positive developments. After the Santa Cruz massacre a diplomat, archbishop De Andrea, was sent to East Timor as a sign of support for the local Church. Nonetheless, in 1993 Mgr Parolin, a Vatican desk officer, expressed the view that 'East Timor's independence is not a viable option' recommending 'a degree of autonomy' in order to preserve the local culture. In 1994 Belo was to declare in an interview for the Portuguese press:

> High ranking church officials give the impression that they are more concerned about caring for Indonesian Catholics than responding to the demands of the Timorese... Moral, spiritual and pastoral support is real enough...but active [political] support is needed... East Timor seems to be a 'taboo subject' for the Church.[30]

In 1996 Portuguese Prime Minister Antonio Guterres disclosed Cardinal Sodano's private assurance to him that diplomatic pressure was being put upon Suharto to release Resistance leader Xanana Gusmao from imprisonment in Jakarta. But in public the Cardinal simply reiterated that the Vatican supported the 'historical, cultural and religious identity of East Timor' and asserted that 'the Holy See has not forgotten Timor...the Timorese must realise they are not alone...the bishop of Dili knows that'.[31] Belo's receipt of the Nobel Peace Prize later that year improved his standing significantly in the Universal Church as in the international community. But still some Vatican officials remained cold towards him and the Secretariat restricted his movements outside of Oslo and put limits upon his contact with the media for the duration of his visit.[32] Nonetheless, the Vatican indicated its commitment to the Church's work in the territory – with all that entailed for the defence of human rights – by the creation that same year of the new diocese of Baucau (although publicly this was declared to have a 'purely pastoral' purpose). In 1998 Sodano met with Kofi Annan regarding the East Timor issue, after the Pope had engaged in his own discussion on the matter with the UN Secretary General.[33]

On September 12th 1999, in the midst of the turmoil following upon the UN-conducted plebiscite *La Republica* reported from Rome that the Secretary of State had pledged that 'the Holy See will do everything possible to bring peace to East Timor'. Noticeably there was no similar commitment to justice for the East Timorese. The Vatican's representative at the UN Human Rights Commission in Geneva, archbishop Bertello, remarked bluntly that 'the Timorese affair...takes on a very special significance because the attackers wanted to annihilate with blood the will of the vast majority of a people, expressed by nearly 80% of the vote'.[34] But in early October Archbishop Jean-Luis Tauran, Deputy Secretary of State in charge of foreign affairs, expressed (an unwarranted) confidence to Jakarta's ambassador Irawan Abidin that his government would not allow the perpetrators of the mayhem to enjoy impunity. Tauran indicated a wish to 'strengthen relations with Indonesia.'[35]

---

[28] See, e.g. *Tapol* Bulletin 91, Feb 1989, p18-19.

[29] Kohen, A. op.cit.p205

[30] *Publico* (Lisbon), 15.6.1994.

[31] Timor Link, Feb 1996; ETAN Docs 43, p102.

[32] Kohen, A. 1999, op.cit. p233, 243.

[33] Archbishop Renato Martino to the author, Vatican Observer Mission, UN, Sept. 1998.

[34] 'Vatican, UN condemn violence in E. Timor', Catholic News Service, Geneva 25.9.1999.

[35] 'Indonesian official: East Timor violence not directed at Church', John Norton, Catholic News Service, Vatican City, 2.10.1999; cf. 'Leader denies religious motive', John Norton, Catholic Times, 10.10.1999.

The Permanent Observer Mission at the United Nations

The Mission was established at the United Nations in 1964 and the Vatican enjoys the status of a 'Non-member State Permanent Observer'. As such it has a voice but no votes on issues discussed in official forums. The Vatican is highly esteemed by the majority of member states that make up the General Assembly although latterly it has had to contend with certain organisations that have a different view of what constitutes human rights. Certainly the involvement of the Vatican in the operation of the United Nations has increased dramatically over the years.[36] The Mission itself describes its purpose as 'making the Church present in the *areopagus* of the United Nations' and its intentions as 'not political, more moral and social'. The Mission is never directly involved 'unless it is asked' and is 'always interested in supporting the initiatives of the Secretary General'.[37] It has made important contributions to a wide range of deliberations and has made appeals to governments on a number of issues – some very pertinent to the East Timor situation, such as the international arms trade[38].

Various commentators have remarked upon the apparent lack of action by the Mission in respect of the East Timor issue, as has been noted already. It does seem to be the case that the Mission did not urge East Timorese political self-determination, as many Timorese, many campaigners, and the Portuguese government felt it should. The development of International Law seemingly provided good grounds from which the Vatican could urge Timorese political rights. But the unresolved nature of some of the legal questions, and the varying degrees of willingness on the part of States to abide by the principles of the Law undermine this base, as noted already. The practical response of the Mission was to make several distinct and continuous appeals.[39] One was that 'a reduction of the military presence in East Timor was indispensable for any solution'. The Mission also called for the provision of information about and accountability for the (many) people who had 'disappeared', and a 'total solution' to the problem of prisoners of war (i.e. one that led to the release from captivity of all such persons). It insisted on 'the preservation of the cultural and religious identity of the native people', and 'supported efforts at dialogue between the parties' intended to effect the goal of 'a just, global and internationally acceptable solution to the conflict.'[40] The Mission also urged the 'inclusion of East Timorese' into the whole social system established by Indonesia in East Timor. This was in order to prevent the marginalisation of the indigenes that was perceived to be a significant cause of continuing social conflict and resistance to the Indonesian administration throughout the territory. The Mission certainly supported 'an increased autonomy' for East Timor - regarding this as a way to overcome the *impasse* of Indonesian (and Portuguese) intransigence on the question of sovereignty (an approach which was also adopted by bishop Belo when his calls in 1989 for a plebiscite had proved fruitless). Evidently the Holy See was far from inactive on the issue and it is noteworthy that these various prescriptions were gradually taken up by many other agencies concerned for East Timorese welfare.

---

[36] The Mission has established the *Path to Peace Foundation* which assists in coping with increased demands upon the Holy See and is responsible for publications, seminars, cultural programmes, etc.
[37] Mgr.George Panikulam, Mission Counsellor, to the author at the Permanent Observer Mission, New York, Sept 1998. Panikulam was subsequently appointed Papal Nuncio to Mozambique.
[38] See Bibliography – Ch12: Vatican Observer Mission at the UN 1997; on the arms trade see (e.g.) Archbishop Renato Martino, Observer, at the First Committee of the UN General Assembly, October 19th, 1998 - 'Vatican call to give up arms, etc', Gerry Leonard, The Universe, 1.11.1998.
[39] Listed by Archbishop Renato Martino & Mgr Panikulam to the author at the Mission, New York, Sept 1998. Martino was subsequently appointed President of the Pontifical Council for Justice & Peace.
[40] i.e. The Tri-partite negotiations between Portugal and Indonesia under the auspices of the UN Secretary General, and other deliberations arising therefrom such as the All-inclusive Intra-Timorese Dialogue [AIETD].

There were many within and outside the institutional Church who believed that for it to be specific in its recommendations in respect of East Timorese political self-determination would be to go beyond the parameters of its Gospel mission and enter into the realm of secular politics. But such distinctions cannot be so easily made - official Social Doctrine itself describes the close interrelationships that exist within the proper functioning of Church and State.[41] It can certainly be argued that the position adopted by the Vatican was one that actually facilitated progress towards a just and internationally acceptable solution, whereas to be confrontational on this substantive issue would have served only to discourage Indonesia from engagement in further deliberations. From this perspective the Permanent Observer Mission acted responsibly with regard to the political question. Moreover, that the Vatican's activity was not publicly known does not mean that no action was taken:

> The Holy See operates in a very quiet way, a silent way... There is no trumpet call... no intention for publicity. The Holy See is discreet in order to save the primary cause. To speak too much about intentions may damage this cause...Propaganda is to be avoided... there must be silent moments...dialogue...well thought-out suggestions. All these form part of a peace process. Sometimes pulling one thread will unravel the whole effort. Useful activity is not necessarily that which is immediate or leads to immediate results... We should wait for God's moment.[42]
> East Timor is very much on the agenda of the Holy See, but its work is not publicised apart from exceptional circumstances.[43]

Observer Mission staff assured the author of their faithfulness to the Church's call to 'oppose violence and remain faithful to its prime directive: the supremacy of love'. There is no doubt that the Mission sought to make a contribution towards the peaceful settlement of a conflict with a complexity of causes. However, the discreet manner of the Mission's operation meant that its voice was a muted one – in particular that there was a deliberate avoidance of the media outlets of public communication. This means that independent evidence to gauge the effectiveness of the Missions' activity in respect of East Timor is hard to come by. Clearly it fell short of the expectations of many – especially in the matter of achieving a truly *just* outcome.

Papal Envoys

The attitude of the Papal Nuncios to Indonesia (and elsewhere) was very pertinent in the matter of Vatican influence upon developments in the East Timor issue. These officials provide the Secretariat of State with information they have accrued and in turn they receive directives from the Vatican as to the posture to be adopted. Their prime function, in common with other ambassadors, is to improve the Church's relations with the government of the country to which they are accredited. Although there is evidence of differences in the approach adopted by successive envoys to Jakarta during the period of the invasion and occupation of East Timor overall there seemed to be greater concern with the welfare of the Church in Indonesia than with the plight of the East Timorese. At the same time it was noticeable that the Nuncios in Lisbon carefully avoided any identification with Portuguese sentiment regarding the matter of East Timorese political self-determination. The influence of the Nuncios in Canberra and Washington in respect of the East Timor issue has been noted already.

The Nuncios to Jakarta were tasked with facilitating the mission of the Church in Indonesia in collaboration with the Indonesian Bishops Conference and directly represented the Holy See's oversight of the Church in East Timor. This put them in a particularly awkward

---

[41] e.g. Vatican II *Gaudium et Spes* Part II Ch IV.

[42] Mgr George Panikulam to the author at the Permanent Observer Mission, New York, Sept 1998.

[43] Archbishop Renato Martino, Observer, to the author at the Mission, Sept.1998.

position in which they were involved in a mediating role between the East Timorese Church - with its increasingly significant role in the nationalist resistance - and the regime of the *Orde Baru* (which was dominated by the Military, themselves responsible for gross violations of human rights in the territory and engaged in the economic and social marginalisation of the native people).

Vincenso Farano (Nuncio to Jakarta 1974-80) demonstrated considerable concern for the East Timorese and is remembered favourably by the clergy: 'a true shepherd according to the Gospel'.[44] In 1974 he reassured the Portuguese bishop in Dili that, in the light of his experience, the Church had nothing to fear from integration into the Republic. But when the invasion and its aftermath in East Timor revealed the oppressive nature of the Indonesian administration in the territory he took considerable risks to assist the local church with material and moral support. He gathered medical supplies in the Nunciature, and often visited the clergy and people in East Timor – even in the areas still under the control of FRETILIN – as well as the many refugees from the civil war and invasion languishing in camps in West Timor. He also duly consulted the East Timorese priests as to who should be appointed as Apostolic Administrator when bishop Ribeiro retired in 1977. However, his personal engagement did not result in any Vatican statements on the issue.

Pablo Puente (Nuncio to Jakarta 1980-86) is not fondly remembered in East Timor. From the outset of his mission he accepted and even promoted the pro-integration perspective presented to him by Indonesian government officials such as Benny Murdani and Frans Seda. Before he had even visited East Timor he stated that the Indonesian administration there was a *fait accompli* and that the situation was an improvement on that which had been the case under Portugal.[45] In 1983 he induced Mgr Costa Lopes to resign and discredited his accounts of Timorese suffering, appointing Carlos Belo as Apostolic Administrator without due consultation of the local clergy.[46] He sought (unsuccessfully) to achieve the integration of the enclave of Oecussi into Indonesian West Timor.[47] Far from supporting the Administrator he had himself appointed, Puente admonished Belo for his publicisation of human rights violations by the Military.[48] Despite being provided with detailed accounts of the abuses being perpetrated by the regime, Puente distanced himself from the carefully worded critique of the Indonesian administration in East Timor produced in January 1985 by the Dili Council of Priests.[49] Puente maintained a close relationship with General Murdani throughout his term as Papal envoy to Indonesia. Many years later in 1997, when he became Nuncio to Great Britain, the reputation Pablo Puente had gained among the East Timorese by his manifest and inexcusable pro-Jakarta prejudice preceded him. Anxiety was widespread among some of the expatriate community in the British Isles as to the malign influence he might still have over the unfolding course of events but the Nuncio denied them any opportunity to convey their concerns to him personally.

Francisco Canalini (Nuncio to Jakarta 1986-1991) was also castigated by the East Timorese for his 'silence', his 'fence-sitting' and for being 'a Pontius Pilate', washing his hands of personal responsibility for the prevailing situation. The Resistance was of the view

[44] Fr.Reinaldo Cardoso and Fr.Domingos da Cunha, to the author Rhode Island, Sept 1998; Rabbitt Roff, S., 1992, *Timor's Anschluss – Indonesian and Australian Policy in East Timor 1974-76*, Edwin Mellin, New York, p55; Bibliography – General (East Timor): Kohen, A. 1999, op.cit. p98; Retboll, T. (ed) 1980; Bibliography – Ch5: Crowe, L. 1996, op.cit. pp56, 137.

[45] Bibliography – Ch8: Walsh P. 1980 (1), p10; 'Church may hold key to Timor's future', Pat Walsh, National Outlook, January 1982, p14; Bibliography – General (East Timor): Horta, J.R.1987, p20.

[46] Interview with Costa Lopes, *Diario de Noticias*, Lisbon July 1983; Bibliography – General (East Timor): Horta, J.R. 1987,op.cit.p203; Taylor, 1991 op.cit. p151f; Bibliography – Ch5: Federer, J.1994, op.cit. p28,30; Crowe 1996, op.cit. p70,134; &c.

[47] Bibliography – Ch2: Budiardjo & Liem, 1984 op.cit.p123.

[48] Bibliography – General (East Timor): Kohen, op.cit.p123.

[49] op.cit. The document is cited above in Chapter 5.

that the Nuncio used his office 'to try to persuade local church leaders not to support the demands of the people'.[50] When bishop Belo wrote to the UN Secretary General in 1989 calling for an authentic referendum, Canalini distanced himself from the sentiments of the letter claiming that its contents were Belo's personal view and insinuating they did not represent that of the local Church and people. This was despite the fact that the Primate of the Indonesian Catholic Church, archbishop Leo Soekoto, had himself publicly supported the aims of Belo's letter to Peres de Cuellar.[51] The East Timorese clergy were outraged at the slight upon their bishop and denounced what they perceived as Canalini's general hypocrisy:

> In our view the Nuncio is questioning the moral integrity of the bishop with the intention of isolating him from the people and thereby serving the politics of oppression of the Indonesian government...The Apostolic Administrator is accused of playing politics. Is it only politics when one talks against this regime in power? Or isn't it politics too when one talks in favour of the government? What do *Gaudium et Spes* and *Evangelii Nuntiandi* and other Church documents teach? ... With the exception of Mgr Farano, every Nuncio has preferred to practice the silence of the corrupt accomplice (sic)... It is not by sacrificing East Timor that Indonesia will be saved.[52]

A few months later, to avoid further strained relations with Jakarta, Canalini refused asylum to East Timorese students at the Nunciature, 'an act of betrayal showing callous disregard for the sufferings of the people.'[53] Criticism of the Nuncio's stance also arose within influential Church organisations outside of East Timor. In 1987 Canalini was interviewed by the Indonesian media outlet *Pembaruan* and declared that the Vatican 'would not take sides while the conflict remained unresolved' and 'awaited a settlement in accordance with international law'. He reiterated that it was for this reason the Vatican 'had kept Dili diocese out of the Indonesian Bishops Conference'. But then the Nuncio went on to suggest that in practical terms the problem was 'only a legal one' as 'Belo attended their [Conference] meetings and there was co-operation over development programmes'. This statement was strongly criticised by the Catholic Institute for International Relations in London because of its implication that there were no issues of substance at the heart of the Vatican's refusal to accept Indonesia's point of view over the issue. It was also regarded as trivialising the significance of the Vatican's commitments to International Law: 'No weight is given to the moral and political principles that underpin the Timor conflict. Gone is any reference to concern for the territory's political identity.'[54] Canalini was present in Dili in September 1990 for the Mass that was the focus of celebrations for the 50th anniversary of the establishment of the Diocese. During the ceremonial there was a demonstration and some of the participants pressed him to clarify the Vatican position on East Timor. No such clarification was forthcoming.[55] Commentators subsequently observed that 'Canalini thought the good of the East Timorese was more than outbalanced by that of Indonesian Catholics and by the beneficial effects of harmonious relations with Indonesia for the Vatican in its dealings throughout the Islamic world.'[56]

Pietro Sambi (Nuncio to Jakarta 1991-1998) was generally credited with paying more attention to the East Timorese viewpoint but the Church's good relations with Indonesia remained his overriding concern. He was under pressure from Jakarta[57] to get the Vatican to di-

---

[50] Xanana Gusmao, interview for *Diario de Noticias*, 27.10.1992.

[51] Bibliography – Ch8: Hull, G. 1992, op.cit.p14.

[52] East Timorese Clergy 'Expression of Support' (July 1989) and 'East Timor Clergy Respond' (August 1989) on file with the author.

[53] *Kompas* Jakarta, 29.6.1989. The cited comment is from *Tapol* Bulletin 94, August 1989, p5.

[54] 'Pope reaffirms concern, doubts remain', Timor Link No12/13, April 1988, p7-9.

[55] Bibliography – Ch2: Pinto, C.1997, pp125-6.

[56] 'Timor time bomb ticks on', Desmond O'Grady, The Tablet, 6.6.1996, p724.

[57] CNRM (Northern Territory) Urgent Action message to Pat Walsh, ACFOA 1993. Copy on file.

vide (and thereby 'weaken') the Dili diocese. He sought (unsuccessfully) for a solution to the Timor issue that did not lessen Indonesian prestige but at the same time 'satisfied the Timorese population'. Sambi endeavoured to sustain positive relations with the military commander in East Timor, expressing appreciation of the 'work done for the people' by the territorial troops, encouraging a reduction of combat forces, and appealing to all military personnel to 'avoid confrontation and employ peaceful collaboration with the people'. Meanwhile he urged the Timorese to 'put the past behind' and for 'disparate groups to reconcile…Violence and hatred are contrary to the Gospel.' [58] At the same time he recommended bishop Belo to adopt a pro-integration posture, and advocated co-operation by all Timorese with the Indonesian government as the 'best way to end their troubles'.[59] Belo opined that:

> The people expect a stronger position from the Nuncio about political issues. Unfortunately we only hear about the pastoral and religious aspect…
> The relation between the East Timor Church and the Nuncio is not one full of sympathy…He will be declared *persona non grata.*'[60]

Renzo Fratini (Nuncio to Jakarta from 1998) was in post during East Timor's Year of Crisis. During that period he made repeated appeals for unity among the East Timorese and for an end to violence. He also supported the efforts of bishops Belo and Nascimento in their attempts to effect reconciliation between those favouring and those rejecting the offer of the Habibie government for East Timor to have a 'limited autonomy' within Indonesia. When the post ballot mayhem subsided he visited the camps in West Timor and called on Jakarta to disarm the militias who were 'creating a climate of fear'. But he blamed the crisis on 'a small group of criminals and thieves… or maybe a group connected to the old regime', and stressed the importance of reconciliation and future good relations with Indonesia 'which had done a lot for East Timor by building schools, hospitals and churches'.[61] Fratini was speaking from within an Indonesia soon to be wracked from east to west by inter-communal violence stirred up by intransigent elements of 'the old regime'. In this strife many adherents of various religious faiths were to lose their lives and property, and many Catholic and other Christian churches and institutions were to be mindlessly destroyed.[62] The Vatican's concern for the precarious situation of the Church in Indonesia surely then seemed justified. But these events also demonstrated the truth of the observation made a decade earlier by the priests of the Diocese of Dili (cited above): 'It is not by sacrificing East Timor that Indonesia will be saved.'

The Pontifical Commission 'Justitia et Pax'

The contribution of the Pontifical Justice and Peace Commission towards a settlement of the East Timor issue was both direct and indirect. One of the ways in which the Commission's work impinged indirectly upon the East Timor issue was through the concerns it expressed over the international arms trade. As already noted its 'reflections' provided material for cogent criticism of those governments and commercial enterprises supplying weapons to Indonesia.[63] Another was the stimulus it gave to the emergence around the world of Diocesan Justice and Peace Commissions and parochial 'J & P Groups' some of whom addressed the Timorese plight and became advocates of their cause.

---

[58] Interview for UCANews 4.5.1992, following a Pastoral Visit to E Timor April 22-28th; Address to Indonesian troops in East Timor, Christmas 1993 - UCANews 31.12.1993.

[59] To the ACR delegation, Bali 1993 – Bishop Ted Collins to the author, Darwin Sept 1997.

[60] Remarks to representatives of CAFOD UK, & *Pax Christi* International 1993-96 (copies on file), and to Louise Crowe (Bibliography – Ch5: Crowe, L. 1996 op.cit.p140).

[61] AFP Kupang 7.10.1999.

[62] See: 'Indonesian Christians face fresh onslaught from Muslim gangs', The Tablet 8.7.2000; 'Jakarta's Heroes and Villains', by John Prior, The Tablet 13.1.2001.

[63] 'The International Arms Trade: an ethical reflection', 1994. In Briefing (CBCEW) 7.7.94., pp4-16.

The influence of the Commission within the Vatican organisation as a whole is not considered to be very strong, nonetheless its activities merited the participation of Catholic senior Indonesian politician Frans Seda who brought his pro-integration views to bear therein.[64] Furthermore, as Seda was appointed to serve as one of the Commission's delegates to the Asia-Pacific region, he was able to use the authority and often the facilities of his position to check criticism of Jakarta's policies as this began to gather momentum in Church circles.[65] In this way the potential of the Commission to support the East Timorese cause was inhibited or diminished for some time. However, in February 1996 the President of *Justitia et Pax* Cardinal Roger Etchegaray visited East Timor, his presence and his words proving to be of great comfort and strength to the local Church leadership and people. He urged 'a dialogue, in which there must be space for the realisation of the legitimate aspirations of the Timorese people to see their special cultural and religious identity recognised', and he called for 'respect for human rights – the only way in which justice and peace can be brought together.' 'There can be no justice without peace, or peace without justice' he declared, and spoke clearly of East Timor being an 'international' political problem (i.e. not an internal matter to be resolved by Indonesia alone). Although he stressed that 'the Church does not interfere in political matters' and that the Holy See had not made any statement on the matter of 'integration' he notably spent time at prayer in the chapel of Santa Cruz cemetery. He also met with the Dili diocesan Justice and Peace Commission whom he asked to keep him informed about human rights violations. Bishop Belo and the clergy spoke of the visit as 'a great encouragement':

> He has boosted confidence in the Vatican... it was a real comfort in the way in which he represented the attention of the Universal Church to the suffering of the East Timorese people, to the bishop, the priests and the religious... We felt also that the Justice and Peace Commissions of all the world [ ] were joined with us.[66]

There is no doubt that the visit of Cardinal Etchegaray was of significant importance and led to a change in Rome's view of the East Timor issue - and of bishop Belo.[67] A few weeks later he publicly declared:

> The situation in East Timor is becoming explosive with the youth growing more conscientised and radical in their options...
> Incontestably East Timor has benefited from the prodigious economic development of Indonesia, but the process of 'integration' has raised various problems...
> A true dialogue would permit the finding of a just and durable solution...[it is] truly the most responsible way, the most humane, and also the most efficacious to build that just and peaceful society in East Timor which is earnestly desired. Times press, and the Timorese are in crisis [les Timorais a tendent febrillement].[68]

Later that year Etchegaray stood at Belo's side at the Nobel Prize awards in Oslo and declared: ' I am proud to be standing next to you'.[69]

---

[64] Views of: Tom Quigley, NCBC-USCC, to the author, USA Sept 1998; Archbishop F.Nguyen van Thuan (Vice President of the Commission) to Justice & Peace Commission, Japan – source, Sr.Monika Nakamura, to the author, Tokyo, May 1998.

[65] On Frans Seda's involvement see: *Tapol* Bulletin 81, June 1987; Federer, J. 1994, op.cit. p25.

[66] Timor Link March 1996 p7-8, and July 1996, p8; cf. Internews Vol 4 No2, 1996 (*KWI* quarterly newsletter). The full text of Cardinal Etchegaray's closing speech in Dili is in *Osservatore Romano*, 27.2.1996 and in Briefing (BCEW), 21.3.1996.

[67] Tamrat Samuel, UN Official, to the author at the United Nations, New York Sept.1998; Bishop Wm Brennan, Chairman BCJDP, to the author, Sydney, Sept.1997.

[68] 'Pour un vrai dialogue au Timor Oriental', Roger Cardinal Etchegaray, *Le Monde*, 22.3.1996 (this author's translation).

[69] Kohen, A. 1999 op.cit. p243

Pope John Paul II[70]

Although various critics of the shortcomings of the Vatican response to the East Timorese plight have included the present Pope in their list of those to be castigated it is also widely remarked that the contribution the Pontiff made towards a satisfactory resolution of the issue was considerable.[71]

There were several ways in which John Paul II brought his influence to bear. One way was somewhat obliquely in his general statements on human welfare, and in his addresses to the Vatican diplomatic corps. More direct opportunities were provided through his personal dealings with Church leaders from East Timor and with statesmen and ambassadors representing countries with a special involvement in the issue. His greatest influence upon the outcome was through his pastoral visits to Indonesia and East Timor itself in 1989. Also of some pertinence were his visits to Portugal in 1991 and - to a much lesser extent - to Australia in 1986. These pastoral journeys require distinct attention.

There is no doubt that in his writings John Paul II has promoted further development of the idea that sin pervades the very fabric and institutions of human society. Social, economic, and political structures can hold human beings captive and be detrimental to their physical, moral and spiritual welfare. Oppressive structures must therefore be recognised and dismissed from human concourse. But while Papal teaching admits that political and other social activity is necessary to bring this about, and urges such activity where it is - and in a manner that is – appropriate, the emphasis of the present Pope has been upon 'integral liberation'. This essentially includes the elements of forgiveness and reconciliation between those who have been in contention and for it to come about a personal or individual renewal of heart is necessary. It is noteworthy that during his pontificate John Paul II encouraged the Church in Poland to identify with a mass revolt against an unjust social order, while in Latin America the Church was urged to distance itself from the proponents of radical change. But the Church in Latin America, unlike the Church in Eastern Europe, was not threatened by the established power. Likewise, the Church in Indonesia was not menaced by the *Orde Baru* regime – in fact it was protected by it from the threat of Communism and/or militant Islam. Hence the emphasis in Vatican dealings with Jakarta over the question of East Timor on sustaining good relations with the government – a posture which was maintained by the Pope himself. Nonetheless, John Paul II was more forthright in his defence of East Timorese rights than various other departments of the Vatican administration proved to be. Furthermore, his appeals for reconciliation and forgiveness within East Timorese society have been interpreted by those well versed in such an art as having the important purpose of achieving greater political unity within the popular struggle for justice, a matter which will be further elaborated below.

In addition to the general approach to social injustice outlined in his various encyclicals the Pope also made more specific reference to the matter of national 'development' which again he described as necessarily 'integral'. In this instance he meant that development must take into account the full affirmation of human rights - such as the right to freedom of assembly, to form trades unions, to a just wage, to take initiatives in economic matters, etc - and generally for people to be participants in decisions affecting their economic and social welfare. 'Does not the denial or limitation of these impoverish the human person as much as, if

---

[70] For detail of the pontificate: Weigel, G. 2000, *Witness to Hope*, Harper Collins, London.

[71] e.g. 'John Paul II had a very limited role' – Federer, J. 1994, op.cit.p40; 'The Pope is a prisoner of the Vatican' – Dom Martins, Bishop of Setubal, to the author, Setubal June 1997. Conversely: 'John Paul II has consistently affirmed East Timorese rights, etc' – Timor Link July 1996, p8; 'The Holy Father is very aware of the East Timorese situation' – Frs R.Cardoso and D.da Cunha, to the author, Rhode Island, Sept 1998; 'The Pope is an influential figure in international circles...[his] views on the East Timor question will continue to be an important guiding light pending a UN sanctioned settlement' – Muladi, leader of Indonesian National Commission for Human Rights, *Komnas Ham* – in 'Soares calls for US mediation', Indonesia Times/ *Antara/AFP*, 18.1997.

not more than, the deprivation of material goods?' he asks.[72] John Paul II also addressed the matter of human rights in his addresses for World Day of Peace when he attended to 'those caught in the midst of bitter conflicts, the marginalised, the victims of all kinds of exploitation, who craved for a life rooted in justice and genuine peace... There can be no complete justice unless everyone shares in it equally'. He also opposed the actions of those 'who attempt to weaken ethnic identity...or have recourse to violence as a means of resolving political and social problems'... and he urged 'the eradication of trafficking in arms.'[73] The derivation of human rights from the innate dignity of the human person in such Papal statements as these, and in the other sources of Catholic Social Doctrine, emphasise the 'universality and indivisibility' of their application. All such teaching is clearly pertinent to the situation experienced by the people of East Timor, among others, especially when the regime of Suharto's *Orde Baru* was one which sought to use cultural specificity as a justification for not abiding by such 'Western concepts'.

As happened with lesser Vatican officials, the Pope was subjected to diplomatic pressure by the governments of Indonesia (noted above) and Portugal[74], and both Portuguese and Indonesian officials claimed the Pope's support for their government's position with regard to East Timor's political status.[75] Conversely, John Paul II made repeated appeals to each country's leading ministers and to their ambassadors to effect a peaceful and just outcome to the contentious issue.[76] The Pope was also in receipt of numerous appeals from various quarters in East Timor itself and from Timorese refugees in the diaspora.[77] He addressed words of comfort to such exiles gathered in his presence at Fatima and in Rome, and via his representatives to the people of East Timor in the territory itself.[78] He gave much-appreciated personal

---

[72] Papal Encyclical *Solicitudo Rei Socialis* (1987), paragraph 15 and *passim*.

[73] Address for World Peace Day, January 1998. Full text in Briefing (BCEW), January 1998.

[74] e.g. 1) President Eanes raised concerns over any division of Dili diocese when the Pope visited Lisbon in 1982 (Budiardjo & Liem, 1984 op.cit.p122). 2) President Cavaco Silva pleaded for Church intervention to end the atrocities in East Timor at a papal audience (1987). 3) President Mario Soares criticised the 'silence of the Pope' as 'complicity in Indonesian aggression' (*Diario de Noticias* 10.5.1990, in *F&D* p437). In 1996 the Pope was pressured for support by the Portuguese Ambassador (text on file with the author) and by the Prime Minister (*Diario de Noticias*, Rome 29.3.1996); and in 1998 by the Foreign Minister (LUSA 9.3.1998).

[75] e.g. Portugal: 'Report by the Eventual Commission', Assembleia de Republica, Lisbon 1987, p15. Indonesia: Frans Seda asserted that the Pope had 'a positive attitude...as he is discussing East Timor with us' (Jakarta Post 17.12.1987; Timor Link 12/13, April 1988, p8); Others asserted that 'no mention of East Timor by the Pope in his New Year message is a positive development for Indonesia' (The Indonesian Times, *Antara*, AFP, etc 18.1.1997).

[76] e.g. To Portuguese envoys: 1993 (text in CCJPD 1993, op.cit. p58), 1996 (text in ETAN docs No43 p99; to Indonesian envoys: 1984, '87, '95 & '96 (see respectively: CCJPD 1993, op.cit p24-25; Timor Link Nos 12/13, April 1988, p8; ETAN Docs Vol 36, p70; citations in 'Timor time bomb ticks on' D.O'Grady, The Tablet, 1.6.1996, p724-5; LUSA, 24.12.1996), to Indonesian FM Ali Alatas 1995 (Cited in ETAN Docs Vol 22, p106)

[77] e.g. Letters from East Timorese protesting the removal of Mgr Costa Lopes (*Diario de Noticias*, interview with Mgr Lopes July 1983); Letter from priests in East Timor (Bibliography – General (E Timor); CIIR 1992, p9; Letters from Timorese in Australia: at time of the Pope's visit to South Pacific (May 1984) and during the Pope's visit to Australia 1986 (copies on file); etc. Young Timorese exiles in Portugal demonstrated during his visit to Lisbon in May 1991 (Portuguese Press 10.5.1991).

[78] e.g. At Fatima in May 1982 the Pope allowed simultaneous translation of the Mass into Tetun (*Pro Mundi Vita* 1984, p31). In Rome he addressed Timorese refugees at a General Audience in 1993, and 1995. In East Timor in 1997 the Pope sent a personal message expressing his concern for all to be read by his representative (bishop Maurilio Quintal de Gouveia of Evora, Portugal) at the installation of bishop Nascimento ('Pope speaks up on East Timor', John Aglionby, The Guardian (UK), Jakarta, 20.3.1997; Timor Link April 1997, p5). He had also heartened the clergy and people by his despatch of Cardinal Etchegaray a year earlier, as noted already.

support to bishop Belo[79], whose appointment he had also personally influenced[80], and was pleased by Belo's receipt of the Nobel Peace Prize in 1996 – not least, but not only, for the protection it afforded the Apostolic Administrator.[81]

The contrast between the Pope's address to successive Indonesian ambassadors in 1984 and 1987 is remarked upon by numerous authors who draw attention to the changed wording in the latter which eliminated all reference to East Timorese 'political' status and laid stress on their cultural and religious identity.[82] But attention must also be given to John Paul's statements in several of his annual addresses to the Vatican diplomatic corps. In 1992 he called for 'a persevering dialogue which will lay the foundations for a political and social life in harmony with the aspirations of the people'. In 1995 he referred to 'the distressing trials to which the East Timorese were still being subjected' and in 1996 to the people who were 'still waiting for proposals capable of allowing the realisations of their legitimate aspirations.' In this last text the reference was to the desirability of recognition of 'their special cultural and religious identity' but the Pope continued in a passage rich in overtones:

> We must admire and support the courage of the many men and women who manage to safe-guard the identity of their peoples and who hand on to the younger generations the torch of memory and hope.

It should be noted that in order to interpret the words of the Holy Father fairly it is necessary to be sensitive to the wider allusions, implications and echoes of his text as well as its bare bones. This is true of 'Vatican-speak' generally and is a matter which will be given some further consideration below in respect of the significance of the Pope's homily during his pastoral visit to East Timor in 1989.

Along with his practical appeals for a just resolution of the issue there was also the purely spiritual engagement of the Holy Father with the suffering East Timorese. On more than one occasion the Pope declared that he prayed for them 'every day'.[83] At the outbreak of the post ballot violence in 1999 he wrote to the bishops of East Timor:

> I am profoundly saddened that the glimmers of hope born of the recent popular consultation have been transformed into the terror of today which nothing and no one can justify... In these hours of suffering I send the expression of my spiritual closeness while remembering in my prayer those who have died, the injured, the refugees, the deportees, and all who are in distress...
> I call on everyone to cling to hope in the victory of the Cross, even as they are living once again the sorrowful experience of the Passion... It is my heartfelt wish that as soon as possible Indonesia and the International Community will put an end to the slaughter and find effective ways to meet the legitimate aspirations of the Timorese population.[84]

A few days later he was publicly very outspoken:

> I cannot keep quiet my profound bitterness for yet another defeat of any sense of humanity when, at the dawn of the Third Millennium, fratricidal hands are raised once more to kill and destroy without mercy...

[79] For examples see especially: Kohen, A. 1999 op.cit. pp 17, 124, 153, 205, 246.
[80] Salesian Provincial Mauricio de Bastos e Pinho to the author, Lisbon, June 1997.
[81] Kohen, A. 1999, op.cit. p243.

[82] See: *Tapol* Bulletin 85, Feb 1988, p14; Taylor, J.1992, op.cit.,p151f; Federer, 1994, op.cit.p40, etc.
[83] CAFOD field officer's interview with bishop Belo, Dili 1994; *Radio Renascenza* interview with John Paul II en route for the Azores, 12.5.1991 (copy of transcript on file).
[84] Source: Vatican Internet web site - 9.9.1999.

I express once again my complete reprobation for the grave human rights abuses perpetrated in that territory in the vain attempt to wipe out the desire expressed by the population and their legitimate aspirations...

I repeat my appeal to the responsible political and military parties and the international community to listen to the cries of the weak and defenceless and help them soon.[85]

When bishop Belo met with him in Rome after his escape from the post ballot violence and destruction his appreciation of John Paul II's contribution was quite unreserved: 'Thank you, thank you – for your concern, your prayers, your support and your solidarity.'[86]

The Papal Visits

Members of the East Timorese expatriate community in Australia, including Fr. Francisco Fernandes, sought to have an audience with Pope John Paul II during his pastoral visit in 1986. But the organisers did not accommodate their wishes on the grounds that Australia's multicultural composition made it impossible to satisfy such requests from the great many immigrant Catholic communities. In an open letter to the Holy Father the Timorese called for his help:

> We ask your Holiness to articulate an alternative to violence and political expediency...by strongly defending our people's rights as human beings ...to make our own decisions and to be East Timorese... and by impressing on the international community the necessity for a just solution based on our internationally recognised right to self determination. ... The only path to peace is the path of principle. It is our sincere belief that a clear enunciation of these principles by the international Catholic Church under your Holiness' leadership would breath new life into the UN process being pursued and significantly advance the cause of peace for our people.[87]

A significant dimension of the Pope's response to this appeal was his visit to Indonesia and to East Timor in 1989, although this was fraught with controversy as different interpretations were put upon the Holy Father's purpose and upon his every word and gesture by different parties to the issue.

John Paul II was invited to Indonesia as a guest of the government, but the pastoral character and purpose of his journey was emphasised by the Vatican at every opportunity. In his numerous addresses the pontiff sought to acknowledge the religious tolerance of the Indonesian Constitution and government, to encourage positive interdenominational and interfaith relations and remark upon the valuable contribution made to the development of Indonesian society by the Church and its institutions. He emphasised the necessity of 'respectful dialogue', 'the promotion of the common good', the need for 'human rights and freedoms to be defended' and for 'justice to be fostered'. His most direct challenge to the Suharto regime's *modus operandi* was made during the State Reception in Jakarta, its allusion to the East Timor situation in particular was indirect, but clear enough:

> At times nations are tempted to disregard fundamental human rights in a misguided search for political unity based on military or economic power alone. But such unity can easily be dissolved...As your national tradition teaches, the most secure basis for lasting unity and development as a nation is a profound respect for human life, for the inalienable rights of the human person, and for the freedom of responsible citizens to determine their destiny as a people...

---

[85] Reuters, Castelgandolfo, 12.9.1999.

[86] 'Pope meets with bishop Belo, hears accounts of violence in Timor', John Thavis, Catholic News Service, Castelgandolfo, 15.9.1999.

[87] 'Letter on behalf of the East Timorese in Australia' by Abel Guterres, Chairman Timorese Cultural & Information Centre, Collingwood, Australia, 17.11.1986 – copy on file with the author.

In acknowledging the presence of legitimate diversity, in respecting the human and political rights of all citizens, and in encouraging the growth of national unity based on tolerance and respect for others, you lay the foundations for that just and peaceful society which all Indonesians wish for themselves and long to bequeath to their children.[88]

Mixed reactions to the Pope's visit to East Timor were evident before, during and after it took place. The Indonesian authorities saw it as a diplomatic achievement that would confirm their policy of 'integration'.[89] The Portuguese were dismayed that the Pope went as a guest of the occupying power which they perceived as contradicting the Vatican's stated position on East Timorese status in the international community. They were also anxious about the violence that might be unleashed by the Indonesian military to keep the people subdued. Nonetheless it was hoped in Lisbon and by the Bishops Conference that the visit might change international passivity and promote the rights of the native people. The Nuncio was duly appraised of these concerns.[90]

In East Timor, and among expatriates, there was grave concern – and even considerable opposition to the Pastoral Visit. This was principally on the grounds that it would consolidate the Indonesian claim to sovereignty over the territory. A Letter from the laity observed that 'the visit of the Pope is the most important aim of the Indonesian government at this time' and the Association of Catholic Students 'strongly requested that the visit be cancelled'.[91] A group of clergy wrote to the Papal emissary Fr.Tucci in similar vein: 'Many wonder if the Holy Father is coming to conclude and approve the atrocious and unspeakable process of integration'.[92] They also expressed their anxiety about the pro-integration interpretations to the Portuguese bishops.[93] Some from within the Resistance wrote to the Portuguese President contesting the visit. From exile in Lisbon Mgr Costa Lopes uncharacteristically accused the Holy Father of 'obedience to the Indonesians' and denounced their attempt to use the visit to imply that East Timor was part of the Republic.[94] Mgr Belo felt it necessary to appeal for spiritual loyalty from all sections of the Catholic community in a special Pastoral Letter which assured everyone of the awareness the Pope had of the dangers of his visit being politicised. He emphasised that 'the Pope is above political parties, ideologies, worldly governments.'[95] Xanana Gusmao wrote to the Pope from his mountain hideout expressing the people's sorrow that they could not greet the Holy Father as they would wish but that they 'had confidence they will not be abandoned' and were 'looking forward to hearing a message of Peace for East Timor'. 'The guerrilla fighters' he declared, 'kneel before you and beg the protection of your blessing upon our struggle to liberate this country.'[96] Within the international solidarity movement there were considerable reservations and misgivings about the Papal Visit - listed succinctly by the Catholic Institute for International Relations:

---

[88] Texts of all the Papal Addresses in Indonesia in 'The Pastoral Journey of the Holy Father in the Far East and Mauritius', *Osservatore Romano* N43, 23rd October 1989, pp3ff.

[89] 'Indonesia counts on Pope's silence', Roy Eccleston, The Australian, 9.10.1989

[90] See, e.g. *O Jornal*, 7.4.1989; *O Independente*, 7.4.1989, 5.10.1989; *Diario de Noticias* 10.6.89; 28.6.1989, 312.8.1989; *O Seculo* 30.8.1989; *Jornal de Noticias* 15.6.1989; *F&D* pp 155, 157, 165, 172, 177, 180, 203-4, 222, 227.

[91] 'The Situation in East Timor', Letter received by various NGOs (e.g. in Australia and Japan) from East Timorese laity, Autumn 1989 – copy on file; 'Letter of Association of Catholic Students to Nuncio Canalini', 23.2.1989 – copy on file.

[92] Full text in 'Pilgrim Pope's road gets rockier', UNIYA, No6, Spring 1989, Melbourne; citations in Timor Link 18/19, Oct 1989, p5-6

[93] *Jornal de Noticias* & other media outlets 5.5.1989; *F&D*, p163.

[94] *Diario de Noticias*, *O Seculo*, etc. 11.7.1989, 12.10.1989; *F&D*, pp196, 227.

[95] Pastoral Letter on the Visit of the Holy Father, September 1989 – copy on file.

[96] For full text of Letter (5.11.89) see Bibliography – Ch2: Gusmao, X. 2000, pp137-8.

John Paul II is being welcomed in Indonesia as head of state hosted (not by the Indonesian Bishops Conference) but by the government... Many fear that Indonesia will exploit the visit as evidence that integration has been recognised by the Vatican – some believe the trip has been planned in a way that implies the Vatican has moved *de facto* towards such recognition... The ambiguities of Vatican policy hitherto have created unease in East Timor. ... Nonetheless, the Vatican is well informed and understands the alienation, anger and trauma of the Timorese people. [97]

In a lengthy 'Reflection' the East Timorese clergy expressed the hopes and fears of their people, concluding: 'This visit could be the salvation or the ruin, with catastrophic consequences, for this Christian community.' [98]

Media accounts of the Visit tended to be selective and partisan in their interpretations, and most concentrated on the demonstration courageously organised by young members of the Clandestine Resistance which was effectively mounted at the very front of the arena at Tacitolu as the Papal Mass ended.[99] Certainly the Indonesian authorities, and their Timorese appointees, did their utmost to make political capital at every opportunity and dismissed the demonstration as the work of an unrepresentative group.[100] Likewise, the Timorese majority opposed to 'integration' clutched at every straw of intimation that the Pope was 'on their side'.[101] Bishop Belo and the East Timorese clergy gained much encouragement from the Visit.[102] In Portugal, the press coverage was largely negative with cartoons lampooning John Paul II as Pontius Pilate.[103] Some among the solidarity groups campaigning around the world for the East Timorese cause were regretful that the Pope did not kiss the ground as he disembarked from the aircraft, a symbolic gesture with political connotations.[104] They also considered his homily as less than forthright, with its references to the need for 'reconciliation' revealing (they thought) the Pontiff's 'acceptance' of the prevailing situation.[105] Even seasoned observers were disappointed:

> The Pope's efforts to accommodate often conflicting expectations and to avoid offending his host, resulted in a cautious oblique approach to dominant issues like economic justice, human rights, and the future of East Timor...
> Positive points were made, but for the most part they were buried in a mosaic of appeals and cautions and lacked clarity and forcefulness...
> The visit will be remembered for the fact that the Pope came, not for what he said...
> But whatever the shortcomings and ambiguities of the Pope's visit, it confirmed that a fundamental problem still exists in East Timor and that the Church at its highest level acknowledges this.[106]

[97] Timor Link 18/19, Oct 1989, pp5-6.

[98] Full text in Bibliography – Ch8: CCJPD 1993, op.cit.p45.

[99] For detail see Bibliography –Ch2: Pinto, C. 1996, op.cit. pp106-114.

[100] See: 'Twenty Years of Occupation; Twenty Years of Resistance', 1995, *CDPM/Paz e Passivel em Timor Leste*, Lisbon, pp32-33; ET Governor Mario Carrascaleo, interview for UCANews Dispatch 529, Oct 19-25th, 1989, p5.

[101] See: CDPM remark in respect of 'A Priest comments' in Timor Link 20/21, Jan-Feb 1990.

[102] Bishop Belo, interviewed by Peter Philp for The Advocate, Archdiocese of Melbourne, Australia.

[103] *O Jornal* 20.10.1989; cf. *O Jornal*, 13.10.1989, *Expresso*, 19.10.1989

[104] The Pope himself had indicated that the gesture should not be understood in this way and was purely a pastoral act - an expression of love. In East Timor the political interpretation was inevitable and so the Pope avoided the gesture altogether and instead chose to kiss the cross placed on the steps of the altar at Tacitolu. See: 'The Kiss of the Pontiff', Asiaweek, Oct 27th, 1989, p26; Belo interview by Philp, The Advocate, op.cit.

[105] Full text of the Homily at Tacitolu, in CCJPD 1993, op.cit.p40-42. For critical analysis see 'Reading the Runes', Timor Link 20/21, Jan-Feb 1990, p5.

[106] 'The Pope rides the Indonesian rapids without rocking the boat', Pat Walsh, National Outlook, January 1990, p12-14

Nonetheless, most commentators recognised the fact that the Visit significantly raised the level of international awareness of the East Timor issue. This was irrespective of the extensive coverage given by the media to the demonstration at the end of the Papal Mass.[107] In itself this heightened awareness made the Visit of great value in the effort to secure a just and enduring settlement.[108] Moreover, some experienced analysts were of the view that 'the actual statements on East Timor were pretty strong...far tougher and more powerful than anything we anticipated. Obviously they will have an international resonance far greater than any other statements [of the Vatican] to date.'[109]

Despite such observations, when John Paul II made a pastoral visit to Portugal two years later there were further calls in the media for the Pope to 'denounce the situation in East Timor', and Timorese expatriates demonstrated, critical of his 'silence' about the matter and appealing for the Vatican to 'use its influence at the United Nations'.[110] En route to the Azores the Holy Father elaborated in a radio interview on the circumstances that had prevailed at the end of the Papal Mass in Dili and reiterated his commitment to the East Timorese cause:

> I went to East Timor not as a politician but as Pope and bishop, as pastor of the Church visiting the various Catholic communities... And that which I wish for that community – which I also said during my visit to Timor – is that it should be able to live in accord with its own principles and customs, its own language and culture...
>
> The political problem is a problem to be taken up in another place: the United Nations...
>
> I hope – I said this there and I must say it again here – that the problem of East Timor is resolved in accordance with the principles of justice, of human and national rights... But I must stress one thing: if you talk about forgetting about Timor, then that does not correspond with my true feelings, because I say a special prayer for that island every day. [111]

Evaluation of the Papal Visit to East Timor depends largely upon the interpretation that is placed upon John Paul II's homily at the Mass outside Dili. There were many people who were critical of its apparent weakness, seeing it as the expression of a desire to seek peace in East Timor at any price, without regard to the justice of the settlement. Such a view assumed that the Vatican itself was reconciled to Indonesia's incorporation of East Timor, and that Vatican policy was designed essentially to shorten the period of transition before the incorporation could be recognised and thereby reduce the suffering of the people.

But a more positive (and arguably more justifiable) interpretation of the homily sees it as recognising not only the ongoing suffering of the people but also the deep divisions within their society, exacerbated by the civil war and by the oppressive occupation.[112] These were matters being addressed at the time by bishop Belo himself and also by the leadership within the East Timorese Resistance who were earnestly seeking a 'national consensus'. In this analysis the reconciliation that the Pope urged is presented in its local context and understood to be pointing up the precondition for the long-term survival of East Timor's culture and people. In other words, John Paul was addressing an urgent and fundamental need for (political) unity, realising that this would remain unattainable unless the bitter divisions of the past were

---

[107] e.g. Kohen, A. 1999, op.cit.p146.

[108] Philp, P., 'Reflection on the E.Timor situation after the Papal Visit', CCJPD 1993, p46-48.

[109] Kohen, A. 1989, East Timor Research Project, Letter to CAFOD, 25.10.1989; cf. Kohen, A. 1999, op.cit., Introduction and pp144-146.

[110] *Publico*, *Diario de Noticias*, etc., 10.5.1991; *Expresso*, *A Capital*, *Jornal de Noticias*, etc., 11.5.1991, cited in *F&D*, op.cit.pp437-8, 440.

[111] John Paul II, interviewed by *Radio Renascenza*, 12.5.1991.

[112] See: 'Reading the Runes', Timor Link 20/21, Jan-Feb 1990, p5.

acknowledged and overcome.[113] Furthermore, such an achievement would necessarily be a human process of healing – interior and social - as much as a political process of development. Expressed in *moral* rather than *political* terms it *required* the profoundly difficult act of comprehending and forgiving others: reconciliation.

With hindsight it can now be recognised that it was their growing unity of opposition to Indonesian rule which ultimately enabled the East Timorese to oust the forces of occupation and to be victorious in their resistance to all the other factors which militated against their national identity and aspirations. History may come to judge more favourably than did many contemporary commentators the contribution of Pope John Paul II and the impact of his Pastoral Visit upon the eventual outcome of the East Timor issue.

The Response of the Vatican – an Evaluation

An application of the criteria delineated in Part One of this thesis serves only to highlight the ambiguity of the Vatican's response to the East Timorese plight. Examination of the attitudes and actions evident at each level of the operation of the Holy See reveals a diversity of approach, or at least a lack of clarity, that inevitably gave rise to misunderstanding among those seeking to discover where the Vatican stood.

This confusion arose in part from misinterpretation by outsiders unfamiliar with the language or the main thrust of Vatican statements which can be better understood when placed in the context of the whole *corpus* of the Church's Social Doctrine as it has developed and been expressed since *Rerum Novarum*. Nonetheless, it was also generated by a lack of consistency within the practice or in the public statements of Vatican officials.

No doubt the security and development of the Indonesian Church was of strategic importance in the Vatican's religious project, but Vatican teaching surely demanded commitment to justice for the East Timorese as an oppressed and marginalised people. Fidelity to this teaching also required unequivocal support of the local Church that was their principal defender against all kinds of human rights violation and abuse. Social Doctrine stresses a preferential option for the poor and is supposedly rooted in respect for the human person. It calls for every effort to ensure that the individual and social rights which derived from that humanity are upheld, and for solidarity to be expressed with those suffering from injustices and exploitation such as arise from the operations of an illegitimate and repressive regime. But the Apostolic Administrators of the diocese of Dili were each distressed in their turn by the apparent neglect by the Universal Church of 'the little people' to whom they ministered and whose innate dignity as human beings they sought to defend.

Certainly there were efforts made by individuals at every level of the Vatican's operation to effect a peaceful settlement of the East Timor issue and bring an end to the suffering of the native people. Such efforts included both prayer and practical action and were carried out by the Pope himself and by his various officials, envoys and diplomats. It is probably true to say that the actions of the Vatican to effect a satisfactory resolution of the problem were ahead of those of many governments. But the Vatican was arguably in a better position than any other agency in the world to know the truth of the situation prevailing in East Timor. Perhaps

---

[113] See:

(1) Belo, Pastoral Letter, Lent 1984 - 'The culture of love and forgiveness must replace the culture of hate and mutual elimination...We either unite and so exist as a Church and a people or we wipe each other out and disappear as a Church and a people'. cf. Belo's Christmas Homily (1994) and his Letter to UN Secretary General (1989) - both cited above, Ch 5 - which also contributed to the unification of the East Timorese political community.

(2) Xanana Gusmao's comment on the Pope's homily was significant - but can be interpreted either way: 'The message of reconciliation given in Tacitolu was, in my opinion, a political speech recognising the existing situation in East Timor, because the very fact of having agreed to come, and under the conditions that we all know about, constitutes a political position.' (*Diario de Noticias* 27.10.1992).

the best use was indeed made of this information in a discreet and productive diplomacy largely hidden from the public eye - but the difficulty of discovering and evaluating this usage arises precisely from its discreet nature. Certainly there was a gathering momentum of support for the East Timorese within Vatican circles over the course of time as their situation did not improve and their resistance to Indonesian rule became more unified and internationally acknowledged. Yet it seems regrettable that the Vatican's unique insight into the distressful realities of the Indonesian administration of East Timor was not communicated more fully through media outlets, including those of the Church itself. No doubt it was important to preserve the Church's political 'impartiality', but at the same time its own Social Doctrine required a strong and clear expression of support for the right of the vulnerable and voiceless East Timorese to a political outcome that was truly just. Silence, or ambiguity, amounted in effect to complicity with the actions of the Indonesian oppressors.

When the measure of the Vatican's official teaching is applied there seems to have been much contradiction and inconsistency both in what was said and what was done by officialdom. In fact overall there appears to have been a distinct bias by the Vatican in favour of protecting the welfare of the Church in Indonesia despite the negative consequences this had for the Church and people of East Timor. There were cogent and powerful pragmatic reasons for the Vatican's posture. But the Church should be the last organisation in the world to be falling back on pragmatic arguments when its moral claim is that it stands for absolute and constant values against the relativistic ethos of the age. Evidently the principles of the Church's Social Doctrine are not easily applied in practice – especially when this would seemingly conflict with religious objectives such as the security and expansion of the Church in a region of strategic importance.

Whatever justifications can be provided for the Holy See's behaviour in respect of the East Timor issue there remains much force in the challenge of the Catholic campaigner and Vatican critic who remarked:

> Surely the Church derives its strength and ensures its future, not through a foreign policy based on rational calculations of convenience, but by being consistent with its mission, and truly identifying with the just aspirations and sufferings of its people.[114]

---

[114] Bibliography – Ch5: Federer, J. 1994 op.cit.p43.

CONCLUSION

The Response of the Church to the East Timor issue – an Overview

Evidence has been put forward to show that the Religious working in East Timor, and other leaders of the local Church, along with the people whom they sought to serve, had good reason to express their sense of being abandoned by the Universal Church and by the Catholic community in other, even neighbouring, countries. It has been demonstrated that in fact the solidarity they desired was not lacking but, with notable exceptions, it was late in coming, and was not consistently expressed at any level or circle of the Church's operation. The response of the Church cannot be described as a corporate effort. Nonetheless the Catholic community abroad played a significant even crucial part in the eventual liberation of the East Timorese people.

Some of the responses discovered within the local Churches studied were based on their thorough research of the situation in East Timor, and were executed with dedication and often with considerable courage. These should be acknowledged - not only for the support they gave to the East Timorese, but for the inspiration they gave to others outside the Catholic community of faith to take up and persistently advocate the East Timorese cause. Among the various activities pursued was the amassing and collation of evidence in respect of human rights violations in East Timor from 1974-99, undertaken by Church personnel in the territory itself and abroad. This was surely one of the most important efforts made on behalf of the indigenous people's welfare - in the past and for their future.

But other responses were uncertain, partial, or partisan, serving to compound or to continue rather than to confront the injustice of the situation. Humanitarian concern was demonstrated from early on, and considerable energy was expended over the years to advance local religious and social development. But advocacy of the rights of the East Timorese to political self-determination and genuine participation in the political process were not addressed as vigorously, as directly, or as publicly, as was necessary and possible. Yet the violation and neglect of these rights were fundamental to their distress and lay at the root of other abuses of their human dignity.

To be sure, a range of responses are appropriate for an organisation such as the Church - from formal statements and declarations through to purely spiritual activities which bear witness to the possibility of 'an alternative history', and including co-operation with secular groups in political activism. But shortcomings on the part of Church leaders (both clerical and lay) meant that the body of the faithful were not always provided with the clear direction they needed, and also diminished the confidence of activists within and outside the community of the Church. Believers were commonly concerned with their own welfare, or anxious to safeguard the work of the Church in their own part of the world.

Most regrettably there were some individual Catholics, and some agencies within the hierarchical structure of the institutional Church – as well as some Catholic organisations outside of it - whose activity presented an obstacle to a just and peaceful settlement of the issue. Indeed, there were those who even contributed to, or whose reaction prolonged, the anguish of the people of East Timor both in their home country and abroad.

Some explanations have been provided for the variegation of the Church's response. Although it is a global organisation with a central focus in the Vatican the Church is internally differentiated with national and regional expressions including episcopal groupings which are affected by local conditions and preoccupations. The distinctive ecclesiastical ethos evident in the various countries studied was a factor in the inadequate understanding of the East Timorese plight which was apparent (even on the part of close neighbours) and which presented a barrier to fruitful inter-communication. Some observers might perceive a Church that is fragmented. Because of the enduring structural and communications links between the Vatican and the local Churches - and between these Churches - which have been observed, the author would consider this view to be a distortion of the reality. But there can be little doubt that the Church is not as monolithic as some (even within its fellowship) would assume or (perhaps) wish. With its many levels or circles of operation from parish faithful through various institutions to the Vatican at 'centre-top' the Church is internally complex. At the highest or most central level there were inconsistencies and a failure to measure up in practice to the standards declaimed in theory. Efforts towards a settlement of the issue were characterised more by the desire for 'peace' than for the justice upon which that would depend. Within the national Churches some individuals bravely demonstrated their readiness for self-sacrifice on behalf of the East Timorese cause, but only in East Timor itself was there such a commitment by the institution itself. Evidently the Church has internal self-contradictions – which it seems comfortable with.

Besides these internal factors, political realities such as the strategic priorities of governments and their institutions, nationally and internationally, obviously affected the response of which the Church was capable. These have been described in respect of some of the countries with an important connection to the East Timor issue, and with regard to the international reaction. However, these considerations do not excuse the Church in such countries from action, they should even have provoked it - and there were instances when that was indeed the case. Moreover, the developments in International Law, attention to which the Church continually invites from the nations of the world, did not feature as significantly or as consistently as might be expected in respect of its own public response to the situation in East Timor.

Another pertinent factor was the disposition of the mass media towards the East Timorese plight. Often this presented a barrier to communication rather than a means of a fuller understanding of the issue, for the reasons outlined and exemplified. But the Church had access to information not afforded to secular agencies. It is to be regretted not only that this knowledge was not more widely disseminated, but that the Church did not prove itself to be outstanding as 'the voice of the voiceless', a function it recognises as belonging to its Gospel mission to the poorest and most vulnerable. By and large the coverage given to the East Timor issue was led by secular agencies in the print and electronic media, with notable exceptions. But this is a subject deserving fuller exploration than was possible in the present work.

The interests of commercial corporations, especially those intent upon exploiting mineral reserves or promoting arms sales, had significant impact upon the course of events. There were admirable instances of a prophetical critique by various individuals and groups within the Church in respect of these practices. There were also efforts by some Church leaders and official agencies to bring such corporations into a heightened ethical awareness, and to encourage greater 'corporate responsibility' on the part of investors. But more generally, in its application of the principles of its own Social Doctrine to these matters in the specific issue under study, the response of the Church overall was far from unequivocal.

Catholics were often active within secular non-governmental organisations expressing solidarity with the suffering East Timorese people, and some agencies of national hierarchies collaborated closely with such groups in advocacy of the Timorese cause and in humanitarian provision. The information exchanged between these organisations enabled both to be more effective in their work. But the biased, mixed or hesitant messages that came from some Church officials scandalised secular activists. At the same time the insensitivity of some of these groups to the broad institutional responsibilities of the Church and to its religious objectives, the tendency of some to exploit the Church's moral capital, and their sometimes narrow agenda made Church officials wary of too close a partnership. This again is a subject that warrants a further exploration not possible here.

The Practice of Catholic Social Doctrine

Presenters of the Social Doctrine of the Church commonly refer to it as the 'hidden gem' or 'best kept secret' of Catholic Teaching. The Doctrine is extolled for its logical coherence and sophistication, its all-encompassing range, and its pertinence for our contemporary 'post-modern' (Western) society - which is judged to be standing direction-less in its search for some moral and social bedrock on which to build and sustain its way of life and institutions. Dialogue with that society, characteristically pluralist and secular, is seen as essential in the matter of discerning and upholding values that can be shared by all as foundational and enduring, but the Doctrine is considered to offer 'useful tools to make progress in human affairs'.[1] These are lofty claims.

There is no doubt that the Doctrine has arisen out of historical circumstances, responding to specific situations, as well as from the Gospel vision. It is not purely conceptual but is grounded in actuality. Furthermore, its moral judgements on what is good and fitting for the social welfare of human beings have a universal character, rooted as they are in the dignity of the human person. They are supposedly binding upon the conscience of Catholics. However, 'their application depends upon reading the signs of the times, which is not an exact science and allows for different interpretations and revision in the light of further experience and knowledge'.[2] The question has to be asked whether Catholic Social Doctrine can fit in with the realities of the working Church in the contemporary world. Can it be applied to complex issues? Is it susceptible to various interpretations, finessing, and evasions? Is the actual practice of its teaching too much to expect of flawed human beings and of a Church that shares in the sinful human condition? The specific issue of East Timor has been revealing.

In the first place it is obvious that the Church's Doctrine, irrespective of its logical coherence, scriptural foundations, or historical origins, was not compelling in its moral force even upon the consciences of those within the community of the Church itself (still less outside of it). The spectrum of responses to the East Timor situation at every level or circle of the Church's life has been described in detail.

Secondly, this study has repeatedly shown that action for 'social justice' is far from recognised as part and parcel of the life of every local Catholic community. Although it was the bishops in Synod (1971) who recognised action for social justice as being a 'constitutive dimension' of faithfulness to the Gospel, bishops (for example, in England) were also quick to elaborate on the 'practical difficulties of applying Gospel values, honoured in the abstract, to specific situations'. Their placing of the task of the 'transformation of human society' upon the laity while pledging themselves 'to keep in mind the need to find the right means for effective action' indicates that Social Doctrine provides no handy rule to resolve each dilemma that comes along.[3]

Thirdly, the manner in which Social Doctrine was applied indicates that while it can indeed be useful, it can also provide a means of evading responsibility. Thus in East Timor the Church was able to find support (and some protection) for its actions in defence of the local people by reference to these official prescripts of the Vatican. Meanwhile in Indonesia the Bishops Conference used high-sounding phraseology from the documents to distance themselves from the issue. Papal Envoys to Jakarta (and elsewhere), and officials of certain social development agencies established by the hierarchy in various countries including Australia and (for a while) the United States, felt it proper to urge general accommodation to the (unjust) *status quo*.

Fourthly, as the historical background to the response of the Church in Portugal and Australia to the East Timor issue has shown, application of the principles of Social Doctrine can generate social entities which are far from its intentions. Thus in Portugal before the Second World War Salazar's interpretation of the Papal Encyclicals brought into existence his authoritarian *Estado Nuovo* regime which protected the institutional interests of the Church but held back national development and neglected the poor. In due course this circumstance affected the response of the Portuguese Church and people to the East Timorese plight. After World War II the well-meaning initiatives of Bob Santamaria in Australia to combat the assertion of Communism were perceived as a threat to the authority of the bishops and caused

[1] Bibliography – Ch4: 'Towards a New Politics', Vallely. P., in Vallely, P. 1998; and see e.g. Schultheis, M.J., DeBerri, E.P., & Henriot, P.J. 1988.
[2] Bibliography – Ch4: Charles, R. *SJ*, 1999.
[3] CBCEW 1980 *Report of the National Pastoral Congress*, p378.

profound disunity within the national Church. Eventually they gave rise to a right wing lay organisation, the National Civic Council, which saw Communist activity in East Timor where none existed – with dire consequences for the hapless people there.

As noted already, there is the question of cultural pertinence. Further elaboration of this issue is to follow later in this text.

Another consideration is the status that has actually been given to the Church's Social Doctrine within the operation of the Vatican itself. Despite the Doctrine's 'logically coherent system' the actual response of officialdom to the East Timorese plight lacked both vigour and consistency. There is a special obligation upon the Universal Church to speak up for 'the little people', but the response within the Vatican was pragmatic as much as it was principled - giving rise to much confusion and disappointment in East Timor and to justifiable criticism within the international solidarity movement. Several Papal Nuncios, supposedly concerned with furthering the *mission* of the Church, seemed pre-occupied with protecting its *social welfare* in their relations with the nation-states to which they were accredited. As has been noted (in Chapter 12), high-ranking representatives of the Pontifical Commission for Justice and Peace have remarked that the influence of the Commission within the overall Vatican operation is not strong. Even the posture adopted by the members of the powerful United States National Conference of Bishops in respect of social justice issues is detrimentally affected by Vatican policy priorities. It was also in the United States, as well as in Indonesia, Portugal, Australia, and in East Timor itself, that the teaching of Social Doctrine regarding the iniquity of Communism gave ideological support to Jakarta's project in the former Portuguese colonial territory. The proposals made by the Vatican Mission at the United Nations were in advance of those made by many governments and non-governmental organisations, and its efforts were appreciated by UN officials – but the discreet manner of the Mission's operation makes it difficult to evaluate its contribution objectively.

Finally, there was evidence of a conflict of interests between the strategic religious aspirations of the Universal Church and the principles of its Social Doctrine. Hopes for the conversion of Indonesia (and neighbouring countries) seemed to some to be put at risk by any advocacy of the East Timorese claim to political independence while their incorporation into the Indonesian State might have strengthened the Catholic presence among predominantly Muslim peoples. But Social Doctrine called upon the Church to prioritise the needs of the poor, the vulnerable, the marginalised, the abandoned – which was indeed the condition of the people in East Timor during the period under study, and in some respects remains so.

On the other hand, evidence has been provided of individuals at every level of the Church's life, acting personally or in the name of official Church agencies, who lived out the Doctrine in practice with zeal and fortitude, disregarding their own safety. Such people furthered the Church's mission in the world for they were true to the Gospel call to self-sacrifice, and their activities did much for the good name of the Church among those who do not share its faith. Nowhere was this more apparent than in East Timor, and it is an important reason for that Church's remarkable growth among the local people during the years of their oppression. There were also some actions taken by some episcopal conferences, and by some of the agencies that they had established or supported, and by groups of Catholic activists in various countries, which were of significant importance in the defence and eventual liberation of the East Timorese people.

The Future Role of the Church in East Timor

At the time of writing, the socio-political situation in the half-island territory is in a period of flux. On October 25th 1999 the United Nations Transitional Administration in East Timor (UNTAET) was evoked by the Security Council (UNSC Res.1272) and entrusted with the task of laying the foundations for reconstruction and with preparing the country for independence. UNTAET facilitated the election of an Assembly charged with the preparation of a national Constitution. This democratically appointed group of East Timorese immediately took on many responsibilities of Government and became the first National Parliament when

Independence was declared on May 20th 2002. A month earlier Xanana Gusmao had been elected to be the first President of the new nation by an overwhelming majority of the people in a direct ballot. President and Government are faced by the huge task of building up the new nation virtually 'from zero'. Meanwhile the local Church must adapt to the developing situation and observers and commentators have remarked upon its present and future role with a mixture of hope and anxiety.[4]

The Church in East Timor is again having to 'listen like a disciple' in order to learn what should be its proper function within the new social order. There are various questions being raised. Will (indeed, should) the Church continue to be the bearer of the national cultural identity? What is its place in the national reconstruction? Can it – should it – offer proposals for the socio-economic field? The Church has had to ask what should be its relationship with the newly emerging/reviving political parties, with the temporary UN administration, and (now) with the elected government of *Timor Leste* (as the sovereign nation is now called). There are important social justice issues to be resolved. These include the pursuit of justice in respect of those who committed, and those who suffered human rights violations during the years of the Indonesian occupation. What should be the relationship of the Church with foreign governments and with the international agencies assisting in social restoration and development? There are aspects of the Church's traditional position in East Timorese society – such as its large land holdings, its relations with the peasantry, and its attitude towards the place of women and their participation in the decision-making process that must be reviewed. For a generation the Church in East Timor has operated in comparative isolation, thrust into the responsibility of being the defender of East Timorese identity and human dignity, the moral bulwark of the Resistance, and the sole institutional expression of East Timorese society. How will it operate within a democratic and increasingly pluralist (and perhaps secularist) State upon which foreign (Western) practices and values will surely impact? What are the new questions that the local Church's theology must address? What will be its new ethical discourse?

While it is too soon as yet to be passing judgements on these matters there is some evidence of a positive response within the local Church.[5] On health grounds bishop Belo resigned his office on November 26th 2002 but he has continued, along with current Church leaders in East Timor, to propose ideals and criteria by which successive political and social developments can be evaluated.[6] Subject matter has included human rights, democracy, reconciliation, the plight of East Timorese refugees, health care, and the general role of the Church in the new order. A priest, Filomeno Jacob *SJ*, held the portfolio of social affairs in the temporary UNTAET Cabinet but withdrew from such office in the transitional government (Constitutional Assembly) in order that separation is maintained between Church and State. The Church made its contribution to the composition of the national Constitution and has called for monitoring of the negotiations with Canberra regarding the exploitation of the mineral resources of the Timor Gap.[7]

---

[4] e.g.: 'East Timor's Transformation into global capitalist outpost', Aditjondro, G.J., 2000. email Conference >reg.easttimor.igc.apc.org< ; Bibliography – General (East Timor): CIIR 2001, p40.

[5] e.g. The following articles by bishop Belo: 'Freedom is not enough', Washington Post 18.5.02; 'My hopes for my nation', The Tablet (UK) 1.6.02; 'Much done but much still to do', International Herald Tribune 30.8.02; 'The next step for East Timor', Boston Globe 5.10.02.

[6] see: Bibliography – Ch5: Belo, C.F.X. 2001: 'Peace Building in East Timor: the role and contribution of the Church', a talk delivered on behalf of Bishop Belo to the Nobel Centennial Symposium in Oslo, December 2001, Timor Link, No 55, March 2002, pp5-8. Diocese of Dili/Baucau Statements: *The Constitution-Making Process in Timor Lorosae: the Church's Position* (2001) – in Timor Link, No 53 (August 2001), pp4-5; *Pastoral Statement for the Election of the Constituent Assembly*, Diocese of Dili, 15.8.01 copy on file.

[7] Sources: RDP Antena 1 Radio, Lisbon, 11.9.01; *Suara Timor Lorosae*, Dili, 3.2.01; 'Bishop of Dili calls for independent control of Timor Sea oil', AFP 29.1.03.

The Church is also participating in the activity of a new national institution – *Comissao de Acolhimento Verdade e Reconciliacao de Timor Leste (CAVR)*, the Commission on Reception, Truth and Reconciliation in East Timor. At the time of writing, Dili Diocesan priest Fr Jovito de Araujo is undertaking the role of Deputy Chairperson. This organisation aims to effect harmonious social relations by seeking the truth in respect of both perpetrators and victims of past humans rights violations and proposing appropriate responses. Besides its participation in this ongoing process the Church's resource of respected pastors, women and men, is also deployed less formally - and in association with village leaders and communities engaging in the traditional methods of conflict resolution. The new nation is faced with the problem of how best to respond to the 'various forms of crimes and violations committed' in the territory since Portugal withdrew in mid-1975. In a 'Pastoral Appeal on Amnesty and the Settlement of Crimes against Humanity' published in Dili on June 29th 2002 bishop Belo presented on behalf of the local Church some practical proposals to be carried out in East Timor itself.[8] He has also supported the call for an International Tribunal to address the crimes against humanity perpetrated against the East Timorese people by agencies of the Jakarta regime from 1975-1999.[9] Repeated efforts have been made by Church leaders to facilitate the repatriation or resettlement of deportees languishing in camps in West Timor. The Church's particular witness may well be in 'the identification of those points at which repentance needs to be made and forgiveness received, and which can be a birthplace for hope'. Its religious ministry will properly include dealing with sins to be repented of, and its social vocation will be to 'transcend the walls of enmity' between those formerly in political opposition. The 'power of the Cross' should enable the Church to continue to be an agent for peace and justice.[10]

Much Church property was destroyed in the post-ballot mayhem in 1999, but its infrastructure is still well established and the Church can capitalise on the confidence of the people that it evoked during the many years of oppression. As an institution the Church continues to be engaged extensively in education and health care provision.[11]

In general the Church appears to be addressing its responsibilities in the matter of 'nation building' – offering its contribution towards the development of law, the economy, and the protection of human rights. Some analysts have suggested that, in order to retain the goodwill and confidence of people within an emergent democratic society, the Church will need to relinquish some of its public power and prestige. Yet it must remain in active solidarity with all those processes that seek to overcome poverty and promote justice and ethical ideals.[12] The Church will also need to act more ecumenically, and with other faith communities (small though they are at present), and in collaboration with national (and international) non-governmental organisations.

Theologically the Church in East Timor should seek to offer a vision of personal and social integration which challenges the *status quo*, and points towards the still-to-be-realised Kingdom of God while offering concrete and sensitive proposals to meet the specific needs of the time. But 'such a theology can only emerge from a thorough and careful understanding of

---

[8] See also: 'No amnesty for crimes against humanity, says E Timorese bishop', CNS 8.7.02; 'No automatic amnesty, says E Timor bishop', The Universe (UK) 14.7.02.

[9] 'An International Tribunal for the restoration of the dignity of humanity', Diocese of Dili, 27th August 2002; this text published also in Timor Link (CIIR, UK) No 56, October 2002, p2-3. See also: 'Nobel Laureate appeals for East Timor', AP, Sydney, 23.4.01.

[10] See Bibliography – Ch5: Smythe, P. 1995, 'The Crucifixion of East Timor'; citations from (Bibliography - General Theology): Clements, K. 1995, p171.

[11] e.g. The Church is undertaking information on HIV/Aids via its network of clinics, and it is a participant in the Timorese led National Steering Committee for Civic Education. Sources: Suara Timor Lorosae, Dili 26.6.01; UNTAET Daily Briefing, 20.8.01.

[12] See: Clements, K. 1995 op.cit.Ch.7.

the nature of the society it is seeking to address. In this sense, it is marked by contextual particularity, while drawing on historical and global insights as a basis for providing a thoughtful and critical social ethic'.[13] The Church's efforts must surely be rooted in prayer, which will evoke its engagement in socio-political affairs and also be the source of that prophetic spirit which can present a critique of the social order that is truly in accordance with the mind and heart of God.[14]

There is no doubt that the political leadership in East Timor desire that the Church be involved in the building of the nation:

> We urge the Catholic Church in East Timor to fully engage itself once again in the process of restoring values that once sustained this society. Without values society will perish...We will set up the institutional mechanisms to ensure consultation with all religious confessions. However, we appeal to the Catholic Church to play a leading role in the fields of education and health...
> The tradition, the institutional structures and experience of the Catholic Church in East Timor are precious assets in the restoration of the ethics needed to develop our new Nation.[15]

> We have to start everything (and) the Church can help this process in a very important way. East Timor's society is still only an 'embryo'. I register here my enormous appreciation for their dedication to the civic education process, in providing to our people the necessary information and support for a better understanding of the importance of their participation in the democratic way of life. ...Now the Church must play an equally important part in building an independent nation. ...The Church has no bias, and people believe in it.
> I see a very important role for the Church in giving a message to the people, not only with respect to democracy, but also to give confidence to people as individuals or as groups.[16]

The Future Role of the Universal Church

Solidarity from neighbouring Churches and the Universal Church is still needed for the people of East Timor. This is not only in the matter of support for the local Church in its religious activity, and in the provision of humanitarian relief and assistance, though all these will remain necessary for years to come. It is also with regard to the advocacy in the international community of East Timorese human rights. These still include the repatriation/resettlement of many thousands of East Timorese refugees in West Timor and elsewhere in Indonesia, and the pursuit of justice in respect of the perpetrators of crimes against humanity committed in the homeland during the Indonesian occupation.

More generally, this investigation has revealed that there is considerable discrepancy between the principles of social justice delineated in Catholic Doctrine and their practice in the life of the Church in the world. Corporate endeavour in such matters is yet to be achieved, even within national boundaries, or by local communities of Catholics. Greater faithfulness to the social implications of the Gospel is obviously desirable - but this is not simply a matter of more conscientious study of the Doctrine or of more wholehearted obedience to its tenets by believers at every level and circle of the Church's operation. Clearly the very manner in which the Doctrine is formulated and effected must also be addressed. Before giving some attention to this issue it is important to note and comment upon certain factors that have inhibited the practice of its principles.

---

[13] Bibliography – General Theology: Villa-Vicencio, C. 1992, p275.
[14] Bibliography – General Theology: 'Between Prayer and Politics', in Hastings, A 1995, Ch2 especially pp19-20.
[15] Mari Alkatiri (Head of Government), Address at the Swearing in of Members of the Transitional Government of East Timor, 21.9.01. e-Conference > east-timor@igc.topica.com <
[16] Xanana Gusmao – acceptance speech following his election as President 14.4.02. He took his oath of office 19.5.02 prior to the declaration of East Timor's statehood. CNS, (Dili) 26.5.02.

One such factor has been the evident tendency of many clergy and laity to urge 'prudence' with regard to public action in socio-political affairs. There are certainly circumstances in which the Church finds itself where restraint and discretion are the better part of valour – in his homilies and speeches bishop Belo often urged prudence so that the local Church and the people it served should not be exposed unnecessarily to further suffering. But he was fearless in advocating the right of the Church to challenge injustice, and in defence of the personal and social rights of the East Timorese that derived from their human dignity. All too often, as this study has revealed, the alleged 'prudence' on the part of Church leaders and members amounted only to timidity. It was either simply self-preserving, or demonstrated an unwarranted conviction that disassociation from contentious issues, or inaction in their respect, will safeguard (and so prolong) the pastoral work of the Church in its social milieu. But the Catechism of the Catholic Church states clearly:

> Prudence is not to be confused with timidity or fear, nor with duplicity or dissimulation...Prudence [should] guide the judgement of conscience.
> With the help of this virtue we apply moral principles to particular cases without error and overcome doubts about the good to achieve and the evil to avoid.[17]

Regarding the issue of East Timor there were many instances within the Church around the world where the virtue of prudence thus defined was evidently lacking.

Another barrier to effective action by the Church in solidarity with one of the poorest, and most defenceless and abandoned people on the planet was the occasions when pragmatism was preferred to principle. Certainly the Church has to act in ways that promise a positive outcome, and carefully, with an eye to all the consequences of its practical action. But, as the Australian government (for example) was eventually to discover in respect of its policy vis-à-vis Indonesia and East Timor, the consequences of unprincipled decisions can also be highly damaging to good relations in the longer term:

> The single most important lesson [from Australian – Indonesian relations 1975-1999] is that the people who say they are being pragmatic are often being too blinkered, too myopic about what constitutes pragmatism, and are sometimes underestimating the importance of principle in determining what is likely to be pragmatic in the long run.[18]

It has been remarked that 'the Church has to be practical – but not unscrupulous; to take complexity into account – but not lose its way'.[19] In the view of this author there were too many instances in the story of the Church's response to the East Timorese plight when its representatives throughout the institution and community lost their way, or at least were not facing in the right direction. As has been noted already, the Church claims to uphold constant and absolute values – and its practice should be at all times consistent with the ideals of its mission. This study has a number of implications for Catholic Social Doctrine, and for its theological basis.

Implications for Catholic Social Doctrine

The argument of this text is rooted in the statement of the Synod of Bishops (1971) that work for social justice is an essential dimension of the Church's mission in the world. But it has called into question the credibility of the Church as a moral authority in social issues. The shortcomings that have been revealed between the principles and practice of the Church's Social Doctrine suggest a number of positive measures be taken to remedy this situation.

---

[17] Catechism of the Catholic Church (1995), Vatican, paragraph 1806.
[18] Rodney Tiffen, author of *Diplomatic Deceits – Government, Media and East Timor* (Bibliography Ch3), in interview for 'Asia-Pacific Report' ABC (Radio), Sydney, 28.5.2001.
[19] Professor Haddon Willmer, Dept of Theology, University of Leeds, to the author September 2001.

There must be greater dialogue on social issues within the family of the Church and between the Church and the society in which it lives both locally and globally. This would encourage the kind of productive co-operation that is required. Within such a dialogue it will be helpful to avoid the language of dogmatism.

There is no doubt that the insights and experience of regional Churches should be given every consideration because they can enrich Catholic Social Doctrine in its theory and in its practice. Yet the leaders and their advisers of such regional churches have also recognised the shortfall in their achievements in respect of social justice issues in general.[20] That this was the case with regard to the East Timor situation has been indicated by the account in this thesis of the response of two national Churches of the Asian region, those of Indonesia and Japan. Indeed, bishop Belo was still appealing for help from the Asian Bishops by the time of the Special Synod in Rome in 1998.[21] In fact, the Church in East Timor had relied on the texts of Social Doctrine which had arisen from Western culture – not one of its published documents cited any of the Statements of the Federation of Asian Bishops Conferences. Of course, the participation of the Church in East Timor in the Oriental ecclesial development was limited by its colonial/ecclesiastical history – and by its current political isolation. Moreover, the principal secular powers with an influence on the political outcome were Western countries where local Churches (to the extent described) brought their own 'regional' heritage of Social Doctrine to bear upon the issue. Nonetheless, this all serves to indicate that more is needed for the Doctrine's theoretical and practical enhancement than attention to the pronouncements of other regional hierarchies.

It is important to recall that the formulation of Catholic Social Doctrine was stimulated from the outset by the organised efforts of the laity attempting to deal with various problems in human society. Greater attention on the part of officialdom in the Church to the activity and reflections of committed ordinary members of the believing community - as well as to agencies established by the hierarchy - concerning social justice would assist in the development of a sound and efficacious social ethic within the Church. The more the Church at all levels is engaged in the formulation of the Doctrine the more the Church at all levels will carry the Doctrine into effect because it will be 'owned' by all concerned. The formulation and the effecting of the Doctrine should be an undertaking that is participatory, collaborative, and involving a range of 'actors'. The Doctrine should, as it were, 'mediate' the promotion of justice and integral development. Particular attention should be paid to the insights of the poor. As this narrative of East Timor has illustrated, the contribution of women is essential. An ongoing cycle of praxis and reflection rooted in local communities is also necessary. Thorough investigation of local situations is a *sine qua non* for pertinent directives. In these ways the large promises made by Church leaders have a better chance of being fulfilled.

There should also be a better balance between the inductive and deductive approaches to the formulation of Catholic Social Doctrine. Contextual derivation is important as local circumstances can shape the norms and have an impact upon their content. Thus 'indicators' provided by the *Magisterium* should have some flexibility and be open to a degree of interpretation by local Churches.[22] But expression of general norms by the *Magisterium* does remain of critical importance. They suggest – and support – appropriate action for social justice and they can command a universal affirmation. In this way 'they assist in the communication of moral wisdom from one situation to another'. There is undoubtedly a value in some central control over thinking and action in the ecclesial family, and in the prophetic statements of the

---

[20] See: Statement of FABC Plenary Assembly III, Samphran, Bangkok, October 1982, in FABC 1984, *For All the Peoples of Asia*, FABC Manila, paragraph 9; Statement of FABC V, Bandung, July 1990, paragraph 4; Statement of FABC VI Manila, January 1995, paragraph 4 - UCANews web-site, FABC.
[21] See: 'Will Rome Listen to the Asian Bishops?' in 'The Church in the World' The Tablet, May 2, 1998, p566.
[22] See Bibliography – Ch4: Tirimanna, V.*CSSR* 1992, pp534-542.

Universal Church. Local issues can compete for attention and all too easily give rise to views that promote sectional interests. Because norms can be compromised the practice of a skilled casuistry is also important in their practical interpretation.[23] In short, the local Church should be acting in continual and close communion with the Universal Church. It is interesting to note how the Church in East Timor is continuing to refer to the (Vatican) statements of Catholic Social Doctrine as it currently plays its part in the building of the nation.[24]

Theological Implications

It is important for there to be the continuation of a theology that will support the development of a sound and effective Social Doctrine. This should be one that is dialogical and inclusive in character, and the basis for such was laid by the Second Vatican Council and in the Papal Encyclicals immediately associated with it, as noted already. The theology should motivate a commitment to action, drawing attention to the Church's vocation and mission to make the Kingdom of God more a reality in this world. The social wisdom of Asian (but also of other non-European) cultures should be embraced. In Asian culture (for example) there is no dichotomy (as in the West) between religious belief and life as it is lived in community but a more holistic vision of the 'good society'. The Church at large in the world should pursue such an integration of faith and life, love and action. In all of this, personal witness to the Gospel is crucial, as this study has indicated repeatedly.

More specifically, there should be an ecclesiology prevailing that encourages the growth of a Church that is more participatory and collaborative. This will engender greater *community* involvement in the formulation and effecting of Catholic Social Doctrine. Vatican II called for a renewal of inner ecclesial structures emphasising the principles of communion, collegiality and co-responsibility. So at the practical level the style of the Church's leadership should consistently be one that is dialogical, inclusive, and collaborative. There must be a consultation of the People of God so as to discern the wisdom of God present within them. The prophetic function of the Church is not limited to the teaching of the hierarchy – there is also the faith instinct or *sensus fidelium* of the whole People. There should also be a continual analysis and evaluation of the role of the Church at all levels. The question must *frequently* be asked as to which of its sectors are on the side of the poor, the victimised – and which are colluding in, even promoting, social injustice.[25] The Church must also endeavour to rid itself of ecclesiocentric attitudes that put institutional interests above the needs of fellow human beings. It must ensure that it puts its resources on the side of those who are suffering the most and is truly 'a voice for the voiceless'. Defending the sacred value of the human person must be the evident as well as the notional priority of a Church that is faithful to its Lord.

A Matter of Faith

The author set out upon this research in the hope of defending the Church against the allegation that it had neglected, even betrayed, one of its component peoples. Faith in the sacred character of the Church instilled a certain confidence in the researcher that this allegation would prove to be unjustified. An identity within the Catholic community as a diocesan priest for over thirty years gave access to sources of information that perhaps might have been denied to an 'outsider', or even to a Catholic layperson. Hopefully, the trust which was bestowed, and which enabled these investigations to proceed as far as they did, has not been betrayed in this presentation of events. But it is also to be hoped that the truth has not been betrayed either. And the truth is that the Church failed often in its duty towards the suffering people of East Timor. Others, confronted by the evidence recounted here, may be more severe in their judgement of the Church's response than this author has been. But they should also be

---

[23] See Bibliography – Ch4: Biggar, N. 1999.
[24] See Bibliography – Ch5: Belo, C.F.X. 2001 'Pastoral Letter on the Participation of the East Timorese Towards Development, etc.
[25] See: Bibliography – Ch4: Dorr, D., 1991, pp 105-125.

willing to accept the happier truth that there were innumerable examples within the community of the Catholic Church of commitment to its Social Doctrine on behalf of the East Timorese which were made at great personal sacrifice. In the noblest instances these were made at the cost of life itself.

In pursuing this research the author admits to the fact that his faith in the Church has been tried. Yet such disappointments as there have been were perhaps inevitable. The Church is, after all, a human society - albeit of Divine institution, inspired by the Holy Spirit and embodying the activity of Christ in today's world. The Church in its human dimension could hardly be flawless. Yet, though evidently sinful, the Church is also redeemed already by the saving grace of her Lord. Her members are called to avail of that redemption by an increased faithfulness to the Gospel. This may be done as history unfolds and provides successive occasions for the growth of the Kingdom in the life of the Church, as in that of the world.

So may the members of the Church – lay, religious, and clergy alike – take to heart the words of the one they believe to be the Vicar of Christ on earth and 'purify themselves, through repentance of past errors and instances of infidelity, inconsistency, and slowness to act'.[26] By 'recognising the truth' about itself may the Church increasingly become 'a source of peace, and bring forth fruits of liberation, reconciliation and joy'.[27] Only in this way will the Church offer 'a service to humanity' that humanity will recognise and appreciate. It must be expected that due to its human condition in this passing world the efforts of the Church will fall short of its ideals. But the Gospel urges us to persist in striving for perfection, for we are called 'the children of God' - and we aim to be followers of our Lord Jesus Christ.

---

[26] Pope John Paul II, *Tertio Millennio Adveniente*, Vatican 1994, paragraph 33-36.
[27] *Memoria e Reconciliazione*, March 2000, Commissione Teologica Internazionale, Vatican.

Select Bibliography

This bibliography covers most but not all of the materials cited in the text .

Bibliographies

Roff, Rabitt S., 1995. 'East Timor: A Bibliography 1970-1994', in Carey, P. & Carter
Bentley, G., 1995, *East Timor at the Crossroads: The Forging of a Nation.* Cassell: London.
Sherlock, K.,
1980. *A Bibliography of East Timor.* Australia National University: Canberra.
1982. 'The Timor Collection'. List of holdings on East Timor (ongoing). Unpublished manuscript: Darwin.

General Theological Works

Bacani, T.C., 1987. *The Church and Politics.* Claretian: Quezon City.
Bonhoeffer, D., 1959. *The Cost of Discipleship.* SCM: London.
Clements, K., 1995. *Learning to Speak.* T&T Clark: Edinburgh.
Guttierrez, G.,1988. *A Theology of Liberation.* SCM: London.
Hastings, A. (ed),
1991. *Modern Catholicism: Vatican II and After.* SPCK: London.
1995. *The Shaping of Prophecy: Passion, Perception and Practicality.* Chapman:London.
Hoffman, S., 1981. *Duties Beyond Borders: On the Limits and Possibilities of Ethical International Politics.* Syracuse University: New York.
Moltmann, J., 1975. *The Crucified God.* SCM: London.
Villa-Vicencio,C., 1992. *Theology in Reconstruction, Nation Building and Human Right.* Cambridge University: Cambridge.
Wogaman, J.P. 1988. *Christian Perspectives on Politics.* SCM: London.
Yoder, J.H., 1972. *The Politics of Jesus.* Paternoster: Carlisle.

General Works on the East Timor issue

Aarons, M., & Domm, R., 1992. *East Timor: A Western-made Tragedy.* Left Book Club: Sydney.
Barbedo de Magalhaes, A.,
1990. *East Timor: Land of Hope.* University of Oporto: Oporto
1992. *East Timor: Indonesian Occupation & Genocide.* University of Oporto: Oporto.
Carey, P., 1996. *East Timor: Third World Colonialism and the Struggle for National Identity.* Research Institute for the Study of Conflict and Terrorism: London.
Carey, P. & Carter Bentley, G., 1995. *East Timor at the Crossroads: The Forging of a Nation.* Cassell: London.
Chomsky, N.,
1978. *Statement to UN General Assembly 4th Committee.*
1979. *Statement to UN General Assembly 4th Committee.*
1979. *East Timor and the Western Democracies.* Bertrand Russell Peace Foundation: Nottingham.
1982. *Towards a New Cold War: Essays on the Current Crisis and How We Got There.* Pantheon: New York.
1996. *Powers and Prospects: Reflections on Human Nature and the Social Order.* Pluto: London.
Chomsky, N. & Herman, E.S., 1979. *The Washington Connection and Third World Fascism. The Political Economy of Human Rights: Volume 1.* Spokesman: Nottingham.
CIIR, Catholic Institute for International Relations: London:
1985. *East Timor.*
1992. *East Timor: An International Responsibility.*
1996. *East Timor: The Continuing Betrayal.*
2001. *East Timor: Transition to Statehood.*
Cristalis, I. 2002. *Bitter Dawn: East Timor, a People's Story.* Zed: London.
Dunn, J.,
1996. *Timor: A People Betrayed.* ABC: Sydney.
2003. *East Timor: A Rough Passage to Independence.* Longueville: Sydney

ETAN, East Timor Action Network: 1991-1996. 'Documents on East Timor'. New York.

Gunn, G.C., 1997. *East Timor and the United Nations: The Case for Intervention.* Red Sea: Lawrenceville, NJ.

Gunn, G.C., with Lee, J., 1994. *A Critical View of Western Journalism and Scholarship on East Timor.* Journal of Contemporary Asian Publishers: Manila.

Horta, J.Ramos, 1987. *Funu: The Unfinished Saga of East Timor.* Red Sea: Lawrenceville, NJ.

Nicol, B.,
1978. *Timor: The Stillborn Nation.* Visa: Melbourne.
2002. *Timor: A Nation Reborn.* Equinox: Jakarta & Singapore

Hainsworth, P., & McClosky, S. (eds), 2001. *The East Timor Question: The Struggle for Independence from Indonesia.* I.B.Tauris: London.

Jardine, M., 1995. *East Timor: Genocide in Paradise.* Odonian: Tucson.

Kohen, A.S., 1999. *From the Place of the Dead: The Epic Struggles of Bishop Belo of East Timor.* St.Martins: New York (Revised 2000).

Krieger, H., 1997. *East Timor and the International Community: Basic Documents.* International Law Research Centre, Cambridge University: Cambridge.

Pro Mundi Vita, 1984. *East Timor* (Dossier 4). PMV: Brussels.

Retboll, T. (ed), International Work Group on Indigenous Affairs. IWGIA: Copenhagen:
1980. *East Timor, Indonesia, and the Western Democracies.* Document 40
1984. *East Timor: The Struggle Continues.* Document 50
1998. *East Timor: Occupation and Resistance.* Document 89

Suter, K., Minority Rights Group. MRG: London:
1982. *East Timor and West Irian.* Report 42.
1997. *East Timor, West Papua/Irian, and Indonesia.*

Tanter, R., Selden, M., & Shalom, S.R. (eds), 2001. *Bitter Flowers, Sweet Flowers: East Timor, Indonesia, and the World Community.* Rowman & Littlefield: Maryland.

Taudevin, L., 1999. *East Timor: Too Little, Too Late.* Duffy & Snellgrove: Potts Point, NSW.

Taylor, J.G.,
1990. *The Indonesian Occupation of East Timor 1974-1989: A Chronology.* CIIR: London.
1991. *Indonesia's Forgotten War: The Hidden History of East Timor*[Revised 1999 as *East Timor: The Price of Freedom*]. Zed: London.

WCC, 1995. *East Timor: Prospects for Peace. Reports and Papers of an Ecumenical Consultation.* World Council of Churches (Unit - Justice Peace & Creation): Geneva.

Chapter 1 – Indonesia: Independence and Repression

Aditjondro, G., 1998. *Soeharto-Habibie: Guru Berdiri - Murid Berlari: Kedua Puncak Korupsi, Kolusi, Nepotisme* [Soeharto-Habibie: Leader in Charge, Leader Aspiring – Twin Peaks of Corruption, Collusion, Nepotism]. PIJAR: Jakarta.

Amnesty International, 1994. *Power and Impunity: Human Rights under the New Order.* Amnesty: London.

Budiardjo, C.,
1991. 'Indonesia's Mass Extermination and the Consolidation of Authoritarian Power' in Alexander, G., (ed) 1991. *Western State Terrorism.* Polity: Cambridge.
1996. *Surviving Indonesia's Gulag.* Cassell: London

Capizzi, E., 1974. *Repression and Exploitation in Indonesia.* Spokesman: London.

Challis, R., 2001. *Shadow of a Revolution – Indonesia and the Generals.* Sutton: London.

Cribb, R.,
1990. *The Indonesian Killings 1965-1966.* Centre of SE Asian Studies: Melbourne
1992. *Historical Dictionary of Indonesia.* Scarecrow: London.

Cribb, R., & Brown, C., 1995. *Modern Indonesia: A History Since 1945.* Longman: London.

Crouch, H., 1993. *The Army and Politics in Indonesia.* (Revised) Cornell: London.

Dahm, B., 1971. *History of Indonesia in the Twentieth Century.* Pall Mall: London.

Feith, H., 1962. *The Decline of Constitutional Democracy in Indonesia.* Cornell: New York.

Fryer, D.W. & Jackson, J.C.,1977. *Indonesia.* Benn: London.

Grant, B., 1996. *Indonesia.* Monash University: Melbourne.

Hill, H. (ed), 1994. *Indonesia's New Order: The Dynamics of Socio-economic Transformation.* Allen & Unwin: Sydney

Kahin, A.R. & Kahin, G.McT., 1995. *Subversion as Foreign Policy.* New Press: New York.

Kingsbury, D., 1998. *The Politics of Indonesia.* OUP: Melbourne.
Kooistra, M., 2001. *Indonesia: Regional Conflicts and State Terror.* Minority Rights Group: London.
Lev, D., 1966. *The Transition to Guided Democracy: Indonesian Politics 1957-59.* Cornell: New York.
Legge, J.D. 1972. *Sukarno: A Political Biography.* Praeger: New York.
Loveard, K., 1999. *Suharto: Indonesia's Last Sultan.* Horizon: Singapore.
Lowry, R., 1996. *The Armed Forces of Indonesia.* Allen & Unwin: St. Leonards, NSW.
May, B., 1978. *The Indonesian Tragedy.* Graham Brash: Singapore.
McDonald, H., 1980. *Suharto's Indonesia.* Fontana, Blackburn: Victoria.
Nugroho, N. & Saleh, I., 1968. *The Coup attempt of the 'September 30th Movement' in Indonesia.* Pembingin Masa: Jakarta.
Polomka, P., 1971. *Indonesia Since Sukarno.* Penguin: London.
Reeve, D., 1985. *Golkar of Indonesia: An Alternative to the Party system.* OUP: Singapore.
Thollen, H. (ed), 1987. *Indonesia and the Rule of Law: Twenty Years of the 'New Order' Government* Francis Pinter: London.
Reid, A., 1968. 'Gestapu: A Hesitant Assessment'. Journal of the Historical Society of Malaya, Vol. VI. Kuala Lumpur.
Shwartz, A., 1994. *A Nation in Waiting: Indonesia in the 1990s.* Allen & Unwin: St.Leonards, NSW.
Southwood, J. & Flanagan, P., 1983. *Indonesia – Law, Propaganda and Terror.* Zed: London.
Vatikiotis, M., 1993. *Indonesian Politics Under Suharto: Order, Development, and Pressure for Change.* Routledge: London.

Periodicals
Inside Indonesia. Van Klinken, G. (ed), (Quarterly). Collingwood, Vic.
Tapol Bulletin. Budiardjo, C. (ed), (Quarterly). The Indonesia Human Rights Campaign (*Tapol*). *TAPOL*: London.

Chapter 2 – East Timor: Occupation and Repression

Aditjondro, G.,
1994 (1). *In the Shadow of Mt. Ramelau: The Impact of the Occupation of East Timor.* Indonesian Documentation and Information Centre: Leiden.
1994 (2). 'Indonesian Monopolies in East Timor'. Occasional Report No24. Tapol: London.
1997. 'Violence by the State against Women in East Timor'. East Timor Human Rights Centre: Melbourne.
Araujo, A. dos Reis, 1976. [Fretilin's] *Massacres in East Timor.* Provisional Government of East Timor: Dili.
de Araujo, A., Jolliffe, J. & Reece, B. (eds), 1975. *Timorese Elites.* Canberra.
Budiardjo, C. & Liem Soei Liong. 1984. *The War Against East Timor.* Zed: London.
Cabral, E., 2002. 'Fretilin and East Timor, 1974 to the present: An examination of the constraints and opportunities for a non-state nationalist liberation movement.' PhD Thesis. Depatment of Politics and International Relations. University of Lancaster: Lancaster.
Costa de Freitas, J.M. *et al.,* 1976. *Fretilin Massacres – Testimonies of Some Survivors.* Usaha: Singapore.
Cox, S. & Carey, P. 1995. *Generations of Resistance: East Timor.* Cassell: London
DGI, 1982. 'East Timor: How the [Protestant] Churches in Indonesia Look At It'. *Dewan Gereja di Indonesia – DGI* [Council of Churches].
FRETILIN [*Frente Revolucionara do Timor Leste Independente*],
1983. 'Fretilin Achieves the Right to Dialogue'. Fretilin External Delegation: Lisbon.
1998. 'Magna Carta: Freedoms, Rights, Duties and Guarantees for the People of East Timor'. East Timorese National Convention in the Diaspora (April 23-27): Lisbon & Peniche.
Galhos, B., 1997. 'The Role of East Timorese Women in our Struggle and Society'. VII *Journadas* Symposium: University of Oporto: Oporto.
Greenlees, D. & Garran, R., 2002. *Deliverance.* Allen & Unwin: Sydney & London.
Gudmund, J., 1998. *The Crocodiles' Tears – East Timor in the Making.* Dissertations in Sociology. Lund University: Sweden.
Gusmao, X.,
1994. *Timor Leste: Uma Povo, Uma Patria.* Publico: Lisbon.
2000. *To Resist is to Win: Autobiography with Selected Speeches & Writings* (ed. Sarah Niner). Aurora: Richmond, Vic.

Hill, H.M., 1978. 'Fretilin: The Origins, Ideologies and Strategies of a Nationalist Movement in East Timor'. Unpublished MA Thesis. Monash University: Melbourne.

Horta, A.R., 1981. *The Eyewitness – Bitter Moments in East Timor Jungles*. Usaha: Singapore.

Jolliffe, J., 1978. *East Timor: Nationalism and Colonialism*. University of Queensland: Brisbane.

Kingsbury, D. (ed), 2000. *Guns and Ballot Boxes: East Timor's Vote for Independence*. Monash Asia Institute: Melbourne.

Kohen, A., & Taylor, J., 1979. *An Act of Genocide: Indonesia's Invasion of East Timor*. Calvert's North Star: London.

Macmillan, A., 1992. *Death in Dili*. Hodder & Stoughton: Rydalmere NSW.

McDonald, H., Ball, D., *et al.*, 2002. *Masters of Terror: Indonesia's Military and Violence in East Timor in 1999*. Strategic & Defence Studies Centre, ANU: Canberra.

Martinkus, J., 2001. *A Dirty Little War*. Random House: Sydney.

Mubyarto, Soetrisno, *et al.*, 1991. 'East Timor: The Impact of Integration'. Gadjah Mada University: Yogyakarta; Indonesia Resources and Information Programme (IRIP): Northcote.

Pinto, C. & Jardine, M., 1996. *East Timor's Unfinished Struggle: Inside the Timorese Resistance*. South End: Boston.

Pires, M. & Scott, C., 'East Timorese Women: The Feminine Face of Resistance', in Retboll, T. (ed), 1998, *East Timor: Occupation and Resistance*. IWGIA: Copenhagen.

Savage, D., 2003. *Dancing with the Devil: A Personal Account of Policing the East Timor Vote for Independence*. Monash Asia Institute: Melbourne.

Scott, C., 1997. 'Women, Faith and Empowerment'. Unpublished MA Dissertation. School of Development Studies: University of East Anglia: Norwich.

Sissons, M.E., 1996. 'From One Day to Another: Violations of Women's Reproductive and Sexual Rights in East Timor'. Yale Centre for International & Area Studies. Yale University: New Haven, Conn.

de Sousa Saldanha, J.M., 1994. *The Political Economy of East Timor Development*. Pustuka Sina Harapan: Jakarta.

Soesastro, H., 1995. 'East Timor's Economic Development Seen from Jakarta'. The East Timor Project, Vol 1. Monograph Series 3/95. Centre for SE Asian Studies. NT University: Darwin.

Storey, S., 1995. 'Coercive Birth Control and Settler Infusion: The Indonesian Prophylactic against East Timorese Self-determination'. Unpublished MSS. University of Melbourne: Melbourne.

Subroto, H., 1996. *Saksi Mata Perjuangan Integrasi Timor Timur* [Eyewitness to the struggle for integration in East Timor]. Pustaka Sinar Harapan: Jakarta.

Sword, K. & and Walsh, P., 1991, 'Opening Up - Travellers Impressions of East Timor 1989-91', AETA, Melbourne.

Traube, E., 1984. 'culutral Notes on Timor'. Unpublished MSS. New York.

Turner, M., 1992. *Telling East Timor – Personal Testimonies*. University of NSW: Sydney.

UDT, [*Uniao Democratica Timorense*] 1974. 'Provisional Statues of the Timorese Democratic Union'. (UDT): Dili.

Winters, R., 1999. *Buibere: Voice of East Timorese Women* (vol 1). East Timor International Support Centre (ETISC): Darwin.

Winters, R. & Kelly, B., 1996. *Children of the Resistance*. Australians for a Free East Timor: Darwin.

Periodicals

Timor Link , Archer, R., and Scott, C. (eds), (Quarterly from 1985 - 2002). Catholic Institute for International Relations: London.

Estafeta, Scheiner, C. (ed), (Quarterly from 1991). East Timor Action Network: New York.

Government of Indonesia Publications

Department of Information (Jakarta)

1975.   Statements on the East Timor Question.

1979.   To Build a Better Tomorrow in East Timor.

1987.   The Process of Decolonisation in East Timor

1991.   East Timor – Fifteen Years of Development.

Department of Foreign Affairs (Jakarta)

1977.   US Congressional Hearing and Visit to East Timor.

1981.   The Province of East Timor: Development in Progress.

1884.   East Timor after Integration.

1985.   East Timor Develops.

1986.   Aspects of Cultural Development in East Timor Province.

1997.   The Untold Story of East Timor.
Regional Government of East Timor (Dili)
1981.   Report of East Timor First Level Regional People's Assembly, Dili.
1983.   East Timor Develops.
1990.   Regional Investment Chart of East Timor.
1991.   East Timor: Building for the Future.

Chapter 3 – International Relations
Aditjondro, G.J., 1999. *Is Oil Thicker than Blood? A Study of Oil Companies' Interests and Western Complicity in Indonesia's Annexation of East Timor.* Nova Science: New York.
Amnesty International:
Statements to: UN Special Committee on Decolonisation (1990>); UNHCR (1984>)
(Selected) Reports on Violations of Human Rights in East Timor (1990-1999)
Barroso, D. 1995. 'East Timor and the International Community'. VI *Journadas.* University of Oporto: Oporto.
Baranyi, S., Kibble, S., Kohen, A., & O'Neill, K., 1997. *Making Solidarity Effective.* CIIR: London.
BCAS, 2000. 'East Timor, Indonesia and the World Community: Resistance, repression, and responsibility'. Bulletin of Concerned Asian Scholars (BCAS),Vol 32, Nos 1&2, January-June. Cedar, MI (USA).
Brewster, M. & Shearer, I. (eds), 1995. *The East Timor Case in the International Court of Justice.* International Law Association: Sydney.
Carey, A., 1995. *Taking the Risk out of Democracy.* University of New South Wales: Sydney.
Chomsky, N., 1992, *Deterring Democracy.* Vintage: London.
Chomsky, N., & Herman, E.,
1979.'Indonesia: Mass Extermination; Investors Paradise', in Chomsky and Herman, *The Washington Connection and Third World Fascism.* Spokesman: Nottingham.
1979. 'Benign Terror: East Timor.' Bulletin of Concerned Asian Scholars (BCAS), Vol 11 No2. Cedar, MI (USA).
Clarke, R.S.,
1992. Petition presented on behalf of IPJET to UN special Committee on Decolonisation. UN: New York.
1993. Petition presented on behalf of the International League for Human Rights (ILHR) to the UN Special Committee on Decolonisation. UN: New York.
CIIR, 1999. *East Timor – From Bullet to Ballot: Report of the CIIR Observer Delegations to the Popular Consultation in East Timor, 1999.* Catholic Institute for International Relations: London.
CIIR/IPJET, 1995. *International Law and the Question of East Timor.* Catholic Institute for International Relations (CIIR): London, & International Platform of Jurists for East Timor (IPJET): Leiden.
da Costa, Z., 1997. 'The East Timor Permanent Representation at the European Union.'. Conference of the British Coalition for East Timor (BCET): London.
Dunn, J.,
1975. 'Portuguese Timior – The Independence Movement from Coalition to Conflict.'. Dyason House Papers, Vol 2 No 1. Dyason House: Melbourne.
1978.'The Timor Affair in International Perspective'. World Review, October, pp13f.
1995.'East Timor: The Balibo Incident in Perspective – The International Setting.' Parliamentary Human Rights Group. PHRG: London.
2001. 'Crimes Against Humanity in East Timor, January to October 1999: Their Nature and Causes'. Report for UN Transitional Administration in East Timor (UNTAET). UN: New York.
Escarameia, P., 1993. *Formation of Concepts in International Law: Subsumption under Self-determination in the Case of East Timor.* Fundacao Oriente: Lisbon.
ENAAT, European Network Against the Arms Trade:
1997. 'Indonesia: Arms to a Military regime'. ENAAT: Amsterdam.
Freney, D., 1975. *Timor: Freedom Caught Between the Powers.* Bertrand Russell Foundation/ Spokesman: Nottingham.
Inbaraj, S., 1995. *East Timor: Blood and Tears in ASEAN.* Silkworm: Chiang Mai.
Leite, P. (ed), 1998. *The East Timor Problem and the Role of Europe.* International Platform of Jurists: Leiden.
Martin, I., 2001. *Self-determination in East Timor: The United Nations, the Ballot, and International Intervention.* Lynne Rienner: London.

221

Vatikiotis, M., 1989. 'Unresolved tensions - Papal visit renews international focus on East Timor.' Far Eastern Economic Revfiew (October 26th). Hong Kong.
International Media
Achbar, M. (ed), 1994. *Manufacturing Consent: Noam Chomsky and the Media.* Black Rose: London.
ARTICLE 19, 1994. 'The Press under Siege: Censorship in Indonesia.' Article 19: London.
Ball, D. & McDonald, H., 2000. *Death in Balibo, Lies in Canberra.* Allen & Unwin: Sydney.
Burke, A., 1990. *The Sad Story of East Timor: A Case Study in Foreign Policy and the Australian Press.* University of Technology: Sydney.
Chomsky, N.,
1979. 'Slaughter in East Timor: Why is the Press ignoring it?' East Timor Research Project: New York.
1992. *Necessary Illusions: Thought Control in Democratic Societies.* Pluto: London.
Herman, E.S., & Chomsky, N., 1994. *Manufacturing Consent: The Political Economy of the Mass Media.* Vintage: London.
Parenti, M., 1993. *Inventing Reality: The Politics of News Media.* St. Martins: New York.
Pilger, J.,
1994. *Distant Voices.* Vintage: London.
1998. *Hidden Agendas.* Vintage: London.
RSF, 1996. 'Report on Mission to Indonesia.' *Reporteurs Sans Frontiers*: Paris.
Rubin, B. *et al*, 1977. *Big Business and the Media.* DC Heath: Lexington, Mass.
Tiffen, R., 2001. *Diplomatic Deceits: Government, Media and East Timor.* University of Sydney: Sydney.
United Nations
New York - Security Council
Proceedings in respect of the East Timor Question, December 1975 to the present.
 - General Assembly
Resolutions 1541(XV), and 1542(XV) (1960); Resolution 1807(XVII) (1962), in respect of the relationship between Portugal and East Timor.
Resolutions in respect of the East Timor Question, December 1975 to the present.
Debates of the United Nations Special Committee on the Situation with Regard to the Implementation of the Declaration on the Granting of Independence to Colonial Countries and Peoples ('Decolonisation Committee') in respect of East Timor, Annually from 1976 - 2000.
1976. Trusteeship and Decolonisation – Decolonisation: Issue of East Timor. Department of Political Affairs.
1980. The Right to Self-determination: Implementation of UN Resolutions. (H.G.Espiell).
1999. *An Agreement Between the Republic of Indonesia and the Portuguese Republic on the Question of East Timor, etc. (May 5th 1999).*
Geneva - Commission on Human Rights
Annual Meetings 1976 - 2001.
1983. *Resolution* 26 of the Sub-commission on Prevention of Discrimination and Protection of Minorities - Question of the Violation of Human Rights and Fundamental Freedoms: the Situation in East Timor (September 6th).
1983. *Report* of the Working Group on Enforced or Involuntary Disappearances (December 9th).
1984. *Report* of the Working Group on Enforced or Involuntary Disappearances (February 2nd).
1992. *Report* of the Special Rapporteur Bacre Waly Ndiaye for Extrajudicial, Summary or Arbitrary Executions on the events at Santa Cruz Cemetery Dili, East Timor 12.11.1991 pursuant to CHR Resolution 1991/71 (January 31st).
1993. *Resolution* 12 of the Sub-commission on Prevention of Discrimination and Protection of Minorities - Question of the Violation of Human Rights and Fundamental Freedoms: the Situation in East Timor (August 20th).
2003. *Report* of the UN High Commissioner for Human Rights: The situation of human rights in Timor-Leste and related activities (March 4th).

Chapter 4 – Criteria for Evaluating the Church's Response
Asian Theologians and Catholic Thinkers, 'Final Statement, 1993: Launching the Second Century: Asian Seminar on the Future of Catholic Social Thought', Hong Kong (March 12-21), in Asia Focus, April 3, 1993, p8f.

222

Biggar, N., 'A Case for Casuistry in the Church', in Modern Theology, Vol 6 No 1. October 1989. Blackwell/Marston: Oxford.

Charles, R.SJ, 1998, Christian Social Witness and Teaching. The Catholic Tradition from Genesis to Centesimus Annus. Vol 2. The Modern Social Teaching. Contexts: Summaries: Analysis. Fowler Wright: Leominster. 1999, An Introduction to Social Teaching. Family: Oxford.

Charles, R. SJ, & Maclaren, D.OP, 1982. The Social Teaching of Vatican II: Its Origin and Development. Plater: Oxford.

Chia, E. (ed), 2001. Dialogue: Resource Manual for Catholics in Asia. FABC, Office of Ecumenical & Religious Affairs, Bangkok.

Coleman, J., 1991. One Hundred Years of Catholic Social Teaching: Celebration and Challenge. Orbis: Maryknoll.

Dorr, D., 1991. The Social Justice Agenda: Justice, Ecology, Power and the Church. Gill & Macmillan: London.

Eilers, F.J. (ed), 1997. For All the Peoples of Asia, Vol 2. Claretian: Manila.

Fernando, T.& O'Sullivan, H. MM, (eds), 1993. Launching the Second Century: The Future of Catholic Thought in Asia. A Study Guide. Asian Centre for the Progress of Peoples: Hong Kong.

Guerry, E.M., 1961. The Social Doctrine of the Catholic Church. St Paul: New York.

Hebblethwaite, P. SJ, 'The Popes and Politics: Shifting patterns in Catholic Social Doctrine', in Readings in Moral Theology, No.5. Paulist: New York.

Herr, T., 1991. Catholic Social Teaching. New City: London.

Lobo, G.SJ, 'Response to the Social Teaching of the Church from the Asian perspective' in Information on Human Development, Vol 20, Nos 1-4, Jan-April 1992. FABC: Manila.

Schulheis, M.J., De Berri, E.P., & Henriot, P.J., 1988. Our Best Kept Secret: The Rich Heritage of Catholic Social Teaching. CAFOD: London.

Tirimanna, V.CSSR. 1992. 'The relevance of Catholic social Doctrine in a non-European world', in Vidyajyoti Journal of Theological Reflection, Vol LVI, No 10, October 1992. A variant of this article is in Fernando, T. & O'Sullivan, H. MM (eds), 1993, Launching the Second Century, etc (see above).

Vallely, P. (ed), 1998. The New Politics: Catholic Social Teaching for the 21st Century. SCM: London.

Walsh, M. & Davies, B. (eds), 1991. Proclaiming Justice and Peace. Collins: London.

The Vatican

Second Vatican Council

General Teaching: Decree on the Church in the World Gaudium et Spes (1965).
On Mass Media: Decree on the Instruments of Social Communication Inter Mirifica (1963)

Papal Encyclicals

General Social Teaching:

Leo XIII - Rerum Novarum (1891)

Pius XI - Quadragesimo Anno (1931)

John XXIII - Mater et Magistra (1961), Pacem in Terris (1963)

Paul VI - Ecclesiam Suam (1964), Populorum Progressio (1967), Evangelii Nuntiandi (1975); Apostolic Letter Octagesima Adveniens (1971)

John Paul II - Redemptor Hominis (1979), Laborem Exercens (1981), Solicitudo Rei Socialis (1987), Centesimus Annus (1981), Christi Fideles Laici (1989), Redemptoris Missio (1990), Tertio Millennio Adveniente (1994)

On Mass Media:

Pius XII – Miranda Prorsus (1957)

Synod of Bishops

Justice in the World (1971)

Synod of Bishops Special Assembly for Asia (1998), Instrumentum Laboris, in East Asian Pastoral Review, Vol 35, No 1. East Asian Pastoral Institute: Quezon.

Pontifical Councils

- Instruments of Social Communication: Communione et Progressio (1971), Aetatis Novae (1992)
- Justice and Peace: The International Arms Trade: An Ethical Reflection (1994)

Congregation for the Doctrine of the Faith

Libertatis Nuntius Instruction on Certain Aspects of Liberation Theology (1984)
Libertatis Conscientia Instruction on Christian Freedom and Liberation (1986)

Special Pontifical Commission (from 1986)

Catechism of the Catholic Church, 1995.

International Theological Commission
Memoria e Reconciliazione: la Chiesa e le Colpe del Passato [Memory and Reconciliation: the Church and the Faults of the Past], 2000.
Bishops Conferences of Latin America (CELAM)
Statement 1968 (Medellin)
Statement 1979 (Puebla)
Federation of Asian Bishops Conferences (FABC)
Statements of Plenary Assemblies I-III. FABC 1984, *For All the Peoples of Asia, Vol 1: The Church in Asia: Asian Bishops' Statements on Mission, Community and Ministry 1970-1983,, Texts & Documents*. IMC: Manila.
Statements of Plenary Assemblies IV-VII. UCA News Internet web site.
Statement of the Colloquium on Social Doctrine of the Church in the Context of Asia (Jan 20-24, 1992), 'Walking Humbly, Acting Justly, Loving Tenderly in Asia'. FABC (Office of Human Development - OHD): Manila.

Chapter 5 – The Church in East Timor

Aditjondro, G.J., 1994. 'East Timor: An Indonesian Intellectual Speaks Out'. Development Dossier 33. Australian Council for Overseas Aid. ACFOA: Canberra.
Archer, R.,
1991. 'The Catholic Church in East Timor.' Social Science Research Council (SSRC) Workshop on East Timor. SSRC: London.
1995. 'The Catholic Church in East Timor'. In Carey, P., & Carter Bentley, G.C. (eds), 1995, *East Timor at the Crossroads*. Cassell: London.
Belo, C.F.X.,
1984. 'Homily in Dili Cathedral', Lent. Diocese of Dili: East Timor.
1985. 'Responsible Parenthood'. Pastoral Letter (March 3rd). Diocese of Dili: East Timor.
1987. Submission to Council of the Federation of Religious in Indonesia. MASRI: Jakarta.
1991.(1). 'The Position of the Catholic Church on the Visit of the Portuguese Parliamentary Delegation to East Timor'. Pastoral Letter (September 17th). Diocese of Dili: East Timor.
1991.(2). 'On the Correct Use of Places of Worship and of Religious Activities'. Pastoral Statement (December 2nd). Diocese of Dili: East Timor.
1993. (1). Sermons and Interviews during Visit to Australia. Documents on East Timor, Vol 25, p47f. East Timor Action Network. ETAN: New York.
(2). 'Family Planning According to the Church's Moral Stance', Pastoral Letter, (28th August). Diocese of Dili: East Timor.
1994. 'Homily in Dili Cathedral', Christmas. Diocese of Dili: East Timor.
1995. 'East Timor in the Catholic Church's Perspective.' UN All-inclusive Intra-Timorese Dialogue (June). Schlaining, Austria. United Nations: New York.
1996. Speech of Acceptance. Nobel Peace Prize Award, Oslo (December 10th) [In Retboll: T. 1998. *East Timor: Occupation and Resistance*. IWGIA:Copenhagen.
1997. See below: Tuekan. P. & de Sousa, D. *Demi Keadilan dan Perdamaian.*
2001. *The Road to Freedom: Speeches, Pastoral Letters, Articles 1997-2001.* Caritas Australia: Sydney.
Pastoral Letter on the Participation of the East Timorese towards Development in East Timor. Diocese of Dili: East Timor (31.12).
Pastoral Statement for the Election of the Constituent Assembly. Diocese of Dili (15.8).
2002. Pastoral Appeal on Amnesty and the Settlement of Crimes against Humanity. Diocese of Dili (29.6).
Boavida, J.F., 1993. 'The Fusion of Religion and Nationalism in East Timor: A Culture in the Making'. Unpublished MPhil Thesis. Institute of Social and Cultural Anthropology. University of Oxford: Oxford.
Boxer, C.R.,
1968. *Fidalgos in the Far East 1150-1770.* OUP: London.
1990, *Portuguese Conquest and Commerce in Southern Asia 1500-1750,* Variorum: Hampshire.
Carey, P., 1997. 'The Catholic Church, Religious Revival and the Nationalist Movement in East Timor 1975-1995.' Dahm, B. & Talib, N. (eds), *Religious Revival in SE Asia, 1997.* ISEAS: Singapore.

Clergy of East Timor, 1996. 'Reflection'. 7th Christian Consultation on East Timor (CCET), Brussels, (January). CIIR: London.

Costa Lopes, M., 1983. 'The Indonesian Occupation of East Timor.'. *Tapol Bulletin*. *TAPOL*:London

Crowe, L., 1996. 'The Impact of the Indonesian Annexation on the Role of the Catholic Church in East Timor 1976-1995.' Unpublished BA (Hons) Thesis. Faculty of Arts. Northern Territory University: Darwin.

Diocese of Dili – Council of Priests.

1985. 'Statement'. (January 1st).

1994. 'Statement on the East Timor Catholic Church Nowadays'.
   'The Outlook of the Catholic Church on Development'.

Federer, J., 1994. 'The Catholic Church in East Timor - its Lone Struggle for Justice.' Unpublished MSS. East Timor International Support Centre. ETISC: Darwin.

Gunn, G.C., 1999. *Timor Loro Sae: 500 Years*. Livros do Oriente: Macau.

Jardine, M., 1993. 'The secret sacrifice of East Timor: amid invasion, massacre and insurrection the Church takes a stand.'. *Christianity & Crisis* Vol 53 No1, Adelaide.

Lennox, R., 1999. *Fighting Spirit of East Timor: The Life of Dom Martinho, a Hero to his People*. Pluto: Annandale NSW.

MASRI 1981. 'Statement'. Submission to *Majelis Serikat Religious Indonesia* [Council of the Federation of Religious in Indonesia] (MASRI): Jakarta.

Neonbasu, G.,

1992. *Keadilan dan Perdamaian di Diosis Dili* [Justice and Peace in Dili Diocese]

1998. *Sejarah Gereja Katolik di Timor Timur.*[History of the Church in East Timor].
   Komisi Komunikasi Sosial Diosis Dili: Dili.

Ribeiro, J., 1975. *Uma Nova Situacao*. Pastoral Letter. Diocese of Dili: East Timor.

Smythe, P.,

1995 'The Crucifixion of East Timor.' Unpublished MA Thesis. Department of Theology. University of Leeds: Leeds.

1998. 'Bishop Belo: Advocate for Justice', and 'The Catholic Church [in East Timor]', in Retboll, T.(ed), 1998, *East Timor: Occupation and Resistance*. IWGIA: Copenhagen.

1999. 'The Role of the Church in East Timor: Resistance and Reconciliation,' in *Studies in Languages and Cultures of East Timor, Vol 2*. University of Western Sydney Macarthur: Sydney.

Tuekan, P & de Sousa, D. (eds), 1997, *Demi Keadilan dan Perdamaian* [For Justice and Peace]; *Suara Kaum Tak Bersuara* [Voice of the Voiceless]. Majelis Agung Waligereja Indonesia (KWI): Jakarta.

Vlazna,V., 1997. 'The Value of Non-violence in East Timor Activism.' VII *Journadas* Symposium. University of Oporto: Oporto.

Walsh, P.,

1982. 'Timor people support the Church in its opposition to Indonesian take-over.' National Outlook (November). Outlook Media: Sydney.

1983. East Timor Report, Melbourne.

Chapter 6 – The Church in Indonesia

Aditjondro, G.J.,

1995. 'From *Ganyang* [crush] *Malaysia* to *Ganyang Fretilin*.' International Conference on Peacemaking Initiatives for East Timor. Department of Political Science. Australia National University: Canberra.

1996. 'Challenges and Prospects of the Indonesian pro-East Timor Movement.' Newcastle University: Newcastle, NSW.

2000. '*Menyongsong Matahari Terbit di Puncak Ramelau* '[Welcoming the Rising Sun at the Peak of Mt.Ramelau], Foundation of Law, Rights & Justice/ *Fortilos*: Jakarta.

Brackman, A.C.,

1969. *The Communist Collapse in Indonesia*. New York.

1989. *The Catholic Church in Indonesia*. Jakarta.

Cabral, E., 1995. 'Whose Case for Integration? A Response to Thomas Michel *SJ.* ' *(see below)*. Unpublished MSS. Praxis: London.

Cambell-Nelson, J., 1998. *Indonesia in Shadow and Light*. Friendship: New York

Clifton, T.M., 1986. 'The History and Present Day Activities of the Catholic Church in Indonesia.' Unpublished MSS. Indonesian Contemporary Studies. Monash University: Melbourne.

Coomans, M., 1988. 'The Catholic Church in Indonesia.' East Asian Pastoral Review (Vol 25 pp379f). East Asian Pastoral Institute: Quezon.

CSIS, 1981. *Kebebasan Beragama* [Religious Liberty]. Centre for Strategic and International Studies: Jakarta.

Darmaatmadja, C. Cardinal *SJ*, 1996. 'An Open letter Concerning the Incident of 27th July.' KWI: Jakarta.

Diocese of Atambua (West Timor)

1995. Septennial (1989-1995) *ad Limina* Report to Holy See (Bishop Anton Pain Ratu).

Diocese of Kupang (West Timor)

1995. *Ad Limina* Report to the Holy See (Archbishop Gregorio Manteiro)

Dirja, A.*SJ*, 1979. 'East Timor: some experiences and thoughts.' Internos (Journal of the Society of Jesus) No2, Jakarta.

FABC, 1984. 'Information on Human Development' (February). Office for Human Development. Federation of Asian Bishops Conferences. FABC: Manila.

Hadi, A.I., 1990. 'The Participation and Role of Catholics in Indonesian National Politics 1945-1973.' Unpublished BA (Hons) Thesis. Schools of Political Science & History. University of New South Wales: Sydney.

Hardowirjono, R. 1977. 'Serving the Faith by Promoting Justice.' Extracts from 'Service of the Faith in Asia' in Teaching All Nations (1977 No2, p112-117, 120f), in England, J.C. (ed), 1981, *Living Theology in Asia*. SCM: London (pp148f).

Heuken, P.A.*SJ*, 1991. *Ensiklopedi Gereja* [Encyclopaedia of the Church]. Missionsprokur: Nurnberg.

KWI, (*Konperensi Waligereja Indonesia*) [Indonesian Bishops Conference] – Jakarta (see also MAWI below):

InterNews (Quarterly Bulletin).

Dokumentasi Penerengan [Documentation Department]:

1971. Pre-election Statement.

1974. *Sereja Gereja Katolik Indonesia* [History of the Catholic Church in Indonesia].

1976. Pre-election Pastoral Letter.

1977. Observations on Developments in the Nation and Society (November).

1980. *Ad Limina* Report to the Holy See.

1983. Letter to the Apostolic Administrator, Priests, Brothers and Sisters of the Diocese of Dili (November).

1984. Pastoral Letter.

1985. *Umat Katolik Indonesia dalam Masyarakat Pancasila: Hubungan gereja dan negara, pedoman.*[The Catholic Community within the Pancasila Consultative Process: The Relationship of Church and State, a Handbook].

1989. The Catholic Church in Indonesia (Revised Edition).

1996. *Pedoman Gereja Katolik Indonesia* [Handbook of the Catholic Church].

    Ad limina Quinquennial report to the Holy See.

1997. Lenten Pastoral Letter.

1999. Pastoral Letter: 'Arise and be unwavering in hope' (Easter).

    Pastoral Letter: 'Let us change' (November).

2000. Resume of the (3rd) National Conference of the Secretariat for Justice and Peace, Prigen (Feb).

LPPS, *Lembaga Penelitian dan Pembangunan Sosial* [Institute of Social Research & Development]

1968. *Ikhtisar Statisk Tentang Gereja Katolik di Indoneis 1949-196* [Summary of Statistics on the Catholic Church in Indonesia]. LPPS: Bogor.

1982. 'East Timor Emergency and Rehabilitation Programme Narrative Report.' Despatched by Fr.Zegwaard. LPPS: Dili.

MAWI (*Majelis Agung Waligereja Indonesia*) [Supreme Council of the Bishops of Indonesia] (From 1987 known as KWI, see above).

Mangunwijaya, Y.B., 1998. *Menuju Indonesia Serba Baru* [Towards a Completely New Indonesia]. Gramedia: Jakarta.

Michel, Th., 1995. 'East Timor: the case for Integration.' The Month, (May). Jesuit Publications: International. [cf. Cabral, E., 1995 (*see above*)]

Muskens, M.P.,

1973. *The History of the Indonesian Catholic Church* (5 Vols). Arnoldos: Ende-Flores.

1979. *Partner in Nation Building: The Catholic Church in Indonesia.* Missio Actuel Verlag / Misereor: Aachen.

Neonbasu, G. *SVD*, 1997. '20 *Tahun Integrasi: "Ut omnes unum sint"'* [Twenty Years of Integration: "That all may be one"]. Kompas Online, Jakarta.

Pain Ratu, A., 1999. [Bishop of Atambua, West Timor] Open letter: 'To whom it may concern: The Refugee Situation in East Timor'. Disseminated by international electronic and print media (Sept 15th).

Pour, J., 1993. *Benny Murdani: Profile of a Soldier Statesman*. Yayasan Sudirman: Jakarta.

PMV, [Pro Mundi Vita]: Brussels.

1971. 'Indonesia and Foreign Religions in Indonesia.'

1977. 'Indonesia.' Bulletin (Jan-Feb) pp17-24.

Sastrapratedja, M., 1995. 'The Indonesian Church – the challenge of Islam' and 'The Indonesian Missionary Church – hopes and problems.' Sedos Bulletin (Vol 27, Nos 6-7). Service of Documentation and Studies. SEDOS: Rome.

Seda, F., 1985. Address to General Assembly of the Pontifical Commission *Justitia et Pax*. Vatican.

Stuart, C., 1991. 'Catholics in Crisis: The Political Response of Catholics in Jakarta to the 30th September 1965 Movement and its Aftermath.' Unpublished BA Thesis, Department of History. Monash University: Melbourne.

Sandyawan Sumardi, I.*SJ*, 1998. 'The Duty of the State - Immediately Return the Rights of the Poor'. Unpublished address at Meeting and Prayer of Concern for the Urban Poor, Bantar Genbang, Bekasi, West Java (March).

Thomson, A., 1968. 'The Churches in Java in the aftermath of the 30th September Movement. South East Asian Journal of Theology (Vol 9, No 3,m pp7-20).

Threes Nio (ed), 1980. *I.J.Kasimo: Hidup dan Perjuanggannya* [Life and Struggle].Gramedia: Jakarta.

Van Lith, 1922. Pamphlet. KWI: Jakarta.

Van Niel, R. 1985. 'Catholics and the Indonesian Revolution.' (Review) – Bank, J., University of Hawaii: Honolulu. Journal of Asian Studies, (Vol 45, No1).

Webb, R.A.F.P., 1978. 'Indonesian Christians and their Political Parties, 1923-1966: the Role of the *Partai Kristen Indonesia* and the *Partai Katolik.'* SE Asian Monograph Series 2. James Cook University: Townsville & Cairns, QLD.

YK, *Yayasan Kasimo* [Kasimo Foundation]:

1993. 'In Brief: The Role of Indonesian Lay Catholics in State Affairs'. Presented to Pope John Paul II upon his Visit to Indonesia in 1989. YK: Jakarta.

Chapter 7 – The Church in Portugal

Barbedo de Magalhaes, A.

1995. *The East Timor Issue and the Symposia of Oporto University.* University of Oporto: Oporto.

1996. 'East Timor: A People Shattered by Lies and Silence.' VI *Journadas*. University of Oporto: Oporto.

Biblioteca Central, *A Historia de Timor e a Prencea Portugesa na Insulindia* [The History of Timor and the Portuguese Presence on the Island]. University of Oporto: Oporto.

CPEP, *Conselho Permanente do Episcopado Portuguese* [Permanent Council of Portuguese Bishops]:

1984.'*Nota sobre a situacao de Timor Oriental'*. CPEP: Lisbon

1989. '*Nota Pastoral sobre Timor Leste'*. CPEP: Lisbon

1991. '*Comunicado Final'*. CPEP: Fatima.

Birmingham, D., 1991. *A Concise History of Portugal*. Cambridge University: Cambridge.

Boxer, C.R.

1968. *Fidalgos in the Far East 1150-1770*. OUP: London.

1969. *The Portuguese Seaborne Empire 1415-1825*. Carcanet: London.

Bruce, N., 1975. *Portugal: The Last Empire*. David & Charles: London.

Costa Alves, M., 1998. *Voltar a Timor* [Return to Timor]. Gravida: Lisbon.

Dunn, J., 1974. 'The East Timor Situation: Report on Talks with Timorese Refugees in Portugal.' (February). Foreign Affairs Group. Legislative Research Service: Canberra.

Egerton, F.C.C., 1943. *Salazar, Rebuilder of Portugal*. Hodder & Stoughton: London.

Fernandes, F.,

1978.Statement to the UN Committee on Decolonisation.

1980.Statement before the House Subcommittee on Foreign Operations of the Committee of Appropriations (June 10th). United States Congress.

1985. Statement to the Christian Conference of Asia (June). CCA: Seoul.

Graham, L.S. & Wheeler, D. (eds), 1982. *In Search of Modern Portugal: The Revolution and its Consequences*. University of Winsconsin: Winsconsin.

Gouveia, J.B., 1993. *Timor Leste – Textos Juridicos Fundamentais (2a-edicao, aumentada)* [East Timor – Basic Legal Texts, 2nd edition with additions]. Associacao Academica de Faculdade de Direito de Lisboa: Lisbon.

Gunn, G.C., 1999. *Timor Loro Sae: 500 Years*. Livros do Oriente: Macau.

Herr, R. (ed), 1992. *The New Portugal: Democracy and Europe*. University of California: San Francisco.

Jolliffe, J., 1988. *Timor, Terra Sagrenta: Historia da Descolonizacao Abortada* [Timor, Bleeding Land: History of an Aborted Decolonisation]. Lisbon.

Kay, H., 1970. *Salazar and Modern Portugal*. Eyre & Spottiswood: London.

Manuel, P.C., 1995. *Uncertain Outcome: The Politics of the Portuguese Transition to Democracy*. University Press of America: London.

Maxwell, K.,
1995. *The Making of Portuguese Democracy*. Cambridge University: Cambridge.

Nataf, D. 1995. *Democratisation and Social Settlements: The Politics of Change in Contemporary Portugal*. State University of New York: New York.

Pelissier, R., 1996. *Timor en Guerre: Le Crocodil et Les Portugais (1847 – 1913)* [Timor at War: The Crocodile and the Portuguese]. Pelissier: Orgeval.

Pires, L., 1991. *Descolonizacao de Timor: Missao Impossivel?* [The decolonisation of East Timor: mission impossible?] Dom Quixote: Lisbon.

Raby, D.L., 1988. *Fascism and Resistance in Portugal*. Manchester University: Manchester.

da Silva Martins, M., 1995. *Fundacao Spes* [Basic Faith]. Casa da Torre da Marca: Oporto.

Soares, M. 1975. *Portugal's Struggle for Liberty*. Allen & Unwin: London.

Stillwell, P., 1990. *A Igreja Catolica e Timor Leste – Factos e Documentos* [The Catholic Church and East Timor – Facts and Documents]. Centro de Informacao e Documentacao Amilcar Cabral. CIDAC: Lisbon.

Vasconcelos, J., 1992. *Timor: Imperativo de Consciencia* [Timor: Obligation upon Conscience]. Produce: Lisbon.

Government of Portugal Publications

Assembleia da Republica Portuguesa: Lisbon

1981. *Relatorio do Governo de Timor (13 Nov 1974 – 7 Dec 1975)*; *Relatorio da Comissao de Analise e Esclaecimento do Processo de Descolonizacao de Timor*. Council of Ministers.

1986. 'Report presented by the Eventual Commission for the Following-up of the Situation in East Timor.'

1991. *Timor-Leste. Factos e Documentos, Vol 1: 1988-1991*.

1992. 'Obligations of Portugal as the Administering Power of the Non-self Governing Territory of East Timor.' Drafted by Maria Fernanda Lima.

1995. '*Timor Leste: Declaracao de Lisboa*' [East Timor: The Lisbon Declaration] Conferencia Interparlamentar Internacional Sobre Timor Leste.

1996. 'United Nations Decolonisation Committee. Hearings on the East Timor Question'.

Chapter 8 – The Church in Australia

Anderson, D. (ed), 1991. *Australia and Indonesia - A Partnership in the Making*. Pacific Security Research Institute: Sydney.

Arndt. H.W., 1976. 'East Timor: Expediency or Principle?' Quadrant (May), Sydney.

Aubrey, J. (ed), 1990. *Free East Timor – Australia's Culpability in East Timor's Genocide*. Vintage, Random House: Sydney.

Ball, D. & Downes, C. (eds), 1990. *Security and Defence: Pacific and Global Perspectives*. Allen & Unwin: Sydney.

Ball, D. & Wilson, H. (eds), 1991. *Strange Neighbours: The Australia-Indonesia Partnership*. Allen & Unwin: Sydney.

Barclay, St.G., 1985. *Friends in High Places: Australia-American Diplomatic Relations Since 1945*. OUP: Melbourne.

Bell, C. (ed), 1980, *Agenda for the Eighties: Contexts of Australian Choices in Foreign and Defence Policy*. Australian National University: Canberra.

Brennan, G. & Williams, J.K. (eds), 1984, *Chaining Australia: Church Bureaucracies and Political Economy*, Centre for Independent Studies, Sydney.

Byrne, W., 1978. 'Notes prepared for the Episcopal Committee for Development and Peace/ National Committee of ACR'. ACR/Caritas Australia: Sydney.

Callinan, B., 1985. *Independent Company: The Australian Army in Portuguese Timor 1941-43.* Heinemann: Melbourne.

Campion, E.,

1987. *Australian Catholics.* Penguin: Ringwood, Vic.

1997. *Great Australian Catholics.* Lovell: Richmond, Vic.

Cathgart, M., 1993. *Manning Clark's History of Australia (abridged).* Revised edition. Penguin: Sydney.

CCJP, East Timor: A Forgotten People. Issues No10. Catholic Commission for Justice and Peace: Sydney.

CCJDP, 1993. *The Church and East Timor: A Collection of Documents.* Catholic Commission for Justice, Development and Peace: Archdiocese of Melbourne.

CISET, 1994. 'Development? Development for What? Report of a Visit to East Timor by members of Christians in Solidarity with East Timor (CISET)'. UNIYA: Kings Cross, NSW.

Clarke, C.M.H.,

1963. *A Short History of Australia.* Revised edition 1995. Penguin: Sydney.

CSIS, 1984. *Regional Dimensions of Indonesia-Australia Relations.* Centre for Strategic and International Studies: Jakarta.

Dowson, H., 1998, 'The Balibo Murders: Balibo and Beyond: An International Cover-up.' in Retboll, T. (ed), 1998, *East Timor: Occupation and Resistance,* Document 89, IWGIA: Copenhagen.

Dunidja, D., (Transl. Pollard, T., 1996), 'Indonesian National Army VII Military Regional Command-Trikora: Guidelines (Directive) of the VIIIth Military Regional Commander/Trikora on behalf of Commander of the Armed Forces of the Republic of Indonesia for Maluku/Irian Jaya concerning Human Rights.' ACSJC: Sydney.

East Timor Project, 1995. 'An Anthology: Essays on the Political Economy of East Timor.' Monograph Series No3/95. Centre for SE Asian Studies. Northern Territory University: Darwin.

Fry, G. (ed), 1991. *Australia's Regional Security.* Allen & Unwin: Sydney.

Hastings, P.,

1975. 'The Timor Problem' (Parts I, II, III). <u>Australian Outlook</u> (Vol 29, Nos 1-3), Australian Institute for International Affairs. AIIR: Deakin, ACT.

1980. 'Timor and West Irian - the reasons why.' in Mackie, J. (ed), *Indonesia, the Making of a Nation.* Sydney.

Henderson, G., 1982. *Mr.Santamaria and the Bishops.* Studies in the Christian Movement No7. SCM: Manley, NSW.

Hill, H., 1985. 'Australia and Portuguese Timor: Between Principles and Pragmatism.' in Scott, R. & Richardson, J., *The First Thousand Days of Labor: Public Policy and Interest Groups, International Relations.* Canberra College of Advanced Education: Canberra.

Hogan, M. (ed),

1990. *Justice Now! Social Justice Statements of the Australian Catholic Bishops 1940-1966.* Department of Government and Public Administration. University of Sydney: Sydney.

1992. *Option for the Poor: Annual Social Justice Statements of the Australian Catholic Commission for Justice and Peace (CCJP) 1973-1987.* Department of Government and Public Administration. University of Sydney: Sydney.

Hull, G., 1992. *East Timor: Just a Political Question?* Occasional Paper No.11. Australian Catholic Social Justice Council: Sydney.

Kerr, N. (ed), 1985. *Australian Catholic Bishops Statements since Vatican II.* St.Paul: Homebush.

Lambourne, W. 1992. 'Australian Foreign Policy Towards Indonesia and East Timor: Realpolitik, Ethics, and the National Interest.' Unpublished Research Essay, MA International Relations, ANU: Canberra.

Lowry, R., 1996. 'Australia-Indonesia Security Co-operation - for Better or Worse?' Working Paper 299. ANU: Canberra.

Modystack, W., 1982. *Blessed Mary Mackillop: A Woman Before her Time.* Rigby: Sydney.

MMIETS, Mary MacKillop Institute of East Timorese Studies, St.Mary's, NSW:

1995. 'Statement of the Sanctuary Movement'. CISET: Uniya, Sydney.

1996. 'East Timor Visit June-July 1996' (Confidential) Report. MMIETS: St.Mary's NSW.

1997. 'Language and Literacy in East Timor - the Role of MMIETS'. (Sr.J.Mitchell *RSJ*). VII *Jornadas* Symposium. University of Oporto: Oporto.

Moloney, J., 1988. *The Penguin History of Australia.* Penguin: Sydney.

Munster, G. & Walsh, R., 1980. *Documents on Australian Defence and Foreign Policy 1968-1975.* Munster & Walsh: Sydney.

O'Farrell, P., 1985. *The Catholic Church and Community, An Australian History.* Revised edition. Nelson: Kensington, NSW.

Roff, R., 1992. 'Timor's Anschluss – Indonesia and Australian Policy in East Timor 1974-76'. Mellin: New York.

Santamaria, B.A., 1997. *Santamaria – A Memoir.* (Revised edition of *Against the Tide* (1981). OUP: Melbourne.

Thatcher, P., 1992. 'Timorese Refugees in Australia – How, When, and Who?' Unpublished MA Thesis. Centre for Migrant and Intercultural Studies Seminar. Monash University: Melbourne.

Walsh, P.,

1980, (1) 'Notes on ET Issues', Action for World Development: Melbourne.

1980, (2) Development Dossier, No 1 (July), Australian Council for Overseas Aid: Canberra.

1981. 'Australia's support for Indonesia's Take-over of East Timor.' Testimony before the Permanent People's Tribunal (June). Assembleia de Republica: Lisbon.

1982. 'Timor Report: Whitlam and Hastings observed.' Arena (No 60), North Carlton, Vic.

1990. 'Timor Gap: oil poured on bloodied waters.' Arena (No 90), North Carlton, Vic.

1997. 'The Politics of Denial: Australia and East Timor.' VII *Journadas* Symposium. University of Oporto: Oporto.

Whiteley, M., 1991. 'Report on a Visit to East Timor December 15-17 1991.' (January 2nd 1992). ACR/Caritas Australia: Sydney.

Whitlam, G.,

1982. 'Gough Whitlam: the truth about Timor.' The Bulletin, Canberra.

1997. *Abiding Interests.* University of Queensland: Brisbane.

Woolfe, T.M., 1988. 'Witness and Teacher – The Catholic Commission for Justice and Peace 1968-87. A Study of the Ideology of a Catholic Church Agency.' Unpublished PhD Thesis. Department of Government. University of Sydney: Sydney.

Government of Australia

1969. Australian Consular Report (James Dunn), February 17th. Lahane: Dili

1983. Report of the Australian Parliamentary Delegation to Indonesia and East Timor.

1991. Report of the Visit of the Australian Parliamentary Delegation to Hong Kong, Singapore and Indonesia.

Treaty Between Australia and the Republic of Indonesia on the Zone of Co-operation in an area between the Indonesian Province of East Timor and Northern Australia. (1991 No 9).

Joint Committee on Foreign Affairs, Defence and Trade

1991. Inquiry into Australia's Relations with Indonesia

1992. Inquiry into Australia's Relations with Indonesia

1993. Australia's Relations with Indonesia: Report.

Standing Committee on Foreign Affairs and Defence

1983. The Human Rights and Condition of the People of East Timor (Hansard 14.5)

Department of Foreign Affairs and Trade (DFAT)

1994. Response to Joint Committee 1991/92 Inquiry.

Expanding Horizons: Australia and Indonesia into 21st Century.

2000. Australia and the Indonesian Incorporation of Portuguese Timor 1974-1976.

2001. East Timor in Transition 1998-2000: An Australian Policy Challenge.

Legislative Research Service

1974. (James Dunn, Aug 27th) 'Portuguese Timor Before and After the Coup: Options for the Future.'

1976. (James Dunn, July 21st) 'The Timor Story'.

Australia-Indonesia Institute (est.1989)

Annual Reports from 1990.Canberra.

Parliamentary Research Service

1995. 'A Pebble in Indonesia's Shoe: Recent Developments in East Timor.' (Stephen Sherlock) Research Paper No 8. PRS: Canberra.

Chapter 9 – The Church in the United States

Ambrose, S.E., 1993. *Rise to Globalism: American Foreign Policy Since 1938.* Penguin: New York.

Blanshard, P., 1949. *American Freedom and Catholic Power.* New York.

Chomsky, N. See: Bibliography – General (East Timor).

Frank, R.W.,
1976. 'East Timor: The Hidden War.' East Timor Defence Committee: New York.
1983. 'East Timor: the responsibility of the United States.' Bulletin of Concerned Asian Scholars (Vol 15, No2, pp42-58). BCAS: Cedar, MI.
George, A., 1991. *Western State Terrorism.* Polity Press: Cambridge.
Hartung, W.D. & Washburn, J., 1997. *US Arms Transfers to Indonesia 1975-1997: Who's Influencing Whom?* Arms Trade Resource Centre. World Policy Institute: New York.
Hitchens, C., 2001. *The Trial of Henry Kissinger.* Verso: New York.
Jardine, M.,
1993.'United States Foreign Policy Towards East Timor: Past, Present, Future, and the Grassroots Response.' Unpublished MSS, East Timor Action Network (ETAN): New York.
Jenkins, P., 1997. *A History of the United States.* Macmillan: London.
Johnson, C., 1996. 'East Timor: Environmental Degradation Linked to Human Rights Violations, the Ability of NGOs to Affect Policy, and a Causal Explanation for the Lack of Action.' Unpublished MSS. University of Washington: Washington DC.
Kahin, A.R. & Kahin, G.McT., 1995. *Subversion as Foreign Policy.* Vinlin: Kuala Lumpur.
Kennan, G.F., 1948. 'Current Trends, US Foreign Policy.' *Foreign Relations of the US 1948.* Washington DC, Vol 1, Part 2. Pp509f.
McMahon, R.J., 1991. *Colonialism and Cold War: The United States and the Struggle for Indonesian Independence.* Cornell: New York.
Morris, C.R., 1997. *American Catholic.* Random House: New York.
Moynihan, D.P., 1978. *A Dangerous Place.* Secker & Warburg: London.
Nordland, R., 1982. 'Hunger: under Indonesia, Timor remains a land of misery.' Philadephia Inquirer (May 28th), Philadelphia.
Novak, M.,
1990. *Toward a Theology of the Corporation* (Revised edition). American Enterprise Institute for Public Policy Research (AEI): Washington DC.
1997. *On Corporate Governance – The Corporation As It Ought to be.* AEI: Washington.
Novak, M. & Cooper, J.W., (eds), 1981. *The Corporation, A Theological Inquiry.* AEI: Washington.
Oshinsky, D.M., 1993. *A Conspiracy So Immense: The World of Joe McCarthy.* Free: New York.
Selden, M., 1975. 'American Global Enterprise and Asia.' Bulletin of Concerned Asian Scholars (Vol 7 No2, pp15-33): Cedar, Mi.
Siddell, S., 1981. 'The United States and genocide in East Timor.' Journal of Contemporary Asian Publishers: Manila.
USCC/NCCB, 1986. *Economic Justice for All: Pastoral Letter on Catholic Social Teaching and the US Economy.* United States Catholic Conference/ National Conference of Catholic Bishops: Washington DC.

Government of the United States
1976. 'Indonesia's importance to US Foreign Policy'. House Committee on Appropriations on Foreign Assistance.
1977. Statement by H.S.Meyer: 'Report on Congressional Delegation Visit to East Timor 1977 (February 28th)'. Subcommittee on International Organisations of the Committee on International Relations.
1977 'Human Rights in East Timor and the Question of the Use of US Equipment by the Indonesian Armed Forces.' Hearing before the Subcommittee on International Organisation and on Asian and Pacific Affairs of the Committee on International Relations (March 23rd).
       Statement by George Aldrich, Legal Adviser before Subcommittee on International Organisations of the House Committee on International Relations. (July 9th).
1982. Statement by J.H.Holdridge, Assistant Secretary for E Asian & Pacific Affairs before Subcommittee on Asian and Pacific Affairs of the Committee on Foreign Affairs (Sept 14th).
1992. 'Crisis in East Timor and US Policy toward Indonesia' Statement by K.M.Quinn, Acting Assistant Secretary for East Asian and Pacific Affairs - House Committee on Foreign Affairs (June 3rd).
1997. Congressional Record of the House Debate on International Military Education and Training (IMET) in respect of Indonesia (June 11th).

Chapter 10 - The Church in Japan

Allinson. G.D., 1997. *Japan's Post War History.* Cornell: New York.
Buckley, R., 1985. *Japan Today.* Cambridge University: Cambridge.

Cary, O., 1975. *A History of Christianity in Japan. Roman Catholic, Greek Orthodox and Protestant Missions.* C.E.Tuttle: Tokyo.

CBCJ (Catholic Bishops Conference of Japan), Tokyo:

1987. 'Let us live together in joy' – Response to NICE I National Catholic Conference (Dec.18th).

1991. 'Letter of condolence to Bishop Belo regarding the massacre of the East Timorese, etc'.

1995. *The Catholic Church in Japan: An Historical Overview.*

'Resolution for Peace' on the anniversary of the end of World War II.

1997. *Statistics of the Catholic Church in Japan.*

1998. *The Catholic Church in Japan: Present Structure and Activities.* Docs in English 1984-1997.

1999. 'Letter of solidarity to Bishop Belo and Bishop Nascimento of East Timor.' (June 20th).

Furusawa, K., 1993. 'Double Standard: Japan's Stand on East Timor.' United Nations World Conference on Human Rights (June). Free East Timor Japan Coalition: Tokyo.

JCCJP (Japanese Catholic Council for Justice and Peace):

Justice and Peace Pamphlet Series.

Letters to international leaders (Church and State) regarding East Timor.

1995. 'Towards a New Beginning.' Declaration on the Occasion of the 50th Anniversary of the Ending of World War II.

1996. Statement by bishop Niakeo Okada (President) to the UN Decolonisation Committee (July 15th).

Koppel, B.M. & Orr, R.M.Jr., 1993. *Japan's Foreign Aid: Power and Policy in a New Era.* Westview: Boulder, Col.

Mendl, W., 1995. *Japan's Asia Policy: Regional Security and Global Interests.* Routledge: London.

Nester, W.R., 1992. *Japan and the Third World: Patterns, Power and Prospects.* Macmillan: London.

Newland, K. (ed), 1990. *The International Relations of Japan.* Macmillan: London.

Osaki, R.S. & Arnold, W. (eds), 1984. *Japan's Foreign Relations: A Global Search for Economic Security.* Westview: Boulder, Col.

Reader, I., 1991. *Religion in Contemporary Japan.* Macmillan: Basingstoke.

Reischauer, E.O., 1994. *The Japanese Today: Change and Continuity.* C.E.Tuttle: Tokyo.

Soma, A. (bishop), (1974-1997):

Letters to international leaders in respect of events in East Timor or relating thereto. JCCJP: Tokyo.

1993. Homily, Dili – East Timor. JCCJP: Tokyo.

1994. Address to UN Decolonisation Committee. JCCJP: Tokyo.

1994. 'The Role of the Asia-Pacific Church and of Japan in the Issue of East Timor'. VI *Journadas* Symposium. University of Oporto: Oporto.

Yamada, N.K., 1994. *Japanese Responsibility in our Times.* Faculty of Economics, Sophia University: Tokyo. 'Asian People's Challenge and Japanese Response.' Sophia Economics Review (Vol XXVII Nos 2,3), University of Sophia: Tokyo.

Yoichi H., 1997. 'The Future Role of Japan in the East Timor Issue.' Keynote Address. Educational Foundation Conference, Sendai (January 7th). Foundation of Japan Teacher's Mutual Benefit & Educational Promotion: Sendai.

Yoshihara, K., 1979. *Japanese Economic Development: A Short Introduction.* OUP: Oxford.

Government of Japan

1990. 'On Japan's Overseas Development Aid (ODA) in Relation to Military Expenditures and Other Matters of the Developing Countries.' Address by Prime Minister Toshiki Kaifu to the Diet (April).

1991. ODA Guidelines (April).

1993. ODA Charter (June).

1999. Statement on the East Timor Issue.

2000. 'Training Human Resources in East Timor.' Ministry of Foreign Affairs. Press Conference, (December 1st).

Chapter 11 – The Church in England

Barber, P., 1995. *Partners in Repression: The Reality of British Aid to Indonesia. TAPOL*: London.

CAFOD, Catholic Agency for Overseas Development, London:

Field Officers Reports (Confidential).

Open Letters to national and international political leaders.

Policy Statements and Press Releases in respect of East Timor.

CBCEW, Catholic Bishops Conference of England and Wales:

'Briefing'. Monthly. CBCEW: Westminster.

National Catholic Directory of England and Wales. Annual. CBCEW: Westminster.

1980. *Liverpool 1980: Official Report of the National Pastoral Congress, 1980.* St.Paul: London.

The Easter People: A Message from the Roman Catholic Bishops of England and Wales in the Light of the National Pastoral Congress Liverpool 1980. St.Paul: London.

1997. *The Common Good and the Catholic Church's Social Teaching.* CBCEW: Westminster.

1998. *Human Rights and the Catholic Church: Reflections on the Occasion of the Jubilee of the 'Universal Declaration of Human Rights.* CBCEW: Westminster.

Childs, D., 1995. *Britain Since 1939.* London.

CIIR, Catholic Institute for International Relations, London:
See Bibliography – General (East Timor), and Bibliography – Ch3 (above).
CIIR News (Quarterly).
1987. *East Timor: A Christian Reflection.*
1990. *I am Timorese: Testimonies from East Timor.*
1999. Statement to the UN Commission on Human Rights Special Session on East Timor (September).

COMECE, Commission of the Bishops Conferences of the European Community:
1999. *Truth, Memory and Reconciliation: Keys to Peace and Reconciliation.* COMECE: Brussels.

Cumming, J. & Burns, F. (eds), 1980. *The Church Now: An Enquiry into the Present State of the Catholic Church in Britain and Ireland.* Burns & Oates: London.

Curtis, M., 1995. *Ambiguities of Power: British Foreign Policy Since 1945.* Zed Books: London.

Davie, G., 1994. *Religion in Britain since 1945.* Oxford.

Greenwood, S., 1999. *Britain and the Cold War.* London.

Hainsworth, P., 2000. 'New Labour, New Codes of Conduct? British Government Policy Towards Indonesia and East Timor After the 1997 Election.' in Hainsworth, P. & McClosky, S (eds), 2000. *The East Timor Question: The Struggle for Independence from Indonesia.* I.B.Tauris: London.

Hastings, A. 1986. *A History of English Christianity 1920-1985.* Burns & Oates: London.

Hornsby-Smith, M.,
1987. *Roman Catholics in England: Studies in Social Structure Since the Second World War.* Cambridge University: Cambridge.
2001. *Catholics in England 1950-2000: Historical & Sociological Perspectives* Continuum: London.

Johnson. P. (ed), 1994. *Twentieth Century Britain: Economic, Social & Cultural Change.* London.

Kennan, G.F., 1948. 'Current Trends, US Foreign Policy.' *Foreign Relations of the US 1948.* Washington DC, Vol 1, Part 2. Pp509f.

Lee, C., 2000. *This Sceptred Isle: The Twentieth Century.* Penguin: London.

McClelland, V.A., 1991. 'Great Britain and Ireland.' Hastings, A. (ed) 1991. *Modern Catholicism.* SPCK: London.

Needham, A., Parker, J. & Wilson, J., 2000. 'Seeds of Hope – East Timor Ploughshares: Disarming the Hawks.' Hainsworth, P. & McClosky, S. (eds), 2000. *The East Timor Question, etc.*

O'Shaughnessy, H.,
1994. *Getting Away with Murder?* British Coalition for East Timor: London.
    'A People's Resistance.' The Tablet (13.8), London.

Ovendale, R., 1998. *Anglo-American Relations in the 20th Century.* Basingstoke.

PHRG, Parliamentary Human Rights Group. Westminster, London:
Correspondence, Petitions & Declarations to United Nations, British MPs, MEPs, etc.
1987. The Forgotten Cause of East Timor's Right to Self-determination (J.Bizot).
1991. 'Hearing on East Timor: The Santa Cruz Massacre'.

Pax Christi, 1997. 'Responses to Questions Put to RC Diocesan Financial Teams Regarding Diocesan Ethical Investments Policy. Pax Christi: London.

Pilger, J., 1994>,
Articles in (e.g.): The New Statesman, *1994* – 29.4, 15.7; *1995* – 27.1, 16.6, 30.6; Guardian Weekend, *1994* – 12.2; New Internationalist, (March) etc.
1994. *Distant Voices.* Vintage: London
1998. *Hidden Agendas.* Vintage: London.

Stahl, M., 1992. 'A Church on Calvary.' The Tablet (January 25th), London.

Tiratsoo, N., (ed), 1998. *From Blitz to Blair: A New History of Britain Since 1939.* Phoenix/Orion: London.

British Government
Documents on British Foreign Policy Overseas. Series 11, Vol 11. HMSO: London.
1992. Debate, House of Lords (June 16th)
    Statement (Baroness Trumpington) to House of Lords (July 16th)

1993. Statement (FO Minister A.Goodlad) to House of Commons (February 10th).
   Statement (Baroness Chalker) to House of Lords (July 21st)
1994. Debate, House of Lords (March 2nd)
Foreign and Commonwealth Office
1999. Human Rights Annual Report (July 21st).
2000. British Support for East Timor and its Displaced People (January)
Department for International Development
1997. Country Report: Indonesia.

Chapter 12 – The Vatican

[See also Chapter 4 – Criteria for Evaluation]

Belo, C.F.X., 1989. *On the Visit of the Holy Father.* Pastoral Letter. Diocese of Dili.
International Secretariat of the Pontifical Missionary Societies:
La Pontificia Cooperazione Missionaria e la Solidarieta tra le Chiese – Rapporto 1994- 95/1996-97
[Pontifical Missionary Societies Aid Disbursement]
Philp, P., 1989. 'Reflection on the East Timor situation after the Papal Visit.' *The Church in East Timor: A Collection of Documents* (1993). CCJPD: Melbourne.
Pope John Paul II., 1989. 'The Pastoral Journey of the Holy Father in the Far East and Mauritius – texts of the Papal Addresses.' *Osservatore Romano* No43 (23.10), Rome.
Vatican Observer Mission at the United Nations,
1997. *Serving the Human Family: The Holy See at the Major United Nations Conferences.* Path to Peace Foundation: New York.
Walsh, P., 1990. 'The Pope rides the Indonesian rapids without rocking the boat.' National Outlook (January). Outlook Media: Sydney.
Weigel, G., 2000. *Witness to Hope: Biography of Pope John Paul II.* Harper Collins: London.
Vatikiotis, M., 1989. 'Unresolved tensions – Papal visit renews international focus on East Timor.' Far Eastern Economic Review (26.10). Hong Kong.

Index

Afterword

The question of solidarity with the oppressed is one of the most important issues in today's world. Whether they be victims of armed conflict, of landmines, or those in the developing world who suffer the human consequences of international debt, it is clear that all of these children of God, and many others, rely on solidarity and support to lighten the terrible burdens that they carry.

The combined effects of more than a quarter century of warfare have left my own native land, East Timor, in special need of such solidarity. As is well-illustrated in Fr Patrick Smythe's important new study, the need for international solidarity was especially pronounced during East Timor's long years of terrible difficulties from 1975-1999. I am therefore most grateful for Fr Smythe's careful attempt to evaluate the responses that the plight of East Timor elicited from the world during those momentous years.

This excellent study carries concrete lessons for the global community as we face the many challenges of the new millennium. In essence, how can we best help our brothers and sisters who often suffer in silence? This book helps to answer that question. I fervently hope that Fr Smythe's painstaking research will receive the attention it deserves.

Signed Monsignor Carlos Filipe Ximenes Belo
Apostolic Administrator of Dili, East Timor (Emeritus)
1996 Nobel Peace Prize Co-Laureate.
20th November 2003.

Religion und Theologie im Asien-Pazifik-Kontext

herausgegeben von John May (Irish School of Ecumenics, Dublin) und Theodor Ahrens (Hamburg)

John D'Arcy May
After Pluralism
Towards an Interreligious Ethic
Do the religions cause war, or is their tendency to intensify violence outweighed by their potential for peace? Are multicultural societies, as Huntington thinks, condemned to ethnic conflict, or is a specifically *interreligious* ethic emerging from their new patterns of relationships? This book examines the liberal agenda of dialogue and pluralism and finds that we need a more radical approach involving indigenous peoples, women and the poor if we are to find solutions – together – to the problems of economic injustice and the threat of ecological degradation. It contains the Ethel Hayton Lectures delivered at the University of Wollongong, Australia, in 1994.
Bd. 1, 2000, 168 S., 20,90 €, br., ISBN 3-8258-4527-3

Carsten Wippermann
Zwischen den Kulturen: Das Christentum in Südkorea
Als der Katholizismus vor 200 Jahren und der Protestantismus vor erst 100 Jahren nach Korea kamen, stießen sie in eine multireligiöse Kultur, die mehr als 1.500 Jahre vom Buddhismus, Konfuzianismus und Schamanismus bestimmt wurde. Mit dem Aufeinandertreffen der westlichen und östlichen Kulturen entbrannte ein Kampf um die gesellschaftliche Dominanz. Das Christentum wurde anfangs als Bedrohung der moralischen und politischen Ordnung betrachtet und blutig verfolgt. Als der Protestantismus jedoch das überkommene Bildungs- und Gesundheitswesen reformierte, wurde das Christentum zum Hoffnungsträger für viele Menschen. So begann seine außergewöhnliche Erfolgsgeschichte: Heute sind etwa 30% der Bevölkerung Südkoreas Christen und damit die größte religiöse Gruppe. Das Christentum hat in der Bevölkerung das Image, Motor der Modernisierung zu sein. Doch innerhalb der christlichen Kirchen gibt es grundverschiedene Kulturen, die einander vehement bekämpfen. Hier geht es nicht nur um theologische Positionen, sondern auch um Mitglieder, materielle Ressourcen und gesellschaftlichen Einfluss. In der historisch, philosophisch und kultursoziologisch angelegten Studie zeichnet der Autor die ambivalente Erfolgsgeschichte des Christentums nach und rekonstruiert auch die Perspektiven von Vertretern der traditionellen Religionen.
Bd. 2, 2000, 304 S., 25,90 €, br., ISBN 3-8258-4574-5

Wissenschaftliche Paperbacks
Theologie

Michael J. Rainer (Red.)
"Dominus Iesus" – Anstößige Wahrheit oder anstößige Kirche?
Dokumente, Hintergründe, Standpunkte und Folgerungen
Die römische Erklärung "Dominus Iesus" berührt den Nerv der aktuellen Diskussion über den Stellenwert der Religionen in der heutigen Gesellschaft. Angesichts der Pluralität der Bekenntnisse soll der Anspruch der Wahrheit festgehalten werden.
Bd. 9, 2. Aufl. 2001, 350 S., 20,90 €, br., ISBN 3-8258-5203-2

Rainer Bendel (Hg.)
Die katholische Schuld?
Katholizismus im Dritten Reich zwischen Arrangement und Widerstand
Die Frage nach der „Katholischen Schuld" ist spätestens seit Hochhuths „Stellvertreter" ein öffentliches Thema. Nun wird es von Goldhagen neu aufgeworfen, aufgeworfen als moralische Frage – ohne fundierte Antwort.
Wer sich über den Zusammenhang von Katholizismus und Nationalsozialismus fundiert informieren will, wird zu diesem Band greifen müssen: mit Beiträgen u. a. von Gerhard Besier, E. W. Böckenförde, Heinz Hürten, Joachim Köhler, Johann Baptist Metz, Rudolf Morsey, Ludwig Volk, Ottmar Fuchs und Stephan Leimgruber.
Bd. 14, 2002, 368 S., 19,90 €, br., ISBN 3-8258-6334-4

LIT Verlag Münster – Hamburg – Berlin – London
Grevener Str./Fresnostr. 2 48159 Münster
Tel.: 0251 – 23 50 91 – Fax: 0251 – 23 19 72
e-Mail: vertrieb@lit-verlag.de – http://www.lit-verlag.de